OPEN SOURCE
GAME DEVELOPMENT

OPEN SOURCE GAME DEVELOPMENT:

QT® GAMES FOR KDE, PDAS, AND WINDOWS

MARTIN HENI

ANDREAS BECKERMANN

CHARLES RIVER MEDIA, INC.
Hingham, Massachusetts

Cover Design: Tyler Creative

CHARLES RIVER MEDIA, INC.
10 Downer Avenue
Hingham, Massachusetts 02043
781-740-0400
781-740-8816 (FAX)
info@charlesriver.com
www.charlesriver.com

This book is printed on acid-free paper.

Martin Heni and Andreas Beckermann. *Open Source Game Development: Qt Games for KDE, PDAs, and Windows.*
ISBN: 1-58450-406-4

Library of Congress Cataloging-in-Publication Data

Heni, Martin, 1968-
  Open source game development : QT games for KDE, PDAS, and Windows / Martin Heni, Andreas Beckermann.
    p. cm.
  Includes bibliographical references and index.
  ISBN 1-58450-406-4 (pbk. with cd-rom : alk. paper)
  1. Computer games--Programming. 2. Open source software. I. Beckermann, Andreas, 1982- II. Title.
  QA76.76.C672H45 2005
  794.8'1536--dc22
                          2005019983

Printed in the United States of America
05 7 6 5 4 3 2 First Edition

CHARLES RIVER MEDIA titles are available for site license or bulk purchase by institutions, user groups, corporations, etc. For additional information, please contact the Special Sales Department at 781-740-0400.

Contents

Acknowledgments

We want to thank all the people who provided support and advice during the writing of this book. First, we want to thank Dave Pallai and his entire team at Charles River Media for giving us the opportunity to publish this book. We thank our families, parents, and friends for their continual love and support, and for actually "enduring" this project. We are extremely grateful to Laura Layland for proofreading the text, checking for inconsistencies, and for the fruitful discussions regarding this work.

We are also grateful to Matthias Ettrich for devoting his time to write the Foreword and for initiating the KDE desktop project in the first place. Many thanks in particular to Rivo Laks for his expert advice and for critically reviewing the "OpenGL®" and "Particle Effects" chapters. Our special thanks also to Inge Wallin and Ian Wadham for reviewing the book and providing valuable suggestions. We appreciate Trolltech's support concerning licenses and permissions.

Last but not least, we want to thank the entire KDE community for making KDE available, and in particular, the KDE games community for their companionship and support.

We hope you enjoy this book and have lots of fun developing games for KDE and Qt.

—Martin Heni and Andreas Beckermann

Preface

Computer games are intriguing, and fascinate old and young alike. Nowadays, many people play computer games occasionally or on a regular basis. As the number of people interested in playing computer games grows, so does the number of people who are interested in the development or the understanding of the development of such games. Do you belong to the group of people who find the development of computer games interesting? If you do, you'll find the basic elements of computer game development in this book. "Isn't game development difficult?" you might ask. Fortunately, with today's computer technology, it is much easier than you might think—and you can get started as a computer game developer today.

The concept of games on a computer dates back to the late 1950s and early 1960s. Given the computer technology at the time, the excellent computer games that are now feasible with modern computer technology were an impossible dream. Nevertheless, as early as 1958, the first game that can be classified as a computer game was developed by William A. Higinbotham at the Brookhaven National Laboratory in New York. Higinbotham used a laboratory oscilloscope to create a simple game named *Tennis for 2*, which was a simple computer version of tennis, and, as in the actual game of tennis, two players had to play a ball back and forth without missing it. Missing the ball would increase the other player's score until one of the two players lost.

The story of computer games then continued on digital computers with Stephen Russell and his team in 1961–1962, who developed *Spacewar*, a game for the PDP-1 computer, which was the size of a large car. *Spacewar* also involved two players, who would fly in spaceships around a planet shooting at each other. In 1973, *Atari*® introduced the first commercial game called Pong (see Figure P.1), the concept of which mirrored that of *Tennis for 2*. Again, two players had to play a ball back and forth in a tennis-like fashion. Because of Pong's success, game development took off, and arcade games such as *Space Invaders*™ and *Asteroids* appeared around the late 1970s.

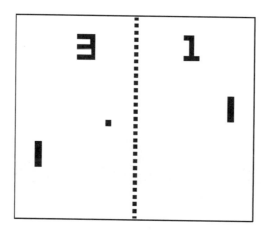

FIGURE P.1   The very early computer arcade game Pong.

In the early 1980s, the introduction of home computers such as the Atari ST, Commodore™ VC20/C64, and the first IBM® PCs brought the computer game world into everyone's home. These computers were able to run a variety of computer games, and even though these games were limited in graphical and sound resources, they soon became very popular. These early games generally belonged to the arcade or adventure genres, since they could be run on limited computer resources.

However, as with most technology, the development and subsequent introduction of more powerful home computers from the 1990s onward led to increasingly complex computer games, involving complicated simulations or graphically superior scenarios. Nowadays, games are approaching movie-like quality in a large variety of game categories, including first-person shooters, simulations, sport games, strategy games, adventures, and role-playing games.

Nevertheless, playing small desktop games or games on handheld computers remains a prominent pastime, and this book introduces the basic principles of game programming for desktop computer systems. We use the term desktop computer games for those games that can be easily programmed by a single programmer or a small team of developers, and run on a standard home desktop computer running, for example, Linux®/KDE (see Figure P.2) or Microsoft® Windows®. Small handheld computers, such as PDAs or cell phones, can also run these types of games. The typical desktop game applications involve card or board games, logic puzzles, and arcade-style games. Well-known games include solitaire, *Tetris*, chess, checkers, *Asteroids*, and *Pac-Man*. Most desktop games are compact and can be easily run during a coffee break. However, the technologies described in this book can be used as a stepping stone to develop something more than just a simple desktop game; for example, a larger strategy game like *Boson*. The simplicity of most desktop games guarantees a wide user community. With reasonable effort, these types of games can be developed and programmed by a single person or a small team who have neither the expert knowledge nor the resources of a large game developing company for graphics, sound, and programming.

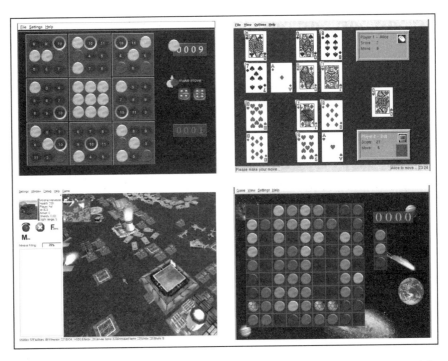

FIGURE P.2   Screenshots of games running on KDE. From top left to bottom right: *Tritoc, Lskat, Boson,* and *Quintalign.*

Desktop game development also serves as an ideal starting point to learn and practice the basic principles of game programming. Once these basic principles are understood, a specialization into a distinct area of game programming—such as fast 3D action games, first-person shooters, or flight simulators—can be accomplished. Moreover, many topics covered by this book (e.g., OpenGL, pathfinding, and artificial intelligence) are used throughout all game genres in both professional and private games.

An uncomplicated way to begin desktop game programming is to use the C++ programming language, with Qt and/or KDE as the graphical environment. KDE is based on Qt and therefore uses many Qt features. Consequently, in this book we chose to use Qt, and where appropriate, KDE for the detailed programming examples. The examples and code snippets we present will provide you with a basis for the development of your own computer games.

For those of you who are used to other platforms, don't worry; games programmed in Qt (and to some extent KDE) can be transferred to platforms such as Linux, Microsoft Windows, and Apple® Macintosh's Mac OS®. Embedded devices running Qtopia™ such as PDAs or cell phones are also compatible. These cross-platform development features are one of the great benefits of Qt-based application programming.

The choice of Qt and KDE is also based on the idea that free software development is easily possible using these platforms. Qt, KDE, and many development tools and libraries necessary for programming are freely available as open source software, which makes it much easier to "get going" and develop a game. Without any of the initial outlay costs for the development tools, you can download the necessary applications from the Internet and immediately start programming games.

The development of open source software has the additional advantage that you can easily and legally gain insight into other people's work, and thus profit from their experience and knowledge. Being inspired by other developers' open source programs and games can serve as a springboard for your own unique ideas. As an added bonus, a wide and very helpful developers' community is available to answer questions from new developers. In open source, this inspiration is actually the core idea of development: you are allowed to access and use other people's software to enhance your own programming development. In turn, you can make your own work available to others. So, let's get started!

To work through the examples described in this book, you will need a few prerequisites. Since all the coding examples are presented in C++, knowledge of the C++ programming language is essential. However, no actual knowledge of game programming itself is required, because the necessary techniques are developed during the course of this book. A little knowledge of Qt or KDE programming would be advantageous, but is not required, as extensive sample applications will demonstrate the specific parts of a KDE/Qt-programmed game.

Furthermore, to keep the examples simple and simultaneously allow the example code to be transferred to other programming languages or target platforms, we minimized the amount of complicated or special features found in C++, Qt, and KDE. We also minimized the dependency of our programming examples on the current versions of Qt and KDE, and since Qt 3 and KDE 3 will be present on the desktop market for quite a while, we kept most of our examples compatible with these versions. However, we do acknowledge the upcoming prominence of Qt 4 and KDE 4, and have therefore indicated where and how the coding examples will have to be extended from Qt 3 to Qt 4. Consequently, you should be able to use all the game programming techniques described in this book for both Qt 3- and Qt 4-based applications.

When transferring our example code to your own games, keep in mind that the examples presented in this book are supposed to show you the principle of an algorithm, not a highly optimized program code. Optional or repetitive parts of the code are omitted, and we use "..." to indicate that the code can or must be extended.

If these parts interest you, you can use or analyze the source code on the companion CD-ROM, on which all the examples are included in full. Transferring our example code into your game is encouraged, but may require some adaptation for the specific Qt/KDE standards, and might need optimizations regarding language, memory, or performance considerations.

ON THE CD

The overall concept of this book is to provide the basic programming skills to design and develop a desktop game. In the first part of the book, we discuss the concept and basic design of an open source desktop computer game with emphasis on object-oriented and event-driven programming (Chapter 1, "Introduction to Desktop Gaming"). To ensure that you have an easy and fast start in your own game development, the book progresses with Chapter 2, "Qt Primer," which recapitulates the key features of Qt used throughout the book. We continue by demonstrating how a generic desktop game application can be written for various target platforms such as KDE in Chapter 3, "Game Development using KDE"; Microsoft Windows and Apple Macintosh's Mac OS in Chapter 4, "Qt Game Development Using Microsoft Windows"; and Qt/Qtopia on PDAs in Chapter 5, "Game Development on PDAs." Throughout these chapters, we demonstrate that by using the Qt library, you can begin to develop your game programming on any of these platforms. In essence, you can choose the platform on which you want to develop your programming skills (e.g., KDE in Chapter 3), and skip the other two chapters until you want to transfer your game to those platforms. If you want to develop your skills on another platform later, you can then refer to those chapters. You can use the generic game application presented in these chapters as a starting point for developing your own desktop games, as it contains all the necessary functions to start the game application, set up all the menus, the game view, and initialize the game.

The second part of the book is devoted to the multimedia features of games. The actual display of the game graphics is often performed using a canvas view (Chapter 6, "Canvas Games"), allowing 2D movement and animations. However, when 3D aspects enter the game, OpenGL (Chapters 7 and 8, "OpenGL" and "OpenGL with Qt") is normally the right choice. Alongside the graphics, another important aspect of computer games is the music and sound effects. We introduce their basic functions and principles for Qt and KDE in Chapter 9, "Sound and Graphics."

The next part of the book focuses on the fundamental principles and ingredients of computer games. The application of this part goes beyond Qt and KDE so you can apply it to other computer languages and operating systems. These principles include artificial intelligence in Chapter 10, "Artificial Intelligence"; pathfinding in Chapter 11, "Pathfinding"; and particle effects in Chapter 12, "Particle Effects." As computer games are representations of the/a (real) world, the correct use of basic physical and mathematical equations is necessary. The most important features useful for desktop computer games are collected in Chapter 13, "Math and Physics in Desktop Games." If you go beyond your own desktop, you will need to enhance your game with network capabilities. In Chapters 14 and 15, "Qt Network Games" and "The KGame Library," we present how such network games can be created in the scope of Qt and KDE, respectively. In Chapter 16, "XML," we further show how Qt allows you to use XML for networking, game saving, or data file handling.

Chapter 17, "Open Source and Intellectual Property Rights," goes beyond the actual programming techniques and provides you with an overview of licenses and intellectual property rights and their effects on open source (game) programming. In the final chapter, we conclude the book by applying all the techniques learned throughout the chapters to develop a fully functional desktop game.

This game is developed and discussed in Chapter 18, "A Practical Summary," and is included on the companion CD-ROM.

ON THE CD

Foreword

Many programmers of my generation wrote their first applications with Turbo Pascal in DOS. Back then, programming was fun! You didn't need to think much about the user interface; you just got on with writing your application, and the "glue code" that connected the user interface with the actual application often comprised less than 10% of the program code.

Later, when graphical user interfaces (GUIs) became popular, things started to change, and not always for the better. Suddenly, putting user interface elements together and managing an event-driven control flow became essential. This sounds like an easy thing to do, but it turned out to be difficult; instead of being able to concentrate on the actual logic of their applications, programmers had to spend a lot of time fighting with toolkits. Unix developers were hit the hardest. Motif™, then the standard user interface toolkit, was notoriously difficult to work with. Often, programmers ended up making their applications fit for Motif, instead of the other way round. The few remaining Motif applications still bear witness to the difficulties every single control element imposed on their developers. A good example was the Netscape® Web browser, whose Unix front end in 1998 consisted of 300,000 lines of Motif code. Trolltech once ported this to Qt and, by doing so, reduced it to 25,000 lines of code. This new front end was significantly smaller, faster, and ran unchanged on both Windows and Unix. It's a pity that Netscape didn't see the potential back then.

However, code size and efficiency are not everything. The basic design philosophy of Qt is simple: programming should be fun, and programmers should be able to concentrate on the task at hand instead of spending unnecessary time fighting with toolkits. Additionally, a program should run on many different platforms, such as Windows, Unix, Linux, and the Macintosh—this important feature is described in the opening chapters of this book.

The requirements for GUIs continue to grow. One example is internationalization. In a shrinking world, it is natural to offer localized versions of applications for different parts of the world. This applies to both Open Source and commercial developers alike. Translating a user interface is not just about changing the text. A simple phrase like "Please enter your name" is much shorter in English than in German ("Bitte geben Sie Ihren Namen ein"). A modern GUI is expected to adapt to this automatically, and Qt does this with an advanced geometry management system. For Hebrew and Arabic, Qt can flip the entire user interface to follow the text flow from right to left.

So far, I have spoken about fun, efficiency, and some of the technical benefits of using Qt. However, there is more to Qt's success: Qt is available in both commercial and Open Source editions. Why does this matter? What is the point of having an Open Source version of Qt? That you do not have to pay? Close, but no cigar! Open Source isn't about money, it is about freedom. Open Source guarantees you four important freedoms: the freedom to use the code, the freedom to study the code, the freedom to change the code, and the freedom to share your changes with others. These freedoms are the foundation of the GNU General Public License (GPL), the purest of all Open Source licenses, and the one under which most free software is published. So what's the catch? There isn't one. All you have to do is pass on the same four freedoms to the users of your code. Applying this principle to a development library like Qt means that, when you build your programs using the Open Source version of Qt, you also have to publish your programs as Open Source. Alternatively, you can obtain a commercial Qt license, which in turn sponsors the development of the free version. Trolltech calls this model "quid pro quo"—something for something.

Is Open Source useful for people who are not interested in programming? Of course! First, they can use the software. Second, they can ask or hire someone to work on the software. Third, they have a certain guarantee that someone will port the software to new operating systems when required. Fourth, there is a good chance that someone will translate the software into his or her own language, even if the market for it is too small for a commercial enterprise to consider. However, the most important advantage is long term: as a computer user, I am interested in good and innovative software, and this requires skillful developers. Reading the open source code available today is a wonderful way to learn programming. In addition, innovations in programming are often based on new combinations of existing ideas. The open source approach to sharing knowledge and code encourages programmers to build on others' work without having to reinvent the wheel.

Game programming is one of the most exciting fields of computing, as I am certain this book will show you. However, right from the start, keep in mind that others should be able to read, understand, and extend your code. A good example is the Patience game that comes with KDE. Right from the start, it was designed as a generic system for card games instead of an implementation of just one specific game. This made it possible for others to add new games to it—and so they did!

I wish all of you a lot of fun when programming games with Qt. I hope you have as much pleasure writing your applications as we at Trolltech have had with the development of Qt itself. I am already looking forward to all the new games this book will inspire, and welcoming those of you who find your way into the open source community.

—Matthias Ettrich
Trolltech, VP Engineering
Oslo, Norway

1 Introduction to Desktop Gaming

In This Chapter

- The Idea for a New Game
- The Game Design Document
- Desktop Game Architecture
- Game Balancing
- Open Source Game Development

Games are a fundamental part of human heritage, played in all cultures and enjoyed by all age groups. Games like chess, for example, have been known for centuries. Today, the concept of classical games is complemented by computer games, which can follow the ideas of board games, imitate stories and movies, or simulate real-world scenarios, from an airplane flight to an entire civilization.

In this book, we present you with the concepts and technologies necessary for the development of your own computer game. Different computer games require different levels of resources, knowledge, and time. A certain class of computer games, desktop games, can be developed relatively easily by one or more developers in their leisure time as a hobby. In this book, we focus on such games.

Regardless of the game you develop, you need to follow a certain procedure to make it a success. The process begins with your basic idea of the game, which you use to create a game concept. The game concept then gives rise to the actual designing and implementing of the code. In this chapter, we provide you with an idea on how to follow these steps, and how to approach developing a new game and those particular issues you need to address. The following chapters then describe the actual setup of the game application and the implementation of the various technologies necessary for a desktop game.

Creating a new game usually follows these eight steps:

1. You want to develop your own game.
2. You have a vague idea about a new game.
3. The idea of the game is refined, and the topic, game play, and goal of the game are chosen.
4. You check whether such a game already exists. If it does, you have three options: drop your idea, or (if the other game is Open Source) join the team of the other game, or develop an alternative version of the game.
5. Make a detailed design of the game and the game architecture.
6. Program the game by developing the source code.
7. Thoroughly test the game, and let other people test the game.
8. Publish the game.

THE IDEA FOR A NEW GAME

A very important step is knowing what game you want to develop. You need a good idea, and the implementation of the idea must be feasible with the resources you have available. Often, this will be just you, or you and a small team, so don't opt for a very complex game that will require 10 years to develop. Doing so is seldom rewarding, and many of these games are never finished. For example, it is a bit unrealistic to start your first project with the idea to develop a game "like Unreal Tournament™, but much better." Games like this are developed by large companies, with many programmers, artists, and writers involved. Hobby programmers have little chance to complete such a project within a few years, so be realistic.

A more achievable goal is to start programming a simple game that does not require too much developmental effort. It is even a good idea to clone existing games from noncomputer games such as board games, computer games from a different platform, or simply from another computer game. You will then enhance the idea or modify the game, which is a good learning process: you've probably also noticed that many commercial games borrow many of their features from other games. However, if you want to publish your game, you must be sure that you do not violate any copyrights or patents (see Chapter 17, "Open Source and Intellectual Property Rights").

Desktop Game Types

There exists a wide variety of possible game types; however, not all are appropriate for a small team of developers and the desktop game environment. To provide you with an overview and help you choose an appropriate topic, listed here are some of the most popular game categories and their relationship to desktop games. Note, however, that many current games are a mixture of several categories, and you can always create a simple version of a complicated game or a complicated version of a simple game. Therefore, the subsequent list just serves as a rough guideline.

The following describes games that are usually low in multimedia and programming complexity. They are well suited for the technologies we describe in this book:

Board games: Games normally following the idea of noncomputer board games (e.g., chess, checkers).

Card games: Games following the idea of noncomputer card games (e.g., poker, patience).

Puzzles: Pieces have to be arranged, inserted, or removed to find the solution to the game (e.g., *Sokoban*, memory, mines).

Maze games: A path through a maze needs to be found (e.g., *Pac-Man*™).

Gambling games: Games based mainly or exclusively on chance or luck (e.g., roulette, slot machines).

Shooting games: Old-style arcade games in which the player has to shoot down waves of enemies (e.g., *Space Invaders*).

Most games within these categories can be implemented in a reasonable amount of time by a single person or a few developers.

Games requiring higher multimedia skills or more specialized programming techniques include:

Strategy games: Economic or military strategies are simulated and employed by the player (e.g., *Civilization*™, *Star Craft*™).

Race games: A target has to be reached in the fastest possible time by racing toward it (e.g., car racing, *Tron*™).

Simulations: Some real vehicles are simulated following real physical laws precisely. Typical examples are flight simulators (e.g., *Microsoft Flight Simulator*™).

Text-based (or still graphics) adventure games: The player follows a story by either solving puzzles or changing the story line by his decisions. This is an old-fashioned type of adventure and more book-like (e.g., *Monkey Island*™).

These games are difficult but not impossible to employ in the scope of Open Source desktop games. However, you will most likely need a team of people for the development, because these types of games comprise many programming techniques and multimedia effects.

Games requiring a lot of multimedia, highly specialized programming techniques, or a great deal of programming effort include:

Multimedia adventure games: The player follows a story by either solving puzzles or changing the storyline by his decisions. Today, adventure games incorporate many graphical and movie effects (e.g., the *Indiana Jones*™ series).

Role-playing games: The player assumes the role of a character and advances its skills. Often, adventure elements are embedded as quests (e.g., *Dungeons and Dragons*™-style games).

Combat games or tactical shooters: The player has to kill all or many opponents (fast). This is typically implemented as fast-paced first-person shooters and involves fast 3D graphics (e.g., *Unreal Tournament*).

Sports games: Sporting events such as tennis, basketball, or football are simulated on the computer (e.g., the *NBA Live*™ series).

These games are difficult to develop without a large team of developers, and the algorithms presented in this book are not sufficient for these games. However, the principle of development is the same, and referring to the advanced algorithms such as those described in the references [DeLoura00], [Kirmse04], [Pallister05], [Rabin02], [Openal05], and [Astle04] will enhance your knowledge in these areas.

Why Play a Game?

Even though you may have the best idea ever for a new game, it still needs to catch players' attention. Therefore, it is important to keep in mind why players actually play games. The following items and Figure 1.1 describe some of the tricks employed to pique a player's interest. Ideally, your game should offer the players one or more of these ingredients to keep them happily playing. [Howland99]:

Rewards: Players like to get rewards. This can be special items, cut-scenes, new levels, or new features. If the player knows a new reward is within reach, he will keep playing.

Winning: Most players play a game to win. However, a game quickly becomes boring if won too easily. Therefore, the ideal game should always maintain a level of challenge so a player can win, but with a struggle. To achieve this, you must implement a skill- or level-dependent artificial intelligence or maps and monsters that can adapt their strengths to the skills of the player.

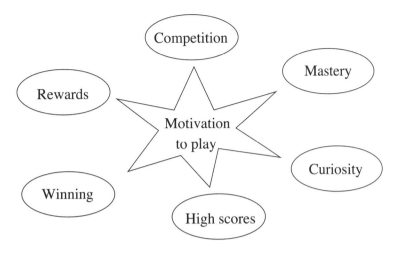

FIGURE 1.1   Motivations to play a game.

Curiosity: Curiosity is another main reason to play a game, and can be distinguished in several areas. First, players want to learn more about a new game; they want to see how it works. Second, players like to explore a game world, learn the different creatures and items, and explore the maps to find what's hidden. This can be encouraged by implementing hidden levels and items. Third, players are often particularly interested to see how the game ends. Therefore, reward the player with a good ending instead of just displaying a plain "game over" message.

Competition: Players like to compete with each other, and beat the competition. This particularly applies to two-person or multiplayer games in which players can compete with other players. Competition can be supported by providing score lists and tables in which the actual proficiency can be easily seen.

High scores: High scores are also a type of competition, and can motivate players even when there are no others with whom they can compete—the players try to beat their own scores.

Mastery: Increasing your skills and techniques is also motivation to keep playing a game. For example, in a flight simulator, the player's goal is to become a proficient pilot, which in itself keeps the user playing. A game of this nature has to give the player a high amount of control over the game so that many features and controls can be learned and applied.

Unless your game aims at the expert player market, it should also have a low entrance barrier; that is, a new player must be able to grasp the rules quickly and learn to play the game without having to read a 200-page manual. Even if the game is complicated in principle, it is a good idea to start simple with a more basic level and reduced features. As the game progresses, the complexity can be gradually added back in so the player makes smooth and steady progress. Note, however, that expert players will be bored by this; therefore, there should be an opportunity for them to progress faster or skip the introduction or tutorials entirely [Howland05].

Key Features of a Desktop Game

Games are complex programs. In contrast to other desktop applications such as text editors, it is not enough that they just work. A player expects more from a game, namely entertainment and fun. To achieve this, a good game has to excel in several key areas:

Multimedia: Games should provide decent sound and graphics effects. Although the desktop games discussed in this book do not require movie-like multimedia effects such as many commercial products offer, it is nevertheless important for a successful game to have good graphics and catchy sound effects. Many desktop games, especially if they are used in an office environment, will be able to work with limited sound effects. However, keep in mind that sound can be quite immersive and can influence the perception of the player.

Goals and rewards: To keep a player playing, a game needs to offer something to strive for—if there is nothing to be achieved, why play? In the previous section, we listed various reasons why a player plays a game.

Game balance: A game should be well balanced. If it is unfair, too difficult, or too easy to play, the game becomes uninteresting.

Configuration and standard interfaces: A game is easier to play if it follows the patterns of other games or applications with which the player is familiar. Standard menu layouts and standard keyboard inputs help people to quickly familiarize themselves with your game. Therefore, follow some standard guidelines like those provided by KDE, or make the interface configurable by the player.

Artificial intelligence or multiplayer: Unless your game is a solitaire-type game where just one player plays, it is important to provide the player with a challenging opponent. This opponent can be the computer—in which case, good artificial intelligence needs to be implemented—or you can create a multiplayer network game so the player can play with other people.

Story or characters: Although less important for desktop games, a good game can also tell an interesting story and implement characters with which the player can identify.

Platform Consideration

In this book, we present the possibility of developing desktop games for a variety of platforms, such as KDE/Linux, Qt/Windows, or Qtopia/PDAs (see Chapters 3 through 5). With relatively little effort, such games can be transferred between all Qt-based platforms. Note, however, that the transfer to another platform is only possible in source code form.

When developing a game, it is important to know which target platforms you plan to publish it on, and whether you need cross-platform features. They will increase the possible user base, but will restrict you from using special target platform-dependent features such as hardware acceleration. If, for example, the game is specifically developed for handheld devices, you will have to limit the complexity, the artificial intelligence, and the graphics to compensate for the lower resources.

The following is a brief list of the advantages and disadvantages of developing for one of the specific platforms discussed in this book:

Pure Qt application: Runs on all platforms supported by Qt; in other words, all main operating systems. However, the user interface does not always conform to typical platform rules.

Qt/Windows application: Qt allows you to address some special features of Microsoft® Windows®; for example, ActiveX. However, by doing so you will not be able to move to another platform.

Qtopia/embedded Qt application: Developing for Qtopia is very similar to the development of a pure Qt application. However, Qtopia provides some special features only available for handheld computers, but these can be replaced or removed quite easily when porting to a desktop computer.

Native KDE application: Developing a native KDE application has the big advantage that you can rely on the many additional library classes that KDE provides to make programming easier. Moreover, your application will integrate seamlessly into the KDE desktop. However, using these additional libraries makes it more difficult to port the game to another Qt platform.

In general, you can create the maximum portability between these platforms by implementing your core game engine in pure Qt, and designing the user interface (the most library-dependent part) in a way that you can easily replace it. Using preprocessor conditions (`#ifdef`) or conditional Makefiles allows you to replace the library-dependent parts without having to redesign the entire game. If the actual game data is additionally available in data files, the game content can be easily adapted (e.g., to provide graphics in different sizes for PDAs and desktop computers).

A typical scenario for such a port would be to transfer a KDE game to a hand-held computer running Qtopia/Qt. From our experience, such a port is possible with moderate effort for most desktop games.

THE GAME DESIGN DOCUMENT

Before starting to code, think about the specific details of the game and create a *game design document*. Depending on the actual game and the size of the project, the design document can be prepared with varying levels of detail.

For Open Source game development, it is particularly useful to have a game design document because it can be published on the Internet, and gives other contributors (programmers or artists) an idea of what the game is about and whether it is worth getting involved. Without a detailed description and a development plan, it will be difficult to convince people to join your project. Furthermore, often the "vision" of the lead developer keeps a project running. In an Open Source project, there are frequently many people with different ideas on where the project should go, and more often than not, they can exclude each other. Therefore, there must be some type of document that fixes the eventual goal; that is, how the game is supposed to be. Otherwise, people may start to work against each other and eventually leave the project.

There is no standard rule on how to write a game design document. In the following list, we describe some of the items usually found in these documents [Gdd03], [Gdd05]. Of course, leave out any items that might not be applicable to your game. Furthermore, in Chapter 18, "A Practical Summary," we present a fully functional example game developed using this form of game design document.

Game Overview: The Game Overview includes the (tentative) name of the new game, a short description of what the game is about, and a general introduction into the game. Also comment on what type of game is actually being developed (e.g., puzzle, flight simulator, etc.), and the target platforms on which the game should run.

Game Rules: Here, the rules of the game are defined in more detail. Included are how the game is played, the actual game flow, what movement rules exist, what is done before the game starts, and how it ends. It is also important to specify how the players achieve scores or other rewards.

Interface: This section goes into more detail about the actual program. A screen description contains preliminary sketches (done with a common paint program) of the screen output. Having such screen sketches allows other people and the artists to form an impression of what the game is about and how it should look. Additionally, the user interface, including the necessary menus, toolbars, and keyboard and mouse inputs are defined.

Multimedia: Another important issue is the definition of the sound and graphics used in the game. This includes the type of graphics (2D or 3D), the graphic libraries necessary to implement this, and the type of sound and the sound library (see Chapters 6 through 9). You can also specify the support you need from artists concerning sprites, background graphics, sound effects, or 3D models.

Artificial Intelligence: If your game is supposed to implement a computer player, you must decide what type of artificial intelligence (AI) you need and how to implement it. Not every type of AI is suitable for every game. Furthermore, an AI player should play with a reasonable strength; that is, it always needs to be comparable to the human player. We discuss AI in more detail in Chapter 10, "Artificial Intelligence."

Story: If your game includes a story, you should think about it before implementing the game. Although many desktop games do not need a story (or do, and don't have one), a captivating story can make a game very attractive. A good tale should cause players to become more engrossed in the game, and identify with their units or characters. However, there is nothing worse than having to read 20 pages of screen text before the actual game starts.

Level and Map Design: You should also include a basic idea on the levels and maps used in the game. Although at this point, not all the levels will be created, it is useful to specify how the levels and maps should essentially look and what elements they contain. Both will affect your game programming, and you should consider it as early as possible. For example, if your 2D strategy game suddenly needs air units or underground levels, the development of your game will be hindered.

Multiplayer: One of the main issues to think about in the early stages of development is who and how many players will play the game. Will this be just one player at one desktop computer (single player), many players on one computer (hot-seat multiplayer), or multiple players over a network (peer-to-peer or host-based network)? This decision will obviously influence your game design, and quite often, games are developed as single-player desktop games and multiplayer features are added later. Although this often can work, it is not guaranteed; therefore, it is wiser to include this consideration in the early design stages. You can find more information on network games in Chapter 14, "Qt Network Games," and Chapter 15, "The KGame Library."

There is one useful way in which actual programming can be applied before the design is finished—rapid prototyping—and you can use it to check whether a particular idea or concept works. Suppose, for example, that you have an idea about a feature of the game but are unsure whether it functions or even makes sense. To test your theory, you can implement a very basic draft version of the game or the feature. Doing this will show you whether there are any difficulties. In such a rapid design, do not pay any attention to the graphics or any other effects; just focus on the particular item you want to test, and implement it. Unless you want to test the artificial intelligence, you should also leave it out and play all the players by yourself. Note, however, that rapid prototyping normally ends with horrible-looking source code. When developing the real game, it is often wise to just delete the source code and start over, thereby profiting from the experiences in the quick test but not binding your overall design to it.

DESKTOP GAME ARCHITECTURE

Once the basic ideas about the game are collected, you need to think about the classes and the class architecture of the game. It is important to spend some time on this design phase before actually starting to code. These designs can be made with either pen and paper or some UML tools that allow you to create a class design on the computer. Several tools are available that are Open Source or at least free for private use [Uml05].

Creating a good class design has the advantage that you have a better overview of the project, and the individual classes have less dependency on one another. Consequently, the project is easier to maintain, features can be added without having to touch many code sections, and the bugs are easier to find and fix. Lacking a good design becomes even more apparent when you have a large project.

One useful way to create a good game architecture is to identify the independent parts of the program and implement them in independent classes. For a desktop game, this will include the actual game data, the game engine, the display of the game, the playback of the sound, the players, and the players' input to the game.

The Document-View Model

Since desktop games are in many respects similar to other desktop applications, we can apply a concept used by many other standard desktop applications called the *document-view* model, and extend it to the desktop games scenario. The document-view model originates from word-processing type programs where the document object represents the data of a document; that is, its text and formatting, and one or more views are used to display the actual text on the screen (see Figure 1.2).

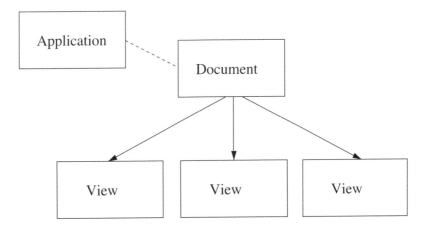

FIGURE 1.2 Conventional document-view architecture.

The idea of the document-view model can be extended to a desktop game. This extension is straightforward and takes into account the particular aspects of a game such as players and player input. Figure 1.3 depicts this form of game architecture, and in the following, the aspects of this architecture are described in more detail.

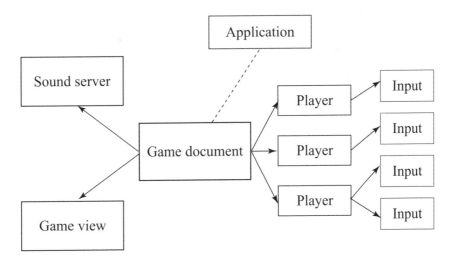

FIGURE 1.3 Desktop game architecture based on the game document, players, input devices, the game view, and sound server.

A game needs one or more graphical *views* to display the actual game on the screen. However, multiple views are often unnecessary for desktop games.

The *game data* or game *document* (the game engine) administers the game flow and the game logic, and collects all information about the game such as the game status and the game data.

A game has a certain amount of players. These players consist of their own specific data (score, equipment, etc.). We will use a *player* object to store exactly this data, and although the player data is in some way also part of the game, it is often beneficial to store it separately; that is, having game data and player data as individual classes.

Each player is connected to the "outside world" with some *input device*; for example, a keyboard, mouse, or joystick. Sometimes, such devices can also act as output devices (force-feedback joysticks), but in the scope of desktop games, this is of little use and we will ignore it. All input devices are represented by their own input class, which handles one particular type of input to the game. These input devices can then be plugged into the player objects and consequently allow the control over that player with one or more inputs (e.g., mouse and keyboard). Note that the artificial intelligence can be seen as an "input" to a player object—in this case, the computer player—and can consequently be treated as an input device. Such input devices make the game engine independent of the actual input. Mouse input, network players, and AI computer players are all treated the same way—they produce input (moves) to the game.

Most games will incorporate sound effects and background music. Playing sound to the user is in some ways very similar to displaying graphics. Consequently, the game also needs a sound "view," which is called the *sound server*.

The Application Framework

In addition to the game-specific architecture described in the previous section, every program for Qt, Qtopia, or KDE needs a certain framework that allows it to be launched and integrates the program with the underlying graphical desktop environment. Therefore, all GUI applications for these platforms are always constructed in the same specific way. Figure 1.4 illustrates this integration into the KDE desktop environment (a Qt application works analogously), and we will now briefly list the various classes needed to set up an application. For the platforms described in this book, these classes are also discussed in greater detail in Chapters 3 through 5. In these chapters, a generic desktop game application is developed that can serve as a starting point for your desktop game.

The *main program* of an application is called at program start. It creates the application object and the main window. This is done in the program `main.cpp` implementing the standard C++ `main()` function.

The *application object* created there represents the game application to the GUI framework. Both Qt and KDE offer an application class (`QApplication`, `KApplication`) for this purpose that can be often used without subclassing.

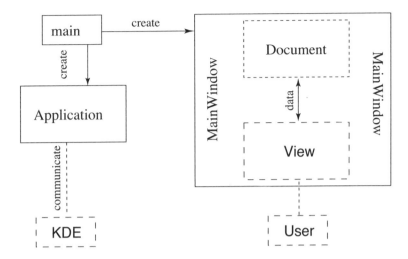

FIGURE 1.4 Standard application framework of a KDE application. The main program creates the application object and the main window. The application interacts with the KDE GUI, while the main window via the game data object and the game view presents the game data to the user.

The application handles all GUI resources and coordinates the communication and interaction of the game with the graphical desktop environment. This is done in the event loop (the main program loop) of the application. Here, all events (GUI events such as mouse clicks, buttons, or inherent game events such as timers) are received and distributed to the game. After this, the task of the application is to just react to the various incoming events (see Chapter 2, "Qt Primer").

One example of such an event is the press of the left mouse button, which might cause the movement of an object in the game. Once the event is processed, the method automatically returns to the event loop. Consequently, every method called by the event loop has to return quickly and must not perform lengthy calculations. Otherwise, the event loop is not continued, and the rest of the program, including the user interface, is blocked. In games in which lengthy calculations for AI or pathfinding are necessary, it is especially important to keep this in mind. There are two possible solutions to the problem: the calculation can be split into smaller steps, or a background thread has to be used that runs independently of the main program.

The *main window* represents and displays the application to the user of the graphical desktop environment. This main window includes the window frame, the menus, the toolbars, and the status bar. Usually, the view of the game is displayed inside the main window. Qt and KDE also provide a superclass for the main window (`QMainWindow`, `KMainWindow`), but to create and set up all the GUI elements such as menus and toolbars, they first need to be subclassed.

Data-Driven Programming

Data-driven game design aims at the separation of the actual game logic from the game data. While the game logic is implemented as standard C++ code, the game data is stored in configuration files. These files are then only read into the game engine at runtime.

Typical game data that can be stored in game data files and then processed by the designers include:

- Game maps and level design
- Units, characters, and game item definitions (properties, looks, etc.)
- Text (stories, messages, translations, etc.)
- Sound and graphics
- AI scripts and AI behavior rules
- General game control scripts (cut scenes, events, etc.)
- Game rules (winning conditions, movement rules, points, etc.)
- Game specifications (player count, etc.)

The ability to separate the code and data leads to a cleaner game design because the development of the game engine concentrates on the main programming task, and the actual game elements are designed and stored outside the program. Both sources are then only combined at runtime when the game engine loads the external data files. A separation of game logic and game data also allows the development of a much more generic game engine because the game engine does not necessarily depend on the actual game. Instead, the actual game is primarily described by the external data, not by the code.

There are several advantages to this type of separation which the programmer and the designer will appreciate:

- The changing of a map, the introduction of a new graphic, or even a new winning condition does not require the program to be recompiled.
- Alongside the coders, both artists and designers are able to make changes to the game.
- The actual game engine code becomes less complex because it only administers data handling, not the game description.
- The game engine can be reused in other games more easily.
- It is much easier to make changes and fine tune in the latter stages of program development or even in the testing phase.

Event-Driven Programming

In your game, many conditions and states will have to be evaluated; for example, program interface conditions such as "is this button pressed," or in-game elements such as "is this enemy attacking me?" There are in principle two programming techniques to handle such conditions. With the first, the states and conditions of your program can be actively queried by the object that is interested in them. This is called *polling*, and with this, your game unit, for example, can ask all other game units whether they just fired. In the second method, instead of actively querying all other objects, it is possible to let the other objects signal a state or condition change to the environment. This is done by sending out *events*. Other game objects can then just passively sit around and wait for an event to happen. Once an event arrives, they react to it. The flow of the program is therefore determined by these events.

A typical application for event-driven programming is a GUI, but the in-game logic can also be built on events. Event-driven programming is often more efficient because a typical polling query will normally return with no interesting results for most of the queries, and therefore, a lot of unnecessary code has to be executed. On the other hand, if you react to events, you will only act when the issue interests you.

In Chapter 2, we will learn two possibilities to handle events in Qt: the GUI event handlers, and the signal-slot framework of Qt, which allows every Qt object to send and receive events.

Reproducibility of Games

Another design issue when writing games is to assure that a particular game situation can be reproduced. This might sound strange for games, because you probably assume that you want as much random behavior as possible. However, this is only partly true. Indeed, a player should find himself with an individual or random game, but not so the developer. The developer must be able to reproduce a game so he can localize and fix bugs.

A game must be able to be started repeatedly in the same situation. This includes being able to repeat all the input, such as the moves of the players or the AI. Such reproducibility can only be achieved by logging the game status, including all game inputs. To be able to repeat the game, it is necessary to allow a "playback" of the log, which then serves as a script input to the game. An additional advantage of this log is that, depending on the game type, a replay feature can be provided, or a movie can be made of the game play. However, this is not easy to achieve, and sometimes it is sufficient if you know what moves to make so you can manually repeat them. For more information about this topic, see [Dickinson01].

A special problem that arises from reproducibility is the treatment of random numbers because they are obviously required to be random. However, in games, pseudo-random numbers (see Chapter 13, "Math and Physics in Desktop Games"), not real random numbers, are used. These numbers are a sequence of numbers appearing to be random but actually are not. A pseudo-random number sequence is entirely determined by an initial seed, and with an identical initial seed, the same random number sequence will be reproduced. For developers, your game should therefore support the explicit setting of the random seed.

Game Ticks

In turn-based computer games, the game flow is naturally split into steps called the *turns*. Real-time computer games appear to run continuously, but actually are broken into little execution blocks of a certain, often fixed, length of time. These blocks are called *game ticks*, and their purpose is to artificially break the game into little portions.

In each game tick, the game has to process all input that occurred, and run the game engine to continue the game flow. Within a tick, nearly all of the relevant game tasks are performed, such as moving units or characters, collision detection, or checking for winning conditions. Usually, all tasks performed within the game engine are performed in a game tick. The actual length of a game tick depends on the type of game, and is often only found by experimenting.

The Qt canvas classes (see Chapter 6, "Canvas Games") already provide all the necessary means to implement game ticks. Qt uses a special periodically-called method (named `advance()`) in which all canvas items are advanced; that is, the game flow is performed. When the Qt canvas is not used, game ticks can be also implemented, and for these cases, some type of "advance" method needs to be added to all game items. This method needs then to be regularly called by the game engine.

Tasks such as updating the game view that are not relevant to the game flow are usually performed outside a game tick method. However, whether the task of updating the game view is separated from the game ticks depends on the actual game and the libraries being used. For a Qt canvas, the advancing of items automatically updates the game view; therefore, both tasks are performed in synchronization.

Note that if the view update and the game ticks run in synchrony, you have to be careful not to make the game ticks depend on the view update; the view update should depend on the game ticks. If this is neglected, the game can become broken when graphic cards become faster and the number of displayed frames per second is increased, since the speed of the game also changes.

Performance Issues

For computer games, performance is often an important issue. Modern state-of-the-art computer games use the latest technologies and require the fastest computers. Desktop games are not as resource hungry, but when displaying extensive graphics or using sophisticated AI routines, you will notice the performance limits of your computer. It is therefore important to optimize a program.

However, optimizing a program is a critical task, and can often make the code more difficult to read or maintain. Eventually, a bug will be introduced, and in the end, more performance could be lost than was originally gained. Therefore, when optimizing is necessary, follow these development steps:

1. Make the game run.
2. Make the game stable.
3. Make the game fast.

Consequently, optimizing should be the last step of development.

It is also important to only optimize when you have a reason to, and to know which parts of the program should be optimized (this requires profiling). For example, there is little point in optimizing a function on which the program spends only 1% of the CPU time. However, if a function takes 20% of the CPU time and it could be improved by 25%, the overall program runs 5% faster (25% of 20%).

There are numerous tools available for profiling, in both commercial and Open Source formats. Actually, a very basic profile can be achieved by just measuring the time used for a particular function by using system functions (`gettimeofday()`). However, keep in mind that these measurements are imprecise, are only performed in accordance with the precision of the underlying clock, and can be affected by other running tasks.

GAME BALANCING

Game balancing is the art of adjusting the game so all elements in the game are in a good relation with one another. This is a necessary aspect because a player will only continue playing a game if it is challenging, interesting, and fair. Balancing is a key issue in all games, including commercial games, and even those sometimes show typical examples of imbalance in characters or units with only supportive or indirect powers, which in turn can become uninteresting to play. Such examples occur in games in which some characters are "weaker" than the others, such as diplomatic or medic figures.

You have to obtain an overall balance in the game to ensure that two players having the same skill will have the same likelihood of winning the game. This is particularly important to make the game fair. Individual items, characters, resources, and units of the game need to be in a balanced relation with each other, and their cost-benefit ratios need to be constant or at least similar. Otherwise, some units are preferred over others, certain units effectively useless. This leads to only very specific options for the player to choose from, and consequently, the game becomes boring.

Besides an overall game balance, the game also needs to maintain a constant balance throughout game play. Of course, when one player gains an advantage, at a certain point in the game, he should be rewarded so that subsequent achievements are easier to obtain and the player has a higher chance of winning the game (positive feedback). However, these positive feedbacks must only be employed at a moderate level so that the slightest advantage will not automatically lead to a guaranteed win—which would make the game unfair and tiresome. However, keep in mind that if there is no positive feedback in the game, it can also be boring.

Therefore, to achieve a proper game balance, try to avoid the following scenarios:

- If a player has a choice between several alternatives in the game—such as building units for a strategy game—but one of them is much more powerful than all the others, he will always choose this one—therefore, the game is boring.
- If during a game, a small advantage of one player is massively enhanced (positive feedback) and leads to a certain win, the game appears unfair.
- If during a game, the advantages of a player have no effect, the game will become uninteresting.
- If one side is much stronger than another side, the game is surely won or lost, which also makes it uninteresting.

One way to achieve a good deal of overall game balancing is by creating a symmetric game; that is, both/all players have exactly the same resources and rules. Most standard board games (e.g., chess or checkers) have this symmetric style. However, games are usually more interesting if they are asymmetric; that is, different players have different resources or rules. Many strategy or role-playing games follow this concept in which one player plays one type of units and another player has a different unit type. It is much harder to obtain a good balance in these types of scenarios, and normally, the balance is only achieved after testing the game.

Game balance can be attained through quality and quantity, which means that if one side has weaker units, it will have more resources to compensate. As a side remark, this trick is normally used to compensate for weak players, which is usually the AI computer player. This player is just equipped with a massive amount of resources and/or units.

Even if the overall game is balanced, you still need to balance the individual resources or units in relation to each other. Each resource needs to have a similar cost-benefit ratio; that is, the advantages gained by having an item need to be in constant relation to its cost. Assuming in a strategy game you can buy three different units A, B, and C for the cost of 10, 20, and 30 coins, respectively, then the relative strength of these units should be more or less 1:2:3. A ratio that is similar to 1:2:3

such as 1:2:4 can also be applicable because having more but weaker units can be advantageous in some game situations, and this can be compensated by increasing the strength of unit C. Of course, the reverse can be true. It is important to respect the cost-benefit ratios; otherwise, if you assume that unit A is as strong as unit C, for example, there would be little reason to obtain unit C.

Note that the cost-benefit ratio is more general than just looking at the strength of a unit in terms of hit-points. Some units are simply required to perform a certain task, whereas other units are quite useless unless they are in their special area. This can be taken into account for the cost-benefit ratio.

A general way to have different units in a game but still keep an overall game balance is to implement the rules of the rock-scissors-paper game. In this simple game, each player has the choice of three possibilities (rock, scissors, paper), and each of them beats one other (rock beats scissors, scissors beats paper, and paper beats rock). Although there exist very different "units" of very uneven strength, the overall game is balanced because each player has the same chance of winning. These rules can be applied in a more general way to many game scenarios, and having many rock-scissors-paper rules built into a game produces an interesting game that can still be fair and balanced. You will find that many games, especially strategy games, employ this rock-scissors-paper concept, although often in a more hidden form (aircraft beats tank, tank beats anti-aircraft gun, anti-aircraft gun beats aircraft). Figure 1.5 depicts the rules of the rock-scissors-paper game when applied to the strategy game example.

Note that a proper game balance is often only found and achieved during game testing. It is therefore very important that the game remain modular even in the final stages, so the strengths of the various resources, items, or units can be adjusted.

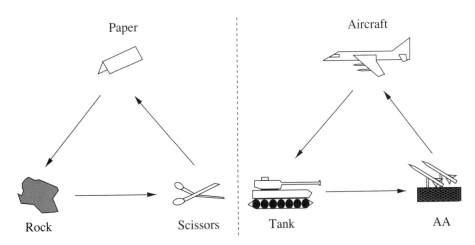

FIGURE 1.5 The rock-scissors-paper game (left) applied to the game balancing of a strategy game (right). The arrows indicate which item beats the other.

OPEN SOURCE GAME DEVELOPMENT

Developing a game is already a huge task; developing an Open Source game adds additional complexity. Although Open Source development can be done by one person, it is often done with a team of developers on the Internet. The advantages of Open Source programs are obvious: you can get a great deal of help from other developers and profit from their source codes. However, typical Open Source development also requires you to consider some additional points. In this section, we comment on a few of them.

Releasing the Game

Open Source programs need to be distributed to many people at very early stages of development. This includes other programmers, artists, or even curious users. However, Open Source developers tend to release only source code, leaving the compilation task to the user. While it may seem reasonable to a programmer to do the full configuration, make, and installation process, it may not be to a nonprogrammer. This becomes even more problematic when the configuration and make parts do not work without additional modifications to adapt the source code to the user's computer system.

To avoid such problems, it is essential to:

- Keep the number of dependencies (on external libraries or programs) low.
- Make it as easy as possible to install a recent version of the game.
- Fix errors in the build system as soon as possible.
- When possible, provide binary packages.

Unfortunately, this sounds easier than it is, since packages made for one system may not work on another system. Furthermore, they will only function when all dynamically linked libraries are installed on the target platform.

Communication

A main issue in Open Source projects is the communication and coordination between the developers. Often, this communication is via e-mail or mailing lists, the more extended form of e-mail. With the latter, an e-mail is automatically forwarded to everyone subscribed to a list. Internet Relay Chat (IRC) is another form of communication, and can be used for instantaneous chats, while announcements made on the project's Web site are more permanent. For most tasks, mailing lists are the most efficient.

Regardless of the form of communication you choose, it is important to distribute all information and news about the project to all relevant developers so they can contribute to the discussion and not develop on an outdated concept.

Tools

Another obstacle that sometimes arises in Open Source programming is that nobody knows what tools can be used to create data or files, such as maps, sound effects, graphics, or 3D models. Often, someone is interested in helping to develop these files, but does not know which tools to use. In such cases, it is important that you can answer this question either in person or within a document on the project Web site. Otherwise, the person who wants to help you needs to first search for the appropriate tools, and might waste time on programs that are not well suited for the particular task. In the end, these helpers are often scared away.

License Issues

Developing Open Source games has several advantages. One of the most prominent is the use of source code from other games, which allows you to gain experience from other projects and developers to use in your own project. Consequently, the rate of achievement in your own progress is accelerated, as you do not have to learn how to do everything on your own.

However, when using other people's work in your code, whether it is actual source code or sound and graphics elements, you have to be familiar with the actual licenses of these items. If something is Open Source, it does not mean that you can do whatever you want with it. What you *can* do depends on the actual license. For example, incorporating items with the GNU General Public License forces you to release your code under the same license. We discuss these license issues in more detail in Chapter 17 "Open Source and Intellectual Property Rights."

SUMMARY

Game development is a fun and interesting task. In the realm of desktop games, everybody can learn how to program a game. Developing small desktop games can be achieved by a single person or in a small team. In the remainder of this book, we present you with the necessary technologies for doing so.

If your games are developed as Open Source software, you will profit enormously from the large amount of Open Source software already available on the Internet. This software can be tools that help you in development, libraries you can use in your game, and even source code that you can legally incorporate into your game from other Open Source programs. However, when using Open Source software, you must respect the details of the different licenses.

Open Source software is often developed on the Internet with a group of developers. This form of distributed development involves some additional consideration on how to communicate between the developers and users, and even how the game should be released. In this chapter, we briefly acknowledged some of the issues that you need to keep in mind when developing Open Source software on the Internet.

When developing a game, even a small desktop game, it is advisable not to immediately start programming. Typing in the source code as soon as you have the first idea is often not a good idea, and many programmers underestimate the importance of planning and designing a project before actually starting to program. Thus, it is advisable to first collect your ideas, and then formulate a game concept and class design. Once the basic concept and design of the game are produced, the actual programming can be started and becomes much easier. In this chapter, we presented the game design document as a way to describe a game and its concept. Additionally, we showed a possible, quite generic, class design that can be used for a variety of desktop games.

The actual implementation, and, in particular, the platform-dependent features such as the integration in the graphical desktop environment, can require the addition of some platform-dependent parts of your game. In the following chapters, we introduce you to Qt and KDE and show you how to set up a desktop game application for platforms such as KDE, PDAs, or Microsoft Windows.

REFERENCES

[Astle04] Astle, Dave, and Kevin Hawkins, *Beginning OpenGL Game Programming*, ISBN: 1592003699; Muska & Lipman/Premier-Trade, 2004.

[DeLoura00] DeLoura, Mark, *Game Programming Gems Vols. 1–2*, ISBNS: 1584500492, 1584500549; Charles River Media, 2000–2002.

[Dickinson01] Dickinson, Patrick, *Instant Replay: Building a Game Engine with Reproducible Behavior*, http://www.gamasutra.com/features/20010713/dickinson_01.htm, 2001.

[Gdd03] *Game Design Document*, http://members.shaw.ca/bsimser/webdesign/sample/default.htm, 2003.

[Gdd05] *Game Design Document*, http://www.digipen.edu/~dquinn/beatman/gdd.html, 2005.

[Howland99] Howland, Geoff, *Game Design: The Addiction Element*, http://www.gamedev.net/reference/articles/article263.asp, 1999.

[Howland05] Howland, Geoff, *Game Design: The Essence of Computer Games*, http://www.lupinegames.com/articles/essgames.htm, 2005.

[Kirmse04] Kirmse, Andrew, *Game Programming Gems Vol. 4*, ISBN: 1584502959; Charles River Media, 2004.

[Openal05] *Cross-Platform 3D Audio, http://www.openal.org*, 2005.

[Pallister05] Pallister, Kim, *Game Programming Gems Vol. 5*, ISBN: 1584503521; Charles River Media, 2005.

[Rabin02] Rabin, Steve, *AI Game Programming Wisdom Vols. 1–2*, ISBN: 1584500778, 1584502894; Charles River Media, 2002–2003.

[Treglia03] Treglia, Dante, *Game Programming Gems Vol. 3*, ISBN: 1584502339; Charles River Media, 2003.

[Uml05] *UML Tools, http://www.jeckle.de/umltools.htm*, 2005.

2 Qt Primer

In This Chapter

- Qt 3 and Qt 4
- The Qt Meta-Object-Compiler
- The Qt Class Library
- Signals and Slots
- Timers
- Qt Events
- Layout Manager
- A Qt "Hello World" Application

Qt is a C++ GUI toolkit and application framework that is mainly used to create windows, buttons, menus, and other graphical objects within a C++ application. Besides the graphical features, Qt also offers a C++ class library that includes a set of utility and template classes often used in standard programming tasks. For many applications, including desktop games, these utility and template classes are powerful enough to allow program development without resorting to the often-used C++ Standard Template Library (STL). This is definitely an advantage, since you have to depend on only one extra C++ library. Alongside these features, Qt has introduced a set of preprocessor keywords that allow you to construct an advanced inter-object communication scheme known as the *signal-slot mechanism*.

Besides being an excellent toolkit, there are two additional reasons why we use the Qt toolkit as a basis for all programming examples in this book. First, Qt is a cross-platform toolkit that allows the development of applications on KDE/Linux, Microsoft Windows, Apple Macintosh Mac OS, and handheld devices such as PDAs and smart phones. Applications developed for one Qt target platform can be transferred, with minimal effort and only small differences in the source code, to other target platforms on which a Qt implementation exists. The distribution of desktop games can profit enormously if they are easily portable and thus available on other target platforms. Second, a main target platform for Open Source game programming is the KDE desktop on Linux. KDE is based on the Qt toolkit; therefore, programming KDE applications requires the use of Qt.

For Open Source programmers, the additional advantage of Qt is that despite being a commercial library, it is also available with an Open Source license (GPL or QPL). This free license incorporates Qt 3 on Linux, Apple Macintosh, and handheld devices, and Qt 4 on all Qt target platforms. Unfortunately, the use of Qt 3 on Microsoft Windows is not possible with an Open Source version of Qt. There is one exception to this problem, which we discuss in Chapter 4, "Qt Game Development Using Microsoft Windows."

Our aim in this chapter is to provide a brief overview of Qt, the main Qt classes, and the additional features relevant for desktop game programming. If you are already familiar with Qt, you can probably skip this chapter. Note that this chapter does not intend to teach you the full extent of Qt or provide a fully comprehensive Qt course.

QT 3 AND QT 4

Currently (2005), Qt is undergoing a changeover in the major version from Qt 3 to Qt 4. For the Qt aspects used in this book, Qt 4 is generally quite source code compatible with Qt 3. In this book, we based our example on Qt 3, but tried to incorporate as few version-dependent features as possible. In some examples where there are special things to consider for Qt 4, we mention the difference between Qt 3 and Qt 4 explicitly.

To allow Qt 3 source code to be ported to Qt 4, Qt 4 can be run in compatibility mode, which allows you to compile Qt 3 source code. To do so, the flag `-DQT_COMPAT` has to be specified to the compiler, and `QT += qt3support` to the project file. Additionally, the tool `qt3to4` needs to be run to replace some naming standards in your source code. To avoid the Qt compatibility mode, we present some key features of Qt important to the desktop games discussed in this book and for these features, we give both a Qt 3 and Qt 4 example: with this knowledge, you can manually enhance your programs to be pure Qt 4 code.

If you develop your own desktop game, the selection of the Qt version is entirely your choice. However, with software libraries it is sometimes difficult to decide when to move to a new version. Qt 3 will have, for still some time, a larger user base than Qt 4 has. In addition, KDE 3 is based on Qt 3 and is very popular and widespread. On the other hand, Qt 4 offers more features, a more consistent handling of the template classes, and better performance. In the same way in which KDE 3 is based on Qt 3, KDE 4 will be based on Qt 4.

The programming examples of this chapter are included on the CD-ROM accompanying the book: the example program myqt3 located in the folder examples/myqt3 is used for Qt 3, and the program myqt4 in the folder examples/myqt4 serves as an example for Qt 4. Note that these example programs will show a graphical window and display some output on a console window. This refers to the application of the utility classes such as regular expressions whose content or output we dump to the console.

THE QT META-OBJECT-COMPILER

Qt introduces a set of preprocessor keywords (macros) that are used to identify and use some of the special Qt features. These special keywords can be inserted into the normal C++ source code typically in the class declaration in a C++ header file. To translate these keywords into standard C++ source code, Qt provides an additional program called the Meta-Object-Compiler (MOC). Running MOC on a source code enriched with these special Qt keywords will transform the source code into a proper C++ program by auto-coding the remaining C++ code necessary to implement these keywords. MOC runs can be included in a Makefile so they are automatically executed before compiling the C++ source code. Examples for these keywords are:

```
// Mark a class for MOC
Q_OBJECT

// Signal declarations
signals:

// Slot declarations
public slots:


...
```

A source code file is recognized by MOC to implement the extended Qt features if the class declaration contains the Q_OBJECT keyword at the beginning of the class declaration.

```
class MyClass : public QObject
{
  Q_OBJECT
  ...
};
```

The primary use of Qt Meta Object systems is to implement the Qt signal and slot mechanism. This is an inter-object communication system and can be used to exchange events, messages, or other notifications between objects. The two keywords `signals` and `slots` are used for this purpose.

```
class MyClass : public QObject
{
  Q_OBJECT

  public:
    ...

  signals:
    ...

  public slots:
    ...
};
```

In this chapter, we describe the signal-slot mechanism in more detail. If any class should use the extended Qt features such as the signal-slot mechanism, it needs to be derived from the `QObject` class, which is the base class of all Qt objects. Note that every `QObject` can have a parent object, which is supplied in its constructor. If a parent object is destroyed, all children are removed, too.

THE QT CLASS LIBRARY

Qt is mainly a graphical toolkit for GUI programming. However, in addition to the GUI programming features, it offers a multitude of useful classes. These classes comprise GUI programming and general programming tasks such as strings supporting Unicode, arrays and lists, and extra supporting classes for file input and output.

We often find that the main problem when using a new class library is that you do not know what features are actually available. Therefore, we view this section as an overview of the Qt classes important for desktop games and do not explain the

classes in great detail, since they are well documented in the Qt manuals [Qtdoc05].
If the manual pages do not suffice, the book of Blanchette [Blanchette04] or the
Web site [Qttut05] provides more detailed tutorials for Qt.

General Qt Classes

Qt offers a variety of C++ classes that can be used for standard programming tasks.
Useful classes for games include string handling, array, list, or lookup table classes.

Strings

The QString class is a convenient way to store ASCII and Unicode strings. It allows
the conversion to and from character arrays as well as number types. Strings can be
searched and replaced, appended, and cut.

```
// Create a string from char* (works only if Qt compiled
// without QT_NO_CAST_ASCII)
QString str;
str = "This is a QString.";

// More generally the following form can be used:
str = QString::fromLatin1("This is a QString");

// Replace parts of the string
str.replace("QString", "Replaced string");

// Find first occurrence of a string or character ('a')
// In Qt3:
int find;
find = str.find("a");
// In Qt4:
find = str.indexOf("a");

// Concatenate two strings
str = str + QString::fromLatin1(" This is more text.");

// Insert arguments into a string
str = QString::fromLatin1("Player %1 has %2 points")
      .arg(2).arg(17.3);
// Results in: "Player 2 has 17.3 points"
```

Arrays

In Qt 3, the class QMemArray provides a template array class for primitive types. It can be easily resized and handles the required memory internally. QByteArray and QCanvasPixmapArray are implementations for two special array types that are valuable for games. QByteArray stores char items and QCanvasPixmapArray QPixmap items for canvas use.

```
// Construct an array
QMemArray<int> array(5);

// Resize array to size 10
array.resize(10);

// Retrieve the size
int size = array.size(); // == 10

// Fill all elements in the array with one value
array.fill(42);

// Set element values
array[0] = 5;
array[1] = 7;

// Get elements
int value0 = array[0];     // == 5
int value1 = array.at(1); // == 7
```

In Qt 4, the template class QVector replaces QMemArray. Its use is similar to QMemArray.

```
// Construct an array
QVector<int> array(5);

// Resize array to size 10
array.resize(10);

// Retrieve the size
int size = array.size(); // == 10

// Fill all elements in the array with one value
array.fill(42);

// Set element values
```

```
array[0] = 5;
array[1] = 7;

// Get elements
int value0 = array[0];      // == 5
int value1 = array.at(1); // == 7
```

Lists

In Qt 3, QPtrList provides a template list operating on pointers, and the QValueList class is the corresponding template for a value-based list class. A useful extension of a QValueList is QStringList, which is a value list based on QStrings. All list types provide an iterator class; here, QPtrListIterator and QValueList::iterator. The following example shows how to implement a value list.

```
// Create a new list
QValueList<int> valList;

// Append some elements
valList.append(1);
valList.append(2);
valList.append(3);

// Iterate list
QValueList<int>::iterator it;
for (it = valList.begin(); it != valList.end(); ++it)
{
  // Get the current list element
  int current = (*it);
  ...
}

// Directly access second list element
int second = valList[1];
```

The next example shows the use of a pointer-based list type.

```
QPtrList<int> ptrList;

// Fill the list
int i = 1;
int j = 2;
ptrList.append(&i);
ptrList.append(&j);
```

```
// Iterate the list
QPtrListIterator<int> it(ptrList);
int* value;
while (it.current() != 0)
{
  value = it.current();
  ++it;
  // Get the list element
  int current = *value;
  ...
}
```

In Qt 4, the pointer and nonpointer list classes are no longer distinguished, and the template classes QList and QLinkedList replace both former list classes. Which list class to choose depends on the application of the list. Usually, QList is the right choice because it provides fast access by item index, while QLinkedList only allows iterator-based access.

The following example shows a QList application for (integer) values.

```
// Create the list
QList<int> list;

// Append elements
list.append(1);
list.append(2);
list.append(3);

// Iterate list
QListIterator<int> it(valList);
while (it.hasNext())
{
  // Retrieve the current element
  int value = it.next();
  ...
}

// Loop the list
for (int i = 0; i < list.size(); i++)
{
  // Retrieve the current element
  int value = list[i];
  ...
}
```

Similarly, a `QList` would work for (integer) pointers.

```
// Create the list
QList<int*> list;

int i = 1;
int j = 2;

// Append elements
list.append(&i);
list.append(&j);
```

Lookup Tables

Lookup tables allow the association of one object (the value) with another object (the key). Accessing the lookup table with a given key will return the corresponding stored value. Loosely speaking, lookup tables are an extended form of array access. In simple arrays, an object (the value) can be looked up with an integer number (the array index), while in lookup tables, this integer index can now be any object (supporting the < operator). Very often, strings are used as lookup keys. Note that in normal arrays, the index keys must be numbered continuously (0,1,...*size*-1). This requirement does not exist for lookup tables; here, arbitrary keys can be used.

In Qt 3, `QMap` provides a value-based lookup table, while `QDict` is a pointer-based table. The following code snippet shows the use of `QMap` using strings as keys to look up their associated values; here, integer numbers. The example program on the companion CD-ROM also includes a `QDict` demonstration.

ON THE CD

```
// Create map and insert the data items. In our example
// we store the points of some players in the map.
QMap<QString,int> map;
map["Jim"]   = 31;
map["Bob"]   = 22;
map["Alice"] = 18;

// Check presence of an element
if (map.contains("Alice"))
{
  ...
}

// Retrieve the data stored for an element, here "Alice"
int value = map["Alice"]; //  == 18
```

```
// It is also possible to iterate all elements
QMap<QString,int>::Iterator it;
for (it = map.begin(); it != map.end(); ++it)
{
  QString key = it.key();
  int value   = it.data();
  ...
}
```

In Qt 4, both the template class QMap and QHash replaces the pointer- and value-based map classes of Qt 3. QMap and QHash work basically the same and differ mainly by access speed (QHash is faster) and in the way the keys are sorted (QMap sorts the keys). For desktop games, usually QHash is preferable, and is shown in the following code snippet:

```
// Create map and insert the data items
QHash<QString,int> map;
map["Jim"]   = 31;
map["Bob"]   = 22;
map["Alice"] = 18;

// Check presence of an element
if (map.contains("Alice"))
{
  ...
}

// Iterate all elements
QHashIterator<QString,int> it(map);
while (it.hasNext())
{
  it.next();
  QString key = it.key();
  int value   = it.value();
  ...
}
```

Pattern Matching

Pattern matching is a powerful way of string processing. Strings can be searched for special patterns called *regular expressions*. These expressions go beyond the simple searching of constant text in strings, since they allow the formulation of text matches such as *Match a string that starts with "A" and has three arbitrary characters; these are then followed by "up" or "down", one or more whitespace and two numbers, the string must end with ".".* This task is not readily achieved by the standard character comparison of text strings. Regular expressions, however, can easily process these types of descriptions. Even though normal desktop games do not generally integrate regular expressions, they are useful when having to parse textual input data or script languages, and when designing file formats.

QRegExp is a class that allows you to use regular expressions so that pattern matching in strings can be performed. A detailed list of the patterns supported by QRegExp is found in the Qt library reference documentation [Qtdoc05].

```
// Create a regular expression, which will match a string
// where: one or more digits (\\d+) are followed by a
// whitespace (\\s) which then is followed by one of the two
// units (meter or feet). After this any number of characters
// (.*) can follow until the side (top or bottom) is found.
QRegExp regexp("(\\d+)\\s(meter|feet).*(top|bottom)");

// Now we create a string which can and will be matched
// by the regular expression
QString str = "This is 42 meter from the top.";

// Search for an occurrence of the regular expression in the
// string
int pos;
// In Qt3:
pos = rexexp.search(str);
// In Qt4:
pos  = regexp.indexIn(str);        // Return the position
bool exact = regexp.exactMatch(str); // Check exact matches

// The expression was found at the resulting position.
if (pos >= 0)
{
  // Do something useful
  ...
}

// Expressions surrounded by round brackets are captured and
// can be retrieved from the regular expression. Note, access
// such captures only if the expression really did match!
QString number = regexp.cap(1);  // "42"
QString unit   = regexp.cap(2);  // "meter"
QString side   = regexp.cap(3);  // "top"
```

File Input and Output

Reading game data or storing save files is an important task in game programming. Qt provides several utility classes that allow easy file and directory handling. Writing or reading data to/from files is usually done with text or binary streams.

Files and Streams

QFile essentially allows the opening and closing of files and supports basic file operations such as checking for the existence of a file. Furthermore, the QFileInfo class permits the retrieval of detailed information about the files, including its size, its absolute paths, the owner, or the file permissions. Alongside QTextStream or QDataStream, the files can be used for file input and output.

```
// Specify the filename
QFile file("demo.txt");

// Open file for writing
// (use IO_ReadOnly to open a file for reading)
// In Qt3:
file.open(IO_WriteOnly);
// In Qt4:
file.open(QFile::WriteOnly);

// Associate file and text stream
QTextStream stream(&file);

// Stream out some test
stream << QString("Hello World\n");

// Close file
file.close();
```

Directories

QDir provides access to the directories and their contents. With QDir, it is also possible to retrieve the contents of the directory, rename it, or create and remove directories.

The QDir path handling is shown in the following code snippet:

```
QDir dir;
QString path;
// In Qt3:
path = dir.absPath();
// In Qt4:
```

```
path = dir.absolutePath();
...

// Change directories
dir.cdUp();
dir.cd(newDirectory);
```

QDir allows you to retrieve a list of all files of a directory. However, the syntax differs slightly between Qt 3 and Qt 4. In Qt 3, it reads:

```
QDir dir;
// Retrieve file list information
const QFileInfoList* list = dir.entryInfoList();
for (QFileInfoListIterator it(*list); it.current(); ++it)
{
  QFileInfo* info = it.current();
  ...
}
```

In Qt 4, the list handling follows the usual QLists convention.

```
QDir dir;
// Retrieve file list information
QFileInfoList list = dir.entryInfoList();
QListIterator<QFileInfo> it(list);
while (it.hasNext())
{
  QFileInfo info = it.next();
  QString filename = info.fileName();
  ...
}
```

GUI Widgets

Since Qt is principally a GUI toolkit, most Qt classes implement GUI features such as windows, buttons, colors, geometrical forms, or fonts. However, in this chapter we do not describe these GUI classes in more detail. Classes that are necessary to set up a desktop game are discussed in the following chapters when we implement a generic desktop game application. For additional Qt GUI classes, we refer to the Qt manuals. Some GUI classes of particular importance for our games include:

QAction: An abstract user interface for menus and toolbars.

QBrush: Represents a brush for drawing areas.

QCanvas: A fast 2D drawing area with automatic update.

QColor: Represents a color based on the RGB or HSV color model.

QFont: A representation of a text font.

QImage: Hardware-independent graphics. Direct pixel manipulations possible.

QLayout: Provides layout managers through its subclasses.

QMainWindow: The main window of the application. Organizes status bars, tool bars, and menus.

QPainter: Direct low-level access to graphics painting.

QPen: Represents a pen to draw lines and outlines.

QPixmap: Hardware-dependent graphics.

QPopupMenu: Represents a menu.

QPushButton: Provides a push button.

QWidget: The base of all Qt window classes. A variety of specialized subclasses exist.

A special feature of Qt GUI objects, which take a parent object in their constructor such as the QWidget or QLayout subclasses, is that they are automatically destroyed if their parent object is removed.

Note the differences between Qt 3 and Qt 4:

QCanvas: All canvas classes exist as Q3Canvas, Q3CanvasSprite, and so on in Qt 4.0. Only in Qt 4.1, the canvas classes will be available as native Qt 4 classes.

QPixmap and QImage: The Qt image classes do implicit sharing of the image data in Qt 3 but not in Qt 4.

QWidget: In Qt 4, the foreground and background handling of widget classes is changed. The widgets are now more flexible and flicker free. However, setting of background and foreground colors cannot be done directly anymore; instead, a QPalette object must be set using setPalette().

Geometrical Classes

To use the graphical elements of a GUI, Qt has also introduced some geometrical classes. These classes can also be used for general-purpose programming.

QPoint: Represents a 2D point.

QRect: Represents a rectangle.

QSize: Represents a size; that is, width and height.

SIGNALS AND SLOTS

Qt uses a mechanism called *signals* and *slots* to allow communication between objects. In essence, the signal from one object can tell surrounding objects that something has occurred, and if the signal is relevant to these other objects, they then react to the notification. This allows you to create a program in which objects specifically react to certain *events* raised by other objects: event-driven game programming becomes possible. Note that this description of events should not be confused with the main event loop of the application, which also handles events, but there we mean GUI events.

With this very efficient event-triggered programming, classes can become very independent, and objects derived from these classes are only connected via signals and slots. Consequently, the amount of code dependencies can been reduced. Figure 2.1 depicts a signal-slot mechanism between Qt objects.

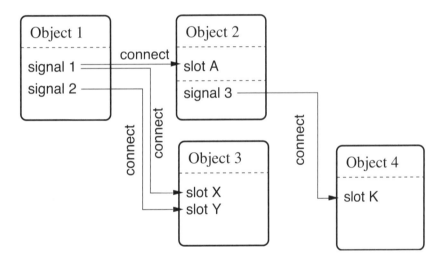

FIGURE 2.1 Basic signal slot mechanism. An object can define signals, which can be connected to its slots or that of another object. If a signal is emitted from one of the objects, the corresponding slots of the connected objects are invoked.

All objects that partake in this Qt communication framework should be derived from the base class QObject and additionally contain the Q_OBJECT macro as the very first line in their class declaration. All Qt classes such as windows, buttons, and timers follow these criteria, but you can also base user-defined classes on QObject and then use the signal-slot mechanism.

Signals and slots are designed to allow an easy and type-safe way to pass information from the sender to the receiver. Type-safe calling implies that only parameters that match the signature of the signal can be passed from the sender to the receiver. This is obvious for standard C++ method calls, but not all communication frameworks work in this manner.

There are generally several possibilities for signals to occur. A signal can be manually emitted by the programmer in any user class. This signal is then available to the rest of the program and will be received by all the objects that are connected to the signal. A good example here is a "*Game Over*" signal, which is emitted by a game class. The main window can pick up this signal and display a message to the user. The Qt and KDE libraries also provide numerous standard signals for a variety of GUI events such as button presses or menu selections. A program can connect and react to these.

An object can react to a signal if it *connects* a *slot* to a *signal*. Once the signal and the slot are connected, every time the signal is emitted the corresponding slot will be called. Note that more than one slot can be connected to any one signal. Signals and slots are marked with special keywords in the class header files. To translate these keywords to standard C++ code, the header files need to be processed by the MOC compiler before the actual C++ compilation is run. MOC then generates additional C++ source code that implements the signal-slot behavior. To notify the MOC compiler that the Qt language extensions should be applied, the macro Q_OBJECT has to be used in the class declaration.

The signals and slots can then be declared as normal C++ methods, but they are listed in the corresponding sections that are marked by the special keywords signals: and slots:, respectively. These definitions are shown in the following code snippet:

```
class MyObject : public QObject
{
  Q_OBJECT
  ...

  public slots:
    void mySlot();

    // Note that signals don't have a public/protected/private
    // modifier, as they are always public
    signals:
    void mySignal();
  ...
};
```

While signals are just a label for the communication, slots are actually normal C++ methods. The only difference between a normal C++ method and a slot declared in the `slots:` section is that this slot method can now be connected to a matching signal. The following example demonstrates the connection of the signal and the slot that were declared in the previous code snippet.

```
connect(this, SIGNAL(mySignal()),
        this, SLOT(mySlot()));
```

Here, the first and third arguments are the sending and receiving objects, which can be different from `this` and thus allow inter-object communication. Assuming we have a button named `button` that can emit the signal `clicked()`, we can connect it to our application.

```
connect(button, SIGNAL(clicked()),
        this,   SLOT(mySlot()));
```

If an object now wants to signal to all the connected objects that a particular event has happened, it just emits the corresponding signal.

```
emit mySignal();
```

The emitting object does not actually know whether anyone is interested in the event, and receives no feedback from any of the recipients. The sender just emits the signal to notify the event to the outside world. However, if there are objects connected to the signal, all objects will receive the signal and all will be called immediately. Note that the `emit mySignal()` command does not return before all connected slots have been called and have returned from processing.

It is also possible to assign parameters to a signal. These parameters are then passed to the signal just like a normal method call.

```
// Emit a signal with two numbers, one integer and one
// double number
emit mySignal(10, 20.4)
```

If a slot wants to connect to such a signal, it has to be defined with an identical method signature. The previous example declaration would therefore resemble:

```
class Object : public QObject
{
  Q_OBJECT
  ...

  public slots:
```

```
        void mySlot(int, double);

    signals:
        void mySignal(int, double);
    ...
};
```

The `connect()` command, which permits the connection between the signal and the slot using two arguments, would look like:

```
connect(this, SIGNAL(mySignal(int, double)),
        this, SLOT(mySlot(int, double)));
```

Signals and slots have to have matching signatures. Otherwise, the slot will not be called and a console warning is issued when the connection is built. This strict signature rule guarantees a type-safe calling of signals and slots. However, it can also be a source for programming errors. Errors occur if you are not careful which parameters are used for the signals and slots. These types of mistakes are unfortunately only observed when the program is running, since the signal-slot connects are performed at runtime. Then, you might wonder why a slot is not called. If this happens, check the console output for Qt warning messages concerning slots.

It is important to notice that inside the actual program, the signal-slot mechanism works like a normal method call. Signals and slots are not processed by the event loop of the application that handles GUI and timer events and so on. This is important to understand the calling sequence of the statements. Signal-slot calls are executed immediately once a signal is emitted, while real (GUI) events are queued and processed once the program returns to the main event loop; that is, when the current method is finished.

A convenient extension when multiple similar signals are used is a `QSignalMapper`. A `QSignalMapper` takes signals from different objects, and for every signal it receives, it emits another distinct signal along with a number or string. This signal/number or signal/string combination then describes the object that emitted the original signal. This concept is described in the following code snippet:

```
// Create a signal mapper with "this" as parent
QSignalMapper* mapper = new QSignalMapper(this);

// Create a button and connect it to the mapper
QButton* button = new QPushButton("Skip move", this);
connect(button, SIGNAL(clicked()),
        mapper, SLOT(map()));
```

```
// Associate this button's signal with the number '42'
mapper->setMapping(button, 42);
// Alternatively: Associate the button with a string
// mapper->setMapping(button, "Skip");

// Connect the mapper instead of the button to our
// target slot, here evaluteButtons(int)
connect(mapper, SIGNAL(mapped(int)),
        this, SLOT(evaluateButtons(int)));
```

TIMERS

Timers and counting are important ingredients for games, and Qt provides the QTimer class for such tasks. This class is very easy to use and allows the integration of periodically repeated events and single notification after a given time period.

The class QTimer implements an internal timer that can be set to an arbitrary countdown. Once started, the timer will then count down, and when zero is reached, the signal timeout() will be emitted. Objects connecting to this signal can therefore receive timed information. There are two types of timers: an interval timer that continually repeats a set amount of time until it is manually stopped; and a single-shot timer that stops completely when the timeout occurs and does not restart. The latter timer is useful for one-time events, delayed actions, or for implementing asynchronous actions.

To use an interval timer in your program, you have to create an instance of the QTimer class and connect a slot to the timer's timeout() signal.

```
// Create a timer object with parent 'this'. Like all
// QObjects, the QTimer is destroyed when the parent is
// destroyed
QTimer* timer = new QTimer(this);

// Connect a slot to the timer's timeout() signal
connect(timer, SIGNAL(timeout()),
        this,  SLOT(mySlot()));
```

A continuous mode timer can be started by calling the method start(), which contains the desired timeout value in milliseconds.

```
// Start the timer to emit the signal every one
// second (1000ms)
timer->start(1000);
```

The timer object can also be used to start a single-shot timer; that is, a timer that times out only once and does not restart afterward.

```
// Start the timer to emit the signal 'timeout()' exactly
// once. The signal is emitted after one second (1000 ms)
// In Qt3:
timer->start(1000, TRUE);
// In Qt4:
timer->setSingleShot(true);
timer->start(1000);
```

A single-shot timer can also be started using the static method singleShot(), which will call a slot after the given time.

```
// Generate a timer event and call the corresponding slot
// event after one second (1000ms)
QTimer::singleShot(1000, this, SLOT(mySlot()));
```

Timers are a convenient way to generate periodic or delayed effects in a game. Note, however, that the accuracy of the timer depends on the operating system and the computer hardware used.

QT EVENTS

The event loop of a Qt application is the permanently running main loop of the program. It is started by the application's exec() method QApplication::exec(), and this is the point from where all the methods of your program are invoked. Once a method is finished, the program returns to the event loop. This event loop is finally left only if the application is quit by calling QApplication::quit().

Qt receives many native events from the underlying windowing system (like X11 or Microsoft Windows) and translates them into Qt events. These events are processed in the event loop and then forwarded to the corresponding Qt objects. Although system events are the main source of events in a program, it is possible to have other events that are created by the application itself. These events can be generated using the QApplication::sendEvent() method.

Typical examples for events are *"the click of a mouse button," "the paint request for a window,"* or *"the size change of a window."* Event handlers for these events would be implemented as:

```
// React to mouse clicks
void MyWidget::mousePressEvent(QMouseEvent* e)
```

```
  {
    ...
  }

  // React to paint requirements, that is the window needs to
  // be repainted
  void MyWidget::paintEvent(QPaintEvent* e)
  {
    ...
  }

  // The window got resized
  void MyWidget::resizeEvent(QResizeEvent* e)
  {
    ...
  }
```

Qt event objects are little containers that contain the actual event parameters relevant for this particular event. An event is passed to the corresponding event handler method to allow its processing. For example, the mouse click event QMouseEvent will hold the position (*x*,*y*) of the mouse when a button is pressed, and information on which mouse button was pressed. This information can be retrieved in the manner shown in the following code snippet:

```
  void MyWidget::mousePressEvent(QMouseEvent* e)
  {
    // Query position of the mouse when the event occurred
    int x = e->x();
    int y = e->y();
    // Check whether the left button was pressed
    if (e->button() == QMouseEvent::LeftButton)
    {
      ...
    }
  }
```

The Qt classes allow you to overwrite many useful event handler methods. Their integration permits more flexible reactions to user input or window changes. However, the majority of Qt classes also translate the most important events into Qt signals. Consequently, the reimplementation of the event handlers is often unnecessary, and more often than not it is sufficient and more convenient to simply connect a slot to these signals.

LAYOUT MANAGER

The function of a layout manager is to offer an automatic or semi-automatic positioning of GUI elements inside a window. If the window is resized or the content of the window changes, the layout inside the window is automatically adjusted by the graphics library. This is particularly beneficial if the user wants different languages or font sizes. In these cases, the actual layout measurements of the window are hard to foresee, and a manually adjusted layout can lead to difficulties.

The Qt library provides a layout manager that can easily handle these adjustments. It deals with resizing font or text changes, and can add or remove graphical elements such as buttons or other widgets to or from the layout. All these actions result in an automatic recalculation of the layout so all the elements are correctly proportioned.

There are three basic layout principles: items can be aligned horizontally or vertically, or placed on a grid. In all cases, the layout manager calculates the size of an individual element by determining the minimum and maximum sizes of all other elements and any additional spacing between those elements. Figure 2.2 depicts these three layout possibilities.

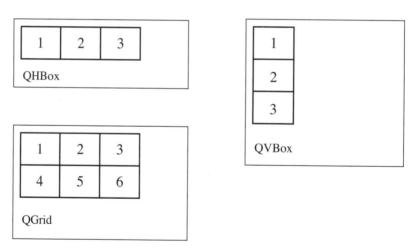

FIGURE 2.2   Basic Qt layout mechanism. Widgets can be arranged in a horizontal (top, left), vertical (top, right), or a grid layout (bottom, left). Resizing the main window will automatically arrange the widgets inside the layouts as well.

To use the layout manager, Qt provides several layout classes that support horizontal, vertical, or grid layout. The one you choose depends on the exact layout requirements of your application. The subclasses of QLayout are termed QGridLayout, QHBoxLayout, and QVBoxLayout, and offer all the features necessary for layout control. To further enhance the layout flexibility, it is also possible to nest layouts; an example would be to place a vertical layout into one cell of the grid layout.

The following example shows how to apply layouts in a normal desktop game situation. For this example, we have a widget that displays a canvas and provides a few control buttons below the canvas view. This type of structure could be found in a card game or a board game.

```
MyWidget::MyWidget(QWidget* parent)
      : QWidget(parent)
{
  // Align subwidgets vertically in this widget.
  // Note that the parent is a widget, meaning this
  // layout will maintain that widget's space.
  QVBoxLayout* topLayout = new QVBoxLayout(this);

  // The widget displaying the canvas (see Chapter 6)
  QCanvasView* canvasView = new QCanvasView(canvas);

  // the canvasView takes most space of this widget,
  // so it is added with a stretch factor > 0
  topLayout->addWidget(canvasView, 1);

  QPushButton* button1 = new QPushButton("Button 1", this);
  QPushButton* button2 = new QPushButton("Button 2", this);
  QPushButton* button3 = new QPushButton("Button 3", this);

  // The buttons are placed at the end of the topLayout in
  // their own child-layout that aligns the buttons
  // horizontally. Note that by giving the topLayout pointer
  // to the constructor the new layout is added to the
  // topLayout
  QHBoxLayout* buttonLayout = new QHBoxLayout(topLayout);
  buttonLayout->addWidget(button1);
  buttonLayout->addWidget(button2);
  buttonLayout->addWidget(button3);

  // Add a stretch area that takes all remaining space of
  // the layout (that is horizontally)
  buttonLayout->addStretch();
}
```

The stretch factor provided when adding the canvas view means that the canvas view is made as large as possible, whereas the buttons receive their minimal (vertical) size only. The stretch area that is added to the button layout has a similar meaning—it adds some type of dummy widget that eats up unused space. Without the stretch area, every button would take one third of the entire width of the widget, which would make them unnecessary wide.

The following example shows how to set up a grid layout for a given widget named widget. Four child widgets are then added to the grid layout, one of them spreading over more than one column. The full example source code can be found in the myqt3 and myqt4 programs on the companion CD-ROM.

ON THE CD

```
// Create a 3x2 grid for an arbitrary widget 'widget'.
QGridLayout* grid = new QGridLayout(widget, 3, 2);

// Add the three widgets ('button', 'label1', 'label2') to the
// grid at the specified row and column. Center align them.
// Row 0, Column 0
grid->addWidget(button, 0, 0, Qt::AlignCenter);
// Row 1, Column 0
grid->addWidget(label1, 1, 0, Qt::AlignCenter);
// Row 1, Column 1
grid->addWidget(label2, 1, 1, Qt::AlignCenter);

// Add a multi cell widget ('label3') in row 2 spanning
// column 0..1. The alignment is to the top-right
// In Qt3:
grid->addMultiCellWidget(label3, 2, 2, 0, 1,
                         Qt::AlignRight|Qt::AlignTop);
// In Qt4:
grid->addWidget(label3, 2, 2, 1, 2,
                Qt::AlignRight|Qt::AlignTop);

// Optionally: Give more room to the latter rows.
// Rows will have the space ratio 1:2:4.
grid->setRowStretch(0, 1);
grid->setRowStretch(1, 2);
grid->setRowStretch(2, 4);
```

Qt layouts (and other GUI elements) can be conveniently constructed using the Qt-Designer, shown in Figure 2.3. This graphical GUI builder is part of the Qt development kit and can be used to set up GUI elements including GUI layouts.

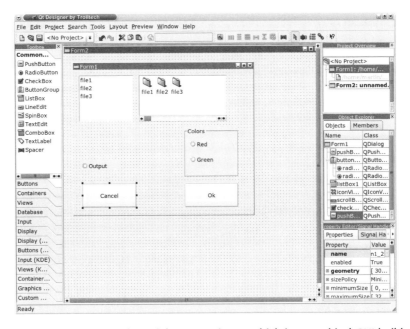

FIGURE 2.3   Screenshot of the Qt-Designer, which is a graphical GUI builder for Qt.

A QT "HELLO WORLD" APPLICATION

We now present a small "Hello World" application for Qt. This application will display a main window with a push button inside that quits the application when pressed.

To implement such a "Hello World" application, we first create a QApplication object. This object serves as a communication device to the operating system and handles the overall features of the application such as the event loop. A standard QWidget is used as the main window of the application, and a button from the QPushButton class is added to this window. This button is then connected to the application so that pushing the button will quit the application.

ON THE CD

The following example shows the "Hello World" application working for both Qt 3 and Qt 4. It can be found on the companion CD-ROM in the folder examples/myqthello.

```
// Qt3 or Qt4: old style headers
#include <qapplication.h>
#include <qpushbutton.h>
#include <qstring.h>
```

```
#include <qwidget.h>
#include <qlayout.h>

// Qt4 only: new style headers
#include <QApplication>
#include <QPushButton>
#include <QString>
#include <QWidget>
#include <QHBoxLayout>

int main(int argc, char** argv)
{
  // Create the main application object
  QApplication app(argc, argv);

  // Create the main window of the application, resize it to
  // a proper size
  QWidget widget(0);
  widget.resize(400, 400);

  // Add a push button to allow quitting the application
  QPushButton button(QString("Click to quit."), &widget);

  // Place the widget into the center of the window
  QHBoxLayout layout(&widget);
  layout.addWidget(&button, 0, Qt::AlignCenter);

  // Show the widget
  widget.show();

  // Connect the button to the 'quit' method of the
  // application. Pressing the button will emit the signal
  // 'clicked()' which in turn will call 'app.quit()' and
  // therefore leave the GUI.
  QObject::connect(&button, SIGNAL(clicked()),
                   &app, SLOT(quit()) );

  // Execute from the applications event loop
  return app.exec();
}
```

Qt offers a tool for automatic Makefile generation called qmake. qmake, which allows you to generate Makefiles for your project from so-called "project" files, which contain a list of all source and header files. qmake assembles this information and builds a Makefile that takes care of the compilation, and in particular, the MOC file generation and compilation.

In our examples, such a project file named `myqthello.pro` could look like:

```
HEADERS += main.h
SOURCES += main.cpp
```

`qmake` allows many optional keywords, but our "Hello World" application does not need them, and therefore we omitted them; that is, kept them at their default values. We only need to list our project source code file(s).

To support the generation of project files themselves, `qmake` can be called with the option `qmake -project`. This will then analyze all files in the current directory and build a default project file. If necessary, you can then manually edit this file to generate your project file. This is also a good way to see how a project file is supposed to look.

A Makefile is generated from a project file by simple calling `qmake`.

```
qmake game.pro
```

More details and advanced options of `qmake` are discussed in Chapter 4.

SUMMARY

In this chapter, we introduced the Qt library, which provides a large amount of classes to support GUI programming. These classes included all types of windows, buttons, pens, or brushes. Additionally, the Qt layout manager allows the flexible and automatic layout of GUI objects so that the layout becomes independent of the actual size of the objects at runtime. Standard programming features such as strings, lists, and arrays are provided by Qt utility classes. These classes are often comprehensive enough, so no other C++ libraries or template class libraries are necessary for desktop game programming.

However, in this book we focus more on the actual game programming rather than on the Qt details. We have therefore limited our examples in the remainder of this book so that the necessary parts of Qt are more understandable and straightforward. Thus, in some places you will be able to optimize or even shorten the demonstration code if you have a more thorough knowledge of Qt.

Desktop game applications can be based on Qt 3 or Qt 4—which one to choose is up to you. Qt 3 is probably for quite a while still more widespread, and KDE of versions 3.x are based on Qt 3. However, Qt 4 introduces performance and usability advantages; especially, the template class handling is more consistent. In this chapter, we showed the main classes useful for desktop games in both Qt 3 and Qt 4 so you can port examples to whichever version you choose.

The Qt signal-slot mechanism is a handy way to implement event-triggered programming in an application. Qt and KDE, which is based on Qt, already offer a range of standard signals for the processing of GUI elements, such as menus, buttons, timer events, and mouse events. However, user-defined signals can also be employed in a game application, allowing easy inter-object communication and event-triggered game programming. In contrast to standard programming, which often has classes that directly depend on one another, Qt only couples the objects that arise from these classes by connect() statements. Therefore, in Qt, the classes remain independent. Typical game signals and events could be the notification of "Game Over," the notification of objects that have been hit or destroyed, and, of course, all types of player or AI input.

An important aspect for games is the availability of an easy-to-use timer. Qt solves this problem by offering the QTimer class. Single-shot events and periodically occurring events can be easily implemented in a few lines using QTimer objects.

To achieve the level of flexibility necessary for the signal and slot processing, Qt introduces some additional preprocessor keywords that can be used in the source code. To allow a standard C++ compiler to compile such Qt programs, they first have to be run through an extra preprocessor called the Qt Meta-Object compiler, or MOC. This then auto-codes the C++ files that are required to implement these Qt features.

The Qt library can be used free of charge in an Open Source GPL or QPL licensed version. This applies to Qt 3 on Linux, Apple Macintosh, handheld operating systems, and all operating systems with Qt 4. You only have to purchase a commercial license when you decide to develop a commercial application. Details on these licenses are discussed in Chapter 17, "Open Source and Intellectual Property Rights." In summary, however, the total concept of Qt and the Qt licenses is well suited for Open Source game programming.

REFERENCES

[Blanchette04] Blanchette, Jasmin, and Mark Sommerfeld, *C++ GUI Programming with Qt 3*, Prentice Hall PTR, ISBN: 0131240722, 2004.

[Qtdoc05] *Trolltech Documentation, http://doc.trolltech.com*, 2005.

[Qttut05] *The Independent Qt Tutorial, http://www.digitalfanatics.org/projects/qt_tutorial*, 2005.

3 Game Development Using KDE

The *K Desktop Environment* (KDE) is a free graphical desktop mainly used on Linux and Unix-like computer systems. KDE allows the user to work on a professional-looking contemporary desktop that provides a consistent look and feel for all KDE applications. A great number of KDE applications are available, and these and new ones are constantly being improved and developed. The most important applications for daily work are bundled together and delivered with the standard KDE distribution.

The major advantage of using such a uniform desktop is that all the applications have a common look and feel, including standardized menus, icons, toolbars, and keyboard shortcuts. Furthermore, in contrast to many other Unix-like systems, KDE has eliminated the nightmare of manually editing all text files, since the configuration settings are collected into a central graphical configuration center.

Finally, due to the excellent internationalization features of KDE, it is currently available in more than 50 languages.

KDE was developed in 1996 by Matthias Ettrich, then a computer science student at the German University of Tuebingen. At that time, most graphical Unix applications did not use a uniform environment that provided a common look and feel. This resulted in programs looking completely different from each other, and due to different user interfaces were not very intuitive to use. This awkward behavior of Unix systems made Matthias suggest the KDE project. His idea was to adopt the Qt library so this powerful toolkit could make Unix systems as easy to use as Microsoft Windows or Apple Macintosh systems. In his famous newsgroup posting [Ettrich96], Matthias proposed the introduction of this new desktop environment for Unix. His focus was to develop a desktop that would be particularly easy to use and would provide a consistent interface to all applications (see Figure 3.1 for a screenshot of KDE). This newsgroup posting attracted much attention and was the birth of the KDE project. Since 1996, KDE has matured a great deal and has attained a modern desktop environment image increasingly seen on home and company computers.

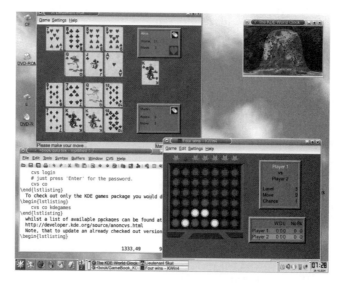

FIGURE 3.1   Screenshot of the KDE desktop.

KDE has been built on top of the free edition of the commercial Qt toolkit. Using Qt as the graphical library allowed the KDE developers to rely on a well-designed toolkit, and therefore concentrate on the key issues of desktop programming rather than on the programming of a graphics library (menus, buttons, windows, etc.). However, although Qt was available for free to Open Source projects, using a product offered by a commercial company was not without problems. Therefore, the decision to use Qt created much dispute in the free software development community. Fortunately, KDE and Trolltech managed to sign an agreement that resulted in releasing the Qt library as a truly free software version following the rules of the GNU GPL. This step was widely accepted and resolved most of the worries of the free software development community.

Today, KDE has reached a fair level of maturity and provides a contemporary-looking desktop environment for Unix/Linux that can compete with commercial desktop systems in both professionalism and ease of use. Several hundreds of programmers all over the world are contributing actively to KDE, and the KDE repository stores roughly 4 million lines of code (for comparison, the Linux kernel comprises roughly 3.7 million lines of code).

KDE is well suited for the programming of desktop games. It provides a set of classes to aid the programmer in the easy creation of an application having a default KDE look, which allows the developer to focus on his game instead of the framework. In addition, KDE offers other classes that can assist in game development; examples of these include the kdDebug technology, KAction for menu and keyboard input, random number generation, and easy program configurations, all of which are discussed in this chapter. Even for advanced games, which might want a distinguished appearance and not the usual look and feel, KDE provides many interesting classes. Powerful file formats developed with KTar are such an example.

Furthermore, with KDE being based on Qt, you automatically have access to the Qt toolkit classes. The combined possibilities of Qt and KDE make the development of desktop games straightforward, and many Open Source desktop games allow contribution or insight into the actual programming mechanisms. Some of these desktop games are part of the KDE standard distribution, while others can be downloaded from external sources; for example, the Web site [KdeApps05].

In this chapter, we present the setup required for a generic desktop game application for KDE, and show all the necessary steps to produce a running game program. We also point out some special KDE development features such as *internationalization* or the *action* concept, which will give further insight into KDE game programming. This chapter is not intended to be a fully comprehensive course in KDE programming, and we concentrate on those features that are typical for desktop games. If you are interested in more details on the actual KDE application programming, we refer to the examples in [KdeDeveloper05] or the books listed at [KdeBooks05].

A STANDARD KDE GAME APPLICATION

Setting up a new application from scratch is often quite difficult. To make this process easier, we've provided a template for a game application that will serve as the basis for the development of a KDE desktop game. During this process, we will create all the main classes necessary for a desktop game, including the application class, its main window, a canvas view for displaying sprites, and a document class to store the game and player data. We will also point out the most important aspects in the creation of such an application. The fully functional program templates can be found on the CD-ROM accompanying this book. The program `mykdeapp` in the folder `examples/mykdeapp` can serve as the programming template and starting point for your own desktop game.

ON THE CD

A typical KDE application contains a main program that sets up the *application* and creates a main window. This *main window* defines the application's frame, menus, toolbar, and status bar, which are all visible to the user. The contents of the main window are usually displayed in one or more *views*. For desktop games, a canvas-based view is normally a good choice, but other KDE or Qt widgets could also serve as views. Finally, the *document* or *game data* object holds all the data of the game such as players, scores, status information, and so forth. Figure 3.2 depicts such a KDE game architecture.

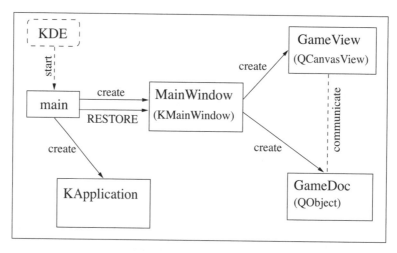

FIGURE 3.2   Basic architecture of a KDE game application. The main program creates the application object and the main window, which in turn creates the game data/document and the view. The main window and the view present the game application to the user. The game document stores the game data.

The Main Program

The main program contains the standard C++ startup function `main()`. It performs the command-line argument handling, creates the application object, sets up the main window, and finally enters the application's event loop. From then on, the program functions are triggered by GUI events including both the user interaction and timer events. The main program `main.cpp` is started by incorporating the necessary header files that define the classes that are used by the main program.

```
// KDE includes
#include <kapplication.h>
#include <kcmdlineargs.h>
#include <klocale.h>
#include <kstandarddirs.h>
#include <kinstance.h>
#include <kaboutdata.h>

#include "mainwindow.h"
```

After this initial step, the `main()` method is defined. First, the *about data* of the application is set. This *about data* is a collection of information about the application and can be automatically seen by the user in the *Help/About* menu of any KDE application. It mainly contains the application's name, the title shown in the title bar, the program version, the author, and the license information.

```
// Define the programs about data
KAboutData* aboutData=new KAboutData(
            "mykdeapp",                   // internal program
                                          // name (lowercase)
            I18N_NOOP("MyKdeApp"),        // public name
            "v1.0",                       // version
            I18N_NOOP("..."),             // description
            KAboutData::License_GPL,      // license
            "(c) 2005, Martin Heni");     // author
// Add additional authors
aboutData->addAuthor("Martin Heni", 0, "martin@example.com");
aboutData->addAuthor("Andreas Beckermann", 0, "andi@example.com");
```

To initialize the GUI application, a `KApplication` object is necessary. This application object is the communication channel to the KDE system. It is set up by creating an instance of the class `KApplication`. Once this instance is created, there are two ways the application can be started. First, the user starts the application manually, and this creates and displays the main window. Alternatively, the appli-

cation is restored by the session management system of KDE. This usually occurs
when the user ended the session with the application still running. KDE then stores
this application with its screen and any other additional attributes the programmer de-
cides to store. Consequently, the next time the user logs in to KDE, the application is
automatically started and the previous data parameters are restored. In our application
startup, we invoke this session management feature by calling the macro RESTORE()
from kmainwindow.h. This macro takes the main window class as parameter and creates
an instance of it, also restoring saved session parameters. It is also possible to restore
additional user configuration parameters in this process if you re-implement the
methods saveProperties(KConfig*) and readProperties(KConfig*) of KMainWindow.
The use of KConfig properties is demonstrated at the end of this chapter.

```
// Create new application object
KApplication app;

// Restore application by session management
if (app.isRestored())
{
  // Call KDE macro definition
  RESTORE(MainWindow);
}
// Create new application
else
{
  // Create new main window
  MainWindow* mainwindow = new MainWindow();
  app.setMainWidget(mainwindow);
  // And show it
  mainwindow->show();
}
```

Finally, the GUI event loop is called by the application's exec() method. When
the program is quit, this method returns and the program exits.

```
// Run the application's event loop
return app.exec();
```

The Main Window

The application's main window is derived from the KDE KMainWindow class, which
supports all necessary functions to set up and control the main window, its menus,
status bar, and toolbars.

In the file `mainwindow.h`, the class `MainWindow`, derived from `KMainWindow`, is defined, and this class does not require many other additional methods and variables. Nevertheless, it is often useful to store the pointers for the document/game object and the game view there.

Additionally, the slots (see Chapter 2, "Qt Primer") for the menu entries are also declared here. These slots are called by KDE when the user selects a menu. As an example, we choose one menu entry, which is just an arbitrary action used as demonstration, and a second one to leave the application. In our demonstration, we use the Qt extension for signals and slots in our class; therefore, we need to declare the object a `Q_OBJECT`. The `Q_OBJECT` macro should be the first line of every `QObject` derived class.

```
class MainWindow : public KMainWindow
{
  Q_OBJECT

  public:
    MainWindow ();        // The constructor
    ~MainWindow ();       // The destructor

  protected:
    void initGUI();       // Set up GUI elements



  protected slots:
    void menuGameDemo(); // A demo menu call
    void menuGameQuit(); // Menu to quit the game

  private:
    GameDoc*  mGameDoc;  // The game/document object
    GameView* mGameView; // The main game view

};
```

The implementation of the class `MainWindow` is done in the file `mainwindow.cpp`. During the initial steps, the necessary header files, which include both the standard KDE and Qt headers and references to the document and canvas view objects, are defined.

```
#include <klocale.h>
#include <kstdaction.h>
#include <kaction.h>
```

```
#include <kstatusbar.h>

#include "mainwindow.h"
#include "gameview.h"
#include "gamedoc.h"
```

The implementation is continued with the main window constructor, and there, the objects for the document and the view are created. The user-defined method initGUI() is called to initialize all actions and menus.

```
MainWindow::MainWindow() : KMainWindow(0)
{
  // Window title
  setCaption("KDE demo program");

  // Initialize view and document variables
  mGameView = new GameView(this);
  mGameDoc  = new GameDoc(this);

  // Set the view as the central widget
  setCentralWidget(mGameView);


  // Set up the menus and so on
  initGUI();

  // Load the GUI from the "mykdeappui.rc" file
  createGUI(QString::null);

  // Get the right widget size
  adjustSize();

  // Save GUI settings
  setAutoSaveSettings();
}
```

An important method call is the createGui() call. This loads an XML resource file for the definition of the menu and toolbar layout, a convenient way to define the program interface layout outside the program source code. If no argument is given createGUI(), the loaded XML file has a name that is constructed from the application's name. Thus, in our example, the file name mykdeappui.rc would be used.

We will now examine how the XML file for our demo application can be set up. We want to implement a *Game* menu containing the entries *Demo* and *Quit*. The following XML file contains both the menu and a menu item.

```
<!DOCTYPE kpartgui>
<kpartgui name="mykdeapp" version="1">
  <MenuBar>
    <Menu name="game"><text>&amp;Game</text>
      <Action name="game_demo"/>
      <Separator />
      ...
    </Menu>
  </MenuBar>
</kpartgui>
```

The *Quit* entry is a standard KDE action and does not need to be listed explicitly in the XML file because it will be added automatically by KDE at the right position. The `Action name` entries refer to the slots that will be invoked when the menu item is selected. We will demonstrate how to connect to them later. More menu entries or menus can be generated by simply repeating the `Menu` or `Action` lines.

In KDE all menu, keyboard, and toolbar inputs are collected in an *action* class. These actions provide the input to the program by calling a slot associated with them regardless of how they are actually involved. Actions can be identified by their name and are collected inside the application in an *action collection* object. Access to this action collection object is provided by the `actionCollection()` function of `KMainWindow`. In our game application, we use the concept of actions only to set up the menus.

Standard actions (KStdAction) do not need to be added to the XML resource file. This is done automatically by KDE.

We employ the user-defined helper method `initGUI()` to define all actions for the menu entries. Furthermore, all actions are linked to the slots defined in the class header file so they can be called if the action is activated by the mouse or the keyboard shortcut.

```
void MainWindow::initGUI()
{
  // Create the 'Demo' menu entry. The parameters are:
  // the menu text "Demo", the object and the slot
  // which shall be called when the action is selected, the
  // action collection and the name 'game_demo' as used in
  // the resource file
```

```
KAction* demo = new KAction(i18n("&Demo"),0,
                                    this,
                                    SLOT(menuGameDemo()),
                                    actionCollection(),
                                    "game_demo");
demo->setStatusText(i18n("Starting demo..."));
demo->setWhatsThis(i18n("Starting demo..."));

// The quit action is already defined in KDE, so
// a standard action can be used here. Its parameters
// are the object and slot which is invoked when the
// action is called, the action collection to store all
// actions and the resource identifier
KAction* quit = KStdAction::quit(this,
                                    SLOT(menuGameQuit()),
                                    actionCollection(),
                                    "game_exit");
quit->setStatusText(i18n("Exiting..."));
quit->setWhatsThis(i18n("Quits the program."));

actionCollection()->setHighlightingEnabled(true);
}
```

Finally, the two slot methods are implemented. These slots will be called when the actions that correspond to the menu entries *Demo* or *Quit* are selected. The first case incorporates anything that is useful for the application, such as starting the game. In the latter, the application is quit, returning from the event loop to the main function.

```
void MainWindow::menuGameDemo()
{
  // Do something useful
  ...
}


void MainWindow::menuGameQuit()
{
  // Close view and main window
  if (mGameView) { mGameView->close(); }
  close();
}
```

The Game or Document Class

The game or document class contains all the data relevant for the game and normally contains links to the player objects, too. In our example application, this particular class does not do anything and thus remains just a container for game data. Consequently, the class definition in the file gamedoc.h is very simple. However, as it is often useful to have access to Qt signals and slots, a QObject is used as the basis for the game class.

```
#include <qobject.h>

class GameDoc : public QObject
{
  Q_OBJECT

  public:
    GameDoc(QObject* parent = 0);

  private:
    // Game data
    ...
};
```

The implementation of the demo game document object in the file gamedoc.cpp is just as simple, since only the constructor for the QObject needs to be defined. However, in a real game application, this is the place to set up and initialize the game data.

```
#include "gamedoc.h"
...
GameDoc::GameDoc(QObject * parent)
        : QObject(parent)
{
  ...
}
```

The Game View

The final class to be defined for the basic game application is the game view, which is the area displayed inside the bordering frame of the main window and which depicts the game, its objects, sprites, and so on. For game applications, a canvas class is usually a good choice. We will briefly describe how such a view can be employed. For further insight into this topic, separate chapters are entirely devoted to the use of the Qt canvas class (see Chapter 6, "Canvas Games") and OpenGL (see Chapter 7, "OpenGL").

The `QCanvasView` class serves as a basis for the displayed canvas whose setup and initialization will be the main task of the view class. The canvas and the other graphical objects are created in the `QCanvasView` constructor. In the following, the view class is implemented in the file `gameview.h`, which again uses Qt signals and slots.

```
#include <qcanvas.h>
...
class GameView : public QCanvasView
{
  Q_OBJECT

  public:
    GameView(QWidget* parent = 0);

  protected:
    void resizeEvent(QResizeEvent* e);

  private:
    ...
};
```

The class implementation in the file `gameview.cpp` first implements the constructor, which will set up and initialize the canvas. The main properties of the canvas are now complete and include its size, the double buffering, its color, and its advance period.

```
// Constructor for the view
GameView::GameView(QWidget* parent)
        : QCanvasView(0, parent, 0)
{
  // Create a new canvas for this view
  QCanvas* canvas = new QCanvas(this);
  // Fit it in the parent window
  canvas->resize(parent->width(), parent->height());
  // Remove flicker by double buffering
  canvas->setDoubleBuffering(true);
  // Choose a nice background color
  canvas->setBackgroundColor(QColor(32, 32, 128));
  // Update/advance
  canvas->setAdvancePeriod(25);
  // Assign the canvas to the view
```

```
   setCanvas(canvas);

   // Set size and position
   move(0, 0);
   adjustSize();


   ...
}
```

At the final stage, the resize method can be re-implemented. This is an important step since the contents of the canvas are then maintained at the same ratio to
the main window if the latter is resized.

```
// Method called by the framework when the window is resized
void GameView::resizeEvent(QResizeEvent* e)
{
  // Adapt the canvas size
  if (canvas())
  {
    canvas()->resize(e->size().width(),
                     e->size().height());
  }
}
```

In our example, we just use one game view. Therefore, we can link the canvas
and the view, and resize them together. This method cannot be applied if more than
one view is associated with the canvas.

BUILDING A GAME

A very easy way to begin a KDE project is to use the free Integrated Development
Environment (IDE) KDevelop (see Figure 3.3). KDevelop is particularly well suited
for KDE program development. It is integrated into most standard Linux distributions or can be downloaded for free from the Web site [Kdevelop05]. KDevelop
integrates all steps of program development, from providing a default project, to a
class browser, a debugger, and document generation. A demonstration project that

ON THE CD incorporates KDevelop can be found on the companion CD-ROM in the folder
`examples/mykdevelop`.

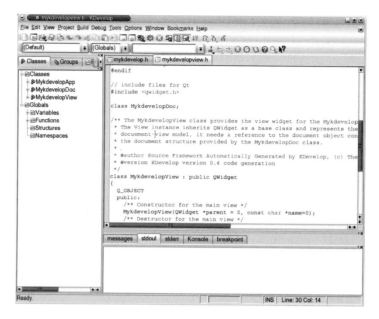

FIGURE 3.3 Screenshot of KDevelop, an Open Source integrated development environment for KDE.

For game development, it is good practice to begin a new project from the category *KDE Normal*. This will create a running application with all menus, toolbars, and status bars. Depending on the type of game, the only main thing that needs to be changed is the type of view. As commented upon earlier, most games will benefit from a `QCanvasView` instead of a standard `QWidget` view. If necessary, this can be simply altered in the view class. However, for mainly text-based games, the standard widget view is also often sufficient.

KDevelop also creates all the necessary configuration, make, and build process files. The configuration scripts generated by KDevelop will scan the target platform for the required libraries, and include files to configure and build the program accordingly. To provide a better understanding of the details of the process of automatic configuration and Makefile generation, we explain them in more detail in the next section.

Primer on `autoconf` and `automake`

The GNU software tools offer a wide variety of useful tools, two of which are `autoconf` [Autoconf05] and `automake` [Automake05]. These tools allow the automatic generation of `configure` and `make` scripts.

A `configure` script allows you to configure the source code for different target computers by respecting the different library, compiler, and include file locations and settings. The Makefile generation allows the production of a complex `Makefile` that respects all the program's dependencies and configuration properties from a simple script that may contain only a few lines defining the source code filenames of the project.

On top of the standard `autoconf` and `automake` scripts, KDE offers a set of enhanced scripts that allows the creation of any KDE application in a similar manner, respecting some additional KDE features.

In the following examples, we give a brief introduction to the use of `autoconf` and `automake` because it is useful to see how these tools can generate a simple "Hello World" program. This program can be found on the companion CD-ROM in the folder `examples/myauto`. To run the demo program, we assume that the `automake` and `autoconf` package are installed on your computer; if not, install them from the packages provided for your distribution. Our KDE and autotool examples are created with version 2.57 of `autoconf` and version 1.7.6 of `automake`. However, the version dependency should be small and the examples will run with most other versions.

To create a "Hello World" application, we first need to set up a small C++ main program, which is done in the file `main.cpp`.

```
#include <stdio.h>

int main()
{
  printf("Hello world!\n");
}
```

For the automatic configuration script generation, a template configuration script is required, which is stored in the file `configure.in`. In a simple form, this could look like:

```
# Initialize autoconf - pass ANY source file here
AC_INIT(main.cpp)
# Initialize automake - pass application and version
AM_INIT_AUTOMAKE(mykdeapp,1.0)
# C++ compiler   (use AC_PROG_CC for C compiler)
AC_PROG_CXX
AC_PROG_CXXCPP
# check installation features to allow 'make install'
AC_PROG_INSTALL
# Output Makefile
AC_OUTPUT(Makefile)
```

where, of course, all comment lines starting with "#" can be omitted.

It is possible to automatically generate a default `configure.in` script by calling `autoscan`. The latter will scan the source code for known compatibility problems and used libraries so that a `configure.scan` file can be produced. This file can be further edited and then copied to `configure.in`.

The final ingredient for the "Hello World" program is the template file for the `Makefile`. This is stored in the file `Makefile.am` and lists the name of the binary program and a list of source codes necessary for building the program.

```
# Application target name
bin_PROGRAMS  = mykdeapp
# Source code file(s)
mygame_SOURCES = main.cpp
# Optional: Create a non standard GNU application
AUTOMAKE_OPTIONS = foreign
```

Or, if more than one source code is available:

```
# More than one file is given like
mygame_SOURCES = main.cpp file1.cpp file2.cpp
```

Finally, we can start the configure and Makefile generation process by calling the following auto tool commands:

```
# Create M4 macro definitions
aclocal
# Create 'configure'
autoconf
# Create 'Makefile.in' and missing GNU files
automake -a
```

At this stage, the `automake` will complain about some missing files, such as NEWS, README, AUTHORS, and ChangeLog. The existence of these files is defined by the GNU build process. If you do not have these files, simply create empty files using

```
touch NEWS README AUTHORS ChangeLog
```

Then, rerun the `automake` command. Alternatively, you can decide to build a nonstandard GNU project by setting the option "foreign" (in AUTOMAKE_OPTIONS). This will allow you to create projects that do not comply with the GNU project rules.

Finally, the configuration and make process can be started. This step will also be performed later by a user installing the released software. It will configure and create the `Makefile` for the target computer and build the program.

```
# 'Configure' program
./configure
# Build program
make
# Optionally: Install program
make install
# Optionally: De-install program
make uninstall
```

The use of the `autoconf` and `automake` tools allows an easy generation of Makefiles which respects all program dependencies and the configuration of the compiler, linker, and libraries, and is computer independent. Beyond the features discussed in this section, the auto-tools allow a much richer set of configuration options. For further details, we refer to the Web sites [Autoconf05] and [Automake05], and the tutorials at the Web site [Gkioulekas98].

The process of build file generation can sometimes be quite tedious when using just the pure `autoconf` *and* `automake` *tools. Instead of manually setting them up, you can use either the templates provided by the KDE project or use KDevelop, which does the* `autoconf` *and* `automake` *handling automatically. In some cases, even* `qmake` *is a good choice since it is easier to use in Qt-based environments. An introduction to* `qmake` *can be found in Chapter 4, "Qt Game Development Using Microsoft Windows."*

Automatic KDE Configuration and Program Making

When developing an application for KDE, KDE itself provides many supporting scripts and tools, so even the `autoconf` and `automake` files are generated more easily.

All KDE applications of one particular package—for example, a games package—are grouped inside a common directory. Inside such a directory, KDE provides some administrative files to support creating all `Makefiles`. These files are listed in:

```
admin/
Makefile.cvs
configure.in.in
Makefile.am.in
mykdeapp/
mygame/
myothergame/
...
```

where the `admin` directory stores the KDE configuration scripts. The `Makefile.cvs`, `configure.in.in`, and the `Makefile.am.in` serve as templates for the `automake` process. Finally, the `mygame`, ... directories store the source code of the actual games. Of course, their names can be chosen arbitrarily. The administrative files are supplied in the archive `admin_kdegames_3_3.tar.gz` on the CD-ROM accompanying this book in the folder `tools`. Alternatively, they can be downloaded from the KDE repository or the KDE Web access [Web05] from the `kdegames` directory.

Inside the application directory, we will choose `mykdeapp` as an example. Here, only one file, `Makefile.am`, has to be adapted to your particular program. It will specify some general administrative features such as the icons, the setup, and data installation relevant for the application. For the demo game application described here, the `Makefile.am` would look like

```
# Recursively apply 'make' to these subdirectories
SUBDIRS =  src

# Options: 'foreign': do not generate a standard GNU
# application
AUTOMAKE_OPTIONS = foreign

# Install the icon names here. The icon files are named
# e.g. cr48-app-mykdeapp.png
KDE_ICON = mykdeapp

# Specify the location of the XML resource files
rcdir = $(kde_datadir)/mykdeapp
rc_DATA = mykdeappui.rc

# Store application date, here the *.desktop file
xdg_apps_data = mykdeapp.desktop
```

We have defined the meaning of the Makefile keywords in the comments inside the code listing.

Most commands can just be copied without changing them into a new application, but the program name `mykdeapp` is an exception and has to be adapted. Of major importance is the `SUBDIRS` command, which tells the make process to also run for the specified subdirectories. In the case shown here, we have stored the actual source code in the `src` directory and would now like to create the binary program from this source code. Therefore, in this directory we also need a `Makefile.am` that lists all the necessary source code files for the compilation process.

```
# Keyword to automatically handle all the include files
INCLUDES = $(all_includes)
```

```
# Tell automake to automatically handle all meta object files
METASOURCES = AUTO

# Optional: Automatically create translation files
POFILES = AUTO

# Define the binary program filename
bin_PROGRAMS = mykdeapp

# List all source code files of the application
mygame_SOURCES = main.cpp mainwindow.cpp gamedoc.cpp \
                 gameview.cpp

# Optional: Add any additional library (e.g. OpenGL,...)
mygame_LDADD  = ...

# Optional: Add additional library paths
mygame_LDFLAGS = $(all_libraries) $(KDE_RPATH)
```

This automake template file will be used by KDE to generate your application's Makefile. In particular, the entries bin_PROGRAMS and mykdeapp_SOURCES are of importance. The first specifies the name or names of the resulting binary program(s), and the second lists the source files for each application. This entry is constructed from the name of the program mykdeapp and the keyword _SOURCES. All other entries can usually be left on standard or default values.

Specifying these two Makefiles is enough to generate a fully competent KDE application. This application will be configured for different target computers, will include an API documentation and translation files, and can be delivered as a *.tar.gz package.

The build process is now started by invoking the default Makefile Makefile.cvs and then configuring the application for the development computer. This example will automatically generate all missing Makefiles.

```
# Generate the automake files
make -f Makefile.cvs
# Configure the application and generate the Makefiles
./configure

# Same as above but use your home directory as target.
# This is helpful if the installation should not be
# done as 'root'.
./configure --prefix=$HOME
```

Of course, these steps have only to be performed when setting up the project the first time. Once the Makefiles are created, a normal call to make is sufficient to rebuild the application.

A working demo application for KDE using these automake features is stored on the companion CD-ROM under the name examples/mykdeapp. These Makefile templates can be adapted for your own game program. The only changes required to adapt them is to replace the application's name.

Makefile command lines are generally required to be indented by real tabulators, not spaces. Make sure your editor does this properly.

NOTE

Packaging the Application

Once the game application is finished, tested, and runs correctly on the development computer, you will probably want to distribute it to other people. In Open Source projects, applications are typically exchanged as source code packages bundled together in *.tar files. These files can be unpacked by the receiver, who can then run the configuration process.

The typical steps a receiver has to perform to get a program running are similar to the steps carried out by the initial developer. If we suppose that the package was provided as a file called mykdeapp-1.0.tar.gz, then the receiver would unpack, build, and install it by executing:

```
tar xzf mykdeapp-1.0.tar.gz
cd mykdeapp-1.0
./configure
make
make install
```

The question now is, how do you create a source code package that only contains necessary files? Fortunately, this task can be easily achieved by a script that is attached to the KDE development tools. It can be found in the kdesdk/scripts directory at the Web site [Web05] or on the companion CD-ROM in the tools folder. This script will package all the files from the development directory that are required for a distribution and place them in a *.tar archive file.

ON THE CD

In the directory one level above your project, simply type:

```
# For versions KDE >3.3
cvs2dist --no-i18n kdegames mykdeapp 1.0
# For versions KDE <3.3
cvs2pack kdegames mykdeapp 1.0
```

Here, the arguments of the tools are the module name (e.g., kdegames), the application's name (e.g., mykdeapp), and the version of the program (here 1.0). Executing this script command will create the aforementioned package mykdeapp-1.0.tar.gz.

INTERNATIONALIZATION AND LOCALIZATION

When creating a game application for distribution in other countries, the different languages, units, or time formats for each country must be considered. To support worldwide application release and accommodate the various features specific to individual countries, KDE produced a set of localization functions that allow the same program to be executed in different languages depending on the user's configuration. This is achieved without changing the source or binary code of the application.

Designing a program for different countries or regions is called *internationalization*, or *i18n* (from: *i, 18 letters, n*). The actual process of adapting program features to these different countries or regions is called *localization*, or *l10n*. In essence, localization means that the program will be aware of the user's location and uses this information for input or output of the local items.

Internationalization affects two areas. First, the language of the text output changes, which means that all text, menus, and output of the program are in the language the new user has chosen. Second, many items such as currencies, time, date formats, flags, units, and so on are unique to that country and need adapting to the local area translations.

For the internationalization of a program, all strings and other texts that are displayed to the user have to be translated before actually displaying them. KDE offers an "automatic" translation process for this. Strings that are passed through the KDE i18n() function are looked up in a table for the specific language, and instead of the original string, the translated version is presented to the user. These "lookup" translation tables are stored in files called PO files and contain the original string and the string of the foreign language.

The "automatic" translation process of KDE does not mean that KDE is actually translating the text for you; this still has to be done by a human translator. However, KDE will automatically import different languages and display the text output of your game in the chosen language if such a translation file is available.

A string made available for translation is written in one of the following possible forms of i18n(). The first way is the standard lookup method. The argument to i18n() is simply looked up in the translation table and replaced by the translation for a particular country.

```
// Simple i18n
setCaption(i18n("Configure Player Names"));
```

In the second form, there is a comment for the translator attached to the first part of the string. This comment is stored in the translation file but is not visible to the user. This comment makes it easier for the translator to figure out in what context the string is used, because often the same string in English can translate to different strings in other languages depending on the context.

```
// Commented i18n, displaying "View" to the user
text->setText(i18n("view a card", "View"));
```

The i18n() function can be used only once a KApplication application object has been created. If text needs to be marked for translation beforehand, the macro I18N_NOOP() can be used instead. This macro marks a string for translation without actually translating it.

A special problem with translated strings arises when the strings contain variable parts or arguments that are inserted at runtime. Intuitively, one could translate the fixed text parts individually and then concatenate them at runtime. However, in the translation of text, the word order of the string can be sometimes totally changed, and simple concatenation of certain text sections will lead to an incorrect translation. The following example shows how this problem can occur. Here, a player's name and the current game number should be inserted into a text. This type of string could resemble the following:

```
// Variable argument strings - Incorrect usage!
QString msg = i18n("Player ") + name +
              i18n(" has won game number ") + number;
```

which would translate to German as

```
"Spieler " + name + " hat Spiel " + number + " gewonnen"
```

Here you can see that in the new language, an additional string needs to be inserted after the variable number. Obviously, this cannot be performed by a simple translation of the two independent i18n() strings from the original English version. To avoid such problems, it is better to put the entire sentence into one big translation string and let the translators figure out the exact placement of the variables. This can be done be using placeholders inside the string and providing the variables as arguments to the i18n() function.

```
// Variable argument strings - CORRECT usage
```

```
QString msg = i18n("Player %1 has won game number %2")
              .arg(name).arg(number);
```

Now the string can be correctly translated to

```
"Spieler %1 hat Spiel %2 gewonnen"
```

and the variables name and number will replace the placeholders %1, %2 at runtime.

Note that it is normally not necessary to translate debug messages or log output, since these were just for debugging purposes and not intended for the user.

Also within KDE is the class KLocale, which provides many functions for developers to make their code i18n() aware. Access to the KLocale object is available in every application through the static method KGlobal::locale(). For example, all KDE applications automatically load a translation file if such a file is available and named after the application. If another translation file should be used or an already existing translation catalog has to be added to the application, the following steps should be executed:

```
#include <klocale.h>

int main(int argc, char** argv)
{
  // Use this to set the main catalog for all locales
  KLocale::setMainCatalogue("mykdeapp");

  // Adds another catalog to search for translation lookup.
  KGlobal::locale()->insertCatalogue("libkdegames");

  ...
}
```

Translatable strings can automatically be extracted from source code files using the xgettxt command. This command will parse the source code for strings, especially for i18n() strings, and write them into a PO file that can be used for translation. Translating such a PO file can be done manually, but it is more efficient to use translation programs that also perform all handling and syntax checking of PO files. Here, KBabel is a good choice [KBabel05].

The xgettxt command can be either used manually

```
xgettext -C -ki18n -kI18N_NOOP   *.cpp
```

on the command line, or it is invoked in the make process by adding

```
POFILES = AUTO
```

into a KDE `automake` file [KDEi18n05].

A generated `PO` file will list all text strings and the resulting translations for all the source code files. A brief excerpt could look like:

```
#: main.cpp:26
msgid "Enter debug level"
msgstr "..."
...
```

When preparing applications for translation, several issues have to be considered. Earlier, we explained that sometimes when strings are translated to another language, they can be altered—both in words and in length. Often, a short string in English might suddenly become very long in another language. Of course, this can also affect how the strings are arranged in a screen layout. The best solution here is to make the layout as flexible as possible by using layout managers, not by manually aligning all strings. Unfortunately, this is sometimes not so easy to achieve in games.

Localizations

Compared to translation, the localization of other items is not a big issue for most desktop games. However, a few things are worth paying attention to, such as date and time formats or the currency settings. Methods to handle these localization issues are again provided by the KDE `KLocale` class. This class offers methods that allow you to present the money

```
// Convert a double value to a localized money string
QString KLocale::formatMoney(double amount,
                             const QString& currency =
                                          QString::null,
                             int digits = -1)
```

or the time and date

```
// Convert a date into a localized string
QString KLocale::formatDate(const QDate& date,
                            bool shortfmt = false)

// Convert a time into a localized string
```

```
QString KLocale::formatTime(const QTime& time,
                            bool includeSecs = false)
```

in a form suitable to the local user. More conversion methods and details on these localization methods can be found in the KDE documentation [Klocale05].

PROGRAM DOCUMENTATION

Doxygen is an automatic interface documentation tool for many programming languages, including C++, and generates documentation similar to *javadoc* or *kdoc*. The principle function of this tool is to analyze classes, their functions, and methods specified in the header files together with some specially formatted comments. This information is then used to produce comprehensive program API documentation. The output of Doxygen can be formatted in various ways, but to date, HTML remains the most common choice. Figures 3.4 and 3.5 show a screenshot of Doxygen output.

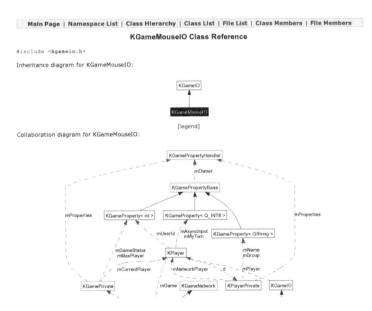

FIGURE 3.4 Screenshot of documentation generated by Doxygen— the class collaboration diagram.

Public Member Functions

KGameMouseIO (QWidget *parent, bool trackmouse=false)
virtual ~KGameMouseIO ()
void setMouseTracking (bool b)
virtual int rtti () const

Protected Member Functions

bool eventFilter (QObject *o, QEvent *e)

Detailed Description

The KGameMouseIO class. It is used to process mouse input from a widget and create moves for the player it belongs to.

Author:
Martin Heni <martin@heni-online.de>

Constructor & Destructor Documentation

KGameMouseIO::KGameMouseIO(QWidget * *parent*,
bool *trackmouse* = false
)

Creates a mouse IO device. It captures all mouse event of the given widget and forwards them to the signal handler **signalMouseEvent**. Example:

```
KGameMouseIO *input;
input=new KGameMouseIO(mView);
connect(input,SIGNAL(signalMouseEvent(KGameIO *,QDataStream &,QMouseEvent *,bool *)),
        this,SLOT(slotMouseInput(KGameIO *,QDataStream &,QMouseEvent *,bool *)));
```

Parameters:
The   widget whose events should be captured

FIGURE 3.5 Screenshot of documentation generated by Doxygen—the class description.

To use Doxygen, the commenting of the program files has to follow a few special rules. Doxygen allows several different ways to do this. KDE applications generally follow the kdoc/javadoc style, which we present in the following code snippet. For this style, all class definitions, methods, or variables that should appear in the output need to have a special comment block before them. This comment block has to start with a double star comment instead of the normal single star comment.

```
/**
 * This is the documentation for this class.
 */
class GameView : public QCanvasView
{
 Q_OBJECT
 public:
  /**
   * The class resize event.
   * @param e The event
   */
  void resizeEvent (QResizeEvent* e );
};
```

Employing these special comments will lead to a fair documentation of all classes and methods used in the program. However, to make the documentation more precise, some special keywords are supported inside the comments:

`@author string:` The author of a class.

`@param string:` The parameter of a method.

`@ref string:` Links to another class or method.

`@return:` The return value of a function.

`@see string:` Reference to another class or method.

`@short string:` A short one-line description of a class.

`@version string:` The version of the class.

Except for the `@ref` keyword, all special commands need to appear on a single individual line.

A typical example for documentation could resemble:

```
/**
 * This is the game view class.
 *
 * The game view shows the graphics in a canvas view.
 *
 * @short The game main view.
 * @author Martin Heni
 * @version 1.0
 * @see GameDoc#GameDoc
 */
class GameView : public QCanvasView
{

public:
  /**
   * The constructor for the game view.
   *  @param parent The parent window
   */
  GameView(QWidget* parent = 0);

  /**
   * A test method for the number of items on the
   * view.
   *
   * @param type   The sprite type to count
   * @return       The number of sprites in this view.
  int spriteNumber(int type);
};
```

Finally, in a typical KDE build process environment, `doxygen` is started by a simple call to

```
make apidox
```

which will generate the documentation in the directory `apidocs`.

Doxygen can also be used with an alternative build process environment that does not include an "apidox" target, or manually from the command line. In this case, `doxygen` needs a configuration file that specifies its operation mode. Such a configuration file is fortunately generated automatically by `doxygen`:

```
doxygen -g mykdeAppConfig
```

In this example, the configuration file `mykdeAppConfig` would be generated. It is then possible to manually edit this file and change some configuration settings. A selection of useful options comprises:

PROJECT_NAME: The name of the project.

PROJECT_NUMBER: A project revision number.

OUTPUT_DIRECTORY: The path to the directory where the documentation will be placed. Leaving this option empty will generate the documentation in the current working directory.

EXTRACT_ALL: Setting this option to YES will extract documentation even for uncommented elements.

INLINE_SOURCE: Setting this option to YES will include parts of the source code in the documentation.

HAVE_DOT: Setting this option to YES will use the dot tool to create graphics. Do this if you want to use call or collaboration graphs.

CALL_GRAPH: If this option is YES, a dependency diagram is generated for functions and methods.

GENERATE_LATEX: Setting this to YES will generate latex output.

GENERATE_HTML: Setting this to YES will generated HTML output.

Once these options are defined, `doxygen` can be started in the appropriate source directory. It will then analyze the source code files and generate the corresponding documentation. This is done by executing:

```
doxygen mykdeAppConfig
```

TRICKS OF THE TRADE

This section provides a collection of useful ways in which game programming for KDE can be made easier.

Naming Conventions

When developing applications, it is often helpful to comply with a uniform naming scheme in the source code. KDE has established a few guidelines on how items are named and labeled. Of course, there are no strict rules, and in your program, you can name things to your liking. However, sticking to some general rules will make it easier for other people to understand your programs.

In class names, all individual words start with uppercase letters, and KDE classes are additionally prefixed with a leading uppercase K. Application programs such as desktop games do not need to start class names with a leading uppercase K.

```
// KDE class
class KAboutPerson

// Game class
class GameView
```

Method and function names begin with a lowercase letter, and all subsequent words start capitalized. Set functions are prefixed with the word set, while get functions are only labeled with the attribute they retrieve.

```
// Boolean query
bool isEnabled();

// Set function
void setName(QString name);

// Get function - 'get' is omitted.
QString name();

// Standard functions
bool updateConnections();
void gameOver();
```

Signals and slots do not need to differ in naming from normal methods. However, some people prefix slot methods with the word "slot," and often, signals are marked with the word "signal." However, contrary to signals, slots are and can be used as normal methods, and an extra naming is not really necessary unless you want to stress that the method is a slot.

```
signals:
  // Normal signal
  void closeEvent(QWidget *);
  // Prefixed signal
  void signalGameOver();

public slots:
  // Normal slot
  void finished(bool);
  // Prefixed slot - not recommended
  void slotWrite(int d);
```

Variable names also start with a lowercase letter, and all subsequent words begin with uppercase letters.

```
QString weekDayName;
QString playerName;
int month;
```

Variables that serve as attributes in a class are often distinguished from normal variables. However, there exists no concise rule on how to accomplish this aspect. Sometimes, a prefix such as "m" or "m_" is used to distinguish class attributes from normal variables.

```
// No prefix
QCanvas* canvas;
// 'm' prefix
QCanvas* mCanvas;
// 'm_' prefix
QCanvas* m_canvas;
```

Generally, it is useful to label class attributes because it is easier to identify them in the source code.

Whatever naming convention you use, the most important rule to remember is, "once chosen, always applied." It usually looks very unprofessional to use different conventions in the same file (e.g., "m" prefix for one variable and "m_" for the other). This etiquette applies even more when working on someone else's code.

Flexible Paths

In applications that should be able to run outside your current computer environment, it is impossible to use hard-coded path names because it is not known where other people or other systems install the files.

KDE provides methods to handle this in the KStandardDirs class. These path-handling features can be accessed via the static method KGlobal::dirs() in every application, and allow the retrieval of path information for certain file categories. Examples are "icons," "script," "data," and so on (see the KStandardDirs manual for a list of all supported file types).

Using these directory accessors in a program allows access to the flexible path system of KDE.

Directories can also be added to the path resource system. Either an existing search path can be extended, or a user-defined category can be introduced. In the following example, the "data" search path is extended so that the data files of the program can also be found somewhere else. In the second example, a subdirectory of the data directory is declared as a directory that stores the game sprites.

```
// Set directories where data can be found (ui.rc + graphics)
KGlobal::dirs()->addResourceDir("data", myPath);

// Set a user defined sprite directory
KGlobal::dirs()->addResourceType("sprites",
                    KStandardDirs::kde_default("data") +
                    "mygame/sprites/");
```

Single files or complete directories can now be retrieved at runtime using

```
// Get the directory if one filename is known
QString dir1 =
        kapp->dirs()->findResourceDir("data",
                                    "pic/piece1.png");
QString dir2 =
        kapp->dirs()->findResourceDir("sprites",
                                    "sprite1.png");
// Get fully qualified path to the file
QString file3 =
        kapp->dirs()->findResource("data",
                                    "pic/piece1.png");
```

where the filenames should be relative to the base directory for the resources.

Use of the Source Directory

During game development, it is often helpful if the game can be directly tested from the source directory without having to install it first to a target directory. In principle, this is possible for all programs without any additional effort. However, sometimes one obstruction can occur: if the program data files such as the XML menu resource files are not installed, KDE cannot find them and will therefore not display the menus of the application correctly. This problem can be overcome by using a compiler flag that allows you to add a definition to the current source directory in the program. Adding this path to the "data" resource directory will then allow KDE to find the data files in the source directory.

Using the KDE automake features in the Makefile.am file such a compiler flag can be added easily,

```
AM_CPPFLAGS = -DSRCDIR="\"$(shell (cd $(srcdir) && pwd))\""
```

and when the source directory is defined in this manner, it can be added to the resource directory of the "data" category.

```
// Set local source directory for data
#ifdef SRCDIR
  KGlobal::dirs()->addResourceDir("data",
                    SRCDIR + QString::fromLatin1("/.."));
#endif
```

Note that the path has to be extended before the GUI is created (createGUI()).

Actions

In KDE, nearly all *interactions* of the user with the application can be encapsulated into a program action that is represented by the KAction class. Regardless of their GUI representation, these actions can bundle several different user interactions into one common program method. Therefore, there exists a one-to-one relationship between the user's interaction and the program's response. For example, the user can achieve particular results by selecting a menu item, clicking a toolbar button, or using a keyboard shortcut. In KDE, all of these different interaction types reside within the same program action, which allows the developer to react to them in a consistent way. This joint handling of the interactions includes the enabling, disabling, checking, or selection of actions, which in turn enables, disables, checks, or selects the respective menu or toolbar items.

In a KDE main window, all of these actions are collected within a KActionCollection class, which is automatically provided by the KMainWindow object. Therefore, all action calls can be made to this action collection. It is often practical to define a shortcut to this collection by

```
// Make actions available
#include <kaction.h>

// Handy define to access an action by name
#define ACTION(x)    (actionCollection()->action(x))
```

In the main application window, these actions can now be used to define the game menus. Some typical actions used in games are presented in the following example. Note that all action names also need to be reflected in the XML resource file of the application as discussed previously.

```
// Standard action to open/start a game.
KStdAction::openNew(this, SLOT(newGame()),
                    actionCollection(), "game_new");

// Standard action to quit a game/exit a program.
KStdAction::quit(this, SLOT(quitGame()),
                    actionCollection(), "game_quit");

// User define action.
new KAction(i18n("&Stop Game"), KShortcut(), this,
                    SLOT(stopGame()), actionCollection(),
                    "game_stop");

// Toggle action switches between two states
new KToggleAction(i18n("View &Names"), KShortcut(),
                    this, SLOT(viewNames()), actionCollection(),
                    "view_names");

// Select action offers a submenu with a choice of items.
new KSelectAction(i18n("&Level"), KShortcut(), this,
                    SLOT(changeLevel()), actionCollection(),
                    "settings_level");
```

The corresponding `mykdeappui.rc` file would read:

```
<!DOCTYPE kpartgui>
<kpartgui name="mykdeapp" version="1">
  <MenuBar>
    <Menu name="file"><text>&amp;Game</text>
      <Action name="game_stop"/>
```

```
      </Menu>
      <Menu name="view">
        <Action name="view_names"/>
      </Menu>
      <Menu name="settings">
        <Action name="settings_level"/>
      </Menu>
    </MenuBar>
  </kpartgui>
```

The file menu is renamed in this example to *Game* to reflect KDE standards.

KStdAction *actions do not need to be added in the XML resource file, as their handling occurs automatically by KDE.*

Any KAction will call the associated slot when it is selected. To further distinguish between the behaviors of actions, a few predefined action classes are available that differ in their effects:

- KStdActions behave like other KActions, but they are already predefined by the KDE libraries. They can be used without any additional definitions in the resource files.
- A KToggleAction will additionally toggle the state of the action in a checkbox-like fashion (checked or not checked).
- A KSelectAction offers a submenu in which a selection of items is presented. Any of these items can be selected and automatically deselects the previous one. Items can be added to a KSelectAction as a list of strings, and the currently selected item can be queried inside the called slot.

Typical operations for actions include enabling, disabling, checking, or selecting them.

```
// Enable/Disable an action/menu by 'graying' it out
((KAction*)ACTION("game_stop"))->setEnabled(true);

// Check/uncheck the toggle action
((KToggleAction*)ACTION("view_names"))->setChecked(true);

// Set one of the items in the select sub-menu to be selected
((KSelectAction*)ACTION("settings_level"))->setCurrentItem(3);
```

Inside the slot called by the action, a game command is either executed (start a new game) or the state of the action is queried (set the level of the game).

```
// Get the currently selected item of the action
int item = ((KSelectAction*)ACTION("view_names"))
            ->currentItem();


// Query whether the action is checked or not
bool checked = ((KToggleAction*)ACTION("settings_level"))
                ->isChecked();
```

Keyboard Shortcuts

Every KAction object can have one or more assigned shortcuts. Default shortcuts are added to all KStdAction objects without any additional code, and you can easily add shortcuts to your custom actions.

```
// Use CTRL+C as shortcut for the action
new KAction(i18n("&Stop Game"),
            KShortcut(Qt::CTRL + Qt::Key_C), this,
            SLOT(stopGame()), actionCollection(),
            "game_stop");


// Same, but shorter:
new KAction(i18n("&Stop Game"), Qt::CTRL + Qt::Key_C, this,
            SLOT(stopGame()), actionCollection(),
            "game_stop");


// Another version, but now CTRL+X is an alternative shortcut
// for the same action
KShortcut shortcut(Qt::CTRL + Qt::Key_C);
shortcut.append(KKey(Qt::CTRL + Qt::Key_X));
// If you use KDE < 3.2 use this instead:
// shortcut.append(KKeySequence(KKey(Qt::CTRL + Qt::Key_X)));


new KAction(i18n("&Stop Game"), shortcut, this,
            SLOT(stopGame()), actionCollection(),
            "game_stop");
```

All actions we have looked at so far have been mainly menu items. These are indeed the usual applications of KAction objects in KDE. However, actions are not required to be used in any menu, and this feature is important for games. The following example might occur in a keyboard-controlled game:

```
new KAction(i18n("Move up"), Qt::Key_Up, this,
            SLOT(moveUp()), actionCollection(),
            "move_up");
new KAction(i18n("Move down"), Qt::Key_Down, this,
            SLOT(moveDown()), actionCollection(),
            "move_down");
new KAction(i18n("Move left"), Qt::Key_Left, this,
            SLOT(moveLeft()), actionCollection(),
            "move_left");
new KAction(i18n("Move right"), Qt::Key_Right, this,
            SLOT(moveRight()), actionCollection(),
            "move_right");
```

By implementing these commands, you already have a complete keyboard interface to your game without writing any actual event handling code.

Some games use many different keys for actions that are nearly identical. For instance, the previous example uses four different keys for moving the character in various directions. Often, there are numerous keys for one task; for example, you may have a game that uses alternative game speeds, and the player can set the speed by pressing a number between 0 and 9. In these cases, you could actually create 10 KAction objects independently and provide 10 different slots. However, many developers prefer to use a single slot that receives an integer value specifying which action is meant. You can achieve this by using a QSignalMapper (see Chapter 2) to combine several KActions. This concept is described in the following code snippet:

```
// Create a signal mapper with "this" as parent
QSignalMapper* mapper = new QSignalMapper(this);

// Create 10 KAction objects in a loop
for (int i = 0; i < 10; i++)
{
  // create an action that connects to the map() slot of
  // the QSignalMapper
  KAction* a = new KAction(i18n("Set speed to %1").arg(i),
                           Qt::Key_0 + i, mapper,
                           SLOT(map()), a actionCollection(),
                           QString("set_speed_%1").arg(i));

  // emit this number for this object
  mapper->setMapping(a, i);
}

// connect the setSpeed() slot to the signal mapper instead
```

```
// of the    actions
connect(mapper, SIGNAL(mapped(int)),
        this, SLOT(setSpeed(int)));
```

Whenever the player presses "0," the slot setSpeed(0) is called. When "1" is pressed, setSpeed(1) is called, and so on.

Configuring Shortcuts

When using KAction, the shortcuts of each action can be automatically configured. All that is required is a GUI to configure them, and this can be easily accomplished with the following few lines:

```
KStdAction::keyBindings(this, SLOT(configureKeys()),
                        actionCollection());
```

and the implementation of the configureKeys() slot will resemble

```
void MainWindow::configureKeys()
{
  KKeyDialog::configure(actionCollection());
}
```

That's all! Note that any user configurations are automatically saved and loaded when the application is restarted.

Desktop Files

Any application that should be an integral part of KDE needs to define a *.desktop file. This file lists the properties of the application visible to the KDE desktop and its users.

Such a desktop file for the mykdeapp example would be called mykdeapp.desktop and could look like:

```
[Desktop Entry]
Encoding=UTF-8
Name=MyKdeApp
GenericName=Strategy Game
Exec=mykdeapp
Icon=mykdeapp
MimeType=
Terminal=false
Type=Application
DocPath=mykdeapp/index.html
Categories=Qt;KDE;Game;StrategyGame;
```

The `Exec` and `Icon` specify the name of the binary and icon files, respectively, and are usually identical to the program name. The `Type` entry defines the type of the application, and the `Name` entries list the user-displayed name for the application.

Random Numbers Using `KRandomSequence`

Most games make use of random numbers in some way. When you need only a single random value,

```
// Get random number from the global KApplication
// object kapp
kapp->random();
```

might be the easiest choice. However, often it is preferable to use the `KRandomSequence` class instead. This class can be instantiated with or without a given seed value. The seed value determines the initial value for a random sequence. The same seed value will always lead to the same sequence of random numbers. If the `KRandomSequence` object is initialized without a seed value, an arbitrary seed value is chosen by KDE, leading to different random numbers each time the program is run. For a finished program, this is usually what you want. However, if you are developing or debugging your game, it is often helpful to have the same random number sequence each time because the behavior of the program is then constantly reproduced.

The following example shows the use of the KDE random numbers:

```
KRandomSequence random;

// Get an integer value in the range (0..max-1)
int max = 1000;
int r1 = random.getLong(max);

// Get a double value in the range (0..1)
double r2 = random.getDouble();

// Get a bool value that is either true or false
bool r3 = random.getBool();

// Shuffle a list of integers
QPtrList<int> list;
list.setAutoDelete(true);
list.append(new int(1));
list.append(new int(5);
list.append(new int(19);
list.append(new int(35);
random.randomize(&list);
```

Game Configuration

A key feature of game development is the configuration of the game. In a good game design, the code should be data driven, which means that you read most values from configuration files. For example, instead of implementing code in this manner:

```
mMaxHealth = 100;
```

your game would follow this alternative method:

```
mMaxHealth = readMaxHealthFromConfig();
```

Such access of configuration information helps you and any other developers of the game to easily change the status ("maximum health") of a game character. More about data-driven design is discussed in Chapter 1, "Introduction to Desktop Gaming," and an even more detailed discussion can be found in [DeLoura00]. Additionally to game data, applications often need to store program configuration data. This can include their window size and position, the network configuration, or sound and graphics settings. In KDE, the KConfig and KSimpleConfig classes provide easy access to configuration files.

KConfig

A very easy way to implement configuration files in KDE is to use the standard configuration file of an application (in our example, mykdeapprc). This file can be accessed by using the kapp->config() pointer, which provides access to the application-wide KConfig object.

```
// Retrieve the config pointer, if "app" is the application
KConfig* conf = kapp->config();

// Choose the default group
conf->setGroup(QString::null);

// Read a "MaxHealth" entry from the configuration file:
// use "100" as default, if the entry is not defined there
int maxHealth = conf->readNumEntry("MaxHealth", 100);

// Read the player name
QString name = conf->readEntry("PlayerName", i18n("You"));

// Read whether or not to start in single player mode
bool singlePlayer = conf->readBoolEntry("SinglePlayer", true);

...
```

```
// Choose the default group
conf->setGroup(QString::null):

// Write entries back to configuration file
conf->writeEntry("MaxHealth", maxHealth);
conf->writeEntry("PlayerName", name);
conf->writeEntry("SinglePlayer", singlePlayer);
```

The resulting configuration file mykdeapprc will now resemble

```
MaxHealth=100
PlayerName=You
SinglePlayer=true
```

KConfig actually integrates the actual KDE application data file into the overall KDE configuration process by merging various configuration files. Although more flexible for KDE, this is often not necessary for games. Additionally, games sometimes require a more complex configuration hierarchy than can be attained with KConfig. These issues are resolved when using KSimpleConfig instead of KConfig.

KSimpleConfig

The actual use of KSimpleConfig is the same as KConfig, with the exception that you have to supply the location of the configuration file.

```
// Load the configuration file "gameconfig"
KSimpleConfig config(app->dirs()->findResource("config",
                                                "gameconfig"));
```

However, while KConfig merges user and system configuration files, KSimpleConfig does not; the latter operates on a single file system only.

KSimpleConfig also allows you to delete entries from the configuration file:

```
config.deleteEntry("SinglePlayer");
```

Configuration Groups

In games with several configuration entries, it is practical to have a more structured order to the configuration entries. KConfig/KSimpleConfig support this task by introducing configuration groups. In brief, a particular group is marked with [String], where "String" identifies the name of the group. All entries below that line belong to a group until the next group line appears. The entries in a configuration file that are not associated to a defined group—that is, the one at the beginning of the file—belong to the default group identified by QString::null.

```
// Choose the default group
conf->setGroup(QString::null);
int players = conf->readNumEntry("Players", 1);

for (int i = 0; i < players; i++)
{
  QString group = QString("Player_%1").arg(i);
  conf->setGroup(group);

  int maxHealth = conf->readNumEntry("MaxHealth", 100);
  QString name = conf->readEntry("Name",
                 QString("Player %1").arg(i + 1));

  setMaxHealthOfPlayer(i, maxHealth);
  setNameOfPlayer(i, name);
}
```

A sample configuration file for this code could look like this:

```
# begin of default group
Players=2

# begin of group "Player_0"
[Player_0]
MaxHealth=60
Name=Player 1

# begin of group "Player_1"
[Player_1]
MaxHealth=80
Name=Player 2
```

An entire group can be also deleted.

```
# Specifying 'true' as second parameter also deletes
# non-empty groups
conf->deleteGroup("Player_1", true);
```

Advanced File Formats Using KTar

Games often require their own file format. This includes the loading of game or configuration data such as maps or levels. However, even when simply saving and loading the user's game, a special file is needed.

If there is only a little data to be saved, a single file in either a binary format or an ASCII format such as XML is sufficient. However, larger games often need a more advanced file format, and often it is more convenient to save different data in different files. For example, such files could contain:

- The actual player data (name, health, position, etc.)
- The map of the current level
- A screenshot of the current game situation, which can be displayed in the load-game dialog
- The current state of any computer opponents, so that they can be (re)loaded

Unfortunately, saving multiple files quickly produces an unstructured mess of save games. Backing up or exchanging these save files will be complicated for the user. One possible solution is to group all files into a single directory. However, this can lead to even more complex problems, since you now have to handle multiple files and perhaps nested directories. This is a great deal of code to write without being actually relevant to the game.

By using the KDE class KTar, many of these problems can be avoided. KTar loads and saves *.tar and even compressed *.tar files (*.tar.gz), and thus provides access to their contents. With KTar, you never have to handle any actual files since the concept relies on using virtual files that are provided by KTar. In addition, KTar provides the ability to compress the files without needing any extra code, which can be very useful when using ASCII or XML files because these files compress very well.

A *.tar.gz file can be easily read using KTar.

```
// Open a tar archive that has been compressed using gzip
KTar tar(filename, "application/x-gzip");

// Open in read mode
if (!tar.open(IO_ReadOnly))
{
  // Error handling
  ...
  return;
}

// Get a pointer to the archive contents
const KArchiveDirectory* contents = tar.directory();

// Get the data of a file "file1.xml" inside the archive
QByteArray data = ((const KArchiveFile*)contents
                  ->entry("file1.xml"))->data();
```

```
// Get a pointer to a subdirectory "subdir"
const KArchiveDirectory* subdir =
        (const KArchiveDirectory*)contents->directory()
         ->entry("subdir");

// Get the data of a file "file2.xml" in the subdirectory
QByteArray data2 = ((const KArchiveFile*)subdir
                ->entry("file2.xml"))->data();


tar.close();
```

These few lines already load a compressed tar archive and provide access to the contents of the files stored in the archive. The program can directly use the loaded data. For the details on how to process the XML data stored in the QByteArray, see Chapter 16, "XML."

As shown in the next example, writing files into the tar archive works basically the same way.

```
// Create a tar archive and compress it using gzip
KTar tar(filename, "application/x-gzip");

// Open in write mode
if (!tar.open(IO_WriteOnly))
{
  // Error handling
  ...
  return;
}

// Get a pointer to the archive contents
const KArchiveDirectory* contents = mTar.directory();

// Write XML data to the archive
QString xml = xmlData.toString();
tar.writeFile("file1.xml", contents->user(),
            contents->group(), xml.length(), xml.latin1());

// Write the same XML data to a subdir of the archive:
// the subdir is automatically added, if not yet present
tar.writeFile("subdir/file2.xml", contents->user(),
            contents->group(), xml.length(), xml.latin1());

tar.close();
```

кTar can be used to create powerful file formats. Moreover, XML files can be easily compressed and written to a кTar archive. Finally, it is often beneficial to add binary data to a save game or a level file, such as a screenshot.

KDE Debugging Using kdDebug

Debugging is an important part of development. Besides using an actual debugger, debug output generated by the program itself can provide a great deal of support to the debugging task. In C/C++ programs, the programmer often uses printf() or cout for this task, but in KDE/Qt programs, these methods are usually inconvenient because they lack the support for QString and other Qt classes.

To support such debugging tasks, KDE introduced the kdDebug() method, which is comparable to cout, but its primary use is for debugging. kdDebug() is defined in kdebug.h and returns a stream that is used for the actual debug output. Its concept is very simple:

```
kdDebug() << "debug statement 1" << endl;
kdDebug() << "debug statement 2" << endl;
```

These lines cause the following output:

```
mygame: debug statement 1
mygame: debug statement 2
```

In this example, mygame is the name of your program. The name of the program is automatically added as a prefix to any kdDebug() debug output line. This helps in distinguishing kdDebug() statements from different programs or libraries.

The stream provided by kdDebug() supports all standard data types, such as int, float, char, and pointers.

```
int x   = 10;
float y = 2.5;
kdDebug() << "x=" << 10 << " y=" << y << " address of x="
          << (void*)&x << endl;
```

This example outputs

```
mygame: x=10 y=2.5 address of x=0xbffff804
```

Besides the standard data types, kdDebug() can also output several Qt classes, such as QPoint, QRect, QObject, and QStringList, to name a few. Furthermore, two special keywords are available that provide extra program information in the debug output,

```
int main(int argc, char** argv)
{
 kdDebug() << k_funcinfo << "debug" << endl;
 kdDebug() << k_lineinfo << "debug" << endl;
 return 0;
}
```

whose output will read

```
mygame: [int main(int, char**)] debug
mygame: [main.cpp:12] debug
```

Additionally, the k_funcinfo will generate information about the function or method, including the class where the debug line was invoked. k_lineinfo gives information about the file and the line in which the debug statement is located. Note that k_funcinfo works only with a GNU compiler; otherwise, it is equal to a k_lineinfo.

Every debug statement issued by kdDebug() *must stream* endl—*that is, the end-of-line notifier—as the final argument. If this is omitted, the KDE libraries generate and output a runtime warning on the console.*

Warnings, Errors, and Fatal Errors

Alongside the normal kdDebug() function, three other functions help classify the debug output:

■   kdWarning() uses the prefix appname WARNING: .
■   kdError() uses the prefix appname ERROR: .
■   kdFatal() uses the prefix appname FATAL: and causes the termination of an application.

The functions kdWarning() and kdError() differ from kdDebug() in terms of the type of prefix they use. kdFatal() additionally causes the application to quit in an abnormal termination. Such sudden program exits are generally better avoided; therefore, another option would be to open a message box telling the user what happened so the application can be stopped more gracefully.

Disabling Debug Output

In the final version for release, the debug output is normally not included because it is usually of little relevance to the user, and having no debug output allows the program to run faster.

To disable the debug output, the program needs to be compiled with the flag
—DNDEBUG; alternatively, this keyword can be placed in a source code file before including kdebug.h:

```
#define NDEBUG 1
#include <kdebug.h>
```

If the debug output is disabled in this manner, all kdDebug() calls in the code do
nothing and are therefore optimized away by the compiler.

Note that from all debug functions, *only* kdDebug() is disabled when compiled
with the NDEBUG flag.

Debug Areas

In large programs, debug output can grow so large that it is difficult to find relevant
information in it. Therefore, an additional filter is required so that only the current
debug data is displayed. Filters such as these are provided by kdDebug() through
debug areas, which can be identified by an integer parameter. By default, this area
is zero. The available areas are defined in the global configuration file kdebug.areas.
Unfortunately, there is no way to add per-application debug files to kdDebug(), but
you can modify the kdebug.areas file on your system for local debugging purposes.
This file also stores a string (such as "libkdegames") labeling the debug area (e.g.,
11000). When such a name is defined, the debug output is then prefixed with the
defined string instead of the name of the application.

```
kdDebug(11000) << "debug line" << endl;
```

This debug statement will output

```
libkdegames: debug line
```

Every debug area can be switched on or off independently of all others. This can
be done by using the *kdebugdialog* tool delivered with KDE. In this tool, an area can
be completely disabled, or its output can be directed to a file. Note that you do not
have to quit your application for these changes to take effect.

Backtraces

An advanced feature of KDE is the possibility to retrieve a *backtrace* from your
program. Backtraces provides information about the entire call hierarchy of the
current function. Sometimes, it can be handy to have this information available so
you can locate which function is responsible for calling another.

The function `kdBacktrace()` returns a string containing a backtrace, or an empty string if backtraces are not supported on your KDE installation. Backtraces can be permanently disabled when the application is ready for release, and this is achieved in the same way as for debug output.

WORKING WITH THE WORLDWIDE KDE PROJECT

KDE is an Open Source project and allows everyone to contribute to the development. This includes the source code, documentation, graphics, and sound. All contributions are welcome. The entire source code of KDE can be downloaded for free to your computer, and you can either make changes or fix bugs to existing programs such as the games, or introduce your own games into the KDE community. Of course, a new game introduced into KDE will have to conform to certain quality standards, and it will have to be discussed whether the new game fits into the general idea of KDE desktop games. Official KDE games are required to fit into the desktop environment by making use of technologies such as KAction and internationalization. Nevertheless, don't be afraid of taking part in KDE; it's fun, and the KDE community is open to all new developers.

Details on contributing to KDE can be found at the main KDE developer page [KdeDeveloper05] or the KDE Games Center [KdeGamesDevel05a]. Many discussions about the development of KDE are conducted on mailing lists, and for game development, the most relevant mailing lists are [KdeGamesDevel05b] and [KdeGamesDevel05c]. Join the discussion on these mailing lists to get an idea of the KDE game developer community.

All the KDE source code can be obtained by either FTP [KdeFtp05] or by using anonymous SVN (subversion). A first glimpse at the KDE repository can be obtained by using the repository Web interface [Web05]. A download of the source code can also be done through the anonymous SVN procedure. For the KDE games package, you would do

```
svn co svn://anonsvn.kde.org/home/kde/trunk/KDE/kdegames
```

A list of available packages can be found at the Web site [KdeModules05]. To update an already checked-out version, an "svn up" is sufficient.

You can use the KDE source code for the basis of your own game development. You can also begin to contribute to KDE with particular emphasis on the KDE games themselves. In the beginning, most people fix some bugs or make some improvements to existing games. These can then be proposed on the mailing list where an existing developer will include them in the KDE repository. If you do this a few times, you probably will want to get your own KDE development account.

This is normally no problem; simply ask on the mailing list. With this personal KDE account, the repository can be used as described previously, and changes can then be committed to the original KDE repository. If you do any of these contributions, you are a KDE developer!

SUMMARY

KDE is a free graphical desktop for Unix and Linux systems that has now reached a professional level in nearly all areas relevant to desktop computers. KDE can be used for anything from word processing to gaming. The development of desktop games for KDE is not difficult and can often be very rewarding. Working together on the Internet with other developers from around the world is especially interesting and usually benefits all parties. In this chapter, we provided a step-by-step introduction to a first KDE game application. This template application can be used as the basis for the development of other desktop games. The easy-to-use KDE build process with either KDevelop or the `autoconf` and `automake` tools allows you to create portable applications for all KDE systems. Together with the internationalization features, the new applications can be distributed around the globe.

One of KDE's most powerful features is the `KAction` technology. In KDE-based applications, this technology is used for most menu/toolbar items and keyboard actions. It is particularly useful to game applications, in which you require custom shortcuts (such as arrow keys). In addition, the details of these key configurations and assignments are already performed by KDE.

For developers who prefer a more graphically-assisted build process, KDevelop provides excellent means to start a program and focus on the actual code. Additionally, being an IDE, it provides many means to aid the process of creating applications. However, you can also use the `autoconf`/`automake` or `qmake` tools directly, which may give you more direct control over your build process system.

As described in this chapter, KDE offers many easy-to-use ways to make a program translatable into different languages. While this feature is not usually the primary goal in a game project, it still is an important feature once a program has become playable and is stable. Nevertheless, it is often difficult to support translations properly without the help of some internationalization library. KDE provides these features, and when using them, you don't need to pay much attention to internationalization because KDE does it for you.

Finally, we presented a comfortable method for API documentation. This issue has a high degree of importance for libraries and larger applications. You have probably noticed in your own programs that even *you* cannot remember the details of something you coded after a couple of months.

REFERENCES

[Autoconf05] *Autoconf, http://www.gnu.org/software/autoconf*, 2005.

[Automake05] *Automake, http://www.gnu.org/software/automake*, 2005.

[DeLoura00] DeLoura, Mark, *Game Programming Gems*, ISBN: 1584500492; Charles River Media, 2000.

[Ettrich96] Ettrich, Matthias, *KDE, http://groups-beta.google.com/group/de.comp.os.linux.misc/msg/cb4b2d67ffc3ffce,*1996.

[Gkioulekas98] Gkioulekas, Eleftherios, *Learning the GNU Development Tools, http://www.st-andrews.ac.uk/~iam/docs/tutorial.html*, 1998.

[KdeApps05] *KDE-Apps.org, http://www.kde-apps.org*, 2005.

[KBabel05] *KBabel, http://i18n.kde.org/tools/kbabel*, 2005.

[KdeBooks05] *KDE Developer's Corner: Books, http://developer.kde.org/documentation/books/index.html*, 2005.

[KdeDeveloper05] *KDE Developer's Corner, http://developer.kde.org/documentation*, 2005.

[KdeFtp05] *KDE FTP, ftp://ftp.kde.org*, 2005.

[KdeGamesDevel05a] *The KDE Games Center, http://games.kde.org*, 2005.

[KdeGamesDevel05b] *KDE-Games-Devel, http://mail.kde.org/pipermail/kde-games-devel*, 2005.

[KdeGamesDevel05c] *KDE-Games-Devel, http://mail.kde.org/mailman/listinfo/kde-games-devel*, 2005.

[KDEi18n05] *KDE Internationalisation, http://i18n.kde.org*, 2005.

[KdeModules05] *KDE Module List, http://developer.kde.org/source/anoncvs.html*, 2005.

[Kdevelop05] *KDevelop, http://www.kdevelop.org*, 2005.

[Klocale05] *Klocale Class Documentation, http://developer.kde.org/documentation/library/cvs-api/kdecore/html/classKLocale.html*, 2005.

[Web05] *The KDE Web Repository, http://websvn.kde.org*, 2005.

4 Qt Game Development Using Microsoft Windows

In This Chapter

- Qt for Windows
- Creating a Standard Qt Application
- `Qmake`—Automatic Makefile Generation
- The Application Icon
- Tricks of the Trade

Microsoft Windows and Apple Macintosh systems are classical desktop operating systems and are installed on most desktop computers throughout the world. However, these systems are not widely used for Open Source program development, because the operating systems neither follow nor particularly support the essence of Open Source. Nevertheless, there are serious advantages to creating a game application for these operating systems, since a much larger user base can be accessed.

The cross-platform features of Qt allow the development of a Qt application for all platforms, as long as the Qt libraries are available. Such platforms include Linux, Microsoft Windows, and Apple Macintosh computers. Any program written initially for a certain platform such as KDE, Qt, or Qtopia can be transferred to alternative Qt platforms with limited effort. Obviously, this aspect of Qt provides a distinct advantage for desktop game development.

In this chapter, we show you how to construct a basic desktop game application using pure Qt. As a demonstration platform, we focus on Microsoft Windows. However, game development for other systems supporting Qt, such as Apple Macintosh or Linux systems, work analogously. However, if you intend to program solely for Linux, it is generally better to create a native KDE application, because this allows a tighter integration into the desktop (see Chapter 3, "Game Development using KDE").

QT FOR WINDOWS

Before starting with the actual application development, we want to draw your attention to one principal issue that arises for Open Source game developers when developing a Qt application for Microsoft Windows. This is the fact that Trolltech only provides a version of Qt 3 for Microsoft Windows with a commercial license. However, starting with Qt 4, Trolltech releases Qt with an Open Source license also for Microsoft Windows systems. Nevertheless, the license issue has to be kept in mind: if you plan to develop commercial games based on Qt 3, it is probably worthwhile to make such an investment since Qt is a good toolkit. Of course, this investment requires more careful consideration if you program free, Open Source games. In this case, you might want to use Qt 4. However, if you require Qt 3, there is one way to obtain a noncommercial version of Qt 3 for Windows: a version of Qt 3.2 is delivered with Blanchette's book [Blanchette04] allowing noncommercial Open Source programming.

Program development with Qt on Microsoft Windows is most easily accomplished with the Borland C++™ or the Microsoft Visual C++® compilers. In both cases, the programming can be performed using powerful graphical IDEs into which Qt integrates seamlessly. Both compilers also allow the generation of Qt programs by using their command-line versions. This is of particular interest because a free version of the Borland C++ command-line compiler accompanies [Blanchette04].

For Apple Macintosh operating systems, these restrictions do not apply because a GPL version of Qt is available as a free download on the Trolltech Web site [Trolltech04a].

CREATING A STANDARD QT APPLICATION

Most application programs follow the same principle when setting up the basic framework. These principles are no different for desktop games that use Linux, Microsoft Windows, or Apple Macintosh as the target platforms.

In this chapter, we demonstrate the code parts necessary for developing a Qt desktop game application for Microsoft Windows in the provided code snippets and explain their relevance to a Qt game program. The CD-ROM accompanying this book includes all the necessary header files and the full source code for the demo program. They can be located in the folder `examples/myqtwin`. The `myqtwin` application (see Figure 4.1) is built upon a canvas view, which is the typical view used for desktop games. A more detailed explanation about canvas games can be found in Chapter 6, "Canvas Games."

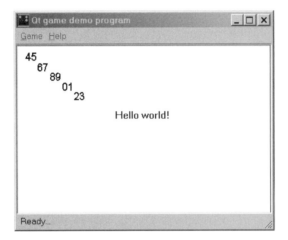

FIGURE 4.1 Screenshot of the example game application template running on Microsoft Windows.

As described in Chapter 1, "Introduction to Desktop Gaming," a desktop game application follows a standard setup procedure. The main files necessary include the main program, the main window, the game view, and the game document. Their principal application is demonstrated in the following using the `myqtwin` example, which can be easily extended to fit your game application.

The Main Program

The application is initialized by the C++ main program. The `main()` subroutine is called by the operating system upon the start of the game. Here, the application and the main window objects are both instantiated and initialized before the application event loop is called. The event loop handles all the processing of GUI events (interaction) and non-GUI events (user, network, and timer events), and once these are processed, the corresponding slots are called.

The main program `main.cpp` reads:

```cpp
#include <qapplication.h>
#include <qstring.h>

#include "mainwindow.h"

int main(int argc, char* argv[])
{
  // Create the Qt application object
  QApplication app(argc, argv);

  // Define the main window, assign it to the
  // application object and show it
  MainWindow* mainwindow = new MainWindow();
  app.setMainWidget(mainwindow);
  mainwindow->show();

  // Run the application event loop
  return app.exec();
}
```

The Main Window

The main window of an application creates the menus, the toolbar, and the actions, and sets up the view object. The "view" is defined as the area inside the main window that displays the actual contents of the application. In the game application, this will consist mainly of sprites and other canvas objects.

We start the main window source code `mainwindow.cpp` by including both the Qt and user-defined header files.

```cpp
// Qt includes
#include <qaction.h>
#include <qdir.h>
#include <qmenubar.h>
#include <qmessagebox.h>
#include <qpopupmenu.h>
#include <qstatusbar.h>
#include <qstring.h>
...

// Application specific includes
#include "mainwindow.h"
#include "gameview.h"
#include "gamedoc.h"
```

The constructor of the main view is used to initialize the menus and the view. However, in the application example here, the initialization of the menus is forwarded to the `initGUI()` method so it does not clutter the constructor with too much code.

```
MainWindow::MainWindow()
          : QMainWindow(0)
{
  // Window title
  setCaption(tr("Qt game demo program"));

  // Reset and initialize class variables
  gameDoc  = new GameDoc(this);
  gameView = new GameView(gameDoc, this);

  // Set the view as the central widget
  setCentralWidget(gameView);

  // Set up the menus etc
  initGUI();
}
```

Note that in this example we introduced the Qt translation function `tr()`. This function works similarly to the KDE `i18n()` function, and its use is explained in more detail later in this chapter in the section "Internationalization."

All menus and actions of the application are now initialized in the `initGUI()` method. As an example, myqtwin uses one menu called *Game*, which is created and plugged into the application menu bar. Conveniently, this menu bar is already supplied by the Qt main window object.

```
void MainWindow::initGUI()
{
  // Create game menu
  QPopupMenu* gameMenu = new QPopupMenu(this);
  menuBar()->insertItem(tr("&Game"), gameMenu);
  ...
```

When required, multiple menus can be added in exactly the same way. To keep the example simple, only one menu entry is inserted into the *Game* menu—we will simply name it *Demo*. In Qt, a menu item is represented by a `QAction`. `QAction`s are more than just menu items; they represent a general user interaction with the program and are achieved via menus, toolbars, or the keyboard. All user interactions are routed through the `QAction`s, which in turn notify the program to respond. The

QAction used in the example program can be called by selecting the menu item or by an associated keyboard shortcut—here, CTRL-x. Additionally, it is possible to have a little help text associated with the action by using the setWhatsThis() method. This text is automatically displayed by the Qt main window as a help to the user when the user highlights the corresponding menu with the mouse arrow. Once the user activates a menu, the slot connected to the QAction is called. In our example, this will be the method menuGameDemo().

```
QAction* gameDemoAction;
...

// Create actions for game menu
gameDemoAction = new QAction(tr("&Demo"), CTRL+Key_X,
                                 this, "demo");

// Set the "help" text for the menu item
gameDemoAction->setWhatsThis(tr("Starting the demo..."));

// Connect the action to a slot method of our program:
// It is activated by clicking on the menu or using the keyboard
// shortcut and then call the slot menuGameDemo().
connect(gameDemoAction, SIGNAL(activated()),
        this, SLOT(menuGameDemo()));
...
```

The new menu entry now has to be assigned to the *Game* menu, and this is achieved by simply adding it to the preferred menu.

```
...
// Add action into game menu
gameDemoAction->addTo(gameMenu);
...
}
```

Other menu entries can be added by creating more actions and plugging them into the corresponding menus.

The View

The "view" of the game application is the visible part of the window inside the frame of the main window. Any Qt widget class (QWidget, etc.) can be used as the application view. However, for game applications, the QCanvasView is often the more appropriate choice since it allows easy definition and use of canvas sprites.

Sprites are often a very natural representation of a desktop game, since most games consist of these little moving objects. However, some games focus more on text input, such as word puzzles. In these games, a simple `QWidget` is usually more than sufficient for the display. All the details of a canvas view, including sprites, are described in Chapter 6.

To begin, we will start programming the view `gameview.cpp` by including any Qt header files and any other user-defined class header files.

```
// Application specific includes
...
#include "gameview.h"
#include "gamedoc.h"
```

Following this step, the view of the main window needs to be set up. We will derive it from the `QCanvasView` class, which allows an association between the canvas and the view so that canvas items and sprites can be displayed. In the following example, some typical initializations of views are shown, such as the setup of scrollbars and the canvas background color.

```
GameView::GameView(GameDoc* doc, QWidget* parent)
        : QCanvasView(0, parent, 0)
{
  // We do not need scrolling so we switch it off
  setVScrollBarMode(AlwaysOff);
  setHScrollBarMode(AlwaysOff);

  // Create a new canvas for this view
  QCanvas* gameCanvas = new QCanvas(this);
  // Fit it in the parent window
  gameCanvas->resize(parent->width(), parent->height());
  // Choose a nice background color
  gameCanvas->setBackgroundColor(QColor(32,32,128));
  // Do more canvas setup here if required
  ...
  // Assign the canvas to the view
  setCanvas(gameCanvas);

  // Set size and position
  move(0,0);
  adjustSize();
  ...
```

In our example, the canvas is linked to the view. Therefore, resizing the view must also automatically resize the embedded canvas objects. This can be achieved by using the Qt event function resizeEvent(), which is called when any changes occur to the window size.

```
void GameView::resizeEvent(QResizeEvent* e)
{
  if (canvas())
  {
    canvas()->resize(e->size().width(),
                     e->size().height());
  }
}
```

The Document

The document class is used to store all the relevant game data, and a simple container class is usually more than sufficient. Nevertheless, it is can be useful to derive the document class from QObject so you can gain access to the Qt signal-slot features.

The following example shows the basic document header file gamedoc.h of the game application.

```
class GameDoc : public QObject
{
  Q_OBJECT

  public:
    // Constructor for the game document object
    GameDoc(QWidget* parent = 0)
    ...

  public slots:
    ...

  signals:
    ...
};
```

Qmake—AUTOMATIC MAKEFILE GENERATION

Qmake is Trolltech's version of the GNU autoconf and automake tools and has been specifically designed for Qt applications. Qmake uses a *project* file to create Makefiles suitable for Qt applications. This project file is a normal text file that collects and defines the properties of the application. The information collected in the project file includes the source code files, the user interface files, and some general commands and parameters. Qmake then compiles all this information into a proper Makefile. Consequently, these Makefiles generated from the project files include all the special Qt features. Particularly useful features are the meta object compiler (MOC) file generation and the code generation from the user interface files (*.ui), which are created with the Qt Designer. Another important feature is that the project file itself can be independent of the actual compiler or operating system platform [Trolltech04b].

For the myqtwin demo application, such a project file myqtwin.pro could resemble

```
TEMPLATE = app
SOURCES  = main.cpp mainwindow.cpp gamedoc.cpp gameview.cpp
HEADERS  = mainwindow.h gamedoc.h gameview.h
CONFIG   += qt warn_on release
```

This project file now includes all of the important aspects that are usually required for game applications.

The keywords of such a project file are:

TEMPLATE: Specifies the type of program that should be built. Here, we require an executable application.

SOURCES: Lists all source code files.

HEADERS: Lists all header files of the application. The header files are used for the generation of the MOC files when using features of Qt such as Q_OBJECT, signals, and slots.

CONFIG: Directs qmake to link the Qt libraries and to modify the build process behavior by either switching warnings on (warn_on) or off (warn_off), or by toggling the debug mode from on (debug) to off (release). Sensible default values often allow the omission of the CONFIG line.

FORMS: Lists all the user interface files.

TRANSLATIONS: Lists all translation language source files (*.ts).

Dialogs from the Qt Designer are stored in the user interface *.ui files. These files are collected together and are added to the build process using a FORMS line such as

```
FORMS        = mydialog.ui
```

In this application example, no dialogs are used, and therefore this line is omitted. In a real application, dialogs are nearly always included. Note, however, that it is also possible to include dialogs as source code, not only as *.ui files.

Within a project file, some of the defined statements can actually contain more than one argument. In these cases, multiple arguments can be listed ordinarily as a whitespace-separated list in one line, or can be added using the += operator in consecutive lines. Taking the example of the source code files that are defined by the SOURCE keyword, the definition of multiple arguments would resemble

```
SOURCES  += main.cpp
SOURCES  += mainwindow.cpp
SOURCES  += gamedoc.cpp
SOURCES  += gameview.cpp
```

and overall, such a format might provide a clearer overview in the project file, especially if numerous files are involved.

Note that qmake allows the addition of specific platform parts that act like a programming if condition. This can be used to include files from different target platforms if necessary.

```
win32 {
  SOURCES += special_windows_code.cpp
  DEFINES += SPECIAL_WINDOWS_DEFINE
}
```

Before starting qmake, some environmental variables have to be set that inform the program about the compiler and the Qt location. This is easily done by executing

```
# For the Borland compiler
SET QMAKESPEC=win32-borland
# For the Microsoft compiler
SET QMAKESPEC=win32-msvc
# The location of the Qt library
SET QTDIR=C:\QT\
```

on the command line or in a startup script such as the autoexec.bat file on Microsoft Windows.

Assuming that qmake and make are in the command path, qmake can be executed with the given project file myqtwin.pro as the argument

```
qmake myqtwin.pro
```

and if it ran successfully, a Makefile is generated. This Makefile can then directly be executed using

```
make
```

which in turn will start the build process for the program. The Makefile contains a few other useful command directives that, for example, allow you to clean up the directory by

```
# Remove object files
make clean
# Additionally remove executable file
make distclean
```

THE APPLICATION ICON

In the Microsoft Windows system, every application can possess a special icon that is depicted in the file manager and in the menu bar of the application (see Figure 4.2). This icon is compiled into the executable file itself. Individual icons are based on special bitmap files, the icon files *.ico. These files can be converted from normal bitmap images or edited using an icon editor tool such as Icon Art™ from the Web site [Conware04]. Nowadays, most integrated developer environments (e.g., the Microsoft Visual Studio) already contain an icon editor. Both methods can be used to create your own icons for use in your game program.

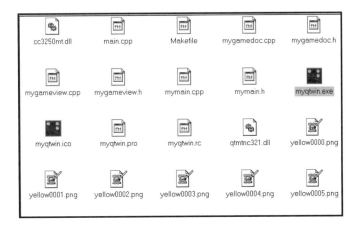

FIGURE 4.2   The application is shown with its icon in the Microsoft Windows file manager.

Once an icon file is available, it can be integrated into the Qt application by simply storing its filename in a resource file. Here we would use the file `myqtwin.rc` with the following simple content:

```
IDI_ICON1              ICON    DISCARDABLE     "myqtwin.ico"
```

To include this resource file into the make process, it has to be specified in the project file for `qmake`. This is easily achieved by adding

```
RC_FILE = myqtwin.rc
```

to the `myqtwin.pro` file. In the final step, by rerunning `qmake` and `make`, the application will be equipped with a user-defined icon.

Note that on Apple Macintosh systems, this procedure would work almost the same way. Here, an icon still needs to be created, and this task can be easily achieved using the icon editor program that is already part of the standard system. This program is used to create `*.icns` icon files, which can be added directly into the `qmake` project file in the following manner:

```
RC_FILE = myqtapple.icns
```

TRICKS OF THE TRADE

This brief section provides a list of useful ways in which game programming for Microsoft Windows can be made easier.

QTime and QDate

Qt offers classes for time and date processing; namely, the `QTime` and `QDate` classes. These classes can be used to retrieve the current time and date and display them in a nice text format:

```
#include <qdatetime.h>
...

// Get the current date
QDate currentDate  = QDate::currentDate();
// Convert it to a text string
QString dateString = currentDate.toString(Qt::TextDate);

// Get the current time
QTime currentTime  = QTime::currentTime();
```

```
// Convert it to a text string
QString timeString = currentTime.toString(Qt::TextDate);
```

Another function of the QTime class is the capability to measure time. This is extremely practical on Windows systems because it allows access to time measurement without actually accessing the functions of the operating system. Furthermore, it permits basic profiling for your application. Although not as accurate as a real profiler, it can help in estimating the amount of time necessary for certain function calls. This feature can be implemented using the following code snippet:

```
#include <qdatetime.h>
...
QTime time;
// Start measurement
time.start();

// Do some lengthy calculation
...

// Measure the elapsed time in milliseconds
int elapsed = time.elapsed();
```

Files and Directories

On Microsoft Windows and Linux systems, the concept of a home directory is often different. These differences are most prominently reflected in the handling of the home directory and open file dialogs. Qt provides access to the home directory using the QDir class:

```
#include <qdir.h>

// Return home directory
QDir homeDir = QDir::home();
```

On Microsoft Windows, a certain logic is applied by Qt to retrieve the location of the home directory. First, the existence of the HOME environment variable is checked. If this is not available, further checks for the USERPROFILE, HOMEDRIVE, or HOMEPATH environment variables are performed. If none of these variables is defined, the last resort is the C: drive.

File open or file save dialogs permit the user to select a file for loading or saving. For example, browsing for a file to open can be performed in the following manner:

```
#include <qfiledialog.h>

// Open a dialog to browse for a file
QString file = QFileDialog::getOpenFileName(
            QString::null,
            "C-Source (*.c *.cpp );;All files (*)",
            this,
            "demo file dialog",
            tr("Demonstration file chooser") );
```

In the working example, the arguments provided to the static method `QFileDialog` are the initial directory, a file filter, the parent window, the dialog identifier, and the dialog title. If `QString::null` is given as the initial directory, the user's `My Documents` folder is browsed on Microsoft Windows systems. Only certain subsets of files in the directory are allowed to be displayed by the file filters. Additional filters can be supplied by separating them with double colons. In our case, the first filter lists C/C++ files ending with `*.c` or `*.cpp`, while the second filter lists all files. Saving a file using `getSaveFileName()` or finding a directory with `getExistingDirectory()` are both executed with a function call analogous to that used for opening a file.

QSettings and the Windows Registry

Qt allows the permanent storage of program settings so they are available even after an application is quit and then restarted. This saving mechanism differs depending on the target platform. On Unix or Linux systems, ASCII configuration files are created in the user's home directory in the folder `.qt` (it is possible to change this location). On Microsoft Windows systems, the Windows registry is used to store the data (see Figure 4.3).

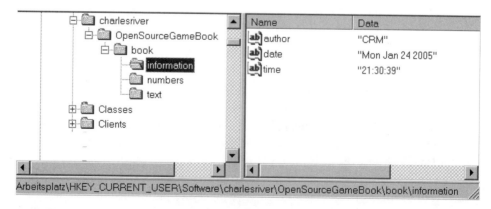

FIGURE 4.3 Screenshot of the Microsoft Windows registry after storing the `QSettings` from this section.

The settings are stored by specifying a key that has a designated value. The key is comprised of at least two strings separated by /; for example, /book/numbers. Values can be specified by numerous Qt/C++ types, and typical examples include int numbers, double numbers, or QString text. The following example shows how you can store a settings key in the Windows registry (see also Figure 4.3):

```
#include <qsettings.h>

// Store settings in a file (Unix, Mac) or the Registry
//(Microsoft Windows)
QSettings settings;
// Set registry main path
settings.setPath("charlesriver.com", "OpenSourceGameBook",
                 QSettings::User);

// Write settings to the given key
settings.writeEntry("/book/numbers/int", 42);
settings.writeEntry("/book/numbers/bool", true);
settings.writeEntry("/book/numbers/double", 7.15);
settings.writeEntry("/book/text/string", "Teststring");

// Write settings in a group. A group path precedes all
// following keys until an endGroup() occurs and can serve
// as a shortcut to long path names.
settings.beginGroup("/book/information");
settings.writeEntry("/author", "CRM");
settings.writeEntry("/time",   timeString);
settings.writeEntry("/date",   dateString);
settings.endGroup();
```

Keys and the list of all possible keys can be retrieved from the settings file or the registry, respectively. This is shown in the following code snippet:

```
// Access settings
QSettings settings;
settings.setPath("charlesriver.com", "OpenSourceGameBook",
                 QSettings::User);

// Retrieve a list of all stored entries of the given key
QStringList keys = settings.entryList("/book/information");

// Retrieve entries stored previously
int number = settings.readNumEntry("/book/numbers/int");
```

```
QString s  = settings.readEntry("/book/information/time");
```

and can be seen in the screenshot depicted in Figure 4.3.

Internationalization

Applications offered worldwide often benefit when translated into the language of
the user. However, it would not be very efficient to compile a new version of the application for each language. Therefore, Qt already includes translation features that
allow all text to be translated into another language. These string translations are
handled via translation files (*.qm) , which are loaded into the application and contain a lookup table between the original text and the translated text. Note that this
file must be loaded before the main window is created.

In our example application myqtwin, a translation file for German would be installed inside the main program main.cpp like:

```
#include <qtranslator.h>
...


// Create the translator
QTranslator translator(0);

// Load German translations
translator.load("myqtwin_de.qm", ".");

// Install the application translator
app.installTranslator(&translator);
```

In the remainder of the program, all text visible to the user (menus, messages,
etc.) are then processed using the tr() function. Using tr() will automatically look
up all strings in the translation file, and if a translation entry exists, present this to
the user:

```
// Apply the translation to a string
QString s1 = tr("Start new Game");
```

Because often there are several possibilities of how to translate a text into another language, it is possible to specify an optional comment to all translation
strings. This string will not appear to the user, but will help the translator determine
the exact meaning of this text:

```
// Translation with an optional comment
// for the translator
```

```
QString s2 = tr("Start new Game",
                "Game menu entry");
```

Similar to the internationalization issues described in Chapter 3, it is important to perform only translation of complete text strings; that is, a string should not be concatenated from partial strings, but instead, one string should contain the entire text, and all variables should be inserted as string arguments.

```
// Translation string using arguments
QString playerName = ...;  // The player name
int points = ...;          // The points
QString s3 = tr("Player %1 scores %2 points").
             arg(playerName).arg(points);
```

To prepare an application for translation, one or more translation entries need to be added to the project file

```
TRANSLATIONS=myqtwin_de.ts
```

and calling the Qt `lupdate` command on this project file will extract all strings marked for translation (`tr()`) from the application and collect them in the XML translation file(s) `*.ts`. Alternatively, you can also run `lupdate` on a set of source files, which would work analogously. Using Qt Linquist, a graphical translation tool also provided with Qt, it is then easy to create the translations for the target language; in our case, German. When all strings are translated, the translation file is "compiled" (`lrelease` or using the *Release* menu entry of Qt Linguist), creating a `myqtwin_de.qm` "object" translation file, and this is what is loaded in the main program.

ON THE CD

The example program `myqtwin` on the companion CD-ROM includes a translation file for German. You can switch `myqtwin` to German by starting the program with the option `German` on the command line:

```
myqtwin German
```

or load the `myqtwin_de.ts` translation file into the *Qt Linguist* to see the translated strings.

SUMMARY

In this chapter, we presented the setup of a standard desktop game application using pure Qt. This application implements the standard main program, the application's main window, a canvas-based view, and a document object for data storage. The application template and the accompanying Makefiles can be used as a starting point for your own game development. Furthermore, we demonstrated how Qt-based game development can be adapted for target platforms such as Microsoft Windows. We demonstrated that because of the extensive cross-platform compatibility in the Qt source code, this program can be further used (that is, compiled) on all other Qt target platforms, including Apple Macintosh or Linux systems.

Furthermore, observe that the source code of a basic desktop game application using pure Qt is very similar to the applications for KDE and PDA game programming (see Chapter 3 and Chapter 5, "Game Development on PDAs"). Note that this is exactly the concept that Qt programs want to provide; that is, almost fully compatible source code that can be easily transferred with minimal alterations from one system to another.

REFERENCES

[Blanchette04] Blanchette, Jasmin, and Mark Sommerfeld, *C++ GUI Programming with Qt 3*, Prentice Hall PTR, ISBN: 0131240722, 2004.

[Conware04] *Icon Art, http://www.conware-pro.com/products/index.php*, 2004.

[Trolltech04] *Qt Download, http://www.trolltech.com/download/index.html*, 2004.

[Trolltech04b] *Qmake, http://doc.trolltech.com/3.0/qmake-manual-1.html*, 2004.

5 Game Development on PDAs

In This Chapter

■ Embedded Game Development
■ Qtopia and Qt/Embedded
■ Creating a Standard Game Application
■ PDA Programming Tips
■ Packaging and Distribution

Personal digital assistants (PDAs), handheld computers, and mobile cell phones have now reached a technical maturity that allows a person to program and develop games for them. Their ever-increasing worldwide popularity also makes the PDA market an interesting target platform for new game development. The desktop games discussed in this book are an especially ideal choice for handheld devices, since these games are the right size and contain the right depth and complexity a player wants on a PDA—a small game of Tetris in the subway going to work or a game of checkers while waiting at the airport. Qt/Linux handhelds and smart phones are up-and-coming, especially in the Asian market, with Sharp developing the Zaurus™ series and companies like Motorola introducing Qt/Linux smart phones, such as the Motorola A760.

In regard to memory size and processing power, the performance of all major PDAs is sufficient to run most desktop games. However, even though small desktop games are no longer a problem, it will still take some time before a 3D first-person shooter can be played on a cell phone. Nevertheless, the combination of Qtopia and embedded Qt provides a platform that allows one to create desktop game applications for all types of mobile devices. In particular, games developed for KDE or Qt can be easily transferred from the KDE/Qt platform to a Qtopia PDA if you follow some general guidelines when designing the game. The compatibility between quite different devices such as desktop computers, PDAs, and even cell phones helps the development of computer game applications enormously. Therefore, it is not necessary to maintain many different software branches for each target platform.

Some popular examples of PDAs that allow Linux and embedded Qt applications to run include:

- The Sharp Zaurus™ series (5500, 5600, 6000, etc.) running Linux and Qtopia.
- The Gmate Yopy™ series (3000, 3500, 3700, etc.) running primarily Linux, but also allowing Qt to be installed.
- The Compaq iPAQ™ series (H3600, H3670, H3870, H3970, H3870, etc.) allowing the installation of Linux and Qt.

Figure 5.1 shows an example of Qtopia running on handheld devices. A more detailed list of Linux and Qt PDAs can be found at the Web sites [Tuxmobil04] and [PDAbuyersguide04]. It is always wise to check pages such as these before buying a new PDA, especially since many new models are constantly added to support Linux and/or embedded Qt [IPAQLinux04a], [IPAQLinux04b], [Underdahl04].

FIGURE 5.1 The Qtopia platform running on PDAs and cell phones (© Trolltech, reprinted with permission).

EMBEDDED GAME DEVELOPMENT

Developing games for embedded devices is generally not much different from developing games for desktop computers. In addition, the high amount of compatibility between Qt/desktop and Qt/embedded software allows the development to occur on the same software branch. In most cases, it is unnecessary to maintain two versions of the software. However, due to the physical properties of a PDA, there are some restrictions when compared to desktop computers. In Table 5.1, we compare some of these performance properties.

TABLE 5.1   Comparison of a typical PDA and Desktop Computer (2005)

Item	PDA	Desktop Computer
Processor	206–400 MHz	1000–3000 MHz
Memory (RAM)	64–128 MB	256–1024 MB
Memory (disk)	128–256 MB (flash)	80.000 MB–160.000 MB
Screen size	3.5"	17-19"
Screen resolution	240 x 320 pixel	1024 x 768 pixel
Networking	11 MBit/s wireless	100 MBit/s
Input devices	Stylus, (keypad)	Mouse, keyboard

With respect to game programming, the main differences between PDAs and desktop computers can be assigned to one of the following categories.

The processor and the available memory of the PDA: As expected, both are typically much smaller than the corresponding ones for a desktop computer. This will affect the amount of data stored and processed. Note that normal program code does not contribute very much to the overall memory consumption. However, large dynamically allocated fields do consume a lot of memory. Therefore, in games, two areas are affected the most. The first is a reduction in the multimedia parts of the game. This includes a decrease in both the graphic size and resolution and a lower quality of sound effects. Second, and usually of less importance, maps or game trees have to be used carefully; that is, they must be limited in size.

The screen size: The PDA screen is smaller and has a much lower resolution than a desktop PC. While modern desktop PCs run with screen resolutions of 1024 × 768 to 1600 × 1200 pixels on a 17"–21" monitor, the typical PDA has only 240 × 320 pixels on a 3.5" display. Smart phones are also produced with similar resolutions, but have even smaller screen sizes. While the resolution determines the amount of detail you can show on the screen, the absolute screen size should also be considered, since a single pixel on a handheld device will be quite small. Consequently, although you might be tempted to squeeze a lot onto those 240 × 320 pixels, it is often better to opt for fewer objects that are larger but more distinct. On handheld devices, this is an important point to consider for the player, since very small graphics will strain the eyes, and in the end, the user will not play your game. Of course, the reduction in graphics will also restrict the amount of additional information that can be shown to the user such as tables, scoreboards, buttons, and menus. Therefore, a careful design is necessary, and the where and how to display information has to be carefully planned.

Dialogs and menus: Due to the limited screen size, dialogs designed for PDAs have to be carefully thought out, since much less information can be shown. Try to keep all dialogs simple, and show only a few entry fields and buttons per dialog. When more information is necessary, it has to be distributed over more than one subpage of the dialog. For menus, consider how many menus you really need. Is it necessary to configure everything in the application? Keep in mind that all user interaction is more tedious on a PDA.

Screen orientation: Most PDAs allow you to rotate the application on the display. Therefore, you can choose either a landscape or a portrait display for the game. This means that your game can be generated wider or taller, an advantage compared to most desktop computers where screen rotation is the exception.

Stylus input: PDAs usually offer a stylus (a pen) as input instead of a mouse. Although this is quite comparable as an input device, its peculiarities have to be considered. For example, a game requiring a massive input of mouse clicks will lead to the player hammering the stylus on the display of the PDA—certainly not ideal for the player or the display.

Keyboard input: PDAs often have no or only a limited keyboard input. Although some PDAs offer a keyboard, and all offer a virtual keyboard or handwriting recognition, this is a bit tedious to use and not a good input for games. This lack of a real keyboard requires one to tailor the input of the programs to low keyboard input. In the majority of cases, it is useful to control the elements of the game with the stylus or with some cursor or application buttons that are easily accessible to the user. Although the (virtual) keyboard should not be used in the game, it can be used to allow input of names in scoreboard lists and so forth.

Floating-point calculation: Many embedded processors—for example, the Strong-ARM processors—do not support built-in floating-point calculations. Consequently, programs that do use floating-point calculations but are run on these types of processors are always much slower than if they were programmed with fixed point or pure integer arithmetic. Therefore, depending on the type of processor within the device, it is good practice to reduce the amount of floating-point numbers, especially when precision is not an issue.

QTOPIA AND QT/EMBEDDED

For the programming of embedded devices, Trolltech offers a special version of Qt called Qt/Embedded. The application framework of Qtopia is built on top of embedded Qt and serves as an additional layer between the program and the device, providing easy access to important features typically found on PDAs and handheld devices.

The Qtopia Development Platform

Qtopia is an application platform and user interface for embedded devices that allows compatible application development for PDAs and smart phones. Qtopia offers a clearly specified software environment and guarantees that all applications developed with Qtopia can be easily transferred to all other devices offering the Qtopia software platform. The Qtopia software is built on top of the embedded version of Qt. Therefore, the Qt library, the graphics system of the embedded device (through a frame buffer), and the underlying Linux operating system can all be accessed. Figure 5.2 depicts the software architecture of the Qtopia software platform.

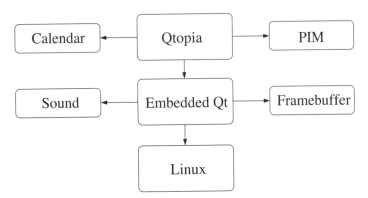

FIGURE 5.2 The Qtopia software architecture. The application layer software Qtopia interacts with the PDA via the embedded Qt and the Linux operation system . To highlight which layers access which components, some examples are listed. Qtopia provides PDA services such as PIM and calendar, while Qt controls the video frame buffer, sound system, and so on. The operating system is provided by Linux.

Qtopia provides access to the special features of a PDA, such as the infrared port, stylus, virtual keyboard, and core applications of the PDA such as the calendar, address book, or personal information manager. Furthermore, additional classes for handling configuration files and the interprocess communications are available.

Qt/embedded is a smaller version of Qt whose API is compatible to any other version of Qt. This advantage of Qt should not be underestimated, as it allows you to use the same software code base for various target systems without having to recode or employ conditional software branches. However, some of the large memory-consuming classes and classes that are of little use on embedded devices are not included [TrolltechQtopia04a]. Examples of these include extra fonts, the Qt properties, desktop motives, splitter and workspace widgets, and some dialogs such as the color and printer dialogs. Unfortunately, Qt/embedded does not contain the Qt `QFileDialog` class. For file selection as needed in load/save game dialogs, this needs to be replaced either by the Qtopia `FileSelector` class or by a listbox imitating the `QFileDialog` functionality (for details on the `FileSelector`, see the PDA example program in the folder `examples/mypdagame` on the companion CD-ROM). Nevertheless, the advantage of this high amount of compatibility is that the same program can be used and developed for both desktop computers and embedded devices if these special classes are used carefully. For games, these restrictions are not really an issue, since in game programming reality, most classes necessary for game development are available for Qt/embedded.

ON THE CD

When comparing PDA game development to KDE/Qt game development, there are only one or two issues to consider for a game running on Qt or KDE and on Qtopia. These few issues have to be pinpointed and included in `#ifdef` lines so the application is hardly changed.

Furthermore, using the Qtopia Standard Development Kit (SDK), which can be downloaded from the Qtopia home page [TrolltechQtopia04b], it is even easier to develop Qtopia applications under a normal Linux desktop. This capability stems from the fact that Qtopia comes with a special program that emulates the Qt virtual frame buffer of the PDA in a Linux window. Therefore, the entire Qtopia environment can be run and tested on a Linux computer system. After completion, a cross compilation run (see next section) to the target platform will create binaries for the PDA, which can then be distributed. Our experience has shown that this procedure works almost perfectly and allows you to develop PDA applications with hardly any interaction with the PDA itself. The use of applications like these makes game development much more compatible and easy.

Cross-Compiling and Developing with the Qtopia Emulator

Development of programs directly on a PDA or smart phone would be tedious, as the devices are small and slow compared to desktop computers. Therefore, programs are usually developed on a desktop computer, typically a Linux/KDE system.

To allow the development on a different platform, two basic ingredients are needed. First, an *emulating platform* is necessary, which allows you to run and test the PDA programs on the development desktop computer. Second, as the development computer and the target PDA have different processors a *cross-compiler* is required, which allows you to compile the program for the PDA target platform.

Both of these requirements are provided by the Qtopia SDK. This kit provides a Qtopia emulator, which runs the entire Qtopia environment inside a window on a Linux desktop. It also allows you to install and run the game programs in this window just as if they would be uploaded to the target PDA. Figure 5.3 shows the Qtopia emulator for Linux. Once the program runs sufficiently enough in the test phase, it can be cross-compiled for the target platform, typically the Strong-ARM or XScale processor series [Intel04].

FIGURE 5.3 Screenshot of the Qtopia games tab page.

After downloading the Qtopia SDK (version 1.7.0 was used for the examples) from the Qtopia download site [TrolltechQtopia04b] and installing the appropriate RPM or source file, the Qtopia emulator can be run as soon as some general environment settings are completed. These environment variables can be either set on the command line or in a startup script. Assuming Qtopia is installed into /opt/Qtopia, the bash shell settings would be:

```
export QPEDIR=/opt/Qtopia
export QTDIR=/opt/Qtopia
export QTEDIR=$QTDIR
export PATH=$QTDIR/bin:$QPEDIR/bin:$PATH
export LD_LIBRARY_PATH=$QTDIR/lib:$LD_LIBRARY_PATH
```

In addition, the virtual frame-buffer emulator can be loaded using

```
qvfb &
```

and, finally, the Qtopia program environment is run by

```
qpe &
```

These commands will execute and load the Qtopia platform including the standard PDA applications into the frame-buffer window (see Figure 5.3). This application is a full emulator of the target PDA; therefore, even without possessing your own PDA, you can run and test the standard PDA programs and your own programs. For details on how and where to install your application, see the later section on iPKG packages.

CREATING A STANDARD GAME APPLICATION

After discussing the theory of PDA game development, it is now time to create a real PDA game application. In this section, we present all the key ingredients in the form of code snippets, which are necessary to set up a basic Qtopia application. These applications can then be immediately run on the Qtopia emulator or transferred to a PDA.

ON THE CD

The CD-ROM accompanying this book includes all header files and the full source code required for the demo Qtopia program `mygame` in the folder `examples/mypdagame`. This basic application also includes some dummy menus and a canvas view, which is the "view" most commonly used for games. This application can be used as a template for your own game development and can be easily extended to a real desktop game.

Assembling the Program

Desktop game programs for PDAs can be set up following the game architecture as described in Chapter 1, "Introduction to Desktop Gaming." The key components required for this architecture include the main application program, the main window, and the game view, which are described in the following sections.

The Main Program

We start the setup of the application by creating the C++ main program. This is then used to start up the application, define some PDA-specific issues such as the virtual keyboard and the stylus operation, and in the end launch the event loop of the application. The event loop checks for GUI and timer events and forwards them to the application.

In the first step, the necessary header files from Qt and Qtopia have to be included in the program alongside any user-defined class header files.

```
#include <qpe/qpeapplication.h>
#include <qstring.h>
#include <qtextcodec.h>
#include <qtranslator.h>


#include "mainwindow.h"
```

The C++ main program is started by the operating system and sets up the GUI application with all PDA parameters.

```
int main(int argc, char* argv[])
{
  // Initialize the application
  QPEApplication application(argc, argv);

  // Set up the language translator
  QTranslator translator(0);
  // Set the location where your .qm files are located to
  // load() as the last parameter instead of "."
  translator.load("mygame.pm", ".");
  // Install the translator to the application
  application.installTranslator(&translator);

  // Initialize the application main window
  MainWindow mainwindow(&application);
  // The stylus creates left mouse events only
  application.setStylusOperation(&mainwindow,
                               QPEApplication::LeftOnly);
  // The virtual keyboard should not be shown
  application.setInputMethodHint(&mainwindow,
                               QPEApplication::AlwaysOff);

  // Display the main window
  application.showMainWidget(&mainwindow, false);
```

```
// Start the actual application with the event loop
return application.exec();
}
```

The Main Window

The main window of an application defines the menus, the toolbar, the actions, and creates the view object. This "view" is the area inside the main window that actually displays the contents; in this case, the game canvas with the sprites and other canvas objects.

To begin, the necessary header files from Qt and Qtopia have to be included alongside any user-defined class header files.

```
// Include the Qt elements for the main window
#include <qaccel.h>
#include <qaction.h>
#include <qmenubar.h>
#include <qmsgbox.h>
#include <qpopupmenu.h>

// Include the user defined classes
#include "mainwindow.h"
#include "gameview.h"
```

The constructor of the main view has to initialize both the menus and the view. For this, we call two subroutines to perform the initialization details.

```
MainWindow::MainWindow(QPEApplication* app)
          : QMainWindow(0)
{
  // Set the title of the application
  setCaption(tr("MyGame"));

  ...

  // Setup the menu
  initGUI();

  // Setup the view
  initView();
}
```

All menus and actions of the application can be initialized with the following method. As an example, we show how a menu entry to start a new game is defined.

It will appear in the menu as *New Game* and can be called via the keyboard using the space bar as a shortcut. Once it is activated by the user, the method gameNew() is called.

```
void MainWindow::initGUI()
{
  // Menu entry to e.g. start a new game.
  QAction* gameNew;
  gameNew = new QAction(tr("New Game"), tr("&New Game"),
                        Qt::Key_Space, this);
  connect(gameNew, SIGNAL(activated()),
          this, SLOT(gameNew()));
  ...
```

All menu entries that are defined in this manner are plugged into the corresponding menus, typically named *Game*, *Edit*, and so forth, and these menus are then inserted into the menu bar.

```
  QPopupMenu* gameMenu;
  gameMenu = new QPopupMenu();
  gameNew->addTo(gameMenu);
  ...


  // Combine the menus to the menu-bar
  menuBar()->insertItem(tr("&Game"), gameMenu);
  ...
}
```

Finally, the canvas view has to be created and stored as the main window's central viewing widget. This is done using the following method:

```
void MainWindow::initView()
{
  // Create a new canvas view
  GameView* view = new GameView(this);
  // Make the game view the central program widget
  setCentralWidget(view);
  ...
}
```

The Canvas View

The "view" of the game application is the visible part of the window inside the window frame of the main window. Any Qt widget class can be used as the application's view. However, for game applications, the `QCanvasView` is normally the preferred choice since it allows easy definition and use of canvas sprites. These sprites are often a very natural representation of a game, as most games consist of small moving objects. However, some games focus more on text input such as Shufflewords or other word-puzzle orientated games. Here, a simple `QWidget` might suffice.

To program the canvas view, we again start by including the necessary header files from Qt and Qtopia alongside any user-defined class header files.

```
// The necessary Qt includes
#include <qcolor.h>
#include <qcanvas.h>

// The includes for the user defined classes
#include "gameview.h"
```

The view of the main window is then initialized. It is derived from the `QCanvasView` class, which allows you to associate it with a canvas and therefore display canvas items and sprites. As we have only one view, we do not distinguish between canvas and view but initialize them simultaneously. In the following example, a typical setup is described. Here, scroll bars are set up and a canvas object is associated with the view. For details on canvas and canvas views, see Chapter 6, "Canvas Games."

```
GameView::GameView(QWidget* parent)
        : QCanvasView(0, parent, 0)
{
  // Switch off the scrollbars
  setVScrollBarMode(AlwaysOff);
  setHScrollBarMode(AlwaysOff);

  // Create a game canvas and set the main parameters like
  // the double buffering, the background color, or the
  // advance period. For details see the chapter on canvases.
  QCanvas* canvas = new QCanvas(this);
  canvas->resize(parent->width(), parent->height());
  canvas->setDoubleBuffering(true);
  canvas->setAdvancePeriod(40);
  canvas->setBackgroundColor(QColor(Qt::darkBlue));

  // Plug the canvas into the window
  setCanvas(canvas);

  // Make a little text sprite
  QFont font;
```

```
    font.setPixelSize(18);
    QCanvasText* text = new QCanvasText(canvas);
    text->setText(tr("Hello world!"));
    ...
    text->move(70.0, 100.0);
    text->show();


    ...
}
```

Because we glue canvas and view together, the resizing of the view has to automatically resize the embedded canvas objects. This is achieved with the Qt event method resizeEvent(), which automatically adjusts the canvas size to the view size.

```
void MyGameView::resizeEvent(QResizeEvent* e)
{
  if (canvas()) canvas()->resize(e->size().width(),
                                 e->size().height());
}
```

Preparations for the Target Platform

The compilation of the source code into executable code depends on the target platform you chose to run the code. The target platform is normally the Qtopia emulator or the target PDA. The first is typically used for development, and the latter is used when you want to play your finished game or distribute it to the consumer. To allow flexible switching between these choices, all compilers and library parameters are set using environment variables. Alongside the Qt and Qtopia directories, these settings also affect the library paths, Makefile generators, and the executable path. Therefore, depending on the employed target platform, all of these variables have to be set to different directories.

Assuming that the Qtopia software was installed into the directory /opt/Qtopia and the Strong-ARM cross-compiler into /usr/local/arm, the settings for the emulator and the PDA platform could follow the following examples.

For the Qtopia emulator development, a bash shell script defining the environment variables could look like:

```
export QPEDIR=/opt/Qtopia
export QTDIR=/opt/Qtopia
export QTEDIR=$QTDIR
export PATH=$QTDIR/bin:$QPEDIR/bin:$PATH
export LD_LIBRARY_PATH=$QTDIR/lib:$LD_LIBRARY_PATH
export TMAKEPATH=/opt/Qtopia/tmake/lib/qws/linux-generic-g++
```

For cross-compiling to a Strong-ARM target PDA—as, for example, the Zaurus series—the corresponding bash shell script defining the environment variables could resemble:

```
export QPEDIR=/opt/Qtopia/sharp
export QTDIR=/opt/Qtopia/sharp
export PATH=$QTDIR/bin:/usr/local/arm/bin:$PATH
export TMAKEPATH=/opt/Qtopia/tmake/lib/qws/linux-sharp-g++
```

ON THE CD

These variables are most conveniently set by a shell script before the project is created. On the companion CD-ROM in the folder examples/mypdagame/scripts, we provide some examples shell scripts setting these environment variables.

Building the Application

Once all source files are created and the environment settings are made, all the source files of the game project have to be compiled into an executable file. To make this process more convenient, a Makefile needs to be created. This can be done either manually or with the help of an automatic Makefile generator.

Here, we introduce the Qt tmake utility. Tmake is a useful tool for the automatic generation of Makefiles. It is simple to use, so you become very quickly accustomed to it. Tmake works well for small projects, and they typically occur for PDA game development. For such small games, we prefer the use of tmake over the more complex automatic Makefile generation tools such as autoconf and automake, because although excellent they are more complex and therefore used for larger projects; for example, in KDE projects. The tmake Makefile generation utility can be downloaded for free at the Web site [TrolltechTMake04].

To use tmake for the Makefile generation, a *project* file has to be defined that lists all program components together with some extra compiler options and flags. The tmake utility will analyze this project file and then proceed to create a normal Makefile. The project file itself is a standard text file (in our project mygame.pro), which could look for the mygame program as follows:

```
TEMPLATE      = app
CONFIG        = qtopia warn_on release
HEADERS       = mainwindow.h gameview.h
SOURCES       = mainwindow.cpp gamwview.cpp main.cpp
INTERFACES    = mygame.ui
TARGET        = mygame
# For the ARM compiler some libraries are possibly needed.
# Remove the '#' in front of each line then
# LIBS          += -ljpeg -luuid
# If necessary some user defined paths and libraries can
```

```
# be defined as well
# INCLUDEPATH    += $(QPEDIR)/include
# DEPENDPATH     += $(QPEDIR)/include
```

Entries in the project file always consist of a key-value pair as shown in the preceding example. The various keywords have the following meanings:

TEMPLATE: The `tmake` program defines two possible program template types. The `app` template is for building applications like our games, while the `lib` keyword allows you to build a library.

CONFIG: This keyword specifies the compiler options and supports the options `qt`, `qtopia`, `opengl`, `warn_on`, `warn_off`, `release`, and `debug`. As the game is a Qtopia application, the keyword `qtopia` is required. The `warning` keywords switch the compiler warnings on or off and are a personal choice. The `release` and `debug` keywords toggle the debug and optimization flags of the compiler. Obviously, `release` should be chosen for the final release version.

HEADERS: Here, all header files of the project are listed.

SOURCES: Here, all program source files of the project are listed.

INTERFACES: Here, all Qt designer files are listed. These are the `ui` files of the project.

TARGET: The `target` keyword determines the name of the executable file.

INCLUDEPATH: Adds some additional include paths to the compiler. This is normally not needed.

DEPENDPATH: Adds some additional dependency paths to the compiler. These are not normally required.

LIBS: Adds some additional library paths to the linker. Again, this option is seldom used.

After specifying all details of the project in the project file, you begin by simply calling `tmake`

```
tmake -o Makefile mygame.pro
```

which will create the Makefile. This Makefile allows you to build the project with a standard call to make

```
make
```

which in turn will build the entire application and create the executable program. Some additional make options for cleaning up of the directory

```
make clean
```

and building a tar file of all project files with

```
make dist
```

are supported too.

PDA PROGRAMMING TIPS

Although we discussed that programming for a PDA platform is very similar to programming a KDE or Qt application, there are some special programming issues to consider. In the following, we point out some of these typical PDA issues and how they can be overcome within Qtopia.

Stylus and Keyboard

With embedded Qt systems, you can choose the stylus operation mode. There are two possibilities. The first method uses the stylus to generate only LeftButton events; this is the default option. The second method allows the stylus to also generate RightButton events and is achieved if the stylus is pressed and held on the display. The two modes can be set by methods of the QPEApplication class.

```
#include <qpe/qpeapplication.h>
...
// Only generate LeftButton events. 'mainwindow' is a pointer
// to the application's main widget
application.setStylusOperation(&mainwindow,
                    QPEApplication::LeftOnly);
...
// OR also generate RightButton events
application.setStylusOperation(&mainwindow,
                    QPEApplication::RightOnHold);
```

In PDA games, the small screen is often a problem because only a few items can be displayed. If the virtual keyboard takes up half the available screen space, there is not much room left to display your game features. Therefore, it is possible to tell the application whether it should provide text input. If the application does not need text input, it can be helpful to switch the virtual keyboard off. The user can still manually reactivate it to fill in the scoreboard results and so on. The keyboard mode can be selected by using another method from the QPEApplication class.

```
#include <qpe/qpeapplication.h>
...
// Set the operating system default mode. 'mainwindow' is
// the application's main widget
application.setInputMethodHint(&mainwindow, QPEApplication::Normal);
...
// OR always switch the virtual keyboard off
application.setInputMethodHint(&mainwindow, QPEApplication::AlwaysOff);
...
// OR always switch the virtual keyboard on
application.setInputMethodHint(&mainwindow, QPEApplication::AlwaysOn);
```

The physical buttons of the PDA are used for special application shortcuts such as launching the calendar or the personal information manager. This behavior can be changed during a game application and is often beneficial, since in a hectic game the player might accidentally press one of these buttons and suddenly have the calendar pop up on top of the game. Furthermore, the buttons can be used for in-game control, and with a device that possesses only a few input possibilities for games, some additional user-defined buttons can be useful.

These special buttons can be assigned solely to your application by "grabbing" the keyboard. This action will then allow only your program to access these buttons. In particular, the special functions, like launching the calendar or PIM, will be disabled. Once the application finishes, these buttons should be released. The "grabbing" of the keyboard buttons is shown in the following example. In brief, the keyboard is "grabbed" directly at the game program start in the main function and "released" after the application's main loop is completed.

```
#include <qpe/qpeapplication.h>

int main(int argc, char* argv[])
{
  // Initialize the application
  QPEApplication application(argc, argv);
  ...

  // Grab the keyboard for the game's use
  application.grabKeyboard();
  ...
```

```
// Run the application's main loop
int result = application.exec();
...

// Release the keyboard
application.ungrabKeyboard();
...
}
```

The most useful key mappings available to the game are given by keyboard definitions in the qnamespace.h definition file (which is automatically included with qt.h). The following list describes the key codes that are typically assigned to physical buttons:

Cursor: Qt::Key_Up, Qt::Key_Down, Qt::Key_Left, Qt::Key_Right

Select: Qt::Key_Space

Calendar: Qt::Key_F9

Address book: Qt::Key_F10

Menu: Qt::Key_F11

Home: Qt::Key_F12

Mail: Qt::Key_F13

Cancel: Qt::Key_Escape

Ok: Qt::Key_F33

These key codes can be used for menu shortcut definitions and key event queries.

Global Functions

Qtopia also offers some additional general-purpose methods that are bundled in the Global class. These methods allow access to the global system resources.

The static method

```
QString owner = Global::ownerName();
```

returns the name the owner entered in the PDA device. This name can be used as a default for the scoreboard list and allows the user to enter names or high scores without or with less typing.

The directory path name to the user's home directory can be accessed via

```
QString homeDir = Global::homeDirPath();
```

which can be used for permanently storing data files.

Another useful method is the possibility to generate temporary files.

```
QString tempName = Global::tempName(QString basename);
```

These are now unique in name and can be used to store temporary game data.

Finally, sometimes it is beneficial to display a brief message to the user. This message is shown in the status bar of the application for a couple of seconds. An example of how to generate such as message is:

```
Global::statusMessage("Message to the user");
```

Internationalization

Applications that are offered worldwide can profit enormously if they are translated into the language of the user. For example, the user could select the game to appear in English, German, Spanish, Japanese, and so on. As it would be very tedious to compile a new application for each language, it is possible to use the Qt translator features. This feature allows all QString objects to be automatically translated into a chosen language (see Chapter 4, "Qt Game Development using Microsoft Windows"). The string translations are handled via a translation file, which is loaded into the application and automatically exchanges all strings to the local language.

Switching into another language will often alter the length of text strings, and therefore alter a carefully designed GUI layout, something you have to consider when designing the GUI. Using a layout manager will automatically accommodate such text.

To perform such a translation procedure, the first step is initiated by creating a translator object and loading the language translation file; here, mylanguage.qm:

```
// Create the application object
QApplication application(argc, argv);
// Create the translator object
QTranslator translator(0);
// Load the language specification file. Here a choice
// of language could happen.
translator.load("mylanguage.qm", ".");
// Install it in the application
application.installTranslator(&translator);
```

Once the language translator is installed, you can apply the `QObject::tr()` method, which will automatically replace all strings in the program with the text stored in the language file. Some typical examples are:

```
# Translate menus
myMenu->insertItem(tr("Choose &level"), levelMenu);

# Translate messages
QMessageBox::about(this,
                   tr("About..."),
                   tr("A nice desktop game.") );
```

Translation files store both the original and the translated texts of the local language. With the help of special tools, such as Qt Linguist or KBabel, all strings from the application can be extracted, translated, and written to these files.

To allow proper internationalization of a program, all literal text—that is, all text displayed to the user—must be captured and displayed with tr(). All strings must be stored in a translated version in the translation file.

Integrated Help

Every application, including those for games, should provide a short help text that describes the purpose of the game, its rules, and how it is operated. The help file has to be written as a standard HTML file. The help file is automatically displayed using the "?" icon in the menu bar of the application, but only when the HTML file is named after the application, such as mygame.html. The help administration is done automatically by Qtopia if the help file is installed into the help/html directory as described in the later section "iPKG Packages."

Persistent Configuration Data

Applications often have to store and keep certain parameters available even after the application is terminated. Furthermore, when the application is restarted, this stored information has to be retrieved. Game application examples of such parameters include high scores, game settings, level settings, and other user parameters.

These defined parameters can be stored using the Qtopia Config class, which allows you to store entries as key-value pairs into a text configuration file. These entries can then be retrieved at any time, even after the application is restarted. The information stored in such a configuration file can be grouped into arbitrarily named groups to allow the storage of information in a more organized way. The keywords of the entries are strings, and the values can be selected from a number of different types such as strings, integers, doubles, or lists.

```
#include <qpe/config.h>
Config* config = new Config("mygame", Config::User);

// Writing the configuration data (sep being a
// list separator string like ',')
config->setGroup("Parameter");
config->writeEntry("level", myLevel);
config->writeEntry("names", myPlayers, sep);

// Reading back the configuration data
config->setGroup("Parameter");
mLevel=config->readNumEntry("level", myLevel);
QStringList list = config->readListEntry(key, sep);

delete config;
```

Portability

Often, when a programmer develops a game for a certain PDA target platform, he also wants that game to run on other systems such as desktop computers, other PDA devices, or even cell phones. This is hardly an issue when using KDE/Qt/Qtopia target systems, since the underlying architecture is quite compatible. Figure 5.4 shows such a game application on both Qtopia and KDE. Furthermore, very few alterations to the source code have to be implemented. A few platform-dependent parts do occur, but they can be easily encapsulated into #ifdef statements.

However, a major difference from desktop computers is the screen size and orientation. PDAs have much smaller screens that are typically in portrait orientation (i.e., rotated at a 90-degree angle to normal desktop screens). Furthermore, the processor speed is slower and the memory size is smaller. A good game design will encompass these differences by designing the game, GUI, and graphic elements so they are portable. This is done most easily by making all areas of the game that could be affected by the target platform configurable; that is, using parameters instead of fixed values. These parameters are then read from configuration files and determine the behavior, look, and setup of the program. Examples for configurable items would be the size, color, or position of your game sprites.

These primary differences mainly affect two areas: the first concerns dialogs and message boxes that have to be altered to accommodate the smaller screen size. Creating these objects with QtDesigner or a similar GUI design tool and storing them in user interface (ui) files allows for easy exchange between GUI elements.

The second affected area relates to graphical objects such as sprites and display design features such as the placement or the coordinates of the elements or objects in the game. These should be configured by parameters loaded from a configuration file. Configuration files are files that can be read using the Qtopia Config class, which is very compatible to the corresponding KDE KConfig or the Qt QSettings class. If all graphic filenames, screen positions, and so on are specified parameters in a configuration file, the application's layout can be changed by simply loading another configuration file. Allowing this at runtime has an additional positive side effect: your game application provides *themes*; that is, various looks of the application that can be chosen and loaded.

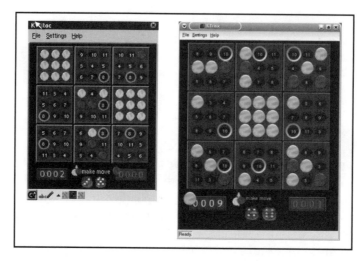

FIGURE 5.4 Comparison of the same game application on Qtopia (left) and KDE (right). Other than the size and resolution, the game is identical.

PACKAGING AND DISTRIBUTION

Once the game application is finished, you need to combine all files into a program package. This package can then be transferred to your PDA, or you can distribute it to other people. The packaging process requires a few additional steps to be performed.

Desktop Files

Any application required to be an integral part of Qtopia and furthermore to be displayed in the application tab pages of Qtopia (see Figure 5.3) needs to follow certain guidelines. The application has to contain:

- A binary file, which is the executable application itself.
- A program icon, which will be shown in the corresponding sections of the application tabs. This has to be a 32 x 32-pixel PNG image.
- A `*.desktop` file that lists the properties of the application.
- An HTML help file describing the functions of the software (optional but recommended).

All these required or optional files have to be installed in certain specified directories on the Qtopia target platform. This also allows the game to appear correctly in the desktop application tab pages. Assuming `$QPEDIR` is the root directory of Qtopia, the files have to be installed into the following directories:

- The `*.desktop` file goes to `$QPEDIR/apps/Games/`.
- The program icon goes to `$QPEDIR/pics/`.
- The program graphic goes to `$QPEDIR/pics/<programname>` (`<programname>` is replaced by the name of your game).
- The binary program goes to `$QPEDIR/bin/`.
- The help file goes to `$QPEDIR/help/html/`.

Typically, the root directory `$QPEDIR` is `/opt/QtPalmtop`, but `/opt/Qtopia` is also possible. When programming on the Sharp Zaurus PDAs, `/opt/QtPalmtop` has to be chosen if the software should also allow the game installation on external memory chips such as SD or CF memory cards. Figure 5.5 shows a typical file structure of the `mygame` program as it is being installed into the Qtopia file system.

Finally, we describe the structure of a `*.desktop` file. This file is a standard Qtopia `Config` configuration file that contains the section `Desktop Entry` and defines some standard entries that describe the application. Such a desktop file for the `mygame` example could look like this:

```
[Desktop Entry]
  Exec=mygame
  Icon=mygame
  Type=Game
  Name=MyGame
  Comment=A one player test game.
```

`Exec` and `Icon` specify the names of the binary and icon files, respectively, which are typically identical to the program name. The `Type` entry defines the application as a game, and the `Name` and `Comment` entries list the title of the game and additional comments about the application.

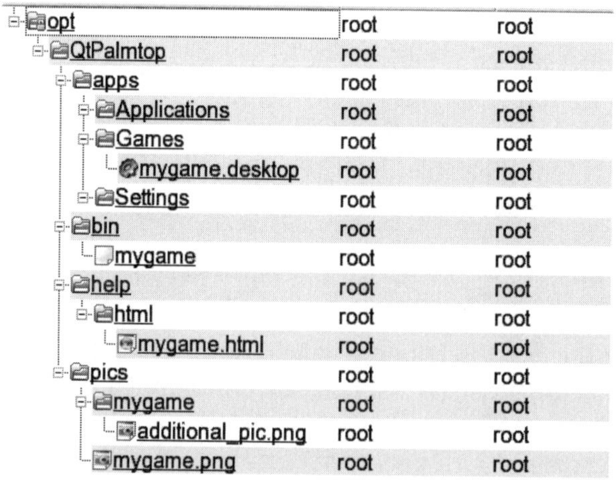

⊟ 📁 opt	root	root
⊟ 📁 QtPalmtop	root	root
⊟ 📁 apps	root	root
⊟ 📁 Applications	root	root
⊟ 📁 Games	root	root
└ 🎮 mygame.desktop	root	root
⊟ 📁 Settings	root	root
⊟ 📁 bin	root	root
└ 📄 mygame	root	root
⊟ 📁 help	root	root
⊟ 📁 html	root	root
└ 🖼 mygame.html	root	root
⊟ 📁 pics	root	root
⊟ 📁 mygame	root	root
└ 🖼 additional_pic.png	root	root
└ 🖼 mygame.png	root	root

FIGURE 5.5 The standard Qtopia file system after installation of the `mygame` program.

iPKG Packages

iPKG is a lightweight software package management system and is comparable to the RPM or Debian `.deb` program installation tools. However, it is optimized for small target computers such as PDAs and therefore only provides the necessary functions to dynamically install, manage, and de-install software. For Qtopia, iPKG is the standard package installation system. Therefore, before uploading your program to the PDA or distributing it on the Internet, it needs to be compiled into such an iPKG package.

The iPKG package building software can be downloaded for free on the Internet at the Web site [Ipkg04]. Older versions of iPKG are Perl shell scripts, while more recent versions (from 0.99 onward) are compiled executables. For creating a game package, this difference does not really matter, since all the versions work equally well in creating the target packages.

Besides the software designated to be installed, iPKG also requires a control definition file that stores information about the soon-to-be-installed software. This file is just an ordinary text file and is placed in the subdirectory CONTROL. An example control file for our game called `mygame` could look like:

```
Package:      mygame
Priority:     optional
Section:      games
Maintainer:   Martin Heni <email>
Architecture: arm
Version:      1.0.0
```

```
License:      GPL
Depends:      qpe-base ($QPE_VERSION)
Description:  A nice desktop game for one or more players.
```

where the fields have the following meanings:

Package: The game package name.

Priority: How important the package is; for games, this is normally set to `optional`.

Section: The category to which the package belongs.

Maintainer: The person who created and maintains the package.

Architecture: The CPU architecture on which the compiled package runs.

Version: The version of the software of this package.

License: The license used for distributing the package.

Depends: Other packages on which this package depends.

Description: The description of this package for the possible users.

There are two ways to create the iPKG package. The first is to use the tool `mkipks`, which is part of the Qtopia SDK. `mkipks` uses the application's control file to create an iPKG package using

```
mkipks mygame.control
```

However, sometimes it is preferable to manually set up the package structure. This action is especially advantageous when some particular directory features must be considered. To manually prepare software as an iPKG package, a temporary package directory has to be created that follows the exact directory naming for the target platform, described in the previous section on desktop files. This procedure is very simple, and since it also provides insight into the operations of a packaging tool, we now show a basic setup for the example application `mygame` on the Qtopia system.

```
# Set up package directories
mkdir PACKAGE
mkdir PACKAGE/opt
mkdir PACKAGE/opt/QtPalmtop
mkdir PACKAGE/CONTROL

# Define target directory to copy files to
TARGET=PACKAGE/opt/QtPalmtop
```

```
# Set up target directories
mkdir $TARGET/bin
mkdir $TARGET/help
mkdir $TARGET/help/html
mkdir $TARGET/apps
mkdir $TARGET/apps/Games
mkdir $TARGET/pics
mkdir $TARGET/pics/mygame

# Copy files to the target directory

# Control file
cp mygame.control PACKAGE/CONTROL/control

# Program
cp mygame $TARGET/bin/mygame

# Help
cp mygame.html $TARGET/help/html

# Desktop info
cp mygame.desktop $TARGET/apps/Games

# Pictures
cp mygame.png $TARGET/pics
# Optionally copy in-game graphics
cp -r pics/* $TARGET/pics/mygame

# Give proper file permissions
chmod -R a+rx PACKAGE
chmod -R ug+w PACKAGE

# Set owner of all files in PACKAGE to 'root'
chown -R root PACKAGE
# run the IPKG package builder (which has to be in your
# $PATH variable)
ipkg-build PACKAGE
```

Note that again we chose QtPalmtop as the target directory. Remember, this step is necessary if you want your application to be installed on both the internal memory and external memory cards.

Uploading the Package

Once the iPKG package is created, it can be transferred to the target platform. Using the local file system, a CF or SD memory card, the provided cradle or a connected (wireless) network, the iPKG packages can be installed on the PDA using the Qtopia package installer. The installer (see Figure 5.6) will automatically list all available packages, including the new mygame one. Installation or de-installation can be done by simple clicking on the package names.

Distributing the Game Package

Once the software is tested and the iPKG package is created, you can transfer it to your own PDA, or if the application is of interest to a larger community, it can be distributed on the Internet. In this case, the program can be made available on your own home page. However, to make the game more popular, it is useful to get it listed in one of the public PDA software indices, some examples being the Web sites of [Killefiz04], [Zaurussoft04] , [SBComputing04], and [Pilotzone04] .

FIGURE 5.6 The Qtopia package installation software provides a graphical interface to install and de-install additional software packages.

Finally, if you want to publish your game programs, you have to consider whether the game should be available to everyone as a free download, or whether you want to have more of a business. The first case is simple; you just allow a normal download of the game. In the second case, you have to find a distribution channel, as you probably do not want to handle the payment methods yourself. An easy way is to register the software with an online software distributor; for example, [Handango04]. They list the software and handle the sales process. Although you will receive the profits from them, the distributors will keep a percentage to cover their own expenses and profit; the exact conditions depend largely on the distributor. This method is a good alternative if you plan to sell your games, as it is very easy and involves no risk. If a game becomes very popular, which can happen to novel and creative games (e.g., Tetris), there will be many interested people and therefore great profits.

SUMMARY

Over the last few years, handheld computers have become powerful enough to allow easy desktop game development and uncomplicated use of these games. Due to their ever-increasing popularity, they have opened up a completely new area for game development. If you want to develop Linux-based games, Qt and Qtopia offer a stable and easy-to-use programming platform. The transfer of games written for KDE or Qt to PDAs is straightforward. Portability between different target platforms is easily achieved with Qt when some general guidelines are respected and critical parts of the program are designed with sufficient configuration parameters.

However, there are a couple of aspects to consider when developing a computer game for PDAs. In brief, the program has to accommodate a slower processor and smaller memory. The smaller screen size and resolution requires you to tailor both the graphics and some game features such as the AI and pathfinding.

To get started with PDA programming, the template game application presented in the course of this chapter can be used. Extending it will provide you with all the necessary ingredients for a canvas-based PDA game. Alongside the Qtopia PDA emulator, the application and therefore your game can be set up, compiled, and run at once on a Linux desktop computer.

REFERENCES

[Handango04] *Handango online, http://www.handango.com*, 2004.

[Intel04] *Intel handheld processors, http://developer.intel.com/design/pca/ applicationsprocessors/index.htm*, 2004.

[IPAQLinux04a] *Nano-X SDK and Developer's Guide, http://embedded. centurysoftware. com/docs/nx/iPAQ-linux-new-install.html*, 2004.

[IPAQLinux04b] *How to port Linux on a new PDA, http://free-electrons.com/ articles/porting/en*, 2004.

[Ipkg04] iPKG *Download, http://docs.zaurus.com/downloads/ipkg-build.sh*, 2004.

[Killefiz04] *Zaurus Software Index, http://www.killefiz.de/zaurus*, 2004.[Tuxmobil04] *Linux with PDAs and Handheld PCs, http://www.tuxmobil.org/pda_linux.html*, 2004.

[PDAbuyersguide04] *PDA Buyers Guide, http://www.pdabuyersguide.com/index.php*, 2004.

[Pilotzone04] *Pilotzone, http://www.pilotzone.com*, 2004.

[SBComputing04] *Zaurus Games Review, http://www.sbcomputing.de/heni/gamesreview/index.html*, 2004.

[TrolltechQtopia04a] *Qtopia, http://doc.trolltech.com/qtopia1.7/index.html*, 2004.

[TrolltechQtopia04b] *Qtopia Download, http://www.trolltech.com/download/qtopia/index.html*, 2004.

[TrolltechTMake04] *Tmake Download, http://www.trolltech.com/download/tmake.html*, 2004.

[Underdahl04] Underdahl, Brian, *iPAQ for Dummies, For Dummies*, 2004.

[Zaurussoft04] *Zaurussoft Software Index, http://www.zaurusoft.com*, 2004.

6 Canvas Games

In This Chapter

- The Canvas View
- The QCanvas Class
- Sprites
- Tiling
- Scrolling

In computer games, drawing graphics on the screen is often done using a *canvas*. The name *canvas* is derived from conventional painting in which paint is applied with brushes to a real canvas. In computer games, this analogy to painting is maintained, and graphical display objects, the equivalent to *paint*, are applied to a "canvas."

In computer terms, a canvas is defined as a class or a set of classes that provide methods to the programmer to draw and paint on such a canvas and even modify its contents. However, the methods available from the canvas classes go beyond simply painting color on the canvas. A canvas also allows the programmer to define objects, often called *sprites*, which can be treated as individual units and can be changed, moved, or animated. Once an item is embedded in the canvas, no manual update or repaint procedures are necessary for display and animation since everything is done internally by the canvas library.

The canvas can be associated with one or more "views" that allow the contents of the canvas to be displayed to the observer, or in this case, the player. Additionally, a canvas can be larger than the physical screen or window, and parts of the canvas can be scrolled into view by the program or the user (see Figure 6.1).

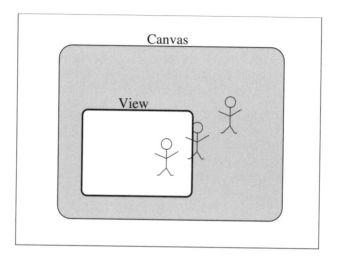

FIGURE 6.1 The widget's view shows part of a larger canvas (light area). Other images are drawn on the canvas (dark area), but are not (yet) visible to the observer.

With respect to desktop games, canvases have a large advantage over a real canvas and other display update techniques. For example, in text processing programs, the programmers must maintain all screen updates. In contrast, a canvas in game programming handles all animation, refreshing, and updating of the screen automatically and transparently in the background. This behavior makes it very easy for the programmer to create game-type movement and animation on the screen.

Furthermore, a canvas provides a highly optimized 2D graphic area suitable for games and fast graphical drawing. A canvas can display a large number of different items at any time; they can possess arbitrary shapes and sizes and are free to move around on the canvas. These items can be easily inserted or removed from the canvas at any point during runtime. Additionally, an important feature for game programming is that collisions between items on the canvas can be registered by the program.

The main advantages of using the concept of canvas programming include:

- For typical desktop games, a canvas provides fast graphic capabilities.
- A canvas can be huge, much larger than the display widget itself. Areas not visible at any one time can be easily scrolled into view.
- Easy-to-use systems to detect collisions between items on the canvas are available.
- Many predefined canvas items already exist and can be used, moved, and animated.

For programmers using Qt or KDE, the Qt library [TrolltechQt04] provides several classes for canvas programming. These classes are well documented and easy to use. The Qt canvas library includes most features necessary for desktop game programming. Qt canvas classes are very well suited for small to medium-sized desktop games and only begin to lose performance when larger games with thousands of canvas items are processed. However, for most desktop games discussed in the scope of this book, the Qt canvas classes are a good choice. In the following sections, we concentrate on this 2D desktop game programming and describe the general application of Qt canvas classes in this field.

THE CANVAS VIEW

The canvas is used to collect and handle all the graphical and text objects in a game program (see Figure 6.1). To display these objects, the canvas has to be associated with one or more views of the actual application. These views are connected to the application and its main window as described in Chapters 3 through 5.

As a basis for the game view, we will use the QCanvasView class, which provides all the methods necessary for a Qt view. A canvas is displayed to the user when it is associated with such a QCanvasView class.

ON THE CD A demonstration of how a canvas view is developed can be found on the companion CD-ROM, labeled mycanvas and located in the folder examples/mycanvas. This program can be used as an example and accompanies the rest of this chapter, as it includes all the basic canvas operations described here. The game view class, defined in the file gameview.h and implemented in the file gameview.cpp, is directly derived from the QCanvasView:

```
#include <qcanvas.h>

class GameView : public QCanvasView
{
  Q_OBJECT
```

```
    public:
      // Standard constructor of the canvas view
      GameView(QCanvas* canvas, QWidget* parent = 0);

    private:
      ...
   };
```

and the canvas object is associated with the QCanvasView in the constructor. This is the basic mechanism to display a canvas in a Qt view and is shown in the following code snippet:

```
GameView::GameView(QCanvas* canvas, QWidget* parent)
           : QCanvasView(0, parent, 0)
{
  // Manually assign the canvas to the view. Note that the
  // canvas could also have been passed to the QCanvasView
  // constructor. But the manual setting shows more what is
  // actually going on.
  setCanvas(canvas);

  // (Optionally) Fit the canvas in the parent window
  canvas->resize(parent->width(),parent->height());
  ...
```

The canvas has been stored in the view and can later be retrieved by the QCanvasView method.

```
QCanvas* QCanvasView::canvas() const
```

If only one view of the canvas is used, it is sometimes handy to couple the size of the canvas to the size of the window to get a one-on-one relationship. This can be done by resizing the canvas to the actual view size. Note that this is a slow operation.

```
// Method called by the Qt framework if the window is resized
void GameView::resizeEvent(QResizeEvent* e )
{
  // Adapt the canvas size to the view size
  if (canvas()) canvas()->resize(e->size().width(),
                                 e->size().height());
}
```

THE `QCanvas` CLASS

We have seen how to associate a canvas object with the application's view class. However, to do so, we first need to create and initialize a canvas object. This is done by creating an instance of the `QCanvas` class.

```
// Create a new canvas as child of a given parent window
QCanvas* canvas = new QCanvas(parent);
```

After creating a canvas, some general properties can be set to it. Most of these properties are optional, but some are essential for proper operation of the canvas. The key properties are discussed in the following sections in greater detail.

Canvas Background and Foreground

An important aspect to any canvas is its background color or background image. This background color or image will appear behind all items drawn on the canvas. Moreover, it will cover all empty spaces on the canvas that are not occupied by any other objects. In most games, this will be a large part of the canvas.

The background color of the canvas can be set using a `QColor` object, which can define arbitrary RGB colors.

```
// Choose RGB color for the canvas background
canvas->setBackgroundColor(QColor(32, 32, 128));
```

Alternatively, instead of a background color, a background image can be used.

```
// Create any pixmap you want ...
QPixmap pixmap = ...
// ... and set it as the background image in the canvas
canvas->setBackgroundPixmap(pixmap);
```

which can be any image stored in a `QPixmap` object.

If a more dynamic background is desired, the virtual method

```
virtual void drawBackground(QPainter& painter,
                            const QRect& clipArea)
```

can be overwritten. The method is called for each canvas update and can draw any user-defined background on the canvas given a certain clipping area. This clipping area defines the part of the canvas that needs to be updated and hence redrawn.

Using a clipping area and drawing only in the given area avoids redrawing the entire background in each update cycle.

The foreground of the canvas will appear in front of all objects on the canvas. However, it is a less-used application and cannot be set directly. Nevertheless, status information or head-up displays can be visualized with a (transparent) foreground. For this task, again the virtual method

```
virtual void drawForeground(QPainter& painter,
                            const QRect &clipArea)
```

can be overwritten. It will be called for each canvas update and is supposed to redraw the canvas foreground in the given clipping area. The foreground drawing works analogously to the background drawing.

Double Buffering

An important feature of a canvas is the so-called *double buffering*. Double buffering is a keyword often heard in computer game programming, and has two main purposes. First, it is used to reduce the flickering that occurs in movement and animation on the screen, and second, it speeds up the graphic operations.

Flickering generally arises when the graphic drawings on the screen are not instantaneous but done step by step or sprite by sprite. This broken translation results in the objects being drawn on the screen without their full scene being completed, and thus only half-completed images can exist. Partially completed images also occur when background objects are visible; that is, before they are covered by foreground objects. Therefore, to the annoyance of the observer, an uneven or flickering movement appears on the screen.

In double buffering, all changes to a canvas are not directly drawn to the screen but to a second virtual screen in the memory that is not visible (hence, the second or double buffer). Only after all the drawings are complete is the entire second buffer shown on the visible screen. This procedure is depicted in Figure 6.2. Since using a double buffer can also reduce the amount of data transferred to the graphics card, an additional positive bonus to the overall performance is achieved.

The double buffering algorithms can also coordinate the switching between the two graphics buffers by synchronizing them with the monitor update frequency. With conventional TVs or cathode ray monitors, an electron beam travels from top to bottom painting the image on the screen multiple times a second. At the bottom of the screen, it is switched off and moves back to the top to start drawing the next image. During this period, a change in the displayed image can occur without being observed by the viewer, and therefore all changes appear very smooth.

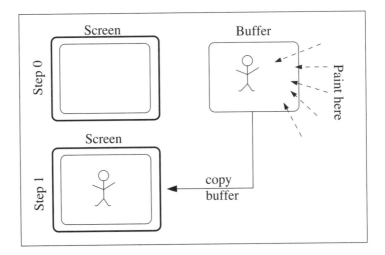

FIGURE 6.2 An example of double buffering: all updates to a canvas are made in a second buffer not visible to the observer. After the updates are finished, this buffer is copied in its entirety to the visible screen.

Using double buffering, the update of the screen is comparable to showing a cartoon movie: one full still picture is displayed after the other. However, if this procedure is done fast enough, the human eye perceives a continuous movement.

Using the QCanvas class, double buffering is switched on using the method call:

```
canvas->setDoubleBuffering(true);
```

In computer game programming, it is recommended to always use the double buffering method. The display and performance advantages easily compensate for the disadvantage of having increased memory usage for storing the displayed graphics twice.

Canvas Updates and Advances

Besides double buffering, the most important technical property of the canvas is its *update period*, a number that signifies the rate at which the canvas library should paint the canvas onto the screen. This is done by an internal timer that will start a repaint of the canvas after each update period. Note that these updates are done cleverly by the canvas library, since the only areas to be repainted are those objects that have changed since the last update. Changes can be caused by movement, removal, insertion, or animation of objects.

To achieve continuous movement, a picture has to be updated roughly 25 times per second (25 Hz). This or a higher frequency tricks the human eye into perceiving an uninterrupted movie instead of individual pictures. Therefore, and not by coincidence, TV devices use update frequencies in this range as well. However, 25 Hz is the lowest limit to trick the human eye. Most computer monitors require a sharper image, and therefore use much higher update frequencies, typically from 70 Hz to 120 Hz. Note that this behavior applies to cathode ray monitors and TV sets and cannot be translated directly to TFT flat screen monitors where lower update frequencies are acceptable.

Consequently, to obtain a smooth nonflickering display, computer games should also update their screen images around the 25Hz frequency. Updates faster than the monitor update frequency yield no additional benefits. On the other hand, if the game only uses very slow or occasional movements (e.g., card games) a much slower update period can suffice.

Besides the direct display updates, Qt also offers a second parameter that is indirectly connected with the update process, the so-called *advance period*. All items on the canvas will be called periodically in this advance period to perform movement, animation, or otherwise change their state (see the section on game ticks in Chapter 1, "Introduction to Desktop Gaming"). This is done by calling the `advance()` method available to all canvas items, which we describe later in more detail for the canvas items.

The `QCanvas` class does not allow you to set the update and advance period independently. Any setting of the advance period will automatically fix the update period at the same value, which can be a disadvantage when you want to change the update period but not the game ticks. Due to this coupling of the update and advance period, it is generally sufficient to directly set the advance period of a canvas by a call to

```
// Update and advance every 25 milliseconds (40Hz)
canvas->setAdvancePeriod(25);
```

which would perform animation, movement, and updates every 25 milliseconds.

If the game does not need any animation or `advance()` calls, a direct setting of the update period would also be possible.

```
// Update every 25 milliseconds (40Hz)
canvas->setUpdatePeriod(25);
```

TIP

When using the Qt canvas library, keep in mind that all object speeds and animations are calculated based on the individual advance and update cycles. Therefore, changing the advance period will affect all movement and animations, making them faster or slower. In a game that allows one to change the advance period, it is necessary to define all speeds relative to this basic time unit. Define your velocities and accelerations in real time (e.g., pixels per second), and calculate the corresponding advance speed (pixels per advance call) in the program.

A slow update or advance frequency will limit the animation and movement speed of the objects on the canvas and cause jumpy movements. Therefore, investing in a higher update frequency is preferable. In contrast, a faster update can cause a high processor load; therefore, the target computer on which the game is played might not be powerful enough to handle this. Professional games often offer a manual or automatic adjustment of the screen update period or the resulting *frame rate*, where frame rate is defined as *screen updates per second.*

Note that the update frequency is 1000 divided by the update time in milliseconds.

Foreground, Background, and z-Order

Usually, a computer monitor displays two coordinates as shown in Figure 6.3. These coordinates are called *x* for the horizontal and *y* for the vertical axis. However, in many games, a third dimension is useful. Even if the game itself is two dimensional, objects can be displayed in front of each other. For example, in the card game *Patience*, cards are constantly being laid on top of each other.

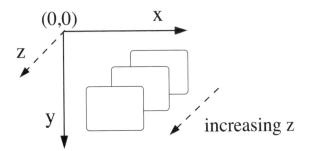

FIGURE 6.3   The coordinate system of a canvas. The *x*-coordinate is horizontal (left to right), the *y*-coordinate is vertical (top to bottom), and the *z*-coordinate determines the *z*-ordering or depth (low to high).

To support this pseudo 3D behavior even in 2D games, a canvas allows the programmer to set a *z-position* for canvas items. Objects with a small *z*-component are drawn behind objects with larger *z*-components. Therefore, these former objects are covered by the items with larger *z*-positions. In the canvas update process, this behavior is achieved by *z-ordering*; that is, sorting the objects with respect to their *z*-coordinate. Objects with smaller *z*-positions are processed and drawn before the objects with higher *z*-positions. This procedure automatically allows the ordered display of the canvas items without any additional programming effort.

The only problem with *z*-ordering is that in each canvas update step, a sorting algorithm has to sort all canvas objects by their *z*-order. In Qt, this can result in a performance loss if many canvas items with different *z*-positions are updated. However, this applies only if you use thousands of items (e.g., for particle effects). In such a case, if you do not need to distinguish a *z*-position, don't, or limit it to just a few different *z*-positions.

In addition to the *z*-order of canvas items, the QCanvas class offers the possibility to place a background image behind all sprites. This background behaves as if it has a lower *z*-position than all other items on the canvas. The background can be changed at runtime, or tiles can be used to cover it with a pattern. Although not often done, it is also possible to define a foreground image that acts as if it has a higher *z*-position than any item on the canvas and is therefore positioned in front of all items.

Chunks

For an overall better organization of display items, the canvas library performs an internal operation to group them into *chunks*. For the majority of games, it is not necessary to know their details or fiddle with them. For the interested reader, we will nevertheless briefly describe the canvas chunk system and a method on how to optimize the performance of some games.

A chunk is defined as a rectangular area on the canvas and consists of a certain width and height. These areas are regularly dispatched on the display, effectively coarse-graining it like a chess-board. All items on the canvas are associated to one or more of these chunks. A canvas item belongs to a chunk if any part of it falls into the rectangular area defined by that particular chunk, and each chunk contains a list of all items that belong to it.

All operations applied to the canvas such as movement and animation will modify one or more chunks. These modifications occur if any pixel inside a chunk is changed. As soon as a modification to a chunk happens, the corresponding chunk is marked *dirty*. When an update of the canvas is due, only the dirty chunks of the canvas are redrawn, which avoids unnecessary updates in areas of the canvas that have not been changed.

It is also possible to manually mark a chunk as dirty, which is sometimes necessary if changes to a canvas item occur but Qt does not recognize them. Examples could be the manual modification of the frames or contents of a canvas pixmap item. Then, a call to one of the following methods:

```
// Mark the chunk containing the given point (x,y) dirty
canvas->setChangedChunkContaining(x, y);

// Mark all chunks in the given rectangular area dirty. The
// area is given as QRect object.
canvas->setChanged(area)
```

will mark the point or the entire area as dirty.

Obviously, the size of an individual chunk determines the overall performance of the canvas. If there are too many chunks, the speed benefit of grouping canvas items into chunks is reduced. If the chunks are too large, it takes too long to process each chunk, and the speed benefit is reduced. However, the Qt canvas library usually chooses a suitable chunk size for most games; however, in some cases, where objects are unusually small or large, it might be worth altering the size of the chunks using

```
// Set chunk size and the number of cluster drawn
int chunksize  = 64;
int maxclusters = 100;
canvas->retune(chunksize, maxclusters)
```

Generally, the chunk size should be roughly the size of a typical object used on the canvas.

Canvas Update versus Paint Update

A canvas provides a very easy and intuitive way to display game objects on the screen. However, the update of the canvas is contrary to the normally used paint update method of a standard desktop program. In the standard approach, the view object is requested to update a part of the screen once its contents have changed. In Qt, this would be done by overwriting the PaintEvent method of the view object

```
void PaintView::paintEvent(QPaintEvent* e)
{
   QPainter p(this)
   ...
}
```

and using the QPainter object to redraw the view contents. Note that these updates do not happen periodically, but only when changes have occurred. Mostly, this is much less often than an update in a canvas view where often permanent movement or animation is occurring. In such a paint procedure, the view object then asks the document object about all data necessary to repaint the display.

A canvas is different in the respect that the programmer has no need to do any manual updates. Although paint updates are also internally used, these updates are done automatically and periodically by the canvas library. The game program just defines graphical objects, including text, images, and geometrical shapes, and tells the canvas library where the objects should be and how they should move or animate. All objects are then automatically drawn, animated, and updated.

You will find that, especially in desktop game programming, this approach is often more intuitive because you would also probably just draw the objects somewhere on the screen and occasionally command them to move.

SPRITES

Sprites are small, independent-acting items on a canvas, and can be text items, geometric forms, or images. Games in particular profit from the concept of sprites, because in a game, the game objects or figures are typically also small, independent-acting units. Therefore, in game programming, the access to a canvas sprite library is very beneficial. Some examples of sprites used in KDE games are shown in Figure 6.4.

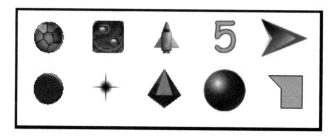

FIGURE 6.4 Example images of typical sprites used in KDE desktop games.

The idea of defining independent graphic objects or sprites on a computer screen dates back to the time of the first home computers. For example, the Commodore C64™ had eight bitmap sprites implemented in the graphics chip itself. Nowadays, canvas sprite libraries implement an arbitrary amount of sprites by simulating them in software.

Each canvas item has a set of properties associated with it. Typically, this includes a position (x,y), a z-order (z), a velocity (vx,vy), and one or more graphic images (frames) or geometrical properties. Canvas items also provide methods that allow them to operate on the canvas; for example, *move, move to, show, hide, animate,* and so on. Another important feature of a canvas item is the capability to detect a collision between two items, or an item and the background. This capacity to detect collisions makes it easy for games to implement realistic behavior such as bouncing balls, or space ships being hit.

In Qt, all sprites derive from a common base class, QCanvasItem, which represents an item on the canvas. This base class already provides the most typical sprite functions, including the setting of the position (x,y), the z-order, and the setting of the velocity in (x,y) direction. In the following example, these general properties are set.

```
// Create a new canvas item associated with the given canvas.
// 'Sprite' can be any class derived from QCanvasItem
Sprite* sprite = new Sprite(canvas)

// Set the position (x,y) using the move command
sprite->move(50.0, 50.0);

// which would be equivalent to
sprite->setX(50.0);
sprite->setY(50.0)

// Set the z-order coordinate
sprite->setZ(10.0);

// Set the velocity in (x,y) direction
sprite->setVelocity(10.0, 3.5);

// which would be equivalent to
sprite->setXVelocity(10.0);
sprite->setYVelocity(3.5);
```

Furthermore, each canvas item can have the status *shown* or *hidden*. A hidden item is not displayed or processed on the canvas. Note, before you can use canvas items on the display, they have to be "shown":

```
// The sprite is now visible on the canvas
sprite->show();

// Hide the still existing sprite from the canvas
sprite->hide();
```

Sprite Subclasses

The canvas library offers various specialized subclasses of sprites designed to cover their most typical uses. These sprite subclasses include:

QCanvasLine: Drawing a line.

QCanvasPolygon: Drawing any polygonal item.

QCanvasRectangle: Drawing a rectangle.

QCanvasSprite: A classic sprite showing a (pixmap) image.

QCanvasText: Drawing some text with any font.

The first three categories of sprites represent geometrical items. They are useful for vector graphics and allow for easy scaling but are seldom used in games. The QCanvasSprite is the classic sprite and normally displays an image or even an animation made from a sequence of images. The QCanvasText is useful for displaying or moving text in a game.

In the following source code snippets, we present examples for three sprite categories: geometrical, text, and pixmap. For all sprites, some basic property settings typical for that sprite category are shown. Additionally, the sprite is moved to the canvas and shown to the user. Because movement and animation are of special importance to sprites, they are explained in more detail in the following sections.

ON THE CD
On the companion CD-ROM, the mycanvas demo program located in the folder examples/mycanvas presents the use and details of all possible sprite types. Here we focus on the most important issues of the different sprite classes.

First, we will create a geometrical sprite; in this case, a sprite representing a simple line.

```
// Create a sprite forming a straight line
QCanvasLine* sprite = new QCanvasLine(canvas);

// Define the line to go from (x0,y0) = (0,0) to
// (x1,y1) = (200, 0)
sprite->setPoints(0, 0, 200, 0);

// Choose the drawing pen being white with width 3
QPen pen(color, 3);
sprite->setPen(pen);

// Position the sprite on the canvas
sprite->move(10.0, 10.0);
```

```
// Display the sprite
sprite->show();
```

Other geometrical sprites work along the same principle, except that the geometrical settings have to be adjusted to the actual geometry. For example, in rectangle and polygon sprites, the width and height or corner points have to be respectively defined.

In the next example, a text sprite is created on the given canvas using the QCanvasText class.

```
// Create sprite displaying some text
QCanvasText* sprite = new QCanvasText(canvas);

// Set the actual text to display
sprite->setText("Hello world!");
// and define its color to be yellow
sprite->setColor(Qt::yellow);

// Optionally a user defined font can be used
QFont newfont = font();
newfont.setPixelSize(16);
sprite->setFont(newfont);

// Position the sprite on the canvas
sprite->move(10.0, 10.0);

// Display the sprite to the user
sprite->show();
```

The pixmap sprites are by far the most often-used form of sprites in computer games, and are created using the QCanvasSprite class. This class provides a sprite type that maintains one or more images, called *frames*. These frames can be displayed individually or can be animated by showing them in a sequence. A pixmap sprite is created by loading the images into the sprite, setting the animation properties, and then showing the sprite.

```
// Load 5 PNG images into the pixmap array. The images must be
// labeled: pic0000.png, pic0001.png, ..., pic0004.png
QCanvasPixmapArray* pixmaps =
                 new QCanvasPixmapArray("pic%1.png", 5);

// Create the actual canvas sprite based on the pixmap images
QCanvasSprite* sprite = new QCanvasSprite(pixmaps, canvas);
```

```
// Select one frame of the loaded images (0,..,4) for display
sprite->setFrame(0);

// Optionally allow animations
sprite->setAnimated(true);

// Move the sprite somewhere on the canvas
sprite->move(10.0, 10.0);

// Show the sprite to the user
sprite->show();
```

It is also possible to create a QCanvasSprite without giving a frame image array. This is done by setting zero as the first argument to the constructor, and then later, the images can be set with a call to

```
// Set the pre-loaded image array into the sprite
sprite->setSequence(pixmaps);
```

Movement of Sprites

One of the most important features of sprites is their movement on the canvas. During a game, both the player(s) and the computer will control sprites going from one screen location to another. Additionally, some extra sprites will move on certain predefined paths on the screen.

For the basic movement, all sprites support movement methods that can be called directly. A movement can be created by either manually putting the sprite in a certain screen position using move(x,y), or with the relative movement moveBy(dx,dy), which moves the sprite by a given amount away from its current position. Furthermore, a movement can be created by giving the sprite a constant velocity along the x-axis and/or the y-axis by setting velocity with setVelocity(vx,vy). A sprite with a nonzero velocity is automatically moved by the given velocity amount (*vx,vy*) measured in pixel per canvas advance cycle if it is registered for animation using setAnimated(true).

Note that the overall speed visible to the user depends on the canvas update or advance period. Changes in this period must reflect in the sprite velocity, too.

To demonstrate the movement principles, the following example shows how a sprite can be moved to a given position and how a certain velocity is set that will move the sprite away from the initial position in each advance step of the canvas.

```
// Move sprite to position (100, 100)
sprite->move(100.0, 100.0);

// Set velocity in x and y direction to (3, 4) pixel/update
sprite->setVelocity(3.0, 4.0);
```

Although on the screen a sprite can only move pixel by pixel, which is an integer quantity, all sprites internally use double numbers for their movement and velocity. This allows a more precise control over the movement. Furthermore, rounding errors are also reduced by the double numbers, and velocities like 1.4 pixels per update are feasible. Therefore, all sprites are moved to the more rounded integer position such as 0, 1, 3, 4, ... in consecutive update steps.

In addition to the position setting and constant velocity movement, all QCanvasItems and thus all sprites provide a virtual method advance(). This method is called during each advance cycle—that is, at fixed time intervals—and allows a more flexible handling of sprite behavior. If this method is overwritten for a certain canvas item, special movements for that sprite can be implemented. Later we will see that special animations and detection of collisions are possible using the advance() method.

The advance() method is called in two phases, with the phase number being given as argument. In the first phase (0), each sprite should not change position, but examine other items on the canvas for which special interchange is required, such as collisions between them. In the second phase (1), all sprites can change positions and do so in ignorance to any other items on the canvas. For movement and animation, only the second phase is of interest.

Using individual movement algorithms in advance() allows a more complex movement than the simple constant velocity approach using the internal setVelocity() methods. Typical examples for these special movements are circular movements, accelerated movements, and so on. Chapter 13, "Math and Physics in Desktop Games," describes physical correct movements in more detail. The following **ON THE CD** example taken from the mycanvas demo program on the companion CD-ROM shows a sprite that has its advance() method overwritten to implement a more complex movement pattern. The sprite will be reflected at the border of the canvas given by (0,0) and (width, height).

```
void Sprite::advance(int phase)
{
  // Phase 1 is for moving
  if (phase == 1)
  {
    // Check whether the sprite hits the canvas x-border
    if (x() >= canvas()->width()-width() || x() <= 0 )
    {
```

```
      // If so exchange the velocity to simulate a
      // reflection at the border
      setXVelocity(-xVelocity());
    }
    // And the same check applies for the y-component
    if (y() >= canvas()->height()-height() || y() <= 0)
    {
     setYVelocity(-yVelocity());
    }
  }

  // Call parents method to do the move for us
  QCanvasSprite::advance(phase);
}
```

It is recommended to give all velocities not as absolute pixel numbers but relative to the advance frequency. Then, an internal change in the update or advance period will not change the velocities of the sprites visible to the user. This can be done by adjusting all velocity settings or more effectively by using position updates in the advance() *method.*

Sprite Animation

The animation of sprites is implemented in a cartoon-like fashion. In each advance cycle of the canvas, a different image frame of the sprite is displayed. Therefore, the individual frames will appear to the observer as a continuous cartoon-like animation. This frame animation allows a sprite to change form, color, and shape. Typical game examples are explosions, rotating pieces, or thrown dice. Such an animation frame sequence is shown in Figure 6.5.

The QCanvasSprite already allows the storage of many image frames in its frame buffer that can then be displayed in sequence. The following example shows how a QCanvasSprite can load several images into its internal frame array. These images can then be used for animation.

```
// Load 5 PNG images into the pixmap array. The images must be
// labeled: pic0000.png, pic0001.png, ..., pic0004.png
QCanvasPixmapArray* pixmaps =
                        new QCanvasPixmapArray("pic%1.png",5);

// Create the actual canvas sprite and store the pixmap images
// as sprite frames
QCanvasSprite* sprite = new QCanvasSprite(pixmaps, canvas);
```

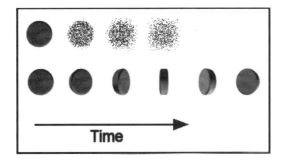

FIGURE 6.5 Sprite frame animation for a dissolving and a rotating game piece. In each animation cycle, one frame taken from the set of all frames is displayed and thus creates the illusion of a dissolving or rotating piece, respectively.

To show any animation, the sprite has to first be registered using a call to `setAnimated(true)`. For animated sprites, two methods are available to display the frames stored in the sprite. The first method is the *cyclic* animation; here, all frames are displayed from the first to the last in sequence. Once the last frame is displayed, the first frame is repeated and the entire procedure starts again. The *oscillating* animation starts like the cyclic animation, but after the last frame is shown, the sequence is reversed and played from the last to the first. After the first frame is reached, it reverses again, and the entire procedure starts from the beginning.

```
// Use the 'cyclic' animation concept
sprite->setFrameAnimation(QCanvasSprite::Cycle);

// Use the 'oscillating' animation  concept
sprite->setFrameAnimation(QCanvasSprite::Oscillate);
```

However, these simple animation types are often not sufficient for games. In addition, for Qt versions earlier than 3.0, these internal animation methods are not available. In both cases, it is possible to use the `advance()` method to create more complex animation patterns. For the sprites, individual frames are selected and can be directly set by:

```
// Set frame with given number 'no' to be displayed by the
// canvas sprite
sprite->setFrame(no)
```

If this is done in `advance()`, a user-defined animation type can be defined. This is particularly useful if more than one frame animation sequence is stored in the sprite. In this scenario, only a subset of frames is selected for the animation depending on the current state of the sprite. For example, a moving spaceship, with smoking rockets would be in sequence one, with, let's say, frames 0–5. The same ship with shields could be defined as sequence two, using frames 6–10. Finally, the ship might be hit and the burning ship could be sequence three with frames 11–20. Each of the sequences consists of a few animation frames that are manually selected and displayed in advance().

A second important use of user-defined animation is the possibility to independently control the speed of the frame animation from the advance period of the canvas. This can be achieved if you choose an advanced period that is faster than the actual animation of your items, and then manually limit the animation of certain sprites. Of course, the animation can only be made slower than the actual advance period.

To change the animation speed, simply change the current frame every n-th step in the advance() method. In the following example, the animation steps are counted by a counter and the animation is only performed when this counter reaches n; therefore, every n-th step.

```
void Sprite::advance(int phase)
{
  if (phase != 0)
  {
    // Suppose a counter is defined in the sprite class as
    //   int counter = 0;
    // we increase the animation counter each advance call
    counter++;

    // The frame is changed only if the counter reached at
    // a given threshold, here n (for example n=10)
    if (counter == n)
    {
      // Increase the frame number. Use the modulo operation
      // to restart if the maximum frame number is reached.
      setFrame( (frame()+1) % frameCount()) ;
      // Reset the counter
      counter = 0;
    }

    // Call parents function to do the remaining advance
    // operation for us
    QCanvasSprite::advance(phase);
  }
}
```

The sprite advance() *method is also the right place to do more than animation and movement of sprites. Using* advance(), *the internal states of the sprites can be changed or events can be initiated. The* advance() *method can also be used as an internal counter or "heartbeat" of a sprite. This is particularly useful if (for performance reasons) no additional timer objects for counting or timing sprites are used.*

Some examples for the use of the advance() method might be the healing of a character in a role-playing game by increasing its hit-points every advance cycle, or the production cycle of a factory in a real-time strategy game where a new unit is produced every *n*-th advance cycle. However, keep in mind how to make the events dependent on the actual number of advance steps or on the amount of "real-time" that has passed. In the first case, a change in the advance period of the game will change the speed of your events; that is, your factory will produce faster or slower. This can be great if you intentionally implemented a "fast-forward" feature, but annoying if you just wanted to optimize the game performance.

Image Masks

An *image mask* is a technical trick to hide parts of an image and is comparable to a real mask that hides part of a face. The "hidden" part of the image is drawn transparently on the canvas, so that in the resulting picture the background shines through the masked area. The nonmasked part of the image is displayed normally.

The mask is implemented as an additional layer within the image. For example, QPixmaps can store such masks, and these pixmaps then contain the actual image data, such as 24 bits per pixel (8 bits red, 8 bits green, and 8 bits blue). Additionally, the mask is stored in the QPixmap as one extra bit per pixel, and in turn indicates to the image whether this pixel should be displayed.

Masking is necessary if you want to show another object or background behind your sprite. It is not necessary if the sprite is just a simple, filled, rectangular shape, or when the background is a single color and no other sprites will pass behind the sprite in question. Masking allows the creation of rings, circles, sprites with holes, or any other nonrectangular forms.

It is not enough to draw the "holes" in the sprite with the canvas background color. This shortcut will only work when the sprite is on a plain background, but not when it covers another sprite or another image.

In Figure 6.6, we show a sprite made out of a dark ring on a light background. The top left image shows the sprite without any mask, and here the sprite simply covers the background. In the top middle image, the same sprite is displayed after a "binary mask" (lower middle) has been applied. Now the mask only allows the ring to be shown. The remainder of the image will be the canvas background that shines through the sprite. The rightmost image displays a sprite using an "alpha mask," the effects of which are explained in more detail in the next section.

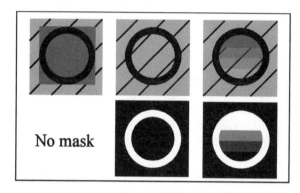

FIGURE 6.6   Image masks and alpha buffer. The top row shows a rectangular sprite with a plain background and a circle of a different color in three different masking situations. The types of masks are shown in the bottom row. The sprites are displayed on a gray background with dark diagonal lines to emphasize the effect of the sprite masks. The top left image shows the sprite without any mask. The top middle image shows the same sprite after the application of the "binary mask" (lower middle). Finally, the top right image is the sprite after applying a "grayscale alpha mask" (lower right).

Soft Overlap Using Alpha Blending

A special form of image mask is the *alpha mask,* and its application is often named *alpha blending.* This concept extends the normal binary image mask (on/1 or off/0) to 256 values. Again, a value of 0 will not draw the corresponding pixel of the sprite, while a value of 255 will draw the pixel of the sprite. All other values in between will gradually (starting from 0 to 255) display more and more of the sprite and therefore blend the sprite image with the current background or any other sprite being covered. This effect is dynamic, and the actual background behind the sprite is always mixed with the sprite's image. Alpha blending allows for smooth corners and edges, anti-aliasing, and semi-transparent effects. A good example of alpha blending is an energy shield of a spacecraft where you can partially see through the shield. In addition, GUIs such as KDE use alpha mask effects for showing semi-transparent menus, smooth fonts, and so on. An alpha mask can be stored and loaded using a PNG image. Alongside the image information (e.g., 24 bit), PNG images also reserve an additional 8-bit graphics channel for the image mask (yielding a total of 32 bits data per pixel).

Figure 6.6 depicts how an alpha mask can be used. The top right image displays the sprite after the addition of the alpha mask shown in the lower right. As you can see, the mask gradually blends in the dark background behind the sprite. In the top part of the inner circle, the image is dominated by the sprite's dark background, while in the lower part of the inner circle, the background behind the sprite appears.

Automatic Frame Generation

A sprite frame animation works along the same principle as a cartoon movie. Each step in the animation, like a movement or a part of an explosion, has to be drawn as an individual picture. This can become quite tedious for many smoothly animated objects. Therefore, it is often helpful to have automatically generated animation frames, and there are some ways to do so.

First, there already exist programs that can provide you with some standard animation types, like explosions. For further details, see Chapter 12, "Particle Effects," which discusses the so-called particle effects.

Second, other programs allow you to interpolate frames in between two existing frames. This is difficult to do yourself, since a good transformation requires you to identify or define some special points on the frame; for example, a person's nose or eye. The differences between the two frames are then analyzed, and the in-between frames are calculated by moving the marked points on a trajectory that connects the points on the two original frames. This powerful but complicated method allows a roughly sketched animation to look very smooth.

Third, it is possible to apply some basic transformations to one frame of a sprite yourself to create new frames. This works particularly well for rotations, size, or color changes, and is very easily applied using standard Qt functions. Size and rotation changes can be applied on any pixmap—that is, on any sprite frame—by using the Qt `QPixmap::xForm()` method. The `xForm()` method applies an arbitrary transformation matrix to a pixmap. With this transformation matrix, a new pixmap object can be created as follows:

```
QPixmap pm;
pm = pm.xForm(matrix);
```

The transformation matrix `QWMatrix` is also a Qt class, and can already produce some standard transformations such as scaling or rotation. Additionally, it allows you to define arbitrary individual matrix transformations. More details on `QWMatrix` transformations can be found in Chapter 13, and as an example, a scaling matrix can be set up by:

```
QWMatrix matrix;
matrix.scale(0.5, 0.5);
```

This process will rescale the pixmap to half its original size. Rotations and shearing are done in a similar manner.

The rotation of an entire pixmap around one of its main axes—for example, the *y*-axis—can be achieved with an easy trick. Simple scaling of the pixmap in the axis perpendicular to the movement with a scale factor proportional to a cosine will create a smooth rotation effect. These effects can be used to simulate the turning of a card or the rotation of a coin (see Figure 6.7). The shrinking of the image appears similar to the real turning of a card. After the image size is scaled to zero, the process is reversed and the image is expanded showing its backside.

FIGURE 6.7 Automatic sprite frame generation. Example of a card being turned over. The effect is achieved by shrinking and growing the pixmaps.

An example for turning a card from its front side to its back side is shown in the following example, which allows the turning to occur: the full front side is scaled down step by step to a thin line, which is then expanded back to a full card showing the back-side image. Here we use the cosine of the angles between 0 and 90 degrees, which corresponds to $\pi/2$ in radians (with π defined as M_PI in the math.h include file).

```
#include <math.h>
...

for (i=0; i<10; i++)
{
   // Create 10 images from 0 .. 81 degree. Note that the last
   // (middle) image for 90 degree is omitted here and inserted
   // in the second loop for the backside to not insert the
   // middle image twice
   matrix.scale(cos( i/10.0 * M_PI/2.0), 1.0);

   // Transform the front side pixmap
   frame = frontPixmap.xForm(matrix);

   // store the frame in any sprite
   ...
```

```
    }
    for (i=10; i>=0; i--)
    {
        // Create the remaining 11 images from 90 .. 0 degree
        matrix.scale(cos( i/10.0 * M_PI/2.0), 1.0);

        // Transform the backside pixmap
        frame = backPixmap.xForm(matrix);

        // store the frame in any sprite
        ...
    }
```

Collisions

An important ingredient in game programming is the detection of collisions between game sprites. Collision detection allows the game programmer to find out if two sprites overlap—that is, hit each other—or if a sprite and the background image are overlapping. Examples of collision detection are the hit of a space ship with a missile, the collision of a space ship and an asteroid, or two bouncing balls hitting each other or a wall. Many games rely on such forms of collision detection.

The difficulty in collision detection is that it is often not enough to just check if two objects are a certain distance from each other or inside a given bounding box. Such a check will ignore the actual shape of the sprites, which could mean that even though sprites are overlapping, the actual sprite images do not collide. Figure 6.8 shows such a situation. Players will certainly feel cheated if their spaceship explodes because it is near an asteroid, but no part of the ship is actually touching it.

Therefore, often a *pixel exact* collision detection is necessary that checks each pixel of the two sprites to see whether they overlap. Unfortunately, checking each sprite object in every update cycle of the canvas during the game depletes a lot of computer power. If pixel exact collision detection is not necessary for your game, it is also possible to ask the collision detection method to perform just a simple bounding box check. In this case, all items are returned where the bounding boxes overlap, regardless of whether the pixels of those items overlap.

The Qt canvas library implements a twofold strategy of collision detection. First, a fast check is performed that checks whether two sprites are actually close enough that a collision could occur. This is done by checking whether their surrounding bounding boxes or the chunks occupied by the bounding boxes overlap. If pixel exact collision is requested, the canvas library makes an additional detailed check on all items that collided in this first check method. This twofold strategy already reduces the amount of pixel exact checks. Despite this optimized strategy, pixel exact collision should only be called for sprites where such a collision has some consequences, because the overall processing is still slow.

Figure 6.8 illustrates the steps toward such a collision. In the left image, two sprites are approaching but are still distinctly apart. In the middle image, the bounding boxes around the sprites overlap, indicating a collision in the first collision check method (bounding box check). However, the images of the sprites do not yet overlap. Only in the right image does the collision really happen and the images of the sprites overlap.

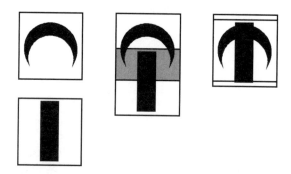

FIGURE 6.8 Sprite collision of two sprites. The sprites are shown together with their bounding boxes. In the left image, the sprites are still clearly apart. In the middle image, the bounding boxes but not the actual images overlap, and in the right image, a real pixel collision has occurred.

In the following examples, we show a single- and two-step collision detection. The collision detection is programmed using an overwritten advance() method to check for a collision between all sprites. If you recall, advance() is called in two phases, where the first phase is used to check for collisions, and the second phase is used for the actual movement. In the following example, the colliding sprites will richochet in the manner of similar hard spheres such as billiard balls. Such behavior is created by simply exchanging their velocity components.

First, we use the collision detection where the pixel exact collision is checked for all sprites (calling the collisions(true) function of a QCanvasItem).

```
void Sprite::advance(int phase)
{
    // Phase 0 is for collision checks
    if (phase == 0)
    {
```

```
    // This checks for EXACT sprite collisions.
    QCanvasItemList collidelist = collisions(true);

    // Walk the list of colliding sprites.
    QCanvasItemList::iterator it;
    for ( it = collidelist.begin();
          it != collidelist.end(); ++it)
    {
      // Apply a type conversion to the sprite used
      Sprite* sprite = (Sprite*)(*it);

      // Exchange the velocities of the two sprites
      double vx = xVelocity();
      double vy = yVelocity();
      setXVelocity(sprite->xVelocity());
      setYVelocity(sprite->yVelocity());
      sprite->setXVelocity(vx);
      sprite->setYVelocity(vy);
    }// end for
  }// end if
  ...
}
```

In the second two-step example, the collision check with all sprites is performed using only the bounding boxes of the items (calling `collisions(false)` from `QCanvasItem`). The resulting collision list can therefore contain items that actually did not collide. Using the initial collision list, a manual pixel exact check can be performed for some of the items that really matter (calling the `QCanvasItem` function `collidesWith(QCanvasItem*)`). Depending on the concept of the game, the rest of the listed items can be ignored or the collision can occur, since it has no significance to the actual game play. If not all items are tested, this two-step algorithm reduces the amount of expensive pixel exact checks.

```
  ...
  // This checks for BOUNDING BOX sprite collisions.
  // The resulting list will contain sprites which
  // actually did not really collide!
  QCanvasItemList collidelist = collisions(false);

  // Walk the list of collision candidates
  QCanvasItemList::iterator it;
  for ( it = collidelist.begin();
```

```
           it != collidelist.end(); ++it)
    {
      // Now make the pixel EXACT collision check only
      // for the items which have a chance of colliding
      // and are of interest for the game (depicted by
      // a call to the 'dummy' isOfInterest() function
      if (isOfInterest(*it))
      {
        // Ask Qt whether the sprite did have a pixel
        // exact collision
        if (collidesWith(*it))
        {
          // Do something useful
          ...
        }
      }
    }
  }// end for
```

TILING

Many arcade-style games use an effective way of filling a huge background with a relatively small amount of graphics memory. This is done by *tiling* the background with a limited set of graphic elements. This set of elements is used to fill the entire background and can be compared to a real tile arrangement on a kitchen wall. Tiling is implemented by defining a basic tile with a constant size; for example, 16 × 16 pixels. The canvas background is then divided into regular cells of exactly this tile size. Each individual cell is then allotted one tile out of a predefined tile set. To benefit from the tiling method, the number of different tiles should be small, and usually at least smaller than the total amount of tiles necessary to fill the construction pattern; in general, the size of the background divided by the size of one tile.

For example, assume you have a background of 320 × 200 pixels and the tiles have a size of 20 × 20 pixels. This results in 16 × 10 = 160 possible background tiles. However, the game will probably work fine with 20–40 different tile patterns to reasonably fill the background. Such an example of tiling is shown in Figure 6.9.

Nowadays, a second more important aspect of tiling is the ability to easily construct a background from a game map or a particular geometrical pattern. The elements of the map, such as rivers or mountains, can be directly translated to background tiles. Furthermore, having defined tiles for the background makes it easy to change parts of the background by exchanging the corresponding tile. Such an example could be the digging of a hole on a game map.

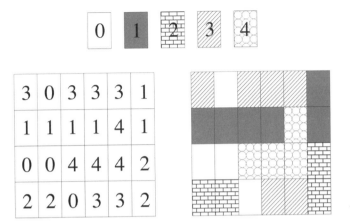

FIGURE 6.9   Canvas tiling. Four possible tiles are defined (top row). Using the four tiles, the canvas is arranged into the depicted construction pattern (left). This resulting canvas background is then displayed on the screen (right).

Tiles are set by defining a master tile bitmap, which is a collection of all possible tiles in one big bitmap arranged from left to right as shown in Figure 6.10. This bitmap can contain multiple rows of tiles, but its overall size needs to be an integer multiple of the size of a single tile. If these master tiles are stored in a QPixmap, they can be set to the canvas by simply giving their number and size.

FIGURE 6.10   The master tile bitmap. It defines all possible tiles, which then can be used on the canvas. The tiles are addressed left to right and then top to bottom.

```
// pixmap:      Contains the master tile pixmap
// x/yAmount:   How many tiles on the canvas in (x,y)
// 16,16:       The size of an individual tile
canvas->setTiles(pixmap, xAmount, yAmount, 16, 16);
```

The canvas is then filled with tiles using:

```
// Set the tile at tile position (x,y)=(1,1) to tile
// number 5.
canvas->setTile(1, 1, 5);
```

The tile position on the canvas can be chosen from the range defined by the setTiles() call; that is (xAmount,yAmount), and the tile number is an integer index to the master tile bitmap. Note that there is no check for the index ranges in the setTile() method; exceeding this range will create a Qt "index out of bounds" error.

When programming a canvas using tiles, you will often notice that many different tiles are needed to properly display a smooth background; for example, the border of a lake or similar patterns in a strategy game. In these cases, there is little reason to use tiles because no advantages in performance are gained when you compare it to just filling in the background with a layer of sprites, which can move or be animated. It is also possible to have an animation of the background tiles by exchanging the tile index numbers periodically, which allows for flashing or changing backgrounds. Typically, arcade style games, strategy games, and maps are applications for tiled backgrounds.

SCROLLING

We mentioned at the beginning of the chapter that a game canvas can be larger than the corresponding window view. The view is then just that current part of the graphic that is shown to the user in the window. To display the other parts of the canvas, there are two principal possibilities.

First, it is possible to allow the window to zoom in and out, which allows a smaller or larger portion of the underlying canvas to be shown. This is useful for overview maps or similar tasks in strategy games. Such a display can be achieved by associating the canvas with more than one view. For each QCanvasView, a transformation matrix can be set.

```
QWMatrix matrix;
...
canvasView->setWorldMatrix (matrix);
```

Note, however, that associating a transformation matrix with a QCanvasView will decrease performance considerably.

Of more importance than the zoom transformations of a canvas view is the scrolling of the canvas. This feature is also less performance consuming. Scrolling is inherently supported by the canvas library and is particularly useful for strategy games or old-style arcade games in which the player walks or flies through a much larger world than the view displays. Using a QCanvasView widget, which inherits from a QScrollView widget, automatic scrolling capabilities are available. You can easily choose which part of the canvas should be displayed in the view. The following example shows how to perform scrolling. We first enable the scroll bars at the side of the window to allow the user to scroll the window, and then we program additional scrolling on the canvas to a certain starting position.

```
// Enable scroll bars for the user
// Note: 'AlwaysOff' would disable the scrollbars
setVScrollBarMode(AlwaysOn);
setHScrollBarMode(AlwaysOn);

// Scroll canvas by 10 pixel in x-direction by the
// program's own scrolling
scrollBy(10,0);
```

Using these predefined methods, scrolling of the canvas becomes very simple and effective.

To summarize the scrolling capabilities: a canvas can be defined to be larger than the view shown in the game window, and Qt offers commands to move the actual canvas around so different parts are displayed. This concept is depicted in Figure 6.1. This is done very effectively so that even scrolling of a very large canvas is feasible.

SUMMARY

Canvas libraries provide a very easy interface to the classical 2D desktop game programming in which a moderate number of moving or animated objects are used. Various types of sprites allow the movement or animation of images, text, and different geometrical objects. The features of the canvas library allow a straightforward implementation of all standard desktop games (e.g., board or card games) and arcade or action games. Once you are familiar with the concept of moving objects around on a canvas, it is very easy to create professional-looking games with hundreds or even a few thousand moving and animated objects in the game. Also useful for game programming is the automatic pixel precise collision detection, which is necessary for many action or arcade games.

There exist two major disadvantages to canvas systems. First, when using the 2D canvas library, true 3D applications are not possible; for this, the use of *OpenGL* (see Chapter 7, "OpenGL") is recommended. Second, if the complexity of the game increases too much, the amount of moved or animated sprites becomes very large (thousands or tens of thousand of items), or there are too many pixel exact collision detections, performance problems may arise.

These performance issues become a particular problem when developing game applications on handheld or embedded computers on which the performance is less than on a desktop computer. On these systems, only a very limited number of sprites can be moved or animated at the same time. For a typical PDA running Qt such as the Sharp Zaurus SL-5500 PDA, only up to a few dozen sprites (depending on the size and animation speed of the sprites) can be used.

Nevertheless, the advantages of canvas programming are overwhelming, and your desktop game will profit enormously from the use of a canvas library. The ease of use, the amount of class methods already available for game use, and the speed and the smoothness of the animations make it an ideal candidate for standard desktop games. Furthermore, it is extremely practical that the Qt canvas library is an integrated part of Qt and KDE. This allows you to produce games that do not require external libraries—always a hassle for people installing your software.

REFERENCES

[TrolltechQt04]   *Qt Developer pages,* *http://www.trolltech.com/developer/index.html*, 2004.

7 OpenGL

In This Chapter

- Introduction to OpenGL
- Coordinate Systems
- 2D Rendering
- 3D Rendering
- Lighting
- Blending
- Reading and Writing Pixel Data
- Text Rendering
- Error Detection
- OpenGL Utility Libraries, Extensions, and Version Detection
- Rendering Performance

This chapter serves as an introduction to fast 2D and 3D graphics programming using the Open Graphics Library (OpenGL). OpenGL is a standardized 3D graphics library that is often used for game programming. Actually, OpenGL is just a specification for a 3D graphics library that defines a set of functions and methods with their parameters and describes what should happen when they are called. OpenGL can also be referred to as a library that actually implements the OpenGL specification. These two meanings are normally indistinguishable, but often the latter is meant.

Implementations of the OpenGL specification in an actual OpenGL library are available from different vendors, usually those of a graphics card. These vendors provide the library files containing a specific OpenGL implementation. On a Linux system, such a library implementing OpenGL is called libGL.so. However, it is also possible to obtain OpenGL implementation by independent vendors. With Linux, you can alternatively use the open source implementation from the DRI project [Dri05], which is based on *Mesa* OpenGL [Mesa05]. However, to benefit from the hardware acceleration of a graphics card, an OpenGL acceleration has to be chosen that supports this particular graphics card, and this is normally the one provided by the graphics card vendor.

Contrary to Qt or other widgets libraries, OpenGL defines only very generic and even low-level functions. Basically, OpenGL only allows the drawing of points and triangles onto the screen. These points and triangles, however, can be painted in various ways with plain colors and complicated graphics. Images used for such surface painting are called *textures*.

In most games, OpenGL is used to draw textured triangles. This is of course an oversimplification of its capability, and you can do many more things including drawing single pixels and bitmaps. However, rendering textured triangles remains the major aspect in games. Therefore, graphics cards of today's PCs are optimized exactly for this application in games. As a result, drawing textured triangles is one of the fastest things a graphics card can do.

When developing a game that is graphically intense, the developers must decide whether they should stay with canvas-based graphic libraries, or if changing to OpenGL would be more beneficial. Text-based or simple desktop games with a limited amount of graphical features are more easily developed using the standard QWidget/QPainter or QCanvas approach. However, if you develop a large game or a game that relies heavily on graphics, you will usually require OpenGL to achieve the level of graphics performance necessary for the game. This is the main reason why OpenGL has been incorporated into the development of many current commercial games. Actually, if you also consider games using DirectX/Direct3D™, which is the Microsoft alternative to OpenGL, you will find that basically all modern games use a 3D graphics library.

Even games that are 100% 2D but use abundant graphical effects can benefit from OpenGL because the latter is simply faster at drawing. Additionally, although not always immediately obvious, games often use OpenGL indirectly through scene graph libraries. These libraries are described at the end of this chapter.

Before we start to take a closer look at OpenGL, we will shortly discuss the situations in which OpenGL should not be applied:

- **Your game is widget based:** OpenGL may still be an option, depending on your situation, but you are probably better off using normal Qt widgets.
- **The game you developed uses very limited graphics:** In this case, a canvas-based solution may be preferred.
- **You are developing for target systems that do not have an acceptable OpenGL implementation:** Nowadays, most PC-based operating systems have at least a basic OpenGL implementation, and the majority of systems have a good

hardware-accelerated implementation. These operating systems include Linux and, of course, Microsoft Windows. Therefore, except for some target systems such as PDAs, OpenGL is generally supported.

However, there are many situations in which OpenGL is virtually the only option:

■ **Your game will use a lot of 2D animations and/or moving objects:** In this situation, a normal canvas drawing might still be sufficient, but a hardware-accelerated solution can make your life much easier and the graphics much faster.
■ **You want to do 3D game applications:** Therefore, if at some point of development you figure out that a substantial part of your game consists of drawing graphics (hopefully, this happens before you even start the project), you should seriously consider working with OpenGL.

OpenGL is a large topic, and therefore this chapter will concentrate on those aspects we consider the most useful for desktop game development. We begin with a general introduction to OpenGL and then proceed to cover 2D and 3D graphics using OpenGL. After a brief introduction to the OpenGL utility libraries GLU, GLX, and WGL, we then discuss some performance-related issues.

Most parts of this chapter are completely independent of Qt, and actually, we will only use Qt for opening the initial window and for loading texture files. If you are already familiar with OpenGL, you can skip this chapter and proceed to the next, which describes how to use OpenGL in conjunction with Qt. To stay compatible and provide you with examples you can use on as many OpenGL implementations as possible, we refer to version 1.2 of the OpenGL standard and use very few special version-dependent features.

For further information, you can refer to additional OpenGL tutorials available on the Internet. A very good and detailed start is also the "OpenGL Programming Guide," the so-called "redbook" [Redbook05], which provides an excellent introduction. However, this guide is not specialized for games.

INTRODUCTION TO OPENGL

Before writing a real OpenGL program, it is useful to have some knowledge about the general design of OpenGL and how to combine the library with the windowing toolkit Qt. The following section contains the fundamental aspects when developing with OpenGL.

Basic Principles

OpenGL is considerably different from the normal window drawing methods to which you are accustomed. In this section, we highlight a few of the basic principles that differ in OpenGL, or at least differ in most OpenGL applications.

Scenes and Models

A game scene typically consists of more than one 3D element. Often, some of these elements are grouped into a *model*; for example, a building or a character. These models can then be displayed in a game scene.

In our concept, the term *scene* determines the entire graphical representation of the 3D world of the game, including both 2D and 3D objects. For example, in a first-person shooter game, *scene* means the complete level currently being played. This includes the player, all enemy objects, the walls, the floor, any items in that level, and the status texts on the screen. Usually, a game displays only a small part of the scene at any time, so a *scene* or *scene-snap* also refers to the currently visible part of the world. Its actual meaning depends on the context.

The process of drawing or displaying a part of the world is called *rendering*. When you render the scene, you produce one picture that will be displayed on the screen. This *snapshot* of the scene is called a *frame*. In contrast to the usual 2D GUI development, in 3D environments you normally redraw the entire scene every time the screen is updated; that is, on every frame. This may sound slow to a GUI developer who is used to windowing toolkits, but it is actually very fast, the reason being that in games, you usually have many objects that are simultaneously moving; sometimes the entire world moves. Thus, it is faster to simply redraw all the objects in the frame instead of keeping track of the objects that have changed since the last frame was drawn. Furthermore, you can apply techniques like frustum culling, which will be explained by the end of this chapter, to make sure only the objects that are actually visible will be rendered.

This drawing principle is very important to understand since it often confuses beginners. Thus, at every frame you first clear the entire screen and then redraw every object, piece by piece or triangle by triangle.

OpenGL does not include any functions to load data from files or display entire 3D models or scenes automatically. Therefore, a model has to be loaded independently of OpenGL and has to be rendered. Your responsibility is to load the model data and any textures from a file into the memory. If you use the combination of OpenGL and Qt for your game, Qt includes methods that can actually load the textures into memory.

Buffers

OpenGL provides multiple buffers when rendering, and while some are consistently present, the availability of others depends entirely on the graphics card. In contrast to normal windowing libraries, such as Qt, OpenGL allows you to modify and read these buffers directly, which is often advantageous when doing advanced tasks. The buffers include:

The color buffer: This buffer is always present and simply contains the color of every pixel (red, green, blue, and alpha components) on the screen, and the graphic card displays this buffer.

The depth buffer: This buffer contains the depth values of every pixel. The depth values for a certain pixel are not equal to the *z* values of the objects represented by pixels. The depth value is a value between 0.0 and 1.0, indicating the distance with respect to the viewer. This buffer is especially used internally in the context of depth testing when 3D objects are rendered.

The accumulation buffer: This buffer is similar to the color buffer and provides color data. It can be also used to produce new images from a series of input images. Therefore, it can be used for scene anti-aliasing.

The stencil buffer: This buffer can be used for several advanced tasks, such as shadows.

Double Buffering

With OpenGL, you will use double buffering most of the time. Fortunately, this aspect is not a concern if you also use the QGLWidget from Qt, because there, double buffering is the default setting. A more detailed explanation of double buffering can be found in Chapter 6, "Canvas Games."

Camera

In normal windowing applications, the visible area is defined by the size of the window. You can draw and see elements inside the rectangle from (0,0) to (width, height) only. Such fixed coordinates are not the normal situation in OpenGL; instead, objects are drawn into a virtual coordinate system at any position you desire. A certain part of this coordinate system is hereby marked as the *view frustum*; that is, the visible area. The actual view frustum is defined by the projection settings, which define the size and form of the frustum. In OpenGL, this is what we think of as the *game camera*. However, we only imagine this is the camera because OpenGL does not use a *camera position* or any *camera* concept at all. Instead of changing the camera position, OpenGL requires that all objects be moved in the opposite direction than the camera would move.

Nevertheless, from the programmer's point of view, the concept of a camera often makes sense. In fact, most games use some type of camera class that specifies where the player currently is and what he is looking at. Placing the camera in the correct position can be tricky, but there is some support by GLU that helps with this task. We will focus on this aspect later.

State Machines

OpenGL is designed as a *state machine*, but what does this mean? It may sound like something "big," but it just means that it maintains many different states, and during the program run these states can be modified. All of these states have a predefined initial value when first starting an OpenGL program. These predefined values are documented on either the corresponding manual or on the actual OpenGL specification, which you can find on the Web site [OpenGL05].

Here is an example:

```
// Set (R,G,B) color state
glColor3ub(255, 0, 0);

glBegin(GL_POINTS);
  // Draw two points in the current color (red)
  glVertex2i(10, 10);
  glVertex2i(20, 10);

  // Change the current color state to blue
  glColor3ub(0, 0, 255);

  // Draw one point in the current color (blue)
  glVertex2i(30, 10);
glEnd();
```

This example first sets the current color state, which in this case is red. After that, it draws three points with the current color. It is not necessary to specify the color for every new point. Everything you draw after the glColor3ub(255, 0, 0) call is drawn with the current color until it is changed.

This scheme of changing the states instead of setting the value every time is used throughout OpenGL, also for the texture currently in use and for the normal vector. Once the principle of this mechanism is understood, it becomes an irreplaceable tool. State values have only to be set once, and additionally, the current states of certain attributes can be saved using glPushAttrib(mask) and restored later using glPopAttrib().

glPushAttrib() takes a parameter that indicates what kinds of states should be saved. Possible values of that parameter include:

GL_CURRENT_BIT: Current color, texture coordinates, and a few other things.

GL_DEPTH_BUFFER_BIT: Depth buffer related states.

GL_ENABLE_BIT: States of possible glEnable() parameters.

GL_LIGHTING_BIT: States related to lighting.

These values can be ORed together so you can save multiple types of states with one call. Additionally, there is a GL_ALL_ATTRIB_BITS, which saves all possible states at once.

The call to glPushAttrib() saves the specified states onto a stack, but does not modify any states. glPopAttrib(), on the other hand, removes the top of the stack and restores the states. Note that you must always have exactly as many glPopAttrib() calls as glPushAttrib() calls. The following snippet is an example on how to use them:

```
// Change the current color to red
glColor3ub(255, 0, 0);

// Save the states in GL_CURRENT_BIT, including the current
// color (red)
glPushAttrib(GL_CURRENT_BIT);

// Change the current color to blue
glColor3ub(0, 0, 255);

// Save all states, including the current color (blue)
glPushAttrib(GL_ALL_ATTRIB_BITS);

// Change the current color to green
glColor3ub(0, 255, 0);

// Draw a green object
renderObject();

// Restore the top of the attrib stack this restores the
// second glPushAttrib() call - the one that used
// GL_ALL_ATTRIB_BITS. The current color becomes blue again
glPopAttrib();

// Draw a blue object
renderObject();
```

```
// This restores the first glPushAttrib() call - the one that
// used GL_CURRENT_BIT. The current color becomes red again
glPopAttrib();

// Draws a red object
renderObject();
```

The combination of `glPushAttrib()` and `glPopAttrib()` allows the states to be changed without having to keep track of them, which is demonstrated in the following example:

```
void renderObjects()
{
  renderObject1();

  // Store lighting attributes
  glPushAttrib(GL_LIGHTING_BIT);

  // The following object needs to be rendered with lighting
  // disabled (for example status text on the screen)
  glDisable(GL_LIGHTING);
  renderObject2();

  // All following objects need lighting enabled again
  // without glPush/PopAttrib(), you would need to keep track
  // of whether lighting is enabled here, or whether the user
  //disabled it for performance
  glPopAttrib();

  renderAllOtherObjects();
}
```

Function Naming Scheme

In the previous section, we encountered a few OpenGL functions, such as `glColor3ub()` and `glVertex2i()`. We will now discuss the meaning behind the various parts of the names, such as `gl`, `Color`, `Vertex`, `3ub`, or `2i`.

OpenGL uses a clearly defined naming scheme. All functions start with `gl`, and all following words are capitalized as shown in the function `glPushAttrib()`. These words describe the actual use of the function or method, such as setting the color (`glColor3ub()`) or the vertex (`glVertex2i()`). This naming scheme is similar to that of Qt/KDE described in Chapters 3 through 5.

Some functions, like glColor*() and glVertex*(), provide several versions of the same basic function that cover different parameters. These functions include the type and number of the parameters in their name. glColor3ub() incorporates three parameters that are unsigned bytes; in contrast, glVertex2i() uses just two parameters, and these are integer values. Table 7.1 lists the possible types of parameters. For portability reasons, OpenGL provides symbol names for the data types (GLfloat instead of float, GLint instead of int, and so forth). Usually, it is practical to use these names instead of the normal C/C++ names. In this book, we have followed other literature, and when glColor*() is written it implies that any of the glColor versions could be used.

TABLE 7.1 OpenGL Parameter Types

Suffix	Parameter Type	OpenGL Type Name
b	8-bit signed integer	GLbyte
ub	8-bit unsigned integer	GLubyte
i	32-bit signed integer	GLint
ui	32-bit unsigned integer	GLuint
s	16-bit signed integer	GLshort
us	16-bit unsigned integer	GLushort
f	32-bit float	GLfloat
d	64-bit float	GLdouble

Many OpenGL functions provide a v suffix in addition to the number and type labels, and this extra suffix indicates an array type of the parameter. Thus, glColor3ubv() takes an array of three GLubyte values, not three separate GLubyte values. These array types are equal to the nonarray type notations of the functions but are sometimes slightly faster.

```
// Array of three GLubyte
GLubyte color[3];
color[0] = 255;
color[1] = 0;
color[2] = 0;
// Change the color state using an GLubyte array as arguments
glColor3ubv(color);
```

This is equivalent to

```
glColor3ub(255, 0, 0);
```

Except for the 2D rendering section, where we will use the *i() versions, we will use the *f() version of the functions. For colors, the glColor3ub() version is mainly used.

Creating OpenGL Widgets with Qt

So far, we have only focused on the very basic principles of OpenGL. Before we can actually have an application that displays something on a screen, we need to open a window. This task is very system-dependent, and OpenGL does not provide the necessary functions. Therefore, you need to use functions of the windowing system or windowing toolkit. One possible choice of a windowing toolkit is glut [Glut05], which is simple and portable. However, since this book focuses mainly on Qt, we will use Qt, which is an equally good choice.

```
int main(int argc, char** argv)
{
  // Create a Qt application
  QApplication app(argc, argv);
  // Create a new OpenGL Qt window
  QGLWidget* gl = new QGLWidget(0);

  ...

  app.setMainWidget(gl);
  gl->show();
  return app.exec();
}
```

Similar to the examples showing an application set up with Qt in Chapters 3 through 5, it is very easy to open an OpenGL widget with Qt. Remember, the Qt installation has to be configured so that OpenGL is enabled. If OpenGL is not enabled, check out the Qt compilation documentation for more information [Qt05].

To benefit from OpenGL functions, you have to subclass QGLWidget and then implement some basic methods.

```
class MyGLWidget : public QGLWidget
{
  Q_OBJECT
```

```
public:
  MyGLWidget(QWidget* parent = 0)
            : QGLWidget(parent)
  {
  }

protected:
  // Initialize OpenGL. this is called automatically by Qt
  virtual void initializeGL()
  {
    // Insert your initializing code here

    // glClear() clears to white background
    glClearColor(1.0, 1.0, 1.0, 0.0);

    // Dithering is usually not needed
    glDisable(GL_DITHER);
  }

  // Called automatically by Qt when the widget is resized
  virtual void resizeGL(int width, int height)
  {
    // Insert resizing code here

    // Make use of the whole widget
    glViewport(0, 0, width, height);

    // Set up a 3D projection matrix. See Projection settings
    // of the 3D rendering section
    glMatrixMode(GL_PROJECTION);
    glLoadIdentity();
    gluPerspective(60.0, ((GLdouble)width) / ((GLdouble)height),
                   0.0625, 512.0);
    glMatrixMode(GL_MODELVIEW);
  }

  // Called automatically by Qt on paint events. Use the slot
  // updateGL() to call update the view manually
  virtual void paintGL()
  {
    // Insert code to render the scene here

    // Reset the modelview matrix
    glLoadIdentity();
```

```
        // Clear the color buffer (contents of the window) and the
        // depth buffer (z-values)
        glClear(GL_COLOR_BUFFER_BIT | GL_DEPTH_BUFFER_BIT);

        // Draw the following objects in red
        glColor3f(1.0, 0.0, 0.0);

        // Draw a triangle
        glBegin(GL_TRIANGLE);
          glVertex3f(0.0, 0.0, -2.0);
          glVertex3f(0.0, 1.0, -2.0);
          glVertex3f(1.0, 1.0, -2.0);
        glEnd();
    }
};


int main(int argc, char** argv)
{
  QApplication app(argc, argv);
  MyGLWidget* gl = new MyGLWidget(0);
  app.setMainWidget(gl);
  gl->show();
  return app.exec();
}
```

The only thing to do in this derived class is to implement `initializeGL()`, `resizeGL()`, and `paintGL()`. A large portion of the code will go to `paintGL()`, which is automatically called by Qt when appropriate; that is, when paint events occur. In case you want to render a frame automatically, you should use the `updateGL()` slot, which calls `paintGL()` and manages tasks such as swapping the buffer (double buffering) and so on. Note that you should not use OpenGL commands in the constructor of `MyGLWidget` to set things up, but rather in the `initializeGL()` method.

The example contains some OpenGL commands, and most are discussed in detail later in this chapter. However, some of them are only required to get the application running and therefore do not need any further discussion.

```
void glClearColor(GLclampf red, GLclampf green,
                  GLclampf blue, GLclampf alpha):
void glClear(GLbitfield buffers);
```

The command `glClearColor()` obtains four float values in the range [0..1] specifying the color. The command `glClear()` clears the specified buffers, which are usually the color and depth buffers. This command is required once per frame at the beginning. The command `glDisable(GL_DITHER)` simply disables dithering, which is enabled in OpenGL by default. Dithering is rarely used in games these days, and therefore we do not cover it in this book. `glViewport(0, 0, width, height)` tells OpenGL that the *viewport* starts at the window coordinates (0,0) and has a size of (`width`, `height`). This aspect of OpenGL is also not discussed any further in this book.

Compiling OpenGL Programs

To compile an OpenGL program, you need to include the files `GL/gl.h` and `GL/glu.h` besides the normal header files into your program. Assuming a standard OpenGL installation, this is performed as described here:

```
#include "myglwidget.h"

#include <GL/gl.h>
#include <GL/glu.h>
// ...
```

For a normal OpenGL installation, you then need to make sure the program is linked against the GL and GLU libraries. If you use `qmake`, this is done by using

```
CONFIG+=opengl
```

in your project file. In an `automake/autoconf` or KDE environment, the line

```
myapp_LDADD=-lGL -lGLU
```

can be used instead.

COORDINATE SYSTEMS

A 3D graphics library like OpenGL requires a 3D coordinate system. In 3D programming, there are usually many performed tasks (such as rotations) that rarely occur in normal 2D GUI development. Therefore, OpenGL provides a way to specify the coordinates of the graphic objects, and a way to influence, and transform them. A basic understanding of how the OpenGL coordinate system works is an important ingredient for developing OpenGL based programs.

The y-Coordinate

Normal window-based applications usually use a normal 2D Cartesian coordinate system, with the origin (0,0) being top left and (`maxwidth`, `maxheight`) being bottom right (see Figure 7.1 (left)). OpenGL uses the mathematical representation with the origin (0,0) at the lower left corner (assuming there are no negative values). Therefore, the y coordinate is flipped (see Figure 7.1 (right)).

Of course, this difference between the coordinates used by windowing toolkits such as Qt and those used by OpenGL can cause some problems, especially when you need to find out the location of the mouse. `QCursor::pos()` provides the location of the cursor in Qt or X11 coordinates only. Fortunately, it is easy to convert one notation into the other by doing

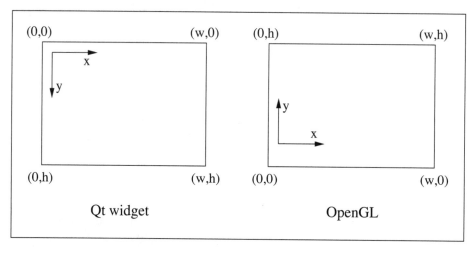

FIGURE 7.1 2D coordinate systems as used in Qt or X11 windows (left) and in OpenGL (right).

```
// maxHeight: Maximum window size in y direction
// givenY: The y value to be converted, e.g. the mouse
//         coordinate
int y = maxHeight - givenY;
```

Transformations such as these are preferably done at the beginning of a method. From then on, the coordinates can be used as usual.

```
void MyGLWidget::mousePressEvent(QMouseEvent* e)
{
    int x = e->pos().x();
```

```
    int y = height() - e->pos().y();
    // from now on you can use x and y
    ...
}
```

Note that this *only* converts the *y*-coordinate to a different coordinate system; it does not apply any active transformations.

Object Coordinates and Modelview Matrix

When going from 2D to 3D, a third axis, the *z*-axis, is required. Instead of using (*x,y*) coordinates, (*x,y,z*) coordinates are used to describe a point in 3D space. Note, however, that this *z*-value is actually a part of the coordinate and is only slightly related to the *z*-order value used for 2D canvas application as described in Chapter 6. Figure 7.2 depicts such a true 3D coordinate system.

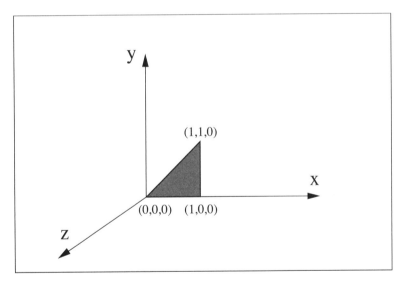

FIGURE 7.2 3D coordinate systems depicting a triangle.

Objects can be at any place in this coordinate system. This includes negative values for each of *x,y,z*. However, parts of the graphics outside the window's coordinates are not rendered on the screen.

To draw objects into the scene (or the coordinate system), the coordinates of an object have to be specified. One method to do this would be to provide absolute coordinates. However, this is not very convenient because these are more difficult to change when the objects move. Imagine that you want to draw a simple triangle in 3D space. You would obviously require three points—for example, (0,0,0), (1,0,0),

(1,1,0)—as shown in Figure 7.2. In the next frame, you want to move the triangle to a different position, as shown in Figure 7.3. When using absolute coordinates, you have to provide all of the new coordinates; that is, you have to duplicate the code, just for a single new position of a single triangle. It is easy to see that absolute coordinates are not practical when it comes to more complex objects, such as a player model in a first-person shooter.

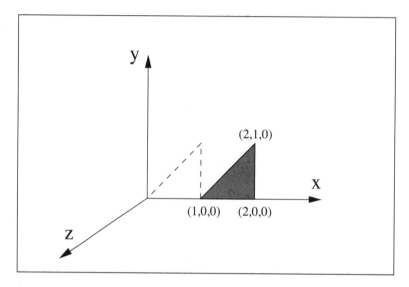

FIGURE 7.3 3D coordinate systems with the triangle from Figure 7.2 that has been moved by (1,0,0).

Therefore, it is more practical to provide a "current position" parameter when drawing the triangle; that is, to use relative coordinates. One way to think of this is that we first "move" the entire coordinate system to that position and then render the triangle (0,0,0), (1,0,0), (1,1,0) with exactly the same (relative) coordinates as before.

The OpenGL *modelview* matrix provides such a "current position" feature. In addition, it provides a "current direction"; that is, the rotation of the coordinate system and a "current scaling." In general, this matrix describes all modifications or transformations that have been made to the coordinate system in which the triangle is being rendered. The modelview matrix, just like most values in OpenGL, is a state, so it only changes when you modify it.

Initially, the current position (0,0,0) is in the center of the screen, and you are looking down the negative z-axis. When a triangle is drawn, it is drawn relative to the current position and is therefore relative to the center of the screen.

In the following section, we use a function termed `renderTriangle()`, which draws a triangle around the current position. Later in this chapter, we present the details on how to implement such a function.

Translations and `glTranslatef()`

To move the triangle away from the center of the screen without modifying the code of `renderTriangle()`, you can use translations. A call to `glTranslatef(dx,dy,dz)` will move the current position where the object is rendered (*not* the position of the camera) by `dx` on the *x*-axis, `dy` on the *y*-axis, and by `dz` on the *z*-axis. For example, a call to `glTranslate(1,2,0)` moves all objects that are rendered from this point on by (1,2,0). In the case of `renderTriangle()`, see Figure 7.4.

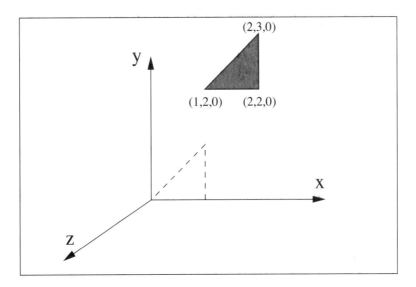

FIGURE 7.4 Coordinate system with the triangle from Figure 7.2 that was rendered after the call to `glTranslatef(1, 2, 0)`.

`glTranslatef()`, like all transformation calls, only modifies the current position; thus, it is accumulative.

```
// Translate the objects by three individual translations
glTranslatef(1, 0, 0);
glTranslatef(5, 0, 0);
glTranslatef(0, 3, 0);
renderTriangle();
```

is equal to

```
// Translate the object in one go
glTranslatef(6, 3, 0);
renderTriangle();
```

And

```
glTranslatef(dx, dy, dz);
glTranslatef(-dx, -dy, -dz);
renderTriangle();
```

is equal to

```
renderTriangle();
```

that is, not calling `glTranslatef()` at all.

Translations only apply to objects that were rendered after the transformation was executed. This may sound obvious, but it is a common mistake to believe that you can change the camera position using `glTranslatef()` calls because OpenGL does not have an actual "camera." The principle is not to first render your objects and then move the camera, but to only change the positions of the objects. This is also why it is sometimes useful to think the other way round. For example, if you want to move the camera position five units to the right, you would instead move all objects five units to the left.

Rotations and `glRotatef()`

3D games become truly interesting if rotations are used. By rotating the graphics, games can be created in which a player can walk through a game world in arbitrary directions.

All rotations also apply to the current position/direction, or in other words, the modelview matrix. In OpenGL, rotations are made using `glRotatef(angle,x,y,z)`. Here, `angle` is the angle (in degrees, not radians) you want to rotate by, and (x,y,z) is the axis you want to rotate around. The axis is described as the vector (x,y,z) and is an extended line from $(0,0,0)$ through (x,y,z). Using this notation, $(1,0,0)$ specifies the x-axis, $(0,1,0)$ the y-axis, and $(0,0,1)$ the z-axis. Rotations are usually done around these three axes, but sometimes it can be beneficial to use an arbitrary rotation axis.

The following example will rotate the rendered triangle by 45 degrees around the current z-axis.

```
glRotatef(45, 0, 0, 1);
renderTriangle()
```

This rotation is also depicted in Figure 7.5.

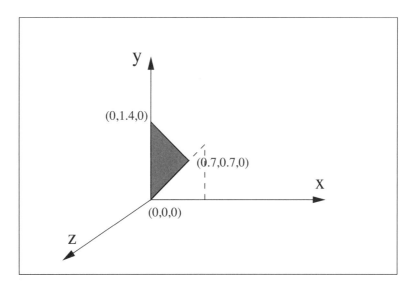

FIGURE 7.5 Coordinate system with the triangle from Figure 7.2 that was rendered after a call to `glRotatef(45, 0, 0, 1)`. Therefore, the original triangle is rotated by 45 degrees around the *z*-axis.

When applying such transformations, it is important to remember that OpenGL is a state machine and therefore always possesses a current position and direction. The direction, however, will be changed by rotations, and consequently, the axes used for rendering objects also change. Figure 7.6 depicts the new coordinate system axis after a 45-degree rotation around the z-axis. A call to `glRotatef(angle, 1, 0, 0)` to rotate around the x-axis will therefore not rotate around the "old" x-axis, but around the new one as depicted in Figure 7.7.

The order of command is important if rotations are involved. The outcome will differ if the command pattern follows first rotate and then translate, or vice versa. The following example and Figures 7.8 and 7.9 depict these two possibilities.

```
glRotatef(90, 0, 0, 1);
// Translation on the x-axis which is the old y-axis
glTranslatef(1, 0, 0);
renderTriangle();
```

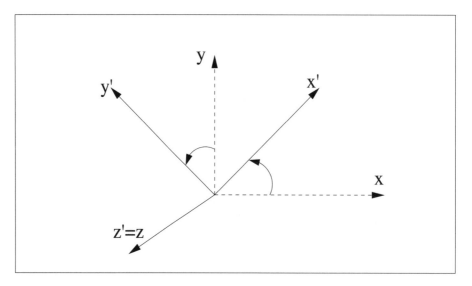

FIGURE 7.6 Coordinate system that is used for subsequent OpenGL commands after a call to glRotatef(45, 0, 0, 1). Note that the z-axis remains the same, because the rotation was made around this axis.

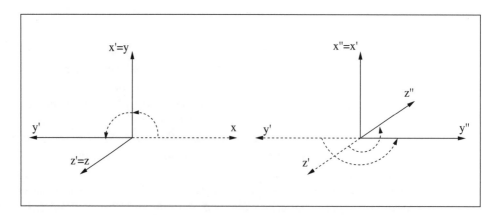

FIGURE 7.7 The effects after first rotating by 90 degrees around the z-axis (left) and then by 180 degrees around the x-axis (right). Note that the second rotation is made around the new x-axis, which is denoted x'.

The preceding code demonstrates the situation in Figure 7.8, whereas

```
// Translation on the x-axis
glTranslatef(1, 0, 0);
glRotatef(90, 0, 0, 1);
renderTriangle();
```

shows the situation presented in Figure 7.9.

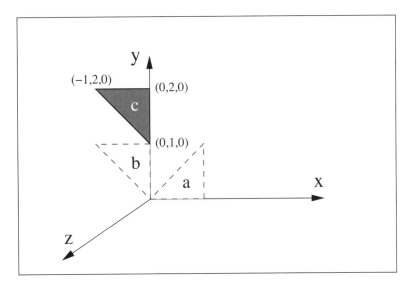

FIGURE 7.8 (a) Marks the original image without precedent rotations. (b) Marks the same triangle, but a call to `glRotatef(90, 0, 0, 1)` was made before rendering it. (c) Depicts the triangle after first rotating and then translating it by (1,0,0).

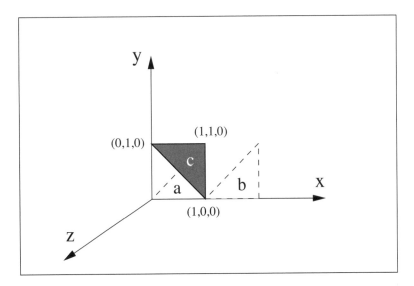

FIGURE 7.9 (a) Marks the original triangle without precedent rotations. (b) Marks the same triangle, but a call to `glTranslate(1, 0, 0)` was made before rendering it. (c) Depicts the triangle after first translating and then rotating by 90 degrees around the z-axis.

Rotations should not be undone by performing a rotation in the opposite direction. Although this might occasionally work, it can also give surprising results due to internal OpenGL rounding errors or a gimbal lock. Therefore, rotations can only be undone by saving the previous state and restoring it afterward using glPushMatrix() *and* glPopMatrix().

Scaling and glScalef()

Scaling objects is achieved in the same manner as all other transformations. glScalef(sx, sy, sz) will apply scaling factors to the three axes. To avoid distortions, the same scaling factors have to be applied in all directions; that is, sx=sy=sz. When a distortion is desired, these values can be set independently. To keep the size of the objects in one axis unchanged, "1" is given as the scaling parameter. Providing a scale factor of "2" will make the objects twice as large, and a scale factor of "0.5" will half the current size. Of course, "0" is an invalid value for these parameters.

As with translations and rotations, the current scaling factors influence all coordinates used from that point on. Therefore,

```
glScalef(0.5, 0.5, 0.5);
glTranslatef(10, 10, 10);
```

is equal to

```
glTranslatef(5, 5, 5);
glScalef(0.5, 0.5, 0.5);
```

Undo Transformations

The modelview matrix needs to be reset at least once per frame to always have a defined starting point for drawing. This means that the current rendering position, direction, and scaling factors are readjusted to their initial values. This is done by the statement glLoadIdentity(), which sets the modelview matrix to the identity matrix (the "1" of matrices). This is usually one of the first statements when rendering a frame.

OpenGL Matrices

As mentioned earlier, in OpenGL the current rendering position, direction, and scaling factors are stored as the modelview matrix. All the calls to glTranslatef(), glRotatef(), and glScalef() will modify that matrix. Additionally, you can do your own modifications to the matrix with glMultMatrixf(), which multiplies the current matrix by any other given matrix.

Sometimes, it is useful to retrieve the current modelview matrix from OpenGL. This is done with this code:

```
// Space for a 4x4 matrix
GLfloat matrix[16];
glGetFloatv(GL_MODELVIEW_MATRIX, matrix);
```

OpenGL stores the modelview matrix as a 4x4 matrix. The matrix is in contrast to the usual mathematical matrix notations transposed. The matrix

$$\begin{pmatrix} a_{11} & a_{12} & a_{13} & a_{14} \\ a_{21} & a_{22} & a_{23} & a_{24} \\ a_{31} & a_{32} & a_{33} & a_{34} \\ a_{41} & a_{42} & a_{43} & a_{44} \end{pmatrix}$$

is stored in the memory in the order $a_{11}, a_{21}, a_{31}, a_{41}, a_{12}$, and so on.

This storage is the opposite order of Direct3D, which uses the usual mathematical notation. For more details on matrices and the use of four coordinates in 3D applications, see Chapter 13, "Math and Physics in Desktop Games."

Introducing a "Camera" Using GLU

All of these transformations only change the current rendering position, direction, or scaling, not the camera position and direction. Even though OpenGL has no camera concept, since all objects are moved, it often makes sense to think of the camera concept instead. Consider the situation in which you have a cube with the center at (0,0,0) and you want to see the right side of the cube from a distance of 10. By default, the "camera" in OpenGL is located at (0,0,0) and you are looking down the negative z-axis. To achieve the desired view, you could translate the cube by (0,0,–10) and then rotate it so the right side is visible.

However, this would not be very intuitive. Preferably, one would actually use some type of camera settings here, which can be imitated using the following GLU function:

```
void gluLookAt(GLdouble cameraX,
               GLdouble cameraY,
               GLdouble cameraZ,
               GLdouble lookAtX,
               GLdouble lookAtY,
               GLdouble lookAtZ,
               GLdouble upX,
```

```
                       GLdouble upY,
                       GLdouble upZ)
```

The parameters cameraX, cameraY, and cameraZ specify the desired camera position; in our example, this would be (10,0,0). lookAtX, lookAtY, and lookAtZ specify
the location the camera should look at, which in this case is where the cube is
(0,0,0). The parameters upX, upY, and upZ dictate the up vector; that is, the direction
where "up" is. In our case, this is the same as the initial values (0,1,0).

The call to gluLookAt() needs to be made before rendering the objects, since
this ensures that all objects are moved and displayed in the desired way.

```
void MyGLWidget::paintGL()
{
  glClear(GL_COLOR_BUFFER_BIT | GL_DEPTH_BUFFER_BIT);

  // Reset the modelview matrix (gluLookAt() modifies this)
  glLoadIdentity();

  // Position the camera at (10, 0, 0) looking at the origin
  gluLookAt(10, 0, 0,
            0, 0, 0,
            0, 1, 0);

  // Now render all objects as usual
  drawCube();

  ...
}
```

2D RENDERING

After discussing the general setup of OpenGL, we can now continue with some
actual rendering. We will begin with 2D rendering, which is used in 2D and sometimes in 3D games. Here, 2D rendering can be used for:

- Startup widgets such as a New Game dialog
- Configuration dialogs
- Status texts such as health, weapon power, or money
- Mini-maps
- Menu bars

To render items, you usually render every frame in at least two passes: first, you render your 3D scene, and then you switch to 2D rendering and draw all of your 2D elements.

Projection Settings

The main task in setting up OpenGL for 2D rendering is to request the correct projection settings. The projection settings tell OpenGL how it should draw the objects that you will render from this point on onto the screen. In 2D mode, these projections are very simple, as OpenGL only needs to know which object coordinates it should consider "visible." This is usually the rectangle defined by the points (0,0) and (w,h), where w is the width and h the height of the display window. In a Qt QGLWidget, this is just its width() and height(). All objects outside this rectangle are not drawn. Additionally the range of z-values that should be drawn needs to be provided. In 2D mode, usually all objects are rendered with z=0.0; therefore, this is the only value that needs to be visible.

The GLU function gluOrtho2D(GLdouble left, GLdouble right, GLdouble bottom, GLdouble top) sets up this 2D projection. It does not take any values for the z-coordinate, but automatically ensures that z=0.0 is a visible value for z. More information about GLU is provided later in this chapter.

gluOrtho2D() does the same as the OpenGL function glOrtho(), but takes no "near" and "far" values; that is, minimal and maximal distance from the viewpoint. gluOrtho2D() assumes near=-1 and far=1, which is perfectly fine for us. For further information on near and far, see the section "Projection Settings." In the following, we will focus on gluOrtho2D().

Calls to gluOrtho2D() should only be added after the current matrix is changed to the projection matrix. This projection matrix is similar to the modelview matrix, but is meant to be used exclusively for projection settings; therefore, the gluOrtho2D() call should only occur there.

```
// Tell OpenGL that we want to modify the projection matrix
glMatrixMode(GL_PROJECTION);

// Reset any previous modifications of this matrix
glLoadIdentity();

// Set a 2D projection
gluOrtho2D(0.0, (GLdouble)width(), 0.0, (GLdouble)height());

// Everything else should go to the normal modelview matrix
glMatrixMode(GL_MODELVIEW);
```

Usually, this code should be placed where the frame is rendered; that is, into `MyGLWidget::paintGL()`. However, if you know that your game does not change the matrix mode within a frame, which is often the case for 2D games, it can also be placed into `MyGLWidget::resizeGL()`. This slightly increases the performance because the projection matrix is kept constant.

Drawing Simple Objects

All complex objects in OpenGL are drawn by splitting them into simple objects, such as triangles, rectangles, lines, or points. Therefore, your OpenGL program will usually be composed by drawing one or more of these simple objects.

Any object is drawn by calling `glBegin(GLenum mode)` with the desired object type as mode parameter (see the following list). After that, `glVertex*()` is used to specify the points that define the object. After `glBegin()`, an arbitrary amount of drawing calls can be made. Once the drawing is complete, `glEnd()` is called and tells OpenGL that all vertices are now complete. These `glBegin()`-`glEnd()` sequences can be repeated and with other mode parameters as well.

The mode parameter can be one of the following values:

- **GL_TRIANGLES:** three vertices per object
- **GL_QUADS:** four vertices per object
- **GL_LINES:** two vertices per object
- **GL_POINTS:** one vertex per object
- **GL_POLYGON:** n vertices per object

Some additional modes behave in slightly different manners to the ones listed, and will be discussed when relevant.

It is interesting to note that you can compose all polygons and even circles using triangles, and this is exactly what happens. For example, a point can be drawn using a very small triangle. Therefore, it can no longer be distinguished whether the object is actually a "point" or a "triangle." This fact is actually the development basis of modern graphics cards, which are heavily optimized for drawing triangles. However, it is not a good idea to replace points or lines by triangles manually. Draw points and lines and leave the conversion to triangles to OpenGL and your graphics card. Polygons are the only aspect that might benefit from manually replacing them with triangles.

When doing 2D rendering, you will most probably use the 2i version of `glVertex*()`, `glVertex2i()`, as you do not need the z-coordinate and there are no half pixels.

```
glBegin(GL_QUADS);
  // Draw first rectangle by given its corner points
  glVertex2i(0, 0);      // bottom left
  glVertex2i(0, 100);    // bottom right
  glVertex2i(100, 100);  // top right
  glVertex2i(100, 0);    // top left

  // Draw second rectangle by given its corner points
  glVertex2i(150, 150);  // bottom left
  glVertex2i(150, 250);  // bottom right
  glVertex2i(250, 250);  // top right
  glVertex2i(250, 150);  // top left
glEnd();
```

This example draws two rectangles by defining their corner points. Inside a glBegin()/glEnd() pair, you can call all "normal" functions or methods from normal C/C++, Qt, or any other library. However, you are limited in the use of OpenGL functions. Most OpenGL functions must not be called between glBegin()/ glEnd() but there are a few exceptions:

- glVertex*()
- glTexCoord*()
- glColor*()
- glNormal*()
- glMaterial*()
- glArrayElement()
- glMultiTexCoord*ARB()
- glEdgeFlag*()
- glCallList()
- glCallLists()
- glEvalCoord()
- glIndex()

All other OpenGL commands are invalid between a glBegin() and its corresponding glEnd() call. Actually, it is usually a good idea to do as little as possible between a glBegin()/glEnd() pair. If possible, you should move most code before the glBegin() call, because all OpenGL data after glBegin() needs to be sent to the graphics card, which should occur as fast as possible.

By default, the objects (polygons) you draw are filled with the current color (see the next section). However, sometimes it is handy to change this behavior so only the edges of the objects are drawn. glPolygonMode(GL_FRONT_AND_BACK, mode) controls this and uses GL_FILL (fill the polygon, the default), GL_LINES (draw only the edges), or GL_POINTS (draw only the vertices).

Colors

Being able to render polygons in different colors is an important and useful task. The OpenGL command glColor*() does exactly this, and there are many versions of this command, including glColor3ub(), glColor3f(), glColor4ub(), and glColor4f(). glColor3*() takes three arguments, representing the amount of red, green, and blue of the desired color. glColor3ub() takes values 0..255 just like the QColor class of Qt. glColor3f() takes float values from 0.0 to 1.0, where 0.0 equals 0 in the ub version, and 1.0 equals 255 in the ub version.

glColor4*() additionally takes a parameter for the alpha component of the color. The alpha value is similar to the one mentioned in the Chapter 6. We discuss this further in the section "Blending." Here, we focus on the glColor3*() versions.

Qt also provides a few convenience methods that allow the use of Qt classes and Qt constants for setting the color. They are described in more detail in Chapter 8, "OpenGL with Qt."

Since the color is a state in OpenGL, it can be easily changed.

```
glColor3ub(0, 0, 0); // black

// Draw 2 black points
glBegin(GL_POINTS);
  glVertex2i(10, 10);
  glVertex2i(10, 20);
glEnd();

// The following line is redundant, because the current color
// will be replaced by the next command. No drawing command
// will use this color
glColor3ub(0, 0, 255); // green - not used
glColor3ub(255, 0, 0); // red   - replaces the green color

// Draw 1 red triangle and 1 blue triangle
glBegin(GL_TRIANGLES);
  glVertex2i(30, 0);
  glVertex2i(30, 10);
  glVertex2i(50, 10);

  glColor3ub(0, 0, 255); // blue
  glVertex2i(50, 0);
  glVertex2i(50, 10);
```

```
  glVertex2i(70, 10);
glEnd();
```

Shade Model

All of the previous examples used only a single color per polygon, and therefore the entire polygon was rendered in one color, a process called *flat shading*. You can enforce this behavior by setting the shading model state to GL_FLAT, using glShade-Model(GL_FLAT). Once set, the entire polygon is the color that was current when the last vertex of one polygon was specified.

```
glShadeModel(GL_FLAT);
glBegin(GL_TRIANGLES);
  glColor3ub(255, 0, 0);
  glVertex2i(0, 0);
  glColor3ub(0, 255, 0);
  glVertex2i(10, 0);
  glColor3ub(0, 0, 255);
  glVertex2i(10, 10); // last vertex of the 1st triangle

  glVertex2i(100, 0);
  glVertex2i(110, 0);
  glColor3ub(255, 0, 0);
  glVertex2i(110, 10); // last vertex of the 2nd triangle
glEnd();
```

The first triangle is rendered in blue, and the second triangle is drawn in red, as red was the current color when the last vertex of the triangle was specified.

Sometimes, flat shading is useful because it is slightly faster than other shadings. However, smooth shading, also called *gouraud* shading, is more appropriate, especially for game programmers. When using smooth shading, the actual color of a point inside a polygon is interpolated from the colors specified at the vertices of that polygon. If you change to flat shading at some point, you need to set the shade model state back to the default smooth shading GL_SMOOTH. One example:

```
glShadeModel(GL_SMOOTH);
glBegin(GL_TRIANGLES);
  glColor3ub(255, 0, 0); // red
  glVertex2i(10, 10);
  glColor3ub(0, 255, 0); // green
  glVertex2i(50, 10);
  glColor3ub(0, 0, 255); // blue
  glVertex2i(50, 50);
glEnd();
```

The color of the vertex (10, 10) will be 100% red and 0% blue and green. At (50, 10) there will be 100% green and 0% red and blue. On the edge between these two colors, the colors are interpolated from red to blue. The same happens with the vertex (50, 50).

Such behavior can be very helpful in most games and is demonstrated here:

```
float factor = ...; // a value 0..1
glPolygonMode(GL_SMOOTH);
glBegin(GL_QUADS);
  glColor3ub(255, 0, 0);
  glVertex2i(0, 0);
  glVertex2i(0, 20);

  glColor3ub(0, 255 * factor, 0);
  glVertex2i(100 * factor, 20);
  glVertex2i(100 * factor, 0);
glEnd();
```

The preceding example describes a horizontal bar with a gradient from red to green. Initially, f is 1.0, and the bar has a height of 20 and a width of 100. As f is reduced, the bar becomes narrower and simultaneously the green component of the rightmost side is reduced. This bar can now be used, for example, as the health indicator of a player, where the factor f is representing the health of the player. When the health is low, the bar will be mostly red, and green when the player has full health.

Note that this practical example can be applied directly to texture mapping as well—just exchange the glColor*() calls with glTexCoord*() calls.

Texture Mapping

A texture map is typically a 2D image that is mapped onto a polygon. OpenGL also supports the mapping of 1D and 3D textures, but they are not relevant to the type of desktop games we are developing in this book. Current graphics cards are heavily optimized for games, and thus the fast drawing of textured triangles or polygons. This is a very fortunate situation for game developers and becomes most obvious when using texture mapping. Games usually rely on the heavy use of textures; in fact, being able to quickly render textured triangles is a key criterion for a good graphics card.

When rendering a polygon using a glBegin()/glEnd() pair, you tell OpenGL which point of the texture image represents a vertex; the rest is done by OpenGL. Specifying texture coordinates is in many ways similar to specifying a color using glColor*(). However, most of the time, the texture coordinates differ for every vertex, whereas the color is often shared by all vertices.

Loading a Texture Image Using Qt

Before textures can be applied to OpenGL, they have to first be loaded into the memory. Although in principle, texture image files can be embedded in the code, this is usually inconvenient and will eventually limit the programming possibilities. However, OpenGL does not provide any functions for loading images and must be performed with other libraries. Consequently, we will use Qt to perform the loading, which provides a convenient way to load images compatible with OpenGL.

Note that there is a restriction to images: both width and height must be 2^n for any positive integer n. However, width and height can be different.

Textures are set up by first loading an image into the memory, and the following normal procedure of loading other Qt images. If you have the choice between QImage and QPixmap, choose the QImage class instead to avoid the slow conversion between a QPixmap to a QImage.

```
QImage qtImage("file.png");

// in case you already loaded the file into a QPixmap:
QPixmap pix = existingPixmap;
qtImage = pix.convertToImage();
```

OpenGL expects the image data to be in a special format. Therefore, QImages must be converted to this OpenGL format after loading them.

```
QImage image = QGLWidget::convertToGLFormat(qtImage);
```

Note that the resulting image object must *not* be used anymore as a parameter with other Qt methods. However width(), height() are still functional, and bits() can be used to retrieve the actual image data.

Qt allows the loading of images for all image formats (jpg, png, bmp, etc.) supported by the actual Qt installation. This might sound obvious, but in non-Qt environments, loading texture images often consumes a great deal of development time and code.

In the following section, we will assume that there is a QImage object named image that contains a loaded texture.

Texture Objects

After loading a texture image into the memory, you need to submit that image to OpenGL:

1. Generate an OpenGL texture object.
2. Bind that object.

3. Load the texture image data to the currently bound texture object.

From a practical point of view, a texture object is just an integer value that identifies a texture. First, you need to generate at least one texture object.

```
GLuint textureObject;
glGenTextures(1, &textureObject);
```

The first parameter to `glGenTextures()` specifies the number of texture objects you want to reserve IDs for. The second parameter takes an array providing space for at least that many IDs. This call just reserves an ID for a texture object; it does not do anything else. It does not make a big difference whether you call `glGenTextures()` 100 times with a count of one, or only once with a count of 100. Of course, calling it only once is faster, but since you need this call only once and only when initializing, this speed difference does not matter.

When you do not need the ID anymore, you can release it using `glDelete-Textures(GLsizei count, GLuint* textureObjects)`. These IDs will be available again.

After creating a texture object, you need to make it current, or in other words, bind it. All texturing commands apply to the current texture only, which is important to remember.

```
glBindTexture(GL_TEXTURE_2D, textureObject);
```

You can safely ignore the first parameter, as in games you will usually use 2D textures only.

Finally, you load the previously loaded image data into the texture object. There are many ways to do so, but with Qt, this is simple and does not require adjusting the parameters. The only small exception to this is included here:

```
QImage image;
// ... load the image
// ... resize the image, if its size was not 2^n * 2^m
// ... create a texture object, make it current.
int internalFormat;
if (useAlphaChannel)
{
  internalFormat = GL_RGBA;
}
else
{
  internalFormat = GL_RGB;
```

```
}
glTexImage2D(GL_TEXTURE_2D, 0, internalFormat, image.width(),
            image.height(), 0, GL_RGBA, GL_UNSIGNED_BYTE,
            image.bits());

// the next call is required because we do not use
// the mipmapping technique
glTexParameteri(GL_TEXTURE2D, GL_TEXTURE_MIN_FILTER, GL_LINEAR);
```

`glTexImage2D()` loads the texture into the currently bound texture object. As you can see, it has many parameters, but since we use Qt to load our images and we focus here on games, only a few are relevant to us. The full declaration of this function looks like:

```
glTexImage2D(GLenum target,
            GLint level,
            GLint internalFormat,
            GLsizei width,
            GLsizei height,
            GLint border,
            GLenum format,
            GLenum type,
            GLvoid* pixels);
```

target: Always `GL_TEXTURE_2D` for us. In desktop games, it is very unlikely that you will use something different.

level: Describes the mipmap level and is set here to the default level 0.

internalFormat: The format OpenGL uses internally to store the texture data. Many different types are supported, but in this book, we discuss `GL_RGB` and `GL_RGBA` only. You can safely use `GL_RGBA` always, but if you know in advance that you do not use the alpha value, you can employ `GL_RGB` instead and save some texture space.

width: The width of the texture. Just use `image.width()`.

height: The height of the texture. Just use `image.height()`.

border: Whether to use a texture border (1) or not (0). We do not cover texture borders in this book, so we always use 0.

type: Always `GL_RGBA`, as that is what `QGLWidget::convertToGLFormat()` produces. This parameter specifies the format of the pixels parameter.

pixels: The actual texture data. Always use `image.bits()` with Qt.

At this point, the texture image has been loaded and you can access it by binding the texture object.

In 2D mode, textures are particularly useful to display an image; for example a logo.

```
// In your initializing code (for example MyGLWidget::initGL())
// you should load texture image into a texture object named
// logoObject.
//In your rendering method (such as MyGLWidget::paintGL()):
...
glEnable(GL_TEXTURE_2D);
glBindTexture(GL_TEXTURE_2D, logoObject); // Do before glBegin()!
glBegin(GL_QUADS);
  glTexCoord2f(1.0, 1.0);
  glVertex2i(width(), height());

  glTexCoord2f(1.0, 0.0);
  glVertex2i(width(), height() - 100);

  glTexCoord2f(0.0, 0.0);
  glVertex2i(width() - 100, height() - 00);

  glTexCoord2f(0.0, 1.0);
  glVertex2i(width() - 100, height());
glEnd();
```

The preceding code displays a logo in the upper right corner of your GL widget. You can also learn from this example that the size of the object does not depend on the size of the actual texture image. Thus, you do not need to do any manual (and very slow) scaling on the texture image, since it is all done extremely quickly by the graphics card as no actual scaling is involved. Of course, the quality of the displayed logo depends on the size of the texture that was loaded. Do not expect a rectangle of size 100×100 to look good if you use a texture image that has a size of 32×32.

The glTexCoord2f() call in the previous example is a straightforward command and tells OpenGL that the following vertex should use the color that is located in the texture at the specified coordinates. It takes two float parameters, with $(0.0, 0.0)$ being the point $(0, 0)$ in the image, and $(1.0, 1.0)$ being the (width, height) in the image. Usually, it is a good idea to use the glTexCoord2f() or glTexCoord2fv() versions only, even though other versions of that function do exist.

3D RENDERING

Fortunately, most things learned in the section "2D Rendering" apply to 3D as well. In the following sections, we discuss the differences for real 3D programming. Generally, you just add another coordinate—the z-coordinate—to the vertices. OpenGL does not provide any functions to render complex 3D objects, such as boxes, cubes, or spheres. There are some functions in GLU to do such things, but most of the time you just use simple triangles and quads.

Before we can actually render some objects, we need to set up the view for 3D rendering.

Projection Settings

In 3D mode, objects are drawn geometrically correctly as you would view them in 3D space or reality. Objects farther away are smaller, whereas objects close up are larger. In addition, if objects are not in the center of your view, you can usually see the sides rather than the front of the objects. For example, when a box is in the center of the screen, only the front side of the box is visible, but when it is moved to the right, the left side of the box is visible as well (see Figure 7.10).

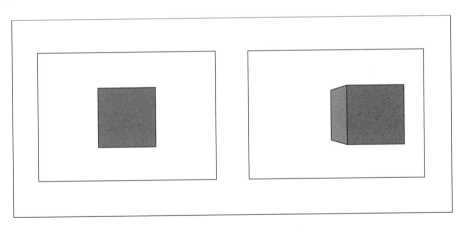

FIGURE 7.10 A box in the center of the screen looks like a rectangle (left image). When moved to the right, you can see the left side of the box as well (right image).

This type of projection is called *perspective projection*, as opposed to *orthographic projection* used for 2D mode.

An orthographic projection can be described by a normal box, or even a rectangle if you ignore the z-coordinates completely. This box can be placed anywhere in the coordinate system (the "world") and describes the contents of the screen. Everything outside this box is not visible.

In a perspective projection, the visible area is not described by a box but by a pyramid with no top, called a *frustum* (see Figure 7.11). OpenGL provides a command to initialize these perspectives, `glFrustum()`. However, this function is normally inconvenient, as the parameters are not so easy to retrieve. We therefore do not take a more detailed look at this function.

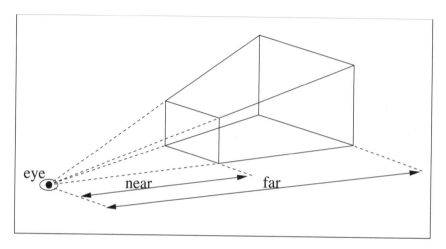

FIGURE 7.11   A view frustum (solid lines) with both the near and the far plane is displayed as part of a pyramid. The top of the pyramid (dashed lines) is not part of the view frustum.

The GLU library also provides a function to initialize a 3D view frustum.

```
void gluPerspective(GLdouble fovy, GLdouble aspect,
                    GLdouble near, GLdouble far);
```

The `fovy` parameter is the angle of the field of view in the *y*-direction. From a practical point of view, this means it specifies the size of the front and therefore also the back rectangles of the frustum, as depicted in Figure 7.12. Increasing the value of `fovy` has the effect of "zooming out," because a larger frustum has to be projected onto the same monitor. Conversely, a small `fovy` value has the effect of "zooming in." The `fovy` angle is specified in degrees and must be in the range of [0...180]. As an initial value, you can choose 60 degrees and experiment a bit for your situation.

The aspect parameter just specifies the aspect of the width/height ratio on the screen. Usually, you can simply use width/height.

The near and far values tell OpenGL what distance in the *z*-direction is "near" the eye and what distance is "far" away. Any object with a *z*-distance smaller than "near" is deleted, just as any object with a z-distance larger than "far." The correct values of "near" and "far" depend on your program. Usually, a small "near" value (e.g., 0.0625) and a large "far" value (e.g., 512.0) are good values. Note that an extremely small value for "near" and an extremely large value for "far" are possible, but not recommended. The distance between "near" and "far" is used to set a depth buffer, so if the distance is too high, the precision of the depth buffer suffers. Also note that "near" must be larger than 0.

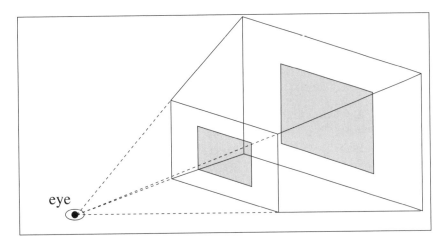

FIGURE 7.12 A view frustum with large `fovy` parameter. The filled inner rectangles depict how the frustum would look with smaller `fovy` parameters.

The following example demonstrates the use of `gluPerspective()`:

```
// Tell OpenGL that we want to modify the projection matrix
glMatrixMode(GL_PROJECTION);

// Reset any previous modifications of this matrix
glLoadIdentity();

// Set a 3D projection
gluPerspective(60.0, ((GLdouble)width())/((GLdouble)height()),
               0.0625, 512.0);

// Everything else should go to the normal modelview matrix
glMatrixMode(GL_MODELVIEW);
```

Drawing Simple 3D Objects

Drawing 3D objects works exactly as in 2D mode, with two exceptions. The first and most obvious exception is that the *z*-values can (and will) differ from 0, so we now need the `glVertex3*()` version of `glVertex*()`.

The second difference is, that instead of using the integer version of `glVertex3*()`, we now use the float version. This derives from the fact that in 2D rendering, we used the integer version only because the coordinates to `glVertex2i()` matched those of the pixels that were drawn on the screen. With a *z*-coordinate, this is not possible, so we use float values for the coordinates, which is more convenient.

The basic mode types for `glBegin()` are the same as for 2D rendering; here is the complete list:

- **GL_TRIANGLE:** three vertices per object
- **GL_QUADS:** four vertices per object
- **GL_LINES:** two vertices per object
- **GL_POINTS:** one vertex per object
- **GL_POLYGON:** *n* vertices per object
- **GL_LINE_STRIP:** *n* vertices for *n*−1 lines
- **GL_LINE_LOOP:** *n* vertices for *n* lines; the last line is connected with the first
- **GL_TRIANGLE_STRIP:** *n* vertices for *n*−2 triangles
- **GL_TRIANGLE_FAN:** *n* vertices for *n*−2 triangles
- **GL_QUAD_STRIP:** *n* vertices for *n*−3 quads

The _STRIP, _FAN, and _LOOP modes were not interesting for the way in which we applied 2D, but when rendering 3D objects, they are important since more polygons are involved. Most important are the line, triangle, and quad strips, which you can draw using GL_LINE_STRIP, GL_TRIANGLE_STRIP, or GL_QUAD_STRIP. They actually allow just lines, triangles, or quads to be drawn, which are interconnected by some of their points.

By using strips, consecutive items do not need to specify all vertices, because the last vertices of the previous item are reused. When drawing triangles, you would normally provide three vertices per triangle. However, with triangle strips you only need to provide the three vertices for the first triangle, since every subsequent triangle will use the last two vertices of the previous triangle as its first two vertices. Thus, you only need to provide one vertex per triangle, which means your program has to send 66% less data to the graphics card, significantly enhancing the rendering speed. Here is an example for when to use triangle strips:

```
glBegin(GL_TRIANGLE_STRIP);
  glVertex3f(0.0, 1.0, 0.0);
  glVertex3f(0.0, 2.0, 0.0);
```

```
glVertex3f(0.0, 3.0, 1.0); // end of 1st triangle
glVertex3f(1.0, 3.0, 1.0); // end of 2nd triangle
glVertex3f(5.0, 3.0, 2.0); // end of 3rd triangle
glEnd();
```

The output of this example is equal to the following, which defines all triangles individually. However, the first example will run faster.

```
glBegin(GL_TRIANGLES);
  glVertex3f(0.0, 1.0, 0.0);
  glVertex3f(0.0, 2.0, 0.0);
  glVertex3f(0.0, 3.0, 1.0); // end of 1st triangle

  glVertex3f(0.0, 2.0, 0.0);
  glVertex3f(0.0, 3.0, 1.0);
  glVertex3f(1.0, 3.0, 1.0); // end of 2nd triangle

  glVertex3f(0.0, 3.0, 1.0);
  glVertex3f(1.0, 3.0, 1.0);
  glVertex3f(5.0, 3.0, 2.0); // end of 3rd triangle
glEnd();
```

The disadvantage of using strips is that all objects need to be inter-connected. Moreover, the triangles must have an order so the complete set of triangles can be represented by strips. Sometimes, this is not possible. For example, a cube cannot be drawn using triangle strips without additional tricks. Note that public algorithms and libraries are available that convert a given set of triangles into triangle strips.

Always keep in mind that the task of "stripping" can cost you much more than you would gain from the reduced amount of data. In theory, it might give you an improvement of up to 66% due to reduced data sent to the graphics card. However, in practice you often do not even notice the difference. Therefore, if you can convert your data easily to triangle strips, you should do so, but think twice before investing lots of work in rearranging your triangles into strips.

Beside strips, two other modes are sometimes useful:

GL_LINE_LOOP is just like GL_LINE_STRIP, but the end of the line strip will be connected to the beginning again.

GL_TRIANGLE_FAN also resembles GL_TRIANGLE_STRIP, but every new triangle uses the very first vertex and the last vertex of the previous triangle, instead of the last two vertices of the previous triangle.

Drawing Complex 3D Objects Using the Depth Buffer

All complex 3D objects (where "complex" means everything not covered in the section about "simple" 3D objects) are made up of simple objects. A cube or box is actually just a set of 6 quads, or alternatively, 12 triangles. For example, a simple colored cube looks like:

```
GLfloat angle = 0.0;
glRotatef(angle, 0.0, 0.0, 1.0);
glBegin(GL_QUADS);
  // front side
  glColor3ub(255, 0, 0);
  glVertex3f(0.0, 0.0, 1.0);
  glVertex3f(1.0, 0.0, 1.0);
  glVertex3f(1.0, 1.0, 1.0);
  glVertex3f(0.0, 1.0, 1.0);

  // back side
  glColor3ub(0, 255, 0);
  glVertex3f(0.0, 0.0, 0.0);
  glVertex3f(1.0, 0.0, 0.0);
  glVertex3f(1.0, 1.0, 0.0);
  glVertex3f(0.0, 1.0, 0.0);

  // left side
  glColor3ub(0, 0, 255);
  glVertex3f(0.0, 0.0, 0.0);
  glVertex3f(0.0, 1.0, 0.0);
  glVertex3f(0.0, 1.0, 1.0);
  glVertex3f(0.0, 0.0, 1.0);

  // right side
  glColor3ub(255, 255, 0);
  glVertex3f(1.0, 0.0, 0.0);
  glVertex3f(1.0, 1.0, 0.0);
  glVertex3f(1.0, 1.0, 1.0);
  glVertex3f(1.0, 0.0, 1.0);

  // bottom side
  glColor3ub(0, 255, 255);
  glVertex3f(0.0, 0.0, 0.0);
  glVertex3f(1.0, 0.0, 0.0);
  glVertex3f(1.0, 0.0, 1.0);
```

```
    glVertex3f(0.0, 0.0, 1.0);

    // top side
    glColor3ub(255, 0, 255);
    glVertex3f(0.0, 1.0, 0.0);
    glVertex3f(1.0, 1.0, 0.0);
    glVertex3f(1.0, 1.0, 1.0);
    glVertex3f(0.0, 1.0, 1.0);
  glEnd();
```

When you execute this example, something strange happens. If you do not notice anything, change the angle value of the `glRotatef()` command. The side of the cube that should be the front is not always at the front. Actually, what will be the front side depends on when that particular side appears in the `glBegin()`/`glEnd()` pair, and not on the *z*-values. The polygon that is drawn last will appear on the screen and overwrites all other polygons, which are then absent or only partially visible.

This is because the *z*-value is used only for projection, and all new polygons just replace the old ones, but no hidden surface removal occurs. To avoid this, the depth buffer needs to be correctly initialized before drawing objects that need to use a depth buffer, which can be done at the beginning of the `MyGLWidget::paintGL()` method.

```
    glEnable(GL_DEPTH_TEST);
```

In some situations, such as drawing status information on the screen, you *want* to have new polygons replace old ones. To do this, just disable the depth testing before drawing such objects.

```
    glDisable(GL_DEPTH_TEST);
```

In addition to enabling the depth test, the depth buffer needs to be reset once per frame, which can be achieved by "clearing" it. In fact, instead of clearing just the color buffer, you clear two different buffers at the same time, and thus replace the command

```
    // Clear the color buffer (widget contents)
    glClear(GL_COLOR_BUFFER_BIT);
```

with

```
// Clear color buffer (widget contents) and z buffer (z values
// of the pixels)
glClear(GL_COLOR_BUFFER_BIT | GL_DEPTH_BUFFER_BIT);
```

This `glClear()` line is the most common. When you use more advanced features, you may need to clear even more buffers, but these two are sufficient for most desktop games. Note that clearing multiple buffers at once is usually faster than independent `glClear()` calls where only a single buffer is cleared.

When you now execute the previous example again, you will see that it appears as you originally expected.

Drawing Very Complex 3D Objects

At some point, hardcoded `glVertex*()`/`glColor*()`/`glTexCoord*()` calls will no longer be sufficient. As long as the most complex object you render is a cube, you can work perfectly well with composing the corresponding OpenGL code by hand. Nevertheless, at some point you will probably need a 3D modeler so the design models will look professional.

OpenGL does not provide a built-in file format, but many file formats are available on the Internet. Before you choose one, it is important to know what you intend to achieve. If it is a simple set of objects along with their colors or texture coordinates, a simple file format is sufficient. Such file formats write the vertex and texture coordinates into ASCII text files. However, when you need advanced features from your modeler, such as animations, materials, hierarchical objects, and vertex sharing, an advanced file format may be required. The `3ds` file format is often used within games, but is now quite old and contains unnecessary overhead.

Whatever your requirements, you should also make sure that the 3D modeler you are using can support that format, especially in terms of import and export. Otherwise, you have to write your own file converters, which can be difficult and time consuming.

Finding the Mouse Positions in 3D Space

In the 3D world, the location of the mouse position is sometimes required. The underlying windowing system (such as X11/Qt) returns only the screen position in 2D space.

To find the 3D world coordinates that belong to these window coordinates, the value of the depth buffer at these coordinates must first be retrieved. With these values, the GLU function `gluUnProject()` can be used to calculate the 3D world coordinates that match the window coordinates at this depth value.

```
void MyGLWidget::mousePressEvent(QMouseEvent* e)
{
  // Window coordinates (remember that y is flipped in OpenGL)
  int x = e->pos().x();
  int y = height() - e->pos().y();

  // Retrieve depth
  GLdouble depth;
  glReadPixels(x, y, 1, 1, GL_DEPTH_COMPONENT, GL_DOUBLE,
               &depth);

  // Retrieve current matrices
  GLdouble m[16];
  GLdouble p[16];
  GLint v[4];
  glGetDoublev(GL_MODELVIEW_MATRIX, m);
  glGetDoublev(GL_PROJECTION_MATRIX, p);
  glGetIntegerv(GL_VIEWPORT, v);

  // Calculate world coordinates
  GLdouble worldx, worldy, worldz;
  GLint ret = gluUnProject(x, y, depth,
              m, p, v,
              &worldx, &worldy, &worldz);
  if (ret != GL_TRUE)
  {
    printf("ERROR\n");
  }
}
```

LIGHTING

Lighting is an important topic in 3D graphics, since distinguishing between an unlit sphere and a simple circle on a 2D screen is extremely difficult. Clever lighting can actually allow the viewer to recognize 3D objects. In addition, lighting can also bring a real feel to objects or a specific atmosphere. An easy effect is to produce day and night by simply rotating the light source around the scene. You can also create lamps that make the area around the lamp brighter. Explosions look more realistic with light; the possibilities are endless.

Lighting is a large topic; therefore, in this chapter, we only focus on the practical aspects of lighting.

Lighting is enabled in OpenGL using

```
glEnable(GL_LIGHTING);
```

and disabled using

```
glDisable(GL_LIGHTING);
```

If you make heavy use of lighting, it is useful to disable it while you draw text elements that are not actually part of the 3D world.

Light Sources

In a specific scene, the light source has to appear as if it comes from the emitting object; that is, from the light source. In an ideal situation, each object that emits light should have its own OpenGL light source. For example, if you have a room without windows but it contains 10 lamps, there should be 10 light sources. Unfortunately, this is sometimes not feasible, since every light source significantly influences performance, and graphic cards usually provide hardware acceleration for only a small number of light sources. When you implement more than this number, your program will become very slow. You can find out how many light sources your OpenGL implementation can use with

```
int maxLights;
glGetIntegerv(GL_MAX_LIGHTS, &maxLights);

// maxLights is the number of lights supported by your OpenGL
// implementation (at least 8) the maximum number of
// accelerated lights can be less than maxLights!
```

Therefore, you should add an OpenGL light source only for the main light sources in your game. However, using materials, which are described later in this chapter, you can sometimes work around this restriction a little by adding an emission component to materials.

An OpenGL light source (a "light") is identified by an ID; the first one being GL_LIGHT0, the next one being GL_LIGHT0 + 1, and so forth until the maximum number of lights supported by your OpenGL implementation is reached. You can enable/disable every light source independently. By default, all lights are disabled. A light is enabled using glEnable() with the corresponding light ID and is disabled with glDisable().

```
// Enable the 1st light source
glEnable(GL_LIGHT0);
```

```
// Disable the 2nd light source
glDisable(GL_LIGHT0 + 1);
```

Usually, a light source is enabled when you initialize your scene or when the object responsible for the light is being constructed. The light is disabled again when that object is removed. Note that even with all light sources enabled, lighting is only performed when GL_LIGHTING is enabled as well.

Of course, a light source can have either a position or a direction. When initializing the light, you need to tell OpenGL which of these possibilities it should implement. This initialization is done with the glLight*() command.

```
// Light coming from the given position
GLfloat position[] = { 10.0, 1.0, 1.0, 0.0 };
glLightfv(GL_LIGHT0, GL_POSITION, position);

// Light coming from the given direction
GLfloat direction[] = { 1.0, 0.0, 0.0, 1.0 };
glLightfv(GL_LIGHT0, GL_POSITION, direction);
```

The first parameter is the ID of the light, the second tells OpenGL that we want to change the position, and the third gives the actual position.

The position or direction array contains four floats instead of the three necessary for 3D space. The fourth value specifies the type of light, either directional where the fourth value is zero, or positional in which case it is not zero. A directional light is a light from the direction specified by the position vector, but is infinitely far away (such as the sun). A positional light comes from a position inside the scene (such as a lamp).

Lights: Ambient, Diffuse, Specular

Light in OpenGL is composed of different types. The *ambient* component is the light that bounces off many surfaces so its direction cannot be determined, and can be considered a surrounding light. The *diffuse* component is light that comes from a clear direction and tends to bounce off a surface in all directions. *Specular* light is similar to diffuse light, but it is mostly reflected in a single direction and therefore is often seen as *highlighting*.

The ambient, diffuse, and specular properties of a light are set just like the position:

```
GLfloat ambient[] = { 0.0, 0.0, 0.0, 1.0 };
GLfloat diffuse[] = { 1.0, 1.0, 1.0, 1.0 };
GLfloat specular[] = { 1.0, 1.0, 1.0, 1.0 };
glLightfv(GL_LIGHT0, GL_AMBIENT, ambient);
```

```
glLightfv(GL_LIGHT0, GL_DIFFUSE, diffuse);
glLightfv(GL_LIGHT0, GL_SPECULAR, specular);
```

Materials

OpenGL objects such as polygons can also have ambient, diffuse, and specular properties that describe a *material* of the object. The material specifies how much of a certain light is reflected by the material. For example, a wooden object would usually have a very small specular component, whereas a metal object would have a big specular component. Furthermore, the materials describe which color of the light is reflected; for example, the material of a green object would contain mostly green ambient, diffuse, and specular values.

Alongside ambient, diffuse, and specular light, materials can also have an emission component, specified using GL_EMISSION. This form describes light that originates from the object.

Materials also have a shininess property, indicating the sharpness and size of the specular highlight. It must be in the range [0...128]. A high value indicates a small but sharp highlight (the light is very focused), while a small value indicates a large but less-sharp highlight.

Material properties can be specified in a similar manner to those of a light source, but using glMaterial*() instead of glLight*().

```
glMaterialfv(GLenum face, GLenum type, const GLfloat* values);
```

Here, face can be GL_FRONT, GL_BACK, or GL_FRONT_AND_BACK, indicating the side of the polygon. The type specifies the light component: GL_AMBIENT, GL_DIFFUSE, GL_SPECULAR, or GL_EMISSION. Additionally, you can use GL_AMBIENT_AND_DIFFUSE. values is the array describing the desired light.

Note that glMaterial*() can be used within a glBegin()/glEnd() pair.

Normals

For lighting to work properly, you need to provide normal vectors for all rendered objects. A normal vector is the vector that is perpendicular to a surface such as a triangle. You provide the normal using glNormal*(), usually glNormal3f(), along with the vertices.

```
GLfloat[] v1 = { ... };
GLfloat[] v2 = { ... };
GLfloat[] v3 = { ... };
GLfloat[] v4 = { ... };
GLfloat[] v5 = { ... };
GLfloat[] v6 = { ... };
```

```
GLfloat[] normal = { ... };
GLfloat[] normal4 = { ... };
GLfloat[] normal5 = { ... };
GLfloat[] normal6 = { ... };
glBegin(GL_TRIANGLES);
  // First triangles uses the same normal for all vertices
  //("face normal")
  glNormal3fv(normal); // first normal vector, then vertices
  glVertex3fv(v1);
  glVertex3fv(v2);
  glVertex3fv(v3);

  // Second triangle uses different normals for all vertices
  //("vertex normals")
  glNormal3fv(normal4);
  glVertex3fv(v4);
  glNormal3fv(normal5);
  glVertex3fv(v5);
  glNormal3fv(normal6);
  glVertex3fv(v6);
glEnd();
```

Often, normals are provided as part of the model file with no additional calculation necessary.

Global Ambient Light

One form of light exists even without a light source present. It is called *ambient light* and does not come from any specific light source, it is "just there." You can define it using `glLightModel(GL_LIGHT_MODEL_AMBIENT, ambient)`, with ambient being an array of size four containing the global ambient light parameters.

Lighting, `glColor`, `glMaterial`

Lighting in OpenGL works with the material of the objects, but not with the current color. Therefore, you usually need to call `glMaterial*()` instead of `glColor*()`, which can be extremely impractical, especially if you want to configure the light. However, you can tell OpenGL to use the current color as current material instead. To do so, you enable the `GL_COLOR_MATERIAL` and tell OpenGL how the current color should be used.

```
glEnable(GL_COLOR_MATERIAL);

// Use the color for front and back materials as diffuse and
```

```
// ambient.
glColorMaterial(GL_FRONT_AND_BACK, GL_AMBIENT_AND_DIFFUSE);

// Set the ambient and diffuse components to this color
glColor3f(0.5, 0.2, 0.1);
renderObjects();

glDisable(GL_COLOR_MATERIAL);
```

Instead of `GL_FRONT_AND_BACK`, `GL_FRONT` and `GL_BACK` could be used. Possible values for the second parameter include `GL_AMBIENT`, `GL_DIFFUSE`, `GL_EMISSION`, `GL_SPECULAR`, and `GL_AMBIENT_AND_DIFFUSE`.

This feature can also be used to update the ambient and diffuse color with a single command instead of two separate `glMaterial*()` calls.

BLENDING

In OpenGL, color data usually consists of four values: red, green, blue, and alpha. If you use `glColor3*()` to specify color data or alternatively use texture images that do not provide an alpha channel, the corresponding alpha values are implicitly set to 1.0 in `float` representation, which is equal to 255 in `ubyte` representation.

The alpha value can be used for many powerful features, one of which is to reject all pixels with an alpha value equal to 0.

```
// In rendering code:
// accept incoming pixels only if their corresponding alpha
// value is > 0.0
glAlphaFunc(GL_GREATER, 0.0);

// Enable alpha test. by default it is disabled.
glEnable(GL_ALPHA_TEST);
glBegin(GL_QUADS);
  glTexCoord2f(0.0, 0.0);
  glVertex3f(0.0, 0.0, 0.0);
  glTexCoord2f(1.0, 0.0);
  glVertex3f(1.0, 0.0, 0.0);
  glTexCoord2f(1.0, 1.0);
  glVertex3f(1.0, 1.0, 0.0);
  glTexCoord2f(0.0, 1.0);
  glVertex3f(0.0, 1.0, 0.0);
glEnd();
glDisable(GL_ALPHA_TEST);
```

This simple code can be used to draw nonrectangular images on the screen by setting the alpha value in the texture image to 0.0 for every pixel that should not be drawn. Figure 6.6 in Chapter 6 depicts this behavior, since the alpha test used here is the same as a mask. The function glAlphaFunc() can be used in different ways to control the behavior of the alpha test; refer to the documentation of that function for further information.

Another way to use the alpha value is through blending. Blending describes the process of combining incoming pixels with already drawn pixels and allows the easy implementation of transparent objects. To achieve this, first draw the background of the scene as usual and then enable the blending. The transparent objects should then be drawn with an alpha value different from 1.0. Here, an alpha value of 1.0 means "full intensity"; that is, the incoming pixel will replace the already existing pixel. This results in no transparency, which is like drawing without any blending. A pixel value with 0.0 describes no intensity; that is, the pixel is not drawn at all. The values in between behave linearly; thus, 0.5 indicates that 50% of the color is drawn, and so on.

A very easy way to achieve transparent or translucent effects is to load the texture in GL_RGB mode (without the alpha value) and then set an alpha value manually using glColor4f().

```
// When initializing:
QImage image;
// Load image, convert to GL format using
// QGLWidget::formatToGLFormatg()
...

glTexImage2D(GL_TEXTURE_2D, O,
             GL_RGB,    // Do not store an alpha value in
                        // the texture
             image.width(), image.height(), O, GL_RGBA,
             GL_UNSIGNED_BYTE, image.bits());

// When rendering:
renderBackground();

// Enable blending (disabled by default)
glEnable(GL_BLEND);

// Set a blending function. This function describes that the
// incoming objects are drawn onto the existing one with an
// intensity factor described by the alpha value
glBlendFunc(GL_SRC_ALPHA, GL_ONE_MINUS_SRC_ALPHA);
```

```
// Make objects translucent (the background shines through)
glColor4f(1.0, 1.0, 1.0, 0.5);
// alternatively
// glColor4ub(255, 255, 255, 127);

// Renders an object translucent using the RGB texture loaded
// above
renderObjectUsingCurrentTexture();

// The following objects are rendered with blending disabled
glDisable(GL_BLEND);
```

As you can see, you need to enable blending explicitly using `glEnable(GL_BLEND)` before you can use it, and disable it using `glDisable(GL_BLEND)` when you are finished. This point should not be forgotten, as blending can make rendering significantly slower, so it should be used only if you actually make use of it.

The example sets a blending function using `glBlendFunc()`.

```
void glBlendFunc(GLenum sourceFactor, GLenum destinationFactor)
```

This function describes how a pixel that has already been rendered (the "destination") is combined with an incoming pixel that is being rendered (the "source"). When blending is disabled, the destination pixel is simply replaced by the source pixel, which equals a `sourceFactor` of `GL_ONE` and a `destinationFactor` of `GL_ZERO` (100% of the source and 0% of the destination form the new value).

In this example, we use a `sourceFactor` of `GL_SRC_ALPHA`, meaning that the alpha value of the source (what is drawn next) specifies the amount of the source RGB pixel that is applied. Here, the alpha is 0.5, so 50% of the source is used. The `destinationFactor` is `GL_ONE_MINUS_SRC_ALPHA`, meaning that the remaining 50% is taken from the color that has already been drawn (the destination).

This combination of the parameters is probably the most common. By using this, you can easily modify the alpha value to make the objects more or less translucent. For example, with an alpha of 0.2, 80% of the background is used, but only 20% of the new objects are used. An alpha of 0.0 would be equal to not drawing the new objects at all, and so forth. You can also use an RGBA texture to provide the actual alpha values in the texture, which makes the process more dynamic, as the texture creator can influence blending more easily. This can be imagined if one part of the texture is transparent, like a window, while other parts of the same texture are opaque.

Since blending is very powerful in OpenGL, there are many additional blending functions other than those presented here.

READING AND WRITING PIXEL DATA

OpenGL provides various ways to modify pixel data directly, such as writing pixels directly to the color buffer. However, most of these functions have little importance in game development, so we will not cover them in depth here.

However, two functions are interesting. The first is `glDrawPixels()`

```
void glDrawPixels(GLsizei w, GLsizei h, GLenum format,
                  GLenum type, const GLvoid* pixels)
```

which places the specified pixels directly in the buffer and thus completely bypasses the modelview matrix and projection matrices. The exact buffer used depends on the format parameter that specifies the kind of pixel data. This can be GL_STEN-CIL_INDEX, GL_DEPTH_COMPONENT, GL_RGB, GL_RGBA, and a few others. In the case of GL_RGBA, the data is written directly to the color buffer. This can be used, for example, to draw images on the screen without reserving additional texture memory.

```
QImage image;
// Load the image, convert it to GL format using
// QGLWidget::convertToGLFormat()
...
// When rendering:
// specify where to draw the image to
glRasterPos(x, y);

// Draw the image to the current raster pos
glDrawPixels(image.width(), image.height(), GL_RGBA,
             GL_UNSIGNED_BYTE, image.bits());
```

As you can see in the example, `glDrawPixels()` uses the current raster position that can be set using `glRasterPos()` to position the pixel data. Keep in mind that (0,0) specifies the lower left corner in OpenGL. The raster position is independent of the projection settings, and you can use the entire widget size.

Another useful function is `glReadPixels()`.

```
void glReadPixels(GLint x, GLint y, GLsizei w, GLsizei h,
                  GLenum format, GLenum type, GLvoid* pixels)
```

This function is the opposite of `glDrawPixels()`. Instead of writing pixels from a buffer, it reads them. This is particularly useful for finding the depth of the pixel under the mouse.

```
void MyGLWidget::mousePressEvent(QMouseEvent* e)
{
  int x = e->pos().x();
  int y = height() - e->pos().y();

  // Find the depth of the pixel under the mouse
  GLfloat depth;
  glReadPixels(x, y, 1, 1, GL_DEPTH_COMPONENT, GL_FLOAT,
               &depth);

  ...
}
```

The depth value can be used to find the world, or more specifically the OpenGL, coordinate for a certain mouse click that is specified in the window coordinates. To do this, you call gluUnProject() with the *z*-parameter set to the depth value.

TEXT RENDERING

Although text rendering is an important feature, it is unfortunately quite difficult and is not covered by OpenGL. For further information, we recommend the "OpenGL FAQ §17" [OpenGLFaq05]. There are a couple of different ways to get text rendering with two different categories of fonts:

Bitmap fonts: Bitmap fonts mean that the fonts of the underlying windowing system (such as X11 or Microsoft Windows) are loaded into the OpenGL bitmap and then drawn on the screen using glBitmap(). We describe this type of font in more detail in Chapter 8. Bitmap fonts have several disadvantages: their appearance, their limitations in font size and orientation (you cannot rotate them), and their slow rendering speed.

Textured fonts: Textured fonts require a custom texture image that can be extracted from the system font. Usually, this is a single image that contains all characters provided by the font. When rendering text, you actually render a couple of quads with blending enabled; this is both fast and better looking. Furthermore, the fonts can be rotated and scaled in many ways. However, they do require additional texture memory, and when over-scaled can appear unprofessional and sometimes unreadable. Often, whereas a textured font becomes unreadable, a bitmap font will still appear clear. This advantage is achieved because a windowing system often provides the same bitmap font in many different sizes. The actual quality of the resulting font depends on the implementation of the textured font. OpenGL, GLU, and GLX do not provide this functionality.

Geometric fonts: Geometric fonts use polygons such as triangles to render text, and in contrast to textured fonts, this allows them to be scaled and rotated without suffering from size problems. Nevertheless, due to the abundant vertices during rendering, they are actually slower than textured fonts. Unfortunately, geometric fonts cannot be generated from normal system fonts. You need to create them from scratch or obtain some special fonts from elsewhere, and creating a good geometric font can be difficult. As with textured fonts, OpenGL does not provide such fonts.

Under X11 there is a GLX function termed `glXUseXFont()`, which creates display lists containing the font. Calling this function is straightforward.

```
QFont font;
GLuint lists = glGenLists(256);
glXUseXFont((Font)font.handle(), 0, 256, lists);
```

The list now contains 256 display lists containing the characters of the font. You can use them like this:

```
// x,y describes position on the screen where the text should
// be rendered
int x = 100;
int y = 100;
const char* string = "hello world"; // text to be rendered
glRasterPos2i(x, y);
glCallLists(strlen(string), GL_UNSIGNED_BYTE, string);
```

Note that `glRasterPos2i()` bypasses the modelview matrix. Therefore, x and y are independent of any `glTranslate*()`/`glRotate*()`/`glScale*()` calls.

ERROR DETECTION

Being able to detect errors is a necessity in every program. OpenGL is a large and powerful library, and therefore it is easy to make mistakes. These errors sometimes have few obvious consequences, as OpenGL usually ignores unexpected commands. Nevertheless, an error can cause a negative effect on performance, or a visible effect may become apparent.

Therefore, you need a way to discover the reasons for these errors. Fortunately, OpenGL provides you with the necessary functions. The OpenGL command glGetError() returns an enum describing the most recent error, or GL_NO_ERROR indicating that no error has occurred. Additionally, glGetError() clears the error state.

```
// Retrieve the most recent error and reset the error state
GLenum error = glGetError();
if (error != GL_NO_ERROR)
{
  printf("An OpenGL error occurred\n");
}

doSomething()

error = glGetError();
if (error != GL_NO_ERROR)
{
  // The error must have been in doSomething(), as no other
  // OpenGL commands have been made since the previous
  // glGetError() command
  printf("An OpenGL error occurred in doSomething()\n");
}
```

The possible values that glGetError() returns are:

GL_INVALID_ENUM: An invalid OpenGL enum value was given; for example, glBegin(GL_TEXTURE_2D).

GL_INVALID_VALUE: An invalid value was given (out of range); for example, glDrawArrays(GL_TRIANGLES, 0, -1).

GL_INVALID_OPERATION: An OpenGL command has been made at a moment in which this command was not allowed; for example, two succeeding glBegin() calls without a glEnd() call in between.

GL_STACK_OVERFLOW: A command has been made that would cause a stack overflow; for example, infinite glPushMatrix() calls would cause this.

GL_STACK_UNDERFLOW: A command has been made that would cause a stack underflow; for example, when more glPopMatrix() calls than glPushMatrix() calls appear.

GL_OUT_OF_MEMORY: There was not enough memory to complete the command. An example would be a glNewList() command when there is no memory left.

GL_TABLE_TOO_LARGE: We do not cover any commands causing this error in this book.

GL_NO_ERROR: No error has occurred since the last glGetError() command.

For convenience there is a GLU function that forms a string from a given error enum:

```
GLenum error = glGetError();
if (error)
{
  printf("An error occurred: %s\n", gluErrorString(error));
}
```

OPENGL UTILITY LIBRARIES, EXTENSIONS, AND VERSION DETECTION

OpenGL primarily provides basic and general-purpose functions. Moreover, when graphics-cards-dependent functions are required, they can be provided through the OpenGL extension mechanism in the OpenGL driver. Certain features of a specific OpenGL version or extension can only be used if they are available on the target system; otherwise that feature cannot be provided unless a fallback implementation exists.

OpenGL, GLU, and GLX

The GLU, GLX (on X11-based systems), and WGL (on Windows systems) libraries often accompany OpenGL, or are at least expected to be installed when OpenGL is installed.

GLU is the OpenGL Utility library. It is a very small library that uses OpenGL commands rather than directly accessing the graphics card; thus, it is not part of the graphics drivers. GLU provides several convenience functions, and in this chapter we have already studied a few of them, such as gluPerspective() and gluOrtho2D(). GLU functions start (similar to OpenGL itself) with glu.

GLX and WGL are window system-dependent libraries. These libraries make sure that OpenGL is made available to the window system by providing several required functions. Most of these functions are handled internally by Qt, and usually it is not necessary to use them yourself, unless you use a different window toolkit such as GLUT.

Extensions

OpenGL provides a powerful extension architecture that allows the vendor of an OpenGL implementation to extend the OpenGL specification with useful functions, which is one of the main reasons why OpenGL has been so successful. Many features have existed as extensions for a long time, and are only included in the new versions when considered useful.

Functions provided by extensions have capital letters appended to the command name that indicate the source of the extension. For example, in versions of OpenGL older than 1.3, the multitexturing feature is an extension approved by the Architecture Review Board (ARB). The commands to specify texture coordinates in multitexturing (similar to `glTexCoord*()`) are thus named `glMultiTexCoord*ARB()`.

Extension Detection

An extension is not necessarily present on every system. Some are even vendor specific, so Nvidia™ extensions are usually not present on ATI™ cards. Therefore, you need to find out whether a certain extension is present before you can use it. There are several ways to do so, the easiest being the compile time check.

```
// Check if the vertex buffer object extension is present
#ifdef GL_ARB_vertex_buffer_object
// use VBOs
glGenBuffersARB(1, &vbo);
// ...
#endif
```

However, the compile time check is often not enough. When the development system is different from the system on which the package is executed (which is the normal case for distributions), the target system may support extensions that the compile system does not, and vice versa.

Therefore, it is often a good idea to test for the extension at runtime. You can use the functions `glGetString(GL_EXTENSIONS)` and `gluGetString(GLU_EXTENSIONS)` to retrieve a list of extensions that are supported on the system.

```
// Create a list of all GL/GLU extensions on this system
QStringList extensions;
QString s = (const char*)glGetString(GL_EXTENSIONS);
s += " ";
s += (const char*)gluGetString(GLU_EXTENSIONS);
extensions = QStringList::split(" ", s);

// Check if multitexturing is supported
if (extensions.contains("GL_ARB_multitexture"))
{
  // multitexturing is supported
}
```

Using Extensions

To use an extension function, you usually need to retrieve the function pointer first. This pointer is necessary to be able to compile on a system without the extension *and* to use the extension on the target system that supports the extension. The function pointer can be retrieved using glXGetProcAddressARBI() (or glXGetProcAddress() on GLX 1.4).

```
typedef void (*_my_glMultiTexCoord2fARB)(GLenum,
                                         GLfloat,
                                         GLfloat);

// This variable is contains the function pointer to
// glMultiTexCoord2fARB(). The "my_" prefix makes sure that
// this code compiles no matter whether glMultiTexCoord2fARB()
// is defined in gl.h or not.
_my_glMultiTexCoord2fARB my_glMultiTexCoord2fARB = 0;

// ...
// In your initialization code:
// retrieve the pointer
if (multiTexturingSupported)
{
  my_glMultiTexCoord2fARB =
      (_my_glMultiTexCoord2fARB)glXGetProcAddressARB((const
       GLubyte*)"glMultiTexCoord2fARB");
 }

// In rendering:
if (multiTexturingSupported)
{
  // ...
  // Use the function pointer like any normal function
  my_glMultiTexCoord2fARB(target, s, t);
  ...
}
```

Version Detection

Often, it is necessary to know whether a certain version of OpenGL or GLU is present on a system so you can determine whether a certain feature is supported. As with extension detection, this can be determined using two different approaches. The easiest way is to test at compile time by checking for specific version definitions.

```
#include <GL/gl.h>
#ifndef GL_VERSION_1_2
#error OpenGL 1.2 not present on this system
#endif
#ifndef GLU_VERSION_1_2
#error GLU 1.2 not present on this system
#endif
```

However, this only states which version of the system your game is being compiled with; to determine which version the running system has, you can use

```
const char* string1 = glGetString(GL_VERSION);
const char* string2 = gluGetString(GLU_VERSION);
```

The returned string uses the format `<major>.<minor>` or `<major>.<minor>.<release>`, each followed by information specific to the vendor of the OpenGL implementation.

RENDERING PERFORMANCE

Regarding speed, it is very important to know when to optimize and when not to. In OpenGL, there are many ways to optimize rendering speed, and consequently many articles on the Internet cover this task. However, be warned: much of this information is now redundant, since several of these performance articles are outdated and recommend avoiding things that today are extremely fast. In the following, we present some possibilities for optimizing the rendering performance of OpenGL.

Immediate Mode, Display Lists, and Vertex Arrays

OpenGL supports several ways to specify vertices and vertex data (color, texture coordinates, normals, etc.), and in the following section we present the three most important.

Immediate Mode

Up to now, we have always used the so-called "immediate" mode. In immediate mode, you have calls to `glVertex*()`, `glColor*()`, `glTexCoord*()`, and so forth, and you explicitly specify them every time you render something.

Display Lists

Immediate mode is, of course, the most flexible way to render objects; however, there is a speed drawback. In every frame you need exactly one `glVertex*()` call for each vertex in your scene. Every function, even one that does nothing, requires a small amount of time when called. This is called the function overhead. Usually, the function overhead is negligible, but with many vertices, the calls performed with the immediate mode can lead to a high value. This is where display lists come into play: a display list contains a number of OpenGL commands that are executed together when the display list is executed. Since you can execute a display list with a single command, it almost completely eliminates the function overhead of the OpenGL commands. However, the details depend on the actual OpenGL implementation.

A display list is generated using

```
GLuint displayList = glGenLists(1);
glNewList(displayList, GL_COMPILE);

// OpenGL commands that follow go to the display list only

glEndList();

...

// Execute the display list
glCallList(displayList);
```

The command `glGenLists(GLsizei count)` reserves count display list IDs and returns the first ID. All IDs are continuous, so the second display list is the returned value +1, and so on.

The command `glNewList(GLuint displayList, GL_COMPILE)` actually creates a new display list. The list will receive the name specified by the `displayList`, which should be created using `glGenLists()`. After the call to `glNewList()`, all following OpenGL commands are no longer executed but are stored in the display list for later execution. A few commands do not follow this rule and are still executed immediately, such as all commands that return a value; for example, `glGet()`. However, all actual rendering commands will be stored in the list. Once the composing of the display list is finished, `glEndList()` is called so the display list can be completed.

Note that instead of `GL_COMPILE` in `glNewList()`, you could also use `GL_COMPILE_AND_EXECUTE`, which additionally executes the commands and functions as if the commands were made outside the `glNewList()`/`glEndList()` pair.

Once a display list is created, it can be called using `glCallList(GLuint list)` or `glCallLists(GLsizei count, GLenum type, const GLvoid* lists)`. The latter just takes an array of display lists and calls them all. You can call a list as often as you like, every time the commands between `glNewList()` and `glEndList()` are repeated.

Note that the commands, and *all* of their parameters, are stored in the display list. This has two important consequences. The first and most important is that it makes the data static, or in other words, all variables become constant.

```
float x = 0.0f;
float y = 0.0f;
float z = 0.0f;
glNewList(list, GL_COMPILE);
  glVertex(x, y, z);
  glVertex(x + 1.0f, y, z);
  glVertex(x + 1.0f, y + 1.0f, z);
glEndList();

glBegin(GL_TRIANGLES);
  glCallList(list);

  z += 1.0f; // this has NO effect!
  glCallList(list);

  x = 10.0f; y = 5.0f; z += 1.0f; // this also has no effect
  glCallList(list);
glEnd();
```

All three triangles in the previous example have exactly the same coordinates because the values of x, y, and z have been saved in the display list. Changing the variables after creation of the display list has no effect. To achieve the result that is intended in the preceding example, you would need to make use of `glTranslate()` and use three independent `glBegin()`/`glEnd()` pairs.

The other consequence of storing the parameters in a display list is the data size. Imagine the following situation:

```
QImage image = ...; // load the image somehow
GLuint list = glGenLists(1);
glNewList(list, GL_COMPILE);
  glTexImage2D(GL_TEXTURE_2D, 0, GL_RGBA, image.width(),
               image.height(), 0, GL_RGBA, GL_UNSIGNED_BYTE,
               image.bits());
glEndList();
```

```
glBindTexture(GL_TEXTURE_2D, texture1);
glCallList(list);

glBindTexture(GL_TEXTURE_2D, texture2);
glCallList(list);
```

This example loads the image into two different texture objects using a display list. However, the parameters are all saved into the display list, including `image.bits()`. Just saving the pointer would be pointless for the display list, because it is invalid once you leave the scope. Therefore, the entire array that the `image.bits()` points to is saved; that is, `image.width()*image.height()*4` bytes! The actual amount of memory required by the display list may be even higher, depending on the actual implementation.

It is usually a bad idea to store commands such as `glTexImage2D()` in a display list. In general, you should try to keep your display lists small. Storing too many commands in display lists may require a lot of memory, and memory is often very limited on graphics cards. Moreover, once you run low on that memory, the program will become even slower.

Vertex Arrays

In regard to rendering modes, display lists will yield the highest performance, but make the data very static, which is often a disadvantage for games.

Vertex arrays allow you to eliminate a lot of function call overhead (and several other related overheads) by maintaining a high degree of dynamic data. Instead of using calls such as `glVertex*()` and `glTexCoord*()` to tell OpenGL about vertex data, you maintain an array that contains the data and then tell OpenGL at which index it can find the data.

```
// In the header:
GLfloat mVertexArray[3 * 3]; // 3 vertices, each 3 floats


// In the initialization code:
// 1st vertex
mVertexArray[0] = 0.0;
mVertexArray[1] = 0.0;
mVertexArray[2] = 0.0;

// 2nd vertex
mVertexArray[3] = 1.0;
mVertexArray[4] = 0.0;
mVertexArray[5] = 0.0;
```

```
// 3rd vertex
mVertexArray[6] = 1.0;
mVertexArray[7] = 1.0;
mVertexArray[8] = 0.0;

// Tell OpenGL about our vertex array
glVertexPointer(3, GL_FLOAT, 0, mVertexArray);
glEnableClientState(GL_VERTEX_ARRAY);

// In the rendering code:
glBegin(GL_TRIANGLES);
  // equal to a glVertex3f() call for the first vertex
  glArrayElement(0);
  // equal to a glVertex3f() call for the second vertex
  glArrayElement(1);
  // equal to a glVertex3f() call for the third vertex
  glArrayElement(2);
glEnd();
```

Note that by "vertex data" we understand the vertex and all related data, such as color, normal vector, and texture coordinates.

In this example, there appear to be two important new functions.

```
void glVertexPointer(GLint size, GLenum type, GLsizei stride,
                     const GLvoid* array)
void glArrayElement(GLint index);
```

The `glVertexPointer()` parameters are:

size: The number of coordinates per vertex, which can be two, three, or four.

type: The data type of the array in the last parameter. One of GL_FLOAT, GL_DOUBLE, GL_INT, GL_SHORT.

stride: We do not discuss this further and just use 0 here. The stride describes an offset (in bytes) of vertex data at an index in the array. It can be used to combine all different vertex array pointers into a single array.

array: The actual array. The array is not copied by OpenGL, so you must make sure that it remains valid as long as you use it.

`glArrayElement()` takes only the index of the vertex as a parameter. The actual address of the first coordinate (x) is index*size, where size is the size parameter of `glVertexPointer()`.

Additionally, to specify a pointer on the vertex array, you need to activate the vertex arrays. This is done using glEnableClientState(GL_VERTEX_ARRAY), and we will see shortly why this is necessary. This can be deactivated again using glDisable-ClientState(GL_VERTEX_ARRAY). However, in many cases you can leave this call out. Note that in contrast to glEnable()/glDisable(), gl*ClientState() calls are not stored in a display list.

At this point, you may ask why so much additional code has to be added, even though the number of function calls has not been reduced; in fact, glVertex*() has only been replaced by glArrayElement(). The answer is that there are similar pointer functions available for glNormal*(), glColor*(), and glTexCoord*(). A single glArrayElement() call will always dereference all currently activated arrays. Look at this example, which extends the previous example:

```
// In the header:
GLfloat mVertexArray[3 * 3]; // just as above
GLfloat mTextureCoordArray[3 * 2];
GLfloat mNormalArray[3 * 3];

// In the initialization code:
// (mVertexArray initialized as in previous example)
mTextureCoordArray[0] = 0.0; // 1st vertex
mTextureCoordArray[1] = 0.0;
mTextureCoordArray[2] = 1.0; // 2nd vertex
mTextureCoordArray[3] = 0.0;
mTextureCoordArray[4] = 1.0; // 3rd vertex
mTextureCoordArray[5] = 1.0;

// This method should calculate the normals of the vertices
// and put them in mNormalArray
calculateNormals();

// Tell OpenGL about our vertex arrays
glVertexPointer(3, GL_FLOAT, 0, mVertexArray);
// Note: only 2 coordinates!
glTexCoordPointer(2, GL_FLOAT, 0, mTextureCoordArray);
glNormalPointer(3, GL_FLOAT, 0, mNormalArray);
glEnableClientState(GL_VERTEX_ARRAY);
glEnableClientState(GL_TEXTURE_COORD_ARRAY);
glEnableClientState(GL_NORMAL_ARRAY);

// In the rendering code:
glBegin(GL_TRIANGLES);
  glArrayElement(0);
```

```
    glArrayElement(1);
    glArrayElement(2);
  glEnd();
```

As you can see, in contrast to the initialization code the rendering code has not changed.

Note that the index specified to `glArrayElement()` always applies to all arrays at once. It is not possible to use one index in the vertex array and another index in the `texturecoord` array.

Using `gl*Pointer()`, you can only tell OpenGL the location of the array, and OpenGL will only use it if you enabled the array with `glEnableClientState()`. You can use this fact to avoid sending the normals to the graphic card if lighting has been disabled. To achieve this, you can modify the previous example like this:

```
if (mDisableLighting)
{
  glDisableClientState(GL_NORMAL_ARRAY);
}
else
{
  glEnableClientState(GL_NORMAL_ARRAY);
}
glBegin(GL_TRIANGLES);
  glArrayElement(0);
  glArrayElement(1);
  glArrayElement(2);
glEnd();
```

Now you can see that the amount of functions per vertex is reduced from two to three (`vertex`, `texcoord`, maybe `normal`) to one. However most of the time, your rendering code will resemble

```
glBegin(GL_TRIANGLES);
  for (int i = 0; i < vertexCount; i++)
  {
    glArrayElement(i);
  }
glEnd();
```

Such loops can be replaced by this:

```
// Note that this is outside (!) of a glBegin()/glEnd() pair!
// start at index 0 and use all vertexCount indices
```

```
glDrawArrays(GL_TRIANGLES, 0, vertexCount);
```

However, because the requirement that the indices you want to render are exactly start, start+1, start+2, and so on, start+count is often very impractical. Often, a random access, as is possible with glArrayElement(), is more applicable. This can be accomplished with a single function call, using glDrawElements().

```
// In the header
GLuint* mIndices;

// In the initialization
mIndices = new GLuint[vertexCount];
for (GLuint i = 0; i < vertexCount; i++)
{
  mIndices[i] = i;
}
// (You can use any other order of the mIndices array)

// In the rendering code:
// note that this is outside (!) of a glBegin()/glEnd() pair!
glDrawElements(GL_TRIANGLES, vertexCount, GL_UNSIGNED_INT,
               mIndices);
```

The glDrawElements() call does exactly the same as calls to all indices of the mIndices array in a glBegin()/glEnd() pair.

Which Mode to Choose

Now that you know about immediate mode, display lists, and vertex arrays, you may be wondering which mode is the best.

At the beginning of development, the answer is usually immediate mode. At that time, you usually cannot predict how your program will evolve or how your rendering code will look in a month or two. If you use display lists at this point, you require the data to be static, but sometimes data needs to become dynamic even if you believe that it will remain static. The same reasons apply to vertex arrays, since using them requires that all data be in a single array, and that this will never change. To impose such strict requirements is not good when a program is in early development.

When your game becomes more or less stable, or alternatively if you have identified the performance bottlenecks that could be eliminated using a different mode, you can then move to vertex arrays or display lists for certain parts of the rendering code. Usually, terrain or model/mesh data are good candidates for vertex arrays, as they consist mostly of vertex/color/normal/texture coordinate data. Display lists are also useful to encapsulate multiple commands into a single `glCallList()` call, because in contrast to vertex arrays, they are not limited to only vertex data.

Frustum Culling

If your game has a large world but usually only a small part is visible, frustum culling may be of interest for you. Frustum culling provides an efficient way to decide whether an object is currently visible.

The view frustum is that part of the game world currently visible on the screen. It is actually a pyramid with the top cut off, and is constructed from six planes or, more simply, six sides (see Figure 7.11).

Frustum culling is used to determine whether an object is inside the view frustum, and then to draw it. When the object lies outside the view frustum, it is not drawn but culled. The principle to test if an object is inside the view frustum works by calculating the position of the object in relation to the planes. An object in front of all six planes is inside the view frustum, whereas an object behind one of the planes is outside.

Extracting the View Frustum

You can extract the view frustum from the OpenGL matrices as described in [Ravensoft05]. The code to do so resembles:

```
// Get projection matrix
GLfloat projection[16];
glGetFloatv(GL_MODELVIEW_MATRIX, projection);

// Combine modelview and projection matrix. You may use your
// own matrix code instead. for convenience we use OpenGL code
// here.
// Save the original matrix
glPushMatrix();

// Multiply modelview by projection matrix
glMultMatrixf(projection);

// Retrieve the result
GLfloat m[16];
glGetFloatv(GL_MODELVIEW_MATRIX, m);

// Restore the original modelview matrix
glPopMatrix();

// Retrieve the view frustum from m. it consists of 4 planes,
```

```
// each 4 floats. the last plane must be the NEAR plane. The
// first three floats specify the normal vector of the plane,
// the last float specifies the distance
GLfloat viewFrustum[6 * 4];

// Extract the numbers for the RIGHT plane
viewFrustum[0 * 4 + 0] = m[3] - m[0];
viewFrustum[0 * 4 + 1] = m[7] - m[4];
viewFrustum[0 * 4 + 2] = m[11] - m[8];
viewFrustum[0 * 4 + 3] = m[15] - m[12];

// Extract the numbers for the LEFT plane
viewFrustum[1 * 4 + 0] = m[3] + m[0];
viewFrustum[1 * 4 + 1] = m[7] + m[4];
viewFrustum[1 * 4 + 2] = m[11] + m[8];
viewFrustum[1 * 4 + 3] = m[15] + m[12];

// Extract the BOTTOM plane
viewFrustum[2 * 4 + 0] = m[3] + m[1];
viewFrustum[2 * 4 + 1] = m[7] + m[5];
viewFrustum[2 * 4 + 2] = m[11] + m[9];
viewFrustum[2 * 4 + 3] = m[15] + m[13];

// Extract the TOP plane
viewFrustum[3 * 4 + 0] = m[3] - m[1];
viewFrustum[3 * 4 + 1] = m[7] - m[5];
viewFrustum[3 * 4 + 2] = m[11] - m[9];
viewFrustum[3 * 4 + 3] = m[15] - m[13];

// Extract the FAR plane
viewFrustum[4 * 4 + 0] = m[3] - m[2];
viewFrustum[4 * 4 + 1] = m[7] - m[6];
viewFrustum[4 * 4 + 2] = m[11] - m[10];
viewFrustum[4 * 4 + 3] = m[15] - m[14];

// Extract the NEAR plane
viewFrustum[5 * 4 + 0] = m[3] + m[2];
viewFrustum[5 * 4 + 1] = m[7] + m[6];
viewFrustum[5 * 4 + 2] = m[11] + m[10];
viewFrustum[5 * 4 + 3] = m[15] + m[14];

// Normalize the result
for (int i = 0; i < 6; i++)
{
```

```
    GLfloat t = 0;
    for (int j = 0; j < 3; j++)
    {
      t += viewFrustum[i * 4 + j] * viewFrustum[i * 4 + j];
    }
    t = sqrt(t);
    for (int j = 0; j < 4; j++)
    {
      viewFrustum[i * 4 + j] /= t;
    }
}
```

Frustum Check

Testing whether an object is inside the view frustum works by finding the location
of the object with respect to every plane. This is done by finding the distance of the
vertices of the object. A negative distance means the vertex is behind the plane, or
not visible, and a positive distance indicates it is in front of the plane.

```
float distanceFromPlane(const GLfloat* v,
                        const GLfloat* plane)
{
  return v[0] * plane[0] +
         v[1] * plane[1] +
         v[2] * plane[2] +
              plane[3];
}


float vertexInFrustum(const GLfloat* v,
                      const GLfloat* viewFrustum)
{
  float distance;
  for (int i = 0; i < 6; i++)
  {
    distance = distanceFromPlane(v, &viewFrustum[i * 4]);
    if (distance <= 0.0)
    {
      return 0.0; // not in frustum
    }
  }
  // distance from the last plane (the NEAR plane)
  return distance;
}
```

This function tells you whether a vertex is in the view frustum, in which case it returns a value larger than zero, and how far that vertex is from the eye/camera position. This can be very useful for further advanced techniques such as implementing a certain level of detail.

Testing every vertex of an object would be too slow; therefore, you usually use bounding volumes, such as bounding boxes or bounding spheres, for the actual test. Instead of testing whether the actual object is inside the view frustum, you simply test whether a box or sphere that encloses the object is in the frustum. The quality of this test depends on the quality of the bounding volume chosen. A simple bounding sphere is usually larger than a simple bounding box, so in many cases the bounding sphere may be partially inside the view frustum, whereas the actual object or the bounding box is not. However, a frustum check for a sphere is extremely easy and is demonstrated here:

```
float sphereInFrustum(const GLfloat* center,
                      GLfloat radius,
                      const GLfloat* viewFrustum)
{
  for (int i = 0; i < 6; i++)
  {
    distance = distanceFromPlane(v, &viewFrustum[i * 4]);
    if (distance + radius <= 0.0)
    {
      return 0.0;
    }
  }
  return distance + radius;
}
```

A simple test for bounding boxes is also easy but requires more code. There, you have to test every vertex of the box for being in front of the plane. If all eight vertices are behind at least one plane, the box is outside the view frustum.

The code example also depicts objects that are only partially in the view frustum. This is intended, as normally you will also need to draw these objects. However, sometimes you may want to know whether the object is partially or completely visible. With this feature, you can often speed frustum culling; for example, by using quad-trees. Basically, you can count the number of planes the sphere is completely in front of. The condition

```
if (distance + radius <= 0.0)
```

is false when a part of the sphere is in front of the plane. This is the case when the center of the sphere is either in front of the plane (distance <= 0.0), or behind the plane, but at most one sphere radius away. Should you want to find out that a sphere is completely in front of a plane, the sphere should not be behind the plane at all (not even partially). Therefore, you could modify the function to resemble this:

```
float sphereCompleteInFrustum(const GLfloat* center,
                              GLfloat radius,
                              const GLfloat* viewFrustum)
{
  // Counts the number of planes the sphere is completely
  // in front of
  int count = 0;
  for (int i = 0; i < 6; i++)
  {
    distance = distanceFromPlane(v, &viewFrustum[i * 4]);
    if (distance + radius <= 0.0)
    {
      return 0.0;
    }
    if (distance >= radius)
    {
      // The sphere is completely in front of this plane
      count++;
    }
  }
  if (count == 6)
  {
    // The sphere is completely inside the view frustum
    return -(distance + radius);
  }
  return distance + radius;
}
```

This code returns 0 if the sphere is outside the view frustum. It returns a value (the distance to the near plane) greater than 0 if it is partially inside the frustum. Finally, a negative value (the negative distance to the near plane) is returned if it is completely inside the view frustum.

Scene Graph Libraries

Using a scene graph library instead of OpenGL directly can make a huge difference in many games. A scene graph library is a higher level library that encapsulates OpenGL commands into (usually) object-oriented functions and methods. In OpenGL, you have to specify all triangles (or similar) of the objects you want to render. A scene graph, however, takes this task from you, and all you have to tell it to do is draw the object only.

Due to this, many performance features, such as frustum culling or similar algorithms, may be implemented in the scene graph library already. In addition, it might have been optimized by people with a great deal of OpenGL experience. Often, such libraries also provide methods to load model files, which can make a game programmer's life much easier. An example of a free scene graph library is plib, which can be found at the Web site [Plib05].

SUMMARY

3D graphic libraries are used in a wide range of games in which extensive graphical effects or fast graphics are required. OpenGL is a good choice for such a 3D graphics library. It offers support for various platforms, including Linux and Microsoft Windows, and is actually the de-facto standard on all non-Windows platforms. Furthermore, OpenGL can be used for 2D applications that require special or fast graphical effects.

Learning how to conceive of the OpenGL coordinate system is a necessary part of understanding OpenGL. OpenGL uses a coordinate system that is different from the one employed by most other windowing toolkits (flipped y-axis). It is also important to know how transformations on these coordinates are performed. In particular, the order in which transformations are made is relevant. Once this step is achieved, OpenGL transformations can be very convenient, and the program can often be made simpler by using matrix math intelligently.

OpenGL does not make a distinction between 2D and 3D mode; however, it does make a lot of sense to implement this distinction for games. Nearly all games need both 2D and 3D rendering, as 2D is required for things such as status texts or mini maps. 2D graphics are achieved by proper projection settings, and 3D scenes are easily implemented using the OpenGL depth buffer. Once a 3D scene is prepared, it can be made more professional looking by incorporating lighting features. Lighting, however, requires a great deal of calculation and can sometimes significantly slow the application; therefore, it should be used carefully.

OpenGL provides an extension mechanism that allows the inclusion of numerous features in an application that are not specified in the official OpenGL specification. If such extensions prove worthy, you will find that they are often incorporated in later versions of OpenGL. Useful extensions include multitexturing, vertex buffer objects, vertex shaders, and texture compression. Some of these are now already officially supported by the OpenGL version 2.0.

However, using 3D graphics in a game also has drawbacks. Due to the immense amount of calculations required, a game can easily become very slow. It is therefore important to regularly profile the code for performance bottlenecks and fix them. There are various ways to perform these tasks, and we presented a few of them in this chapter.

Considering the improvement of the visual appearance of a computer game gained by using OpenGL, it is definitely worth the additional effort.

REFERENCES

[Dri05] *Direct Rendering Infrastructure, http://dri.freedesktop.org/wiki*, 2005.

[Glut05] GLUT—*The OpenGL Utility Toolkit, http://www.opengl.org/resources/libraries/glut.html*, 2005.

[Mesa05] *The Mesa 3D Graphics Library, http://www.mesa3d.org*, 2005.

[OpenGL05] *OpenGL, http://www.opengl.org*, 2005.

[OpenGLFaq05] *OpenGl FAQ, http://www.opengl.org/resources/faq/technical/fonts.htm*, 2005.

[Plib05] *The Portable Game Library, http://plib.sourceforge.net*, 2005.

[Qt05] *Qt Documentation, http://doc.trolltech.com*, 2005.

[Ravensoft05] *Plane Extraction, http://www2.ravensoft.com/users/ggribb/plane_extraction.pdf*, 2005.

[Redbook05] *The OpenGL Programming Guide, http://www.opengl.org/documentation/red_book_1.0*, 2005.

8 OpenGL with Qt

In This Chapter

- Creating OpenGL Widgets
- Coordinates
- Textures
- OpenGL Context Properties
- Convenience Methods
- Text Rendering
- Multiple Widgets and Context Sharing

When developing an OpenGL-based game, one of the first tasks is to create an OpenGL widget. This includes setting up an OpenGL context using functions and libraries that are very system dependent and time consuming to learn, such as the GLX library on X11 systems, WGL on Microsoft Windows systems, or AGL on Apple Macintosh systems.

The Qt library is one possibility to easily combine these functions and open an OpenGL widget. Furthermore, with the cross-platform capabilities of Qt, this will also work on all platforms supported by Qt. However, if opening an OpenGL window is the only task your project requires from such a library, Qt is not necessarily the right choice since other powerful and popular libraries are also available [Glut05] that do the same. Nevertheless, Qt can also support game development in many other ways, and if you are already using Qt, it is logical to open OpenGL widgets with Qt. In this case, you do not need to create additional library dependencies in your project.

In addition to opening OpenGL widgets, Qt provides several features that make OpenGL development much more convenient, so that overall, you can save time and avoid bugs. In this chapter, we demonstrate how to use Qt to create OpenGL widgets, and present the most important features that Qt provides regarding OpenGL such as font display and texture image loading.

CREATING OPENGL WIDGETS

Qt provides a widget class that gives access to OpenGL and supports OpenGL commands. The `QGLWidget` can be used like any other Qt widget, and can therefore coexist with a normal Qt GUI, a trait that is often very handy when developing desktop games. Starting with Qt 4, even normal Qt widgets such as labels and buttons can be used in a `QGLWidget`.

To create an OpenGL widget an instance of the `QGLWidget` class is needed. To make use of rendering, you first need to subclass this `QGLWidget` class and re-implement `paintGL()`, `resizeGL()`, and `initializeGL()`. Especially, `initializeGL()` deserves a special note since it should contain all OpenGL commands that you otherwise might want to place in the constructor of the class. The reason for this is that the OpenGL context may not yet exist when the constructor of the class is called. To avoid this initialization problem, all OpenGL initializing commands are collected in the `initializeGL()` method. Note that these three methods are all automatically called by Qt.

A simple class subclassing `QGLWidget` is shown in the following example:

```
class MyGLWidget : public QGLWidget
{
  Q_OBJECT

  public:
    MyGLWidget(QWidget* parent = 0)
            : QGLWidget(parent, 0)
    {
    }

  protected:
    // Initialize OpenGL
    virtual void initializeGL();

    // Called when the widget is resized
```

```
    virtual void resizeGL(int width, int height);

    // Called on paint events
    virtual void paintGL();
};
```

The `initializeGL()` method is called automatically by Qt for initialization purpose and can be implemented like:

```
void MyGLWidget::initializeGL()
{
  // Insert your initializing code here
  glClearColor(1.0, 1.0, 1.0, 0.0);
  glDisable(GL_DITHER);
  ...
}
```

In addition, widget resize events are automatically processed by Qt and then forwarded to the `resizeGL()` method, which could look like:

```
void MyGLWidget::resizeGL(int width, int height)
{
  // Insert your resizing code here
  glViewport(0, 0, width, height);

  // Setup a 3D projection matrix
  glMatrixMode(GL_PROJECTION);
  glLoadIdentity();
  gluPerspective(60.0, (GLdouble)width, (GLdouble)height,
                0.0625, 512.0);
  glMatrixMode(GL_MODELVIEW);
  ...
}
```

Finally, the key method of a Qt OpenGL implementation will be the reaction to paint events. Again, the corresponding method `paintGL()` is automatically called by Qt. If a manual update is required, the slot `updateGL()` should be called instead, which in turn invokes `paintGL()`. An example implementation of `paintGL()` could resemble:

```
void MyGLWidget::paintGL()
{
  // The code to render the scene goes here
```

```
glClear(GL_COLOR_BUFFER_BIT | GL_DEPTH_BUFFER_BIT);

glLoadIdentity();

// As example draw a red triangle
glColor3ub(255, 0, 0);
glBegin(GL_TRIANGLE);
  glVertex3f(0.0, 0.0, -2.0);
  glVertex3f(0.0, 1.0, -2.0);
  glVertex3f(1.0, 1.0, -2.0);
glEnd();

// Draw more stuff
...
}
```

Finally, the widget can be instantiated and shown, for example, in the main program of your application.

```
int main(int argc, char** argv)
{
  // Create the application and the OpenGL widget
  QApplication app(argc, argv);
  MyGLWidget* gl = new MyGLWidget(0);
  app.setMainWidget(gl);
  gl->show();
  return app.exec();
}
```

Note that none of the three methods paintGL(), resizeGL(), and initializeGL() is to be called directly. During initialization, Qt automatically calls initializeGL(). When resizing the widget, which works like resizing any other Qt widget, Qt also calls resizeGL(). The contents of the widget can be redrawn by calling the slot updateGL(), which in turn calls paintGL(), and organizes related issues such as double buffering.

COORDINATES

In contrast to Qt and most other windowing toolkits that use (0,0) to denote the top-left corner, OpenGL considers (0,0) the lower left corner. Therefore, it is often necessary to convert between these different coordinate representations. This is especially the case when you use mouse coordinates. Fortunately, the conversion between Qt and OpenGL coordinates is very easy and needs to be done only once at the beginning of a method. The following example retrieves the Qt cursor position and converts it to OpenGL coordinates:

```
// Obtain a position in Qt coordinates
QPoint pos = QCursor::pos();

// Convert to OpenGL coordinates
int x = pos.x();
int y = height() - pos.y();
...
```

Conversion from OpenGL coordinates to Qt coordinates can be done exactly the same way:

```
// Convert to Qt coordinates
int qtX = openGLX;
int qtY = height() - openGLY;
...
```

TEXTURES

Textures are vital components of most OpenGL-based games; therefore, loading image files, to use them as textures, is an important task. There exist numerous different image formats such as bmp, jpg, png, and gif, and libraries are available to load these files. All of these libraries differ in complexity and portability and usually have a very different API. However, Qt provides support to all common file formats; therefore, it is logical to use Qt classes to load image files in Qt-based games. This can be easily performed using the QImage or the QPixmap class.

```
// Load an image in different ways
QImage img1("image.jpg");

QImage img2;
img2.load("image.jpg");
...

QPixmap pix1("image.jpg");
...

QPixmap pix2;
```

```
pix2.load("image.jpg");
...
```

If you use the images only for OpenGL textures, QImage would be the most sensible choice, since it can be immediately converted to an OpenGL texture. However, if an image has already been used somewhere else and was therefore loaded using QPixmap, it can be directly converted to a QImage by performing the following command:

```
QPixmap pix("image.jpg");
QImage img = pix.convertToImage();
```

Note, however, that the conversion between the two image classes is slow.

OpenGL prior to version 2.0 requires texture images to have the size $2^n + 2 \times$ border with any integer value $n = n_x$ in the x-direction, and another integer value $n = n_y$ in the y-direction. Therefore, each image must be of size $2^{n_x} 2^{n_y}$ if no borders are used (and indeed we do not use borders in the scope of this book). It is possible to ensure that the images will be of this size when loading them, but generally, it is more convenient to maintain all image files in the right size. If a conversion is necessary, it can be done as shown in the following code snippet:

```
// Load an image
QImage img("image.jpg");

// Calculate correct size
int newW = 1;
int newH = 1;
while (newW < img.width())
{
  newW *= 2;
}
while (newH < img.height())
{
  newH *= 2;
}

// Scale the image
img = img.smoothScale(newW, newH);

// Alternative scaling which is faster but lower quality
img = img.scale(newW, newH);
```

Scaling an image results in a loss of image quality and thus should be avoided.

Images loaded as `QImage` cannot be directly used in OpenGL, and therefore require an extra conversion step. Fortunately, this conversion to the format understood by OpenGL is easy using `QGLWidget::convertToGLFormat()`. The resulting image can then be directly given to OpenGL using `glTexImage2D()`. However, once this conversion is applied to an image, the image can no longer be used as a normal Qt image because the internal image structure has been altered; these images are now only valid for OpenGL and not for other Qt methods or classes.

```
// Load an image
QImage img("image.jpg");

// Convert the image to an OpenGL format
QImage glImage = QGLWidget::convertToGLFormat(img);

// The format the texture will be stored in
GLint internalFormat = GL_RGBA;

// Load the image as OpenGL texture
glTexImage2D(GL_TEXTURE_2D, 0, internalFormat,
             glImage.width(), glImage.height(),
             0, GL_RGBA, GL_UNSIGNED_BYTE,
             glImage.bits());
```

OPENGL CONTEXT PROPERTIES

When creating an OpenGL widget, Qt will create an OpenGL context, which has some initial properties. These properties can be configured by providing a customized `QGLFormat` instance to the widget constructor. These properties include

- Enabling double buffering ("on" by default)
- Presence of a depth buffer ("on" by default)
- Presence of an alpha channel ("off" by default)
- Presence of a stencil buffer ("off" by default)
- Presence of an accumulation buffer ("off" by default)
- Enabling direct rendering ("on" by default)

An OpenGL context that supports an alpha channel and a stencil buffer may be requested as shown in the following example:

```
QGLFormat fmt;
fmt.setAlpha(true);
```

```
fmt.setStencil(true);
QGLWidget* widget = new QGLWidget(fmt, this);
```

Although the default settings of QGLFormat are usually more than suitable for game development, the ability to alter them can sometimes be advantageous. For example, it may be useful to explicitly use software rendering instead of hardware acceleration by requesting a widget without direct rendering. Software rendering is much slower, but is much more compatible with debuggers.

CONVENIENCE METHODS

Other than providing a means to set up the OpenGL environment and texture loading routines, Qt also provides features that make development easier. By using these convenience methods instead of plain OpenGL functions, the code usually becomes more readable and therefore easier to understand and maintain.

Color

Normally, the current color and the clearing color are set by using OpenGL commands such as glColor*() and glClearColor(). However, Qt provides alternative convenience methods to these so the QColor class can be used as a parameter. qglColor() is equivalent to calling glColor3*(), and qglClearColor() is equivalent to glClearColor().

```
// Both calls do the same:
qglColor(Qt::red);
glColor3ub(255, 0, 0);

// Both calls do the same:
qglClearColor(Qt::black);
glClearColor(0.0, 0.0, 0.0, 0.0);
```

It is often more convenient to use one of the Qt methods instead of the original OpenGL versions.

Paint Events

Qt makes sure the implementation of QGLWidget::paintGL() is called when appropriate; that is, when paint events occur. When manual rendering is desired, the slot updateGL() should be called, which in turn calls paintGL(). Furthermore, when following this procedure, Qt also takes care of technical issues such as making the OpenGL context current, swapping buffers (double buffering), and ensuring that the OpenGL widget has been initialized. The `updateGL()` slot can also be used to regularly re-render the scene, by calling it from a timer routine. Such a regular update is something usually desired for games that contain continuously moving objects.

```
MyGLWidget::MyGLWidget(QWidget* parent) : QGLWidget(parent)
{
  ...
  QTimer* timer = new QTimer(this);
  connect(timer, SIGNAL(timeout()),
          this, SLOT(updateGL()));

  // Repaint every 25 ms
  timer->start(25);
}
```

This code example will redraw the scene every 25 ms; that is, 40 times per second. Note that the `QTimer` involves some system-dependent inaccuracy; if that turns out to be a problem, more complicated solutions need to be developed, such as using a modified event loop.

TEXT RENDERING

Many tasks in game development require drawing some text on the screen. Such tasks include drawing status and player information such as health or points. Additionally, it can also be useful to print out debug information for developers. However, OpenGL does not directly support text rendering, but requires the user to implement functions for this task. Fortunately, Qt provides a method to do exactly this: `QGLWidget::renderText()`.

There are several different ways of text rendering such as bitmap fonts, texture fonts, and geometric fonts (see Chapter 7, "OpenGL"). Using the Qt method `renderText()`, one type of font, bitmap fonts, can be displayed. These bitmap fonts use the system fonts of the underlying windowing system for display and thus provide a wide range of professional-looking fonts. However, bitmap fonts also have some disadvantages; for example, they cannot be rotated or scaled and are slower in rendering compared to texture fonts. Nevertheless, for most desktop game applications, they are still fast enough.

The application of `renderText()` is straightforward and shown in the following code snippet:

```
// Render text at position (10,10) in Qt coordinates -
// the text is drawn in the current color
renderText(10, 10, "Text");

// Render some other text with a custom font
QFont font;
font.setSize(16);
renderText(10, 100, "Other Text", font);
```

The coordinates of the text are specified in Qt coordinates with (0,0) in the upper left corner. Note that in contrast to `glXUseXFont()`, starting with Qt 3.3.2, `QGLWidget::renderText()` can even render outline fonts, giving a wider choice of excellent fonts.

MULTIPLE WIDGETS AND CONTEXT SHARING

All OpenGL drawings usually go into a single `QGLWidget`; that is, to one OpenGL context. Even though it is sometimes useful to have another instance, especially for debugging purposes, this second context should generally be avoided for the core functionality of the game. The reason for this is that some drivers and card combinations may have problems with more than one OpenGL context with respect to both stability and performance.

All `QGLWidgets` maintain their own OpenGL context containing the texture objects and display lists, for example. These settings remain unknown to any other `QGLWidget` instances. Actually, using texture objects in a widget different from the one in which they have been originally declared will lead to graphic corruption. However, this sharing is exactly what is sometimes desired. Texture objects and display lists should be used in a second (debug) widget as well. To address this issue, `QGLWidget` provides context sharing. By providing an already existing `QGLWidget` to the constructor of a new `QGLWidget`, the OpenGL context of the first widget will be reused if possible.

```
// Creates a new OpenGL context
QGLWidget* firstWidget = new QGLWidget(this);

// Shares the OpenGL context of the first widget
QGLWidget secondWidget = new QGLWidget(this. 0, firstWidget);

// Find out whether sharing has succeeded
if (!secondWidget->isSharing())
{
```

```
    // Sharing failed
    ...
}
```

Once sharing is successfully established, the second widget may use all display lists and texture objects that have been declared in the first widget. However, even if texture objects and display lists are shared like this, both widgets still use two different OpenGL contexts, which may be slow on some systems. Therefore, it is usually better in games to use a single QGLWidget only.

SUMMARY

Many toolkits are available that can create a display for OpenGL applications. Inside a Qt application, the use of Qt for this task is both natural and straight-forward. Qt contains the QGLWidget class, which can open such a display for OpenGL and therefore provides Qt-based games with easy access to all the features of OpenGL.

Furthermore, Qt encapsulates the often-difficult task of employing GLX function calls that are necessary to set up an OpenGL context in the easier to use Qt wrapper classes. This allows the programmer to focus more on the actual 3D OpenGL programming than on all the details of the function calls.

Additionally, Qt aids the developer by providing useful methods for text rendering in OpenGL, something OpenGL does not inherently support. Qt's support for images and its capability to convert these images into the OpenGL image format also allow the easy load of OpenGL game textures.

REFERENCES

[Glut05] *GLUT—The OpenGL Toolkit, http://www.opengl.org/resources/ libraries/glut.html, 2005.*

9 Sound and Graphics

Multimedia—music, sound effects, and graphics—is a very important aspect when trying to create a professional-looking computer game. In contrast to normal desktop applications in which the function of the application is much more important than the appearance, this does not apply to computer games. Games are played for their functions and for their visual and audio appearance. Generally, for the majority of games, those that look "cool" have a much better chance of being noticed by players than games that have only a plain command-line interface. Admittedly, this is not always good or even fair, but only a handful of games have captured the game market's interest with just plain graphics and no sound.

Desktop games, such as those described in this book, do not require the excessive multimedia effects necessary to produce a movie-quality game production. However, even for small desktop games, it is a good idea to invest some effort into

267

graphics and/or sound effects (SFX), since these extra details will appeal to the player.

Implementing sound and graphics into a Qt or KDE application is easy and straightforward. The difficult part is to actually create the graphics, sound effects, or music, and this part essentially lies in your own creative talents or those of your graphic or audio designer. In this chapter, we cannot provide help with respect to the actual drawing or composing. Therefore, we provide an introduction to digital sound and graphics and how these can be stored on a computer. We further discuss how to load and use music, sound effects, and graphics on the target platforms KDE, Qt, or Qtopia on PDAs.

AUDIO AND SOUND EFFECTS

Sound effects and music are key features for human senses. People often underestimate how much sound effects contribute to a dramatic scene in a movie they are viewing. Tense, exciting, or peaceful moments in the movie are accompanied by the appropriate music. This concept also applies to the theatrical quality of computer games, and to a large extent good sound effects and background music can capture a player's interest much more than just good graphics can. Try this yourself: switch off the sound in a thriller movie or in your favorite action-based computer game and observe the differences.

In computer games, sound effects and music are used in two main areas. First, computer games can have background music. Although continually heard, this musical composition is not directly related to an actual game effect taking place. Nevertheless, nowadays, the background music in computer games is often automatically selected by the game engine to match specific scenes of the game play. For example, as in a movie, more exciting music is played when the player approaches a dangerous scene, and such adapted music selections make the playing experience more intense. The second main area for sound is the sound effects heard when an individual action on the screen is accompanied by an appropriate sound. These short sound pieces produce an actual effect—such as an explosion, shot, or running engine—and will be played when the game displays the corresponding graphics elements. These effects are important to support the visual experience on the screen.

Digital Sound

In general, sound and music are just oscillating or vibrating air. This vibrating air is generated by a sound emitter, which can be a musical instrument, a human voice, or a loudspeaker. This vibrating air is then perceived by our ears as music or sound effects.

To transport music or sound into or out of the computer, the "vibrating air" has to be translated into numbers that a computer understands. This conversion is performed by a microphone (for recording) or a loudspeaker (for playback) (see Figure 9.1), and these devices translate the air vibrations to (microphone) or from (loudspeaker) an electric current that is then suitable for electronic processing. Note that if the music or the particular sound effect is directly generated on a computer, the process of recording the sound into the computer is unnecessary.

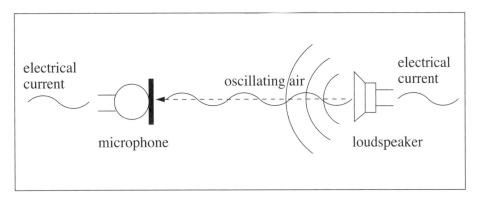

FIGURE 9.1 A sound wave is emitted by a loudspeaker, which transforms the electrical oscillation into airwaves, which in turn are received by the microphone. The microphone converts the air oscillations back to an oscillating electrical current.

Sound itself is an analog phenomenon; that is, a continuous oscillation of sound intensity and frequency. The electric signals generated from a microphone or sent to a loudspeaker are similar analog signals. If these signals from a microphone are then transferred to the computer, they must first be converted into a binary, digital format; only then can the sound from the microphone be used further on the computer. For playback purposes, this process is reversed and the digital data from the computer is converted back to an analog form, which can then be fed to the loudspeaker.

The process of converting the analog signal into its digital counterpart is called *digitization* and requires the quantization of the analog audio input signal and the storage of the previously continuous signal into a discrete set of numbers. This is achieved by sampling (measuring) the original signal multiple times per second. For CD-quality sound or music, the sampling is performed 44100 times per second; that is, with a sampling rate (sampling frequency) of 44.1 kHz. This set of 44100 numbers per second is then stored on the computer. Each of these individual measurements will measure the current amplitude of the sound signal by dividing it into a given amount of digital steps. For CD-quality sound, 16 bits

(65536 steps) are used to describe the amplitude at any given moment. Using this procedure, the original continuous signal is transformed into a little digital staircase signal. Figure 9.2 depicts this process of converting an analog sound wave into a digital signal.

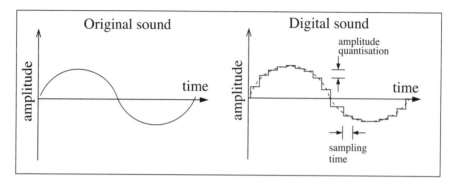

FIGURE 9.2   An original analog sound wave (left) is digitized with a given sampling time and a certain amplitude quantization, resulting in a digital "staircase" representation of the sound (right).

Sampling rate and quantization steps can be chosen differently from the CD example. Nevertheless, if the sampling rate is too small or the quantization steps are too large, the resulting signal will be audibly different from the original signal and the quality will be poor. On the other hand, when more samples are measured each second or a higher precision is used for the amplitude quantization, the resulting signal corresponds better with the original analog audio signal. However, when these values are higher, more storage space for the data is required. Generally, the sampling frequency must be twice the highest frequency that should be heard in the digitized sound [Shannon05]. As an example, the former CD-quality example would store 88200 bytes per second (16bit * 44100 samples/second) for mono audio, and twice as much (176400 bytes per second, or approximately 10 MB per minute) for stereo audio. Its frequency limit would be 22 kHz, which is beyond what the human ear can perceive.

Sound Formats

Audio data that is recorded on the computer or is generated on the computer needs to be stored in a standardized file format so other applications can load, use, and play it back. There are numerous standardized audio file formats available, and these audio file formats can be roughly grouped into three different categories. Files in each category have similar properties even if the actual file formats differ. In the following section, the presented formats are those most commonly used in computer games.

Uncompressed Audio Files

The first category of file formats is uncompressed audio files (sometimes, these audio files can be additionally compressed with a standard *lossless* compression algorithm). These files contain the raw audio information in a digital form as it was obtained from the quantization process. Except for quality losses during the digitalization process, this data is identical to the original audio file and is therefore of very good quality.

WAV files used with Microsoft Windows and Linux systems or AIFF files used mainly in the Apple Macintosh world belong to this audio file category [Wav05]. Essentially, except for additional administrative information, audio CDs also store music in this format.

However, digital sound generates a lot of information, and storing all this information in uncompressed formats can generate very large files.

Audio Files with Lossy Compression

To overcome the large size of digital format files, this second category of audio files compresses the information using *lossy* compression algorithms. These algorithms compress the information in such a way that after decompression, the original data is not restored identically, and thus some information is lost.

MP3 files, OggVorbis, or Windows WMA fall into this category [Hacker00]. Here, the raw digital information, as it would appear in a WAV file, is compressed using sophisticated psycho-acoustic algorithms. These algorithms use the characteristics of the human ear to actually not perceive all sound bits that are present in a sound: the human ear actually overhears parts of the sounds. For example, a very weak sound at the same time or shortly after (or even before) a very loud sound is not perceived (simultaneous or temporal masking). Additionally, not all sound frequencies are perceived equally by the ear. 20 Hz–20 kHz (decreasing with age) is the normal frequency range the human ear can hear. However, not all frequencies are equally as important to the human ear.

Using this psycho-acoustic knowledge of the human ear allows the compression format to miss information from the original music and thus reduce its size. Alongside standard compression algorithms, this technique allows a drastic reduction of the file size. For example, MP3 files are much smaller when compared to a WAV file. Size reduction of factors 10 to 20 is possible without significant quality loss.

The actual amount of compression and therefore the resulting file size can be determined by the creator of the file, and the higher the compression the worse the quality. However, most people cannot distinguish the loss in quality when the original file is compressed to a MP3 format using moderate compression, which results in a data stream of 160–192 kBit/s. This retains good quality combined with small file sizes and makes the MP3 format an ideal choice for large music or speech effects in computer games.

MP3 encoding is a lossy compression and will therefore not contain all information present in the original sound data.

Synthesizer Files

Another audio format used for computer games is the MIDI format [White00], which is totally different from the WAV or MP3 format. In the MIDI format, the original sound is not digitized; rather, the sound is built with a musical language where notes are "played" on a virtual synthesizer. The MIDI files just store the melody together with the particular instruments that should play the tune.

The quality of WAV or MP3 files is superior to those of MIDI files, and there are additional requirements to the installed software or to the sound card. However, MIDI files are even smaller than the MP3 files; thus, MIDI files were once primarily used for the background music in games. Nowadays, however, MP3 files are usually employed for that task, making MIDI files less important to games.

What Audio Format to Choose?

In computer games, it is often preferable to chose file size aspects instead of quality; after all, your main aim is the game, not to have a symphony playing. Therefore, MP3 files for the background music and even the sound effects are usually the ideal choice.

One disadvantage of MP3 is that it requires more computer power to play back MP3 files due to the decoding of the file before playing. If this becomes an issue or a decoder is not available, you could change to WAV files instead. WAV files have the additional advantage that basically all target systems can play them back. Additionally, if you only use small sound effects, like explosion sounds, which do not require much space, WAV files might be more appropriate.

Sound in KDE

There are several ways to play back sound and music in KDE. Since KDE 2.0 the *aRts* sound server has become the central backbone for audio playback in KDE. aRts provides a lot of functionality, including loading/decoding and playing sound files. Many of the aRts features are provided by plug-ins, such as the decoding of compressed sound files. For the purposes of game programming, it is not necessary to know the intricate details of the aRts design and its plug-in architecture.

aRts is usually shipped along with KDE; however, aRts does not depend on KDE or Qt but uses its own template classes. This has some advantages when trying to use aRts in projects other than KDE or Qt. However, this independence can initiate a few disadvantages in terms of API consistency, as you need to get used to a different API form. Therefore, KDE offers some convenience wrapper classes that aid in developing sound codes with aRts.

The following sections show you how to play sound in KDE. The example program `mysound` included on the companion CD-ROM in the folder `examples/mysound` implements these various possibilities.

KAudioPlayer

The easiest way to play a sound file in KDE is to use the `KAudioPlayer` class, which provides a play-and-forget asynchronous audio playing facility. Furthermore, it does not require any special sound libraries to be linked to the application, as it uses the KDE Desktop Communication Protocol (DCOP) to communicate with the aRts sound server. Unfortunately, this indirect interface does not allow fast response times, and only WAV files are guaranteed to be played back. The audio player class `KAudioPlayer` can be used in the following straightforward manner:

```
#include <kaudioplayer.h>
...
KAudioPlayer::play("mysound.wav");
```

This solution is extremely easy to implement, but the high latency is a disadvantage that makes it barely usable for most types of games. However, if latency is not a concern and you require a simple interface, `KAudioPlayer` might be an acceptable choice.

Play Objects

When the features of the `KAudioPlayer` are not sufficient for your application, it will be necessary to access aRts more directly. The first step in this process is to set up a communication link with aRts by creating an instance of the class `KArtsDispatcher`. Once this is done, you will need to initialize a sound server object. By using the KDE class `KArtsServer`, you can make sure that aRts is properly started and initialized. This procedure is most appropriately done during the startup of the application.

```
#include <arts/kartsdispatcher.h>
#include <arts/kartsserver.h>
...
```

```
// Setup communication
KArtsDispatcher mDispatcher;


// The sound server object
KArtsServer mSoundServer;

// Initialize the object and check for errors
if (mSoundServer.server().isNull())
{
  // An error occurred
  return;
}
```

Both objects should be created only in the application, and should be retained until the destruction of the program. Note that the dispatcher object will not be touched anymore, but it needs to remain to maintain the communication link between aRts and your program.

At this point, the program is prepared to play simple WAV files.

```
// Play the sound using the sound-server
mSoundServer.server().play("mysound.wav");
```

This example repeats the same features as the KAudioPlayer, yet the audio response is quicker because the communication with aRts is more direct. Note, however, that now the aRts libraries have to be linked to the application using the compiler flag-lartskde, which was not necessary when using the simple KAudioPlayer interface.

By using aRts directly, it is now possible to play back any other type of sound object supported by aRts. This is achieved by using the aRts *play objects*, and is particularly interesting for playing back MP3 files. A play object is requested from aRts using the KPlayObjectFactory class, for example. aRts then handles the loading and decoding of the file. Once a play object is retrieved, it can be played, paused, and played again as desired.

```
#include <arts/kartsdispatcher.h>
#include <arts/kartsserver.h>
...
// Setup communication
KArtsDispatcher mDispatcher;

// The sound server object
KArtsServer mSoundServer;
```

```
// Initialize the object and check for errors
if (mSoundServer.server().isNull()) { return; }
...

// Create the play object factory
KPlayObjectFactory factory(mSoundServer.server());

// Request the play object
KURL file;
file.setFileName("mysound.mp3");
KPlayObject* playObject = factory.createPlayObject(file, true);

// Play the play object if it got created
if(!playObject->isNull())
{
  playObject->play();
}
```

Again, the aRts libraries have to be linked to the application (`-lartskde`) to allow direct access to aRts.

Note that aRts is still not that well suited for advanced operations in game environments. It is optimized for playing music files, and therefore sometimes the aRts plug-ins have problems with short sound files such as those that are used for sound effects. Most of these problems can be avoided by using WAV files only. For very advanced uses, a gaming sound library such as OpenAL may be preferred over aRts. We present OpenAL later in this chapter.

MIDI Music

MIDI files are rarely used in games these days. However, if you really want to apply them, KDE delivers a library that is able to play back MIDI files. `libkmid` provides a very simple interface that can load and play MIDI music. The following example loads a MIDI file after the library has been initialized:

```
#include <libkmid/libkmid.h>
...
KMidSimpleAPI::kMidInit();
...
KMidSimpleAPI::kMidLoad("mysound.mid");
KMidSimpleAPI::kMidPlay();
...
KMidSimpleAPI::kMidStop();
...
KMidSimpleAPI::kMidDestruct();
```

Note, however, that it depends on the actual target computer installation whether MIDI file playback is supported, and you must consider this when creating music and sound intended to be played on other computers [Kmid05].

Sound in Qt

If you are not using KDE and/or aRts, it is still possible to use the Qt capabilities to play back sound effects. Qt offers the QSound class to access the audio facilities of the target platform. The following example from the example program mysound included on the companion CD-ROM in the folder examples/mysound implements Qt sound playback. Similar to the KDE class KAudioPlayer, a sound file can be loaded and played back asynchronously using:

ON THE CD

```
#include <qsound.h>
...
QSound::play("mysounds.wav");
```

This allows the direct playback of a sound that is stored in a sound file. A more indirect method is to first load the sound file into the memory. Then, the sound can be played without additional access to the file.

```
#include <qsound.h>
...
QSound sound("mysounds.wav");
sound.play();
```

To loop a sound in Qt, it is possible to use the setLoops() method call.

```
// Loop the sound 5 times
sound.setLoops(5);

// Loop the sound indefinitely
sound.setLoops(-1);
```

The sound file formats that can be played back depend on the underlying multimedia system. Generally, only WAV files should be used, as they are supported on all platforms. On X11, the Network Audio System (NAS) is used for playback supporting WAV and AU files. Note that on KDE systems, NAS is often not installed, and therefore no sound will be heard! On Microsoft Windows, Qt can also play back sound files using the underlying multimedia system, but again, only the WAV format is supported.

The availability of sound can be tested using QSound::isAvailable(). If a sound cannot be played back or the particular file format is not supported, QSound does nothing; that is, no error is displayed and no sound is heard.

Sound on PDA Systems

On embedded systems, two possibilities for playing audio files exist. With embedded Qt, sound can be played back using the Qt sound features described in the previous section. Additionally, on PDA systems, the Qtopia framework slightly extends the Qt sound features by implementing the class Sound. This class is a wrapper class for QSound and allows the use of sound on PDAs more easily. For sound playback, Qtopia uses a built-in mixing sound server that accesses the sound driver of the PDA directly. Again, only WAV file sound formats are supported.

A sound file can be loaded into memory and then played back using:

```
#include <qtopia/sound.h>

// Locate and read the audio file
Sound sound("mysound.wav");
sound.play();
```

By using the Sound class, the audio files are automatically searched in the Qtopia resource path. The analogous QSound example might resemble:

```
#include <qsound.h>
#include <qpe/resource.h>
QSound::play(Resource::findSound("mysound.wav"));
```

To continuously loop a song, it is possible to use the playLoop() method calls.

```
#include <qtopia/sound.h>

// Locate and read the audio file
Sound sound("mysound.wav");

// Start the playback
sound.playLoop();
...

// And to stop it
sound.stop();
```

OpenAL

OpenAL, or the "Open Audio Library," is a cross-platform 3D sound library designed primarily for games [Openal05]. In many ways, it resembles OpenGL and is therefore extremely compatible when used in conjunction with this graphics system. Many games are now using OpenAL, including commercial high-end games such as Unreal Tournament 2004™. Similar to OpenGL, OpenAL is strictly speaking only a specification for a sound library, but has been implemented for various platforms, including Microsoft Windows, Linux, and Apple Macintosh. OpenAL can be downloaded for free from the Web site [Openal05].

One important issue arising from the OpenAL specification is that it does not cover the actual loading of files from disk, or the decoding of compressed audio files such as MP3 files. However, to allow such tasks, many OpenAL implementations have added support through utility functions. Obviously, this is a very important issue, and therefore we recommend that you use some form of extended OpenAL implementation. In the following examples, we demonstrate the capabilities of OpenAL.

Before you can do anything useful with OpenAL, it requires initialization.

```c
#include <AL/al.h>
#include <AL/alc.h>
#include <AL/alut.h>

int main()
{
  // Open the (default) device
  ALCdevice* device = alcOpenDevice(0);
  // Error?
  if (device == 0) { return 1; }

  // Create the context
  ALCcontext* context = alcCreateContext(device, 0);
  // Error?
  if (context == 0) { return 1; }

  alcMakeContextCurrent(context);

  ...

  return 0;
}
```

Before playing back a file, it needs to be loaded into memory. For this task, we use the utility function `alutLoadWAVFile()` that is normally issued with the OpenAL implementation. The function signature may look slightly different, because the function is not actually part of the OpenAL specification.

```
ALenum format;
ALvoid* bufferData;
ALsizei size;
ALsizei frequency;
ALboolean loop;

alutLoadWAVFile((ALbyte*)"sound.wav", &format, &bufferData,
                &size, &frequency, &loop);
```

In short, this procedure loads the WAV file `sound.wav` along with some required data. Note that `alutLoadWAVFile()` loads the data only into the variables, which are given as parameters, but does not forward this data to OpenAL. To achieve this next step, it is necessary to additionally reserve a buffer ID and forward the data from `alutLoadWAVFile()` to the actual OpenAL buffer.

```
// Load the data into an OpenAL buffer
ALuint buffer;
alGenBuffers(1, &buffer); // reserve one buffer ID

// Fill the buffer
alBufferData(buffer, format, bufferData, size, frequency);

// Free memory
alutUnloadWAV(format, bufferData, size, frequency);
```

The function `alBufferData()` copies the specified audio data into an OpenAL buffer where OpenAL maintains its own copy of the data. The loaded data can now be discarded using `alutUnloadWAV()`.

Instead of `alutLoadWAVFile()`, any other function that loads an audio file into the variables required for `alBufferData()` could be used. Additionally, an OpenAL implementation may provide functions such as `alutLoadVorbis_LOKI()`, which is the case with OpenAL Linux extensions from Loki. This particular function will then load a compressed Ogg Vorbis file directly into an OpenAL buffer, and take care of all decoding of the compressed file.

In a 3D sound library, it is important where the sound source is actually located. Depending on the distance, position, and velocity of the sound source, the sound will appear different. This sound source in OpenAL has several properties, such as position and velocity. However, for simple sound playing it is already sufficient to just assign a buffer to a source. Every buffer can be assigned to as many sources as desired, and because these buffers are internally shared, this procedure consumes far less memory than loading the same file into several buffers.

```
// Set up a source that plays the buffer
ALuint source;
alGenSources(1, &source);
alSourcei(source, AL_BUFFER, buffer);

// Optional: loop the sound
alSourcei(source, AL_LOOPING, AL_TRUE);

// Start playing
alSourcePlay(source);
```

Playing back a sound is a nonblocking operation; that is, the sound is played in the background and does not interfere with the actual game program.

Once the sound processing in the game is completed, it is advisable to remove the sound objects that are no longer required.

```
alDeleteSources(1, &source);
alDeleteBuffers(1, &buffer);
```

To compile a program with OpenAL, you need to add the flag `-lopenal` to the linker settings.

Sources and Listeners

The purpose of OpenAL is to be a 3D sound library. In such a 3D scenario, the sound sources and the listener can be moved to different locations. The position of the listener and the sources are properties of the library and can therefore be easily manipulated.

```
// The position of the listener
alListener3f(AL_POSITION, posX, posY, posZ);

// The position of a source
alSource3f(source, AL_POSITION, posX, posY, posZ);
```

In OpenAL, there is only one listener, but there can be many sound sources. Therefore, the position is specified for a specific source, while there is no need to identify the listener.

A 3D effect that can be implemented very easily is a source moving from one side to the other. An example to implement this effect would resemble:

```
// Listener position
alListener3f(AL_POSITION, 0.0, -0.5, 0.0);

// Initial source position
alSource3f(source, AL_POSITION, 9.0, 0.0, 0.0)


// Start playing
alSourcePlay(source);

// Move the sound source
for (int i = 9; i >= -9; i--)
{
  alSource3f(source, AL_POSITION, (ALfloat)i, 0.0, 0.0);
  // Do something else, e.g. sleep(1)
  sleep(1);
  ...
}
```

ON THE CD You can find this example, named `myal` on the companion CD-ROM, in the folder `examples/myal`.

OpenAL supports numerous other interesting effects. For example, every source and the listener can have a velocity property that changes the positions, and generates a Doppler effect.

GRAPHICS

Alongside good sound effects, graphics are the next key feature for a good game. The same principles that achieve the movie-like qualities of a top commercial game also apply to the small desktop games. In both situations, the graphics need to fit the idea and scheme of the game. Furthermore, the graphics need to look professional and be well integrated into the game.

For computer games, there are several possibilities to use graphics; for example, 2D bitmap graphics, vector graphics, or even 3D graphics (see Figure 9.3). In the following sections, we present the concept of computer graphics and information on the various different concepts.

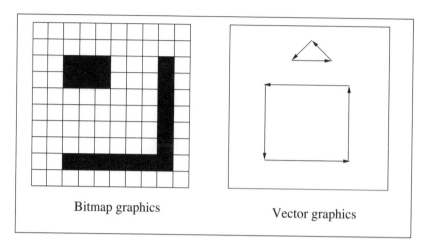

FIGURE 9.3 Comparison between a bitmap image (left) and a vector graphics image (right). Bitmap images are constructed from small colored pixels, while vector graphics define the coordinates, shape, and size of geometrical objects.

Digital Graphics

Images need to be available in a digital form to be of any use on the computer. On a computer screen, digital images are displayed as rectangular arrays of small points, called *pixels* (from picture elements). Each pixel can have one color from a given set of colors.

Partitioning an image into such discrete amounts of pixels will affect the quality of the digital image in two ways. First, the resolution of the image, or more accurately the amount of pixels per displayed size, needs to be sufficient. For example, if the resolution is too low, the fine details will be lost. For display on a computer monitor, one pixel of the image should normally correspond to one pixel of the display. Scaling or zooming an image will result in blurred images. Such artifacts resulting form enlarging a bitmap image are shown in Figure 9.4. Second, the number of possible colors available for each pixel can differ, and thus the color resolution/quality also varies. The number of different colors that can be distinguished is determined by the amount of color data stored per pixel.

The color of a pixel can be stored in two ways. The direct method is to store the amount of color for the three basic color components red, green, and blue (RGB) for each pixel. Mixing these basic colors creates all other possible colors. Nowadays, this storage concept is the one mainly used for computer graphics. Alternatively, it is also possible to store the color as an index number in the pixel. This index number refers to a lookup table or the *palette*, which contains the actual color value, again as an RGB value. Even though this indirect storage is hardly used anymore,

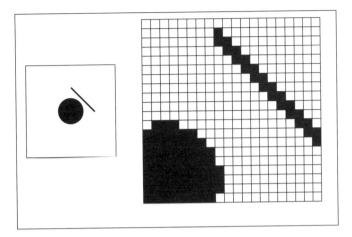

FIGURE 9.4 Scaling bitmap images will reduce their quality.
To the left, an original bitmap image is depicted. This image is
then zoomed in, resulting in the typical staircase effect of enlarged
bitmap images (right).

there are some applications in which palette-based color storage is useful (see Chapter 12, "Particle Effects").

The image data stored per pixel or per palette entry can vary. Typical values include:

1 bit: Black and white images

8 bits: Grayscale (256 gray shades), palette-based or low-color pictures (256 colors)

16 bits: High color images (65536 colors)

24 bits: True color images (16.7 million colors)

32 bits: Combines 24-bit true color image and 8-bit alpha channel

Even higher values are possible but are rarely used for games, and are normally only found in digital photo processing.

An image stored as an array of pixels is called a *raster* image or a *bitmap* image. Most computer images are stored this way because it allows an easy display of the images by directly copying them to the graphics card for display. However, bitmap images have one big disadvantage in that the size of these images basically cannot be changed. Any scaling will lower the quality of the image because there is simply not enough information available to display (enlarging or zooming in), or the information is deleted due to reducing or zooming out. Even though sophisticated algorithms do exist that can reduce the effects of scaling, it is generally not a good idea to do so. When necessary, you can usually reduce the size of an image, but enlarging it will result in serious quality loss.

To avoid the scaling problems of bitmap graphics, so-called vector graphics were introduced into computer graphics. These graphics do not store the information as individual colored pixels, but construct the image out of vectors, which constitute lines, curves, and other general geometrical forms. For these vector elements, only the coordinates, sizes, and length are defined. Changing the size of an image will then automatically readjust the coordinates and sizes of the vector elements without actually changing their basic appearance. Using vector graphics overcomes the scaling problem, but has two other disadvantages. First, not every picture can be easily described as a set of vectors. Although this functions extremely well for schematic drawings, it is not so easily possible for photo images. Second, the natural display of the computer is pixel based; therefore, all vector graphics still need to be rendered into a pixel graphics format before they can be displayed. This rendering requires additional computer power and a graphics library that implements the actual rendering process. Because of the more problematic use of vector graphics, computer games usually use a bitmap-oriented graphics format.

Graphic Formats

There are several possibilities to store graphics on a computer. The most important for computer games are the bitmap graphics that can be stored with different compression algorithms. However, some games can profit from the scaling capabilities of vector graphics. In this section, we describe the graphic formats of importance to desktop computer games.

Quality-Preserving Bitmap Graphics

For computer games, the principally used bitmap file formats that ensure that quality is preserved include PNG, GIF, and BMP. These formats use either no compression (simple BMP) or employ a *lossless* compression algorithm for storing the image data (PNG, GIF, or RLE compressed BMP) [Wikipedia05a].

The *lossless* compression for images removes redundant information in the image data to reduce the overall size. We show the working principle of such a compression algorithm with the RLE algorithm as example, because RLE uses a simple and straightforward compression algorithm. Suppose you have 20 bytes of image information:

0 0 0 0 0 0 0 0 4 4 4 2 2 2 2 2 2 2 2 2

RLE would store this as "8 times 0," "3 times 4," and "9 times 2," or in short, which is only 6 bytes long. Therefore, our example could compress the original 20 bytes to 6 bytes without losing any information.

Clearly, the application and compression efficiency of such compression algorithms depends on the actual image data. For example, a uniform picture can be easily compressed with such a compression algorithm. Note that the more advanced compression algorithms such as those implemented by the PNG file format can use less obvious redundancies in images. Therefore, nonuniform images can also be compressed well.

The advantage of such lossless image compression is that compressing and uncompressing the image will always result in the same image, and this image will contain exactly the same information and quality as the original. However, when compared to the original image, only a moderate amount of reduction can be achieved when using the lossless compression algorithms.

For a true color bitmap picture (24-bit), the original image size is *size = width × height × 3byte*. For example, the original size of a picture of size 100×100 pixels with 24 bits color depth would be 30 KB. By employing the lossless compression algorithm, the reduced image would be approximately 15 KB.

Quality Lossy Bitmap Graphics

In comparison with the MP3 format of audio compression, it is also possible to store images with a compression algorithm that actually loses information from the original image and therefore results in a reduced image quality [Wikipedia05b]. The typical file format employing such a *lossy* data compression is JPEG. Why would you want to lose quality in an image? The most obvious reason is that a much higher compression can be achieved if some information is sacrificed, and therefore less storage space is required. However, like the MP3 system, the compression algorithm is clever and tries to drop information that is not too obvious or even noticeable to the viewer. Generally, what the image is to be used for and the image itself determines whether such a quality loss is acceptable. Figure 9.5 depicts the quality loss that can occur in lossy image compression.

In brief, the JPEG compression works as follows: first, the image is converted from the normal RGB color space to the luminance-chrominance (YUV) color space. The compression algorithm benefits from this transformation because the human eye can notice more details in brightness (luminance) than in saturation or hue (chrominance), and therefore the algorithm can be optimized to store the luminance but reduce the chrominance information. After this step, the original image is split into rectangular tiles of 8×8 pixels and a discrete-cosine-transformation is applied to each of these blocks to convert them into the frequency domain. You may have already noticed these 8×8 blocks in a badly compressed JPEG image. Now, since the human eye cannot distinguish high-frequency brightness variations very well, these components are dropped, resulting in the main compression and quality loss of the image.

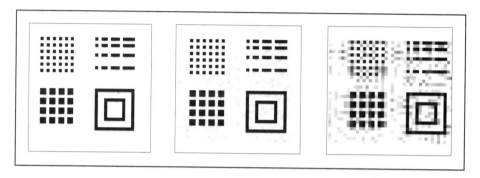

FIGURE 9.5 Difference between lossless and lossy image compression. The same image showing some black-white patterns is shown using three different compression settings. The left image shows a lossless compression (PNG), the middle image shows a slightly lossy compression (JPEG, 15% compression), and the right image shows a strong loss compression (JPEG, 85% compression). Going from left to right, the loss in quality that occurs, especially with distinct patterns, can be clearly observed.

Using a true color bitmap picture with an original size of 30 KB (100×100 pixels with 24-bits color depth), this can be easily reduced to a size of 5–10 KB. The amount of compression and subsequent loss in quality can be determined by the creator of the image. You have to choose a compression that results in an acceptable size and quality for your application.

Vector Graphics

Vector graphics store only the coordinates, sizes, and length of geometrical objects such as lines and curves. The SVG (Scalable Vector Graphics) file format has become the most prominent and standardized file format specification for vector graphics [Eisenberg02].

Before displaying SVG images, they need to be rendered; that is, converted into a bitmap image of the actual size. This is a crucial step, since the graphics display of a computer can only display bitmap-type graphics. Qt 3, Qt 4, and KDE 3 support vector graphics to a certain extent [Ksvg05]. KDE 4 has improved support for SVG graphics as well.

What Graphics Format to Choose?

Lossless compression file formats maintain the quality of the original image. This is particularly important for distinct screen graphics or icons. In most cases, games will rely on such graphic formats, and these are often in the form of PNG images.

Photos, background images, or other smooth images can be compressed well with lossy compression. The JPEG image format is widely used for these types of graphics because it saves a great deal of disk space. However, if disk space is not an issue, there is no reason to use such a file format. In particular, images that incorporate distinct graphics such as line drawings or geometrical images will look blurred when using JPEG compression, producing an overall unprofessional image.

Vector graphics are a good alternative when the game needs to incorporate scalable graphics so images can be displayed at different sizes or zoom levels. Moving to different displays or target platforms will not lose any quality in the images. Unfortunately, the support for vector graphics in Qt and KDE is still limited, and consequently only a few Qt/KDE desktop games use such vector graphics. However, in the KDE project there is an ongoing effort to use more scalable graphics.

Graphics in Qt and KDE

Fortunately, it is very simple to load graphics into Qt and KDE. Qt provides all the necessary classes to load the most commonly used bitmap file formats. Additionally, Qt has some support for loading and rendering vector graphics.

Bitmap Graphics

Qt provides the classes QPixmap and QImage to process graphical data. Both classes support the loading of images from files. The difference between these two classes is the way Qt internally stores the image data.

Both classes implement image loaders that can load all image file formats supported by the current Qt installation. These formats include the often-used PNG, BMP, and JPEG file formats (note, however, that it is possible to compile a Qt version without JPEG support).

Graphic files can be loaded by either specifying the filename in the object constructor

```
QPixmap pixmap("mygraph.png");

QImage image("myimage.png");
```

or by explicitly calling the `load()` method.

```
QPixmap pixmap;
pixmap.load("mygraph.png");
```

```
QImage image;
image.load("myimage.png");
```

The Qt image classes support an alpha transparency channel, which will be automatically loaded from PNG files if available.

The class QPixmap is optimized for drawing on the screen, while QImage is optimized for direct pixel access. Therefore, if you require the image for display purposes only and do not need to manipulate the individual pixels, QPixmap is the best choice. When you require both functions, you can refer to the Qt conversion method, which will transform a QImage into a QPixmap, and vice versa.

```
// Convert QPixmap 'pixmap' to QImage
QImage image = pixmap.convertToImage();

// Convert QImage 'image' to QPixmap
pixmap.convertFromImage(image);
```

These conversion methods are slow and should be avoided during parts of the game where critical timing is prominent.

In addition to the loading of images, the Qt image classes also allow basic image transformations such as scaling and rotations. For more details on these aspects, refer to the Qt documentation [Qt05].

Vector Graphics

Qt offers some limited support for loading SVG formats. It does not, however, support the full SVG standard, and therefore not all features of an image will be displayed.

A SVG file can be loaded and displayed using a QPicture object.

```
// Create a new picture object
QPicture* myPict = new QPicture();

// Load image information. Set the file type to "svg"
// If the file cannot be loaded 'false' is returned!
myPict->load("mysvg.svg", "svg");

...

// Somewhere in the paint code where a QPainter object
// is available, e.g.
QPainter paint(this);
```

```
// Draw the whole SVG graphics
paint.drawPicture(*myPict);
```

If you are developing for KDE only, a more extensive SVG support is available by using the KSVG2 library, which will be part of KDE 4 (or is independently available as a beta version in the kdenonbeta directory of the KDE repository). Note that the KSVG1 library, which is part of KDE 3, is not well suited for implementing vector graphics in games. For more details on this topic, refer to the documentation [Ksvg05].

3D Graphics

Storing 3D objects in a file is an important task for 3D games. Usually, such objects are stored in a model file format that primarily stores vertex coordinates and other vertex data (such as texture coordinates or colors). Such 3D models can be created by using the Open Source modeler Blender [Blender05] that runs on various platforms. Other tools include the commercial AC3D ™ [Ac3d05], which is applicable for Microsoft Windows and Linux, or 3D Studio Max™ [Discreet05], which runs on Microsoft Windows. Of course, these are just some examples; numerous other 3D tools exist.

There are many different file formats available for storing 3D files, among them are the rather simple *.obj format and the powerful but complex *.3ds file format.

ARTISTS IN THE OPEN SOURCE PROJECTS

Good graphics and sounds are an important part of game projects; however, many Open Source game projects have only a little of both. Usually, game projects are started, like most Open Source projects, by programmers. Unfortunately, not all of the programmers possess the artistic skills required to create the right atmosphere in terms of graphics or sound effects. Consequently, the games are well programmed, but lack good graphics and sound. Therefore, it is particularly important to Open Source programmers to attract artists to join their project and to make sure they remain motivated to contribute their skills over the entire length of the project.

A popular belief among Open Source programmers is that few artists are familiar or contribute to Open Source development. However, various projects such as *gnome-look.org* or *kde-look.org* prove this wrong. Nevertheless, to aid development of artistic work, it is useful to maintain a list of artistic "jobs" that are available, such as necessary sounds, graphics, or models. Some sample drafts that give an interested person an impression of what is wanted can also be very helpful.

Another important factor is that, even in early stages of development, you have a version of the game available that the artists can run easily on their computers so they can see what the work is aiming at. Often, we programmers tend to release source code that cannot run easily without additional modifications of the code or the installation system. An artist might not want to do this; therefore, it is important to offer an installation package of your game that can be easily run on another system. This should be accomplished as early as possible in the development process.

SUMMARY

Using sound effects in computer games is a very important feature for improving the game. Good sound effects and background music can drastically increase the atmosphere of a game. Therefore, it is advisable for good games to have sound effects, background music, and if applicable, speech dialogues. However, the effects have to be well adjusted to the game play, because annoying sound effects can make people stop playing the game just as good effects can improve the game experience. Desktop games, especially in an office environment, can be annoying if they force you to play sound. Therefore, it is useful to make the sound effects easily configurable.

There are several possibilities of how to incorporate music and sound effects into your game. The good quality-to-size relation of MP3 music has led to this format being the most commonly used. If MP3 playback is not supported, the fallback to the simple WAV format is a good alternative, because WAV files can be played on nearly all platforms. In both cases, the quality of the music is determined by the digitalization parameters such as the sampling rate and amplitude quantization.

The appearance of a game is determined foremost by its graphics, which need to look consistent and professional. It is important to implement good graphics and graphic effects in your game, because it will attract more people to play.

There are several possibilities of how to load and use graphics in your game. Depending on the actual application, this can be the static but easy-to-use bitmap graphics, scalable and zoomable desktop games using vector graphics, or even 3D games with full 3D vector graphics.

If you are a better programmer than an artist, it is often a good idea to form a small team with people who can create artistic work. Often, these people also want to create a game but lack the programming skills. Here, the KDE game developer mailing lists or the KDE games Web site can serve as a starting point to coordinate a team [Kdegames05]. Note, as with any project in life, a common goal must be present within all team members, as only this will lead to good cooperation. When developers and artists understand each other, a better coordination, and often a mutual motivation, can be achieved.

REFERENCES

[Ac3d05] *AC3D, http://www.ac3d.org*, 2005.

[Blender05] *Blender, http://www.blender.org*, 2005.

[Discreet05] *Discreet, http://www.discreet.com*, 2005.

[Eisenberg02] Eisenberg, J. David, *SVG Essentials*, ISBN: 0596002238; O'Reilly, 2002.

[Hacker00] Hacker, Scot, *MP3: The Definite Guide*, ISBN: 1565926617; O'Reilly, 2000.

[Kdegames05] *The KDE Games Center, http://www.kde.org/kdegames*, 2005.

[Kmid05] *KMid, http://developer.kde.org/~larrosa/kmid.html*, 2005.

[Ksvg05] *KSVG, http://svg.kde.org*, 2005.

[Openal05] *Cross-Platform 3D Audio, http://www.openal.org*, 2005.

[Shannon05] *Nyquist-Shannon sampling theorem, http://en.wikipedia.org/wiki/Nyquist-Shannon_sampling_theorem*, 2005.

[Qt05] *Trolltech Documentation, http://doc.trolltech.com*, 2005.

[Wav05] *WAV PCM Sound File Format, http://ccrma.stanford.edu/courses/422/projects/WaveFormat*, 2005.

[White00] White, Paul, *Basic Midi*, ISBN: 1860742629; Sanctuary Publishing, Ltd., 2000.

[Wikipedia05a] *Lossless Data Compression, http://en.wikipedia.org/wiki/Lossless_data_compression*, 2005.

[Wikipedia05b] *Lossy Data Compression, http://en.wikipedia.org/wiki/Lossy_data_compression*, 2005.

10 Artificial Intelligence

Artificial intelligence (AI) in computer games describes the ability of the computer to provide computer-controlled players or characters to the game that appear realistic to a human player. Although it is not possible to create real intelligence in a computer program, it is important to create at least the illusion of intelligence. Ideally, the computer AI should behave as if it were another player or a natural environment.

In computer games, AI can be used in several different ways:

- The computer assumes the role of one or more of the main players. The computer can either play as an opponent against the human players or play with them as an ally.
- The computer controls aspects of the game such as additional characters, units, and cities that the player cannot or does not want to control.

■   The computer generates a certain "intelligent" environment such as background characters or animals that inhabit that game world.

Typical desktop games such as board or card games usually implement an AI where the computer has to simulate another player. For example, a human player wants to play chess but has no partner available. To be able to play, the computer has to undertake the part of the opponent. Despite the increasing popularity of online games, most games still need this computer player, and a game developer will need to implement these AI aspects in the game.

Computer AI must also be able to play the game reasonably well. If the computer's technique is too weak or too strong, a game can soon become uninteresting. Ideally, the AI should play with comparable strength to the human player. Therefore, most games have different levels of AI so the human player can choose the most appropriate level. Sometimes, games will automatically adjust the strength or level of the computer player to match the human player.

One of the most important aspects of game AI is the requirement to play realistically. Human players tend to play neither perfectly nor always predictably, and a good AI designer should keep this in mind. Seldom is an AI fun if it never makes a mistake. Note, however, that this depends on the type of game you are developing. A chess program on a high level should certainly not make stupid mistakes, while the same program on a lower level perhaps should.

When designing an AI player for a computer game, keep in mind that you develop the game for the human player, not for the AI. Although it is often exciting for game developers to see that their created AI is able to slaughter every human player, this form of AI is usually only frustrating for the players. Players normally play games to win or at least compete with a similar strength AI. As a game developer, you should support this, since clever and competitive AI will make your game more popular.

This chapter discusses some of the major types of AI programming useful for desktop games. The first of these categories includes game evaluation and game trees that are used for conventional board or card games. In these games, the players take it in turn to play and the possible moves are chosen from a clearly specified set of moves at each instance. Games such as chess or checkers are good examples of this category. Other AI classes include AI scripts, finite state machines, and behavioral AI. AI scripts can be used in all types of games, and the latter two are useful for games in which the interaction of the AI with the game characters and units is important. In these games, the interaction within the game is often continuous and not limited to a defined set of possible moves (real-time games). In addition, combinations of different AI categories are often applied.

GAME EVALUATION

Game evaluation is an analysis of the current situation of a game with respect to finding out what to do next, and is performed in two steps. In the first part, you need to judge a game situation, which means you have to be able to determine whether the current situation is good or bad for a certain player. This is actually not as easy as it seems. Second, to be able to plan a move, you have to be able to see the effect of that move. This is done by performing trial moves and then analyzing the resulting situations.

Evaluating a Game Position

A key issue for any player in a game is to be able to judge a given game situation (position). You and the computer AI have to be able to say, "This game position is good for player A" or "This position will result in a loss for player A." Ideally, the evaluations of these different situations should be summarized with just one number. This description might sound trivial, but is actually quite complex, and the analysis is a crucial feature for all board and strategy game AI algorithms. It will determine how well the AI will play, and make each AI algorithm unique.

Once such a game evaluation has been established, it can be used as a basis to enhance the AI algorithm, such as generating trial moves or building a Min-Max game tree. These standard procedures are thus all based on the game position evaluation, and we present them later in this chapter in more detail.

The game evaluation should assign a number between plus and minus infinity (in practice, a large number) to the current game situation. A large positive number means the position is good for the current player; a large negative number means the position is bad for the current player. Values around zero indicate an even game situation.

The form of game evaluation you choose clearly depends on the type of game you are developing. Even though there is no general recipe, there are a few general rules that provide a rough guideline for what to look into when developing an AI for a desktop game:

- A won or lost game will be respectively assigned the maximum or minimum evaluation values (or values close to them).
- Near win or loss situations are assigned a high positive or negative value, but not quite the won/lost values.
- If the game has points or a score, this score can be used for evaluation.
- The material of the players can be evaluated. For example, in chess the pieces of the game can be assigned values. The sum of all pieces for both players is

then totaled and the value for one player is subtracted from the other. This results in a material value of the game but neglects any positioning scores.

■ Complementary to the material value is the position value. A value can be assigned to reflect the potential of a position in the game. For example, if you need to get four pieces in a row, having already three pieces in a row (and room to place another piece in that row) is good. On a chessboard, a pawn approaching the opponent's base line is good. Both of these examples would be rewarded in the evaluation value.

■ A more sophisticated game evaluation also takes the relative placement of pieces or units into account. In a strategy game, it can be good (or not, depending on the game and situation) if the units are in a line or group, but bad if they are dispersed over the game board.

■ To generate more diverse AI behavior, it can be useful to add small random numbers to the evaluated value. The computer is then prevented from making the same move in the same situation. Note, however, that this will decrease the computer's play performance, but it will appear more interesting to the player.

More details on rules for game evaluation can be found in Steve Rabin's books [Rabin02] and [Rabin03].

ON THE CD The following example shows more details on the game board evaluation algorithm for the example game myai included on the companion CD-ROM in the folder examples/myai. This small game follows the rules of tic-tac-toe; that is, it is played on a rectangular game board of 3 × 3 fields. A player will win if he has three pieces in any row, column, or diagonal. The game ends in a draw when the game board is filled before one of the players manages to reach this winning condition. Note that tic-tac-toe can't be won if both players avoid errors. Therefore, we use it only as demonstration of the AI algorithm principles in this chapter, while the example program on the CD-ROM allows an easy extension to larger game boards and modified rules so you can experiment with the AI algorithm.

The evaluation algorithm of myai is based on the addition of the amount of (1,2,3) pieces in all rows, columns, and diagonals of the game board. These numbers are then multiplied with heuristic values, so that the essential part of the algorithm reads:

```
// Values for the various game situations:
// reward 1s, 2s, etc
#define EV_ONE           1
#define EV_TWO           500
#define EV_THREE         1500
...
```

```
// Rewarding full over empty lines will play
// more (or less) defensive
#define EV_LINE_FULL         5
#define EV_LINE_EMPTY         0
...


// Evaluate the game board
// current: The current player
// other:   The opponent
int MyAi::evaluateBoard(int current, int other)
{
  // Piece counter
  int cnt[2];

  // Board value
  int value = 0;

  // Start counting pieces in rows
  for (y=0; y<3; y++)
  {
    // Count the amount of pieces in the given
    // row for both players and store it in 'cnt'
    countPiecesInRow(y, cnt);

    // Evaluate a single line given the amount
    // of pieces for both players in it
    value += evaluateLine(current, other, cnt);
  }

  // Start counting pieces in column
  ...

  // Start counting pieces in diagonals
  ...

  return value;
}
```

The counting of the pieces per row is done by the function `countPiecesInRow()`, which we will omit here, and the actual evaluation of any row, column, or diagonal is forwarded to the following line evaluation function:

```
// Calculate the value of a single line with an
// empirical formula.
// current: The current player
```

```cpp
// other:   The opponent
// cnt:     Array holding the amount of pieces in this
//          line for player 0/1
int MyAi::evaluateLine(int current, int other, int[] cnt)
{
  // Line position value
  int curValue = 0;

  // Current line is already occupied by both players
  if (cnt[current]>0 && cnt[other]>0)
  {
    curValue = EV_LINE_FULL;
  }
  // Current line is empty
  else if (cnt[current]==0 && cnt[other]==0)
  {
    curValue = EV_LINE_EMPTY;
  }
  // Current line 'belongs' to one player
  else
  {
    // Who 'owns' the current line? We or the opponent?
    int owner;
    int mult;
    if (cnt[current]>0)
    {
      owner = current;
      mult = 1;
    }
    else
    {
      owner = other;
      mult = -1;
    }
    // Calculate position value
    if (cnt[owner] == 1) { curValue = mult*EV_ONE; }
    if (cnt[owner] == 2) { curValue = mult*EV_TWO; }
    if (cnt[owner] == 3) { curValue = mult*EV_THREE; }
    ...
  }
  return curValue;
}
```

The resulting value of `evaluateBoard()` gives an indication of how good the current game situation is for the `current` player. If it is positive, the `current` player has the advantage.

During the actual game development, it is often a good idea to start with one or two simple rules to check the basic working principle of the AI. If the AI algorithm works as expected, it can be refined by adding more rules. The problem with too many rules is that it becomes very difficult to check whether the AI is functioning correctly. For debugging purposes, it is also a good idea to have access to the calculated values for each game position. You can then verify whether you agree to the value of the position.

Using different rules or a different amount of rules also allows you to easily implement levels into your AI. An AI player on a higher level will analyze more rules and consequently play better.

Trial Moves

We are now able to analyze the current game situation. However, besides saying, "Oops, this doesn't look good for me!" the analysis of the game situation alone does not provide any help to find a good move. Both the human player and the AI are faced with this problem. With regard to the human player, you would resolve this problem by thinking rationally: "What would happen if I move this unit to that place? Does the situation improve for me or not?" This type of analysis shows that you are performing *trial moves* in your head to perceive which of those moves would have the best possible outcome for your current situation.

The game AI actually follows the same type of procedure. Basically, it will try all possible moves from the current moment and analyze the resulting game values. In comparison to the real player, who does these trial moves in his head, the AI performs them on a virtual game board that is comparable to the real board. After performing these trial moves and analyzing their outcome, the best move for the AI player is simply the one that creates the highest game evaluation value. This move is then incorporated by the AI and played on the real game board.

In most circumstances, the actual game state or position is stored in a class `Position` that describes all the properties of the actual game situation (not just the position of one player). This class should be able to copy, evaluate the position, and allow you to perform a selected move. A move can be specified in its own class `Move`. However, often it is sufficient to have one or two integer numbers representing the move (e.g., the (*x,y*) position on the game board).

For simple board games like our example, the class `Position` stores little more than the actual game board, which is often just an integer or `char` array. The class `Position` could then resemble:

```
class Position
{
  public:
    // Construct a game board/position
    Position();

    // Copy a game board
    Position copy();

    // Perform a move
    void doMove(const Move& move);

    // Evaluate the position
    int evaluate();

  private:
    // The game board (e.g. for a chess game: SIZE = 64)
    int mBoard[SIZE];
    // The player to move
    int mToMove;
    ...
};
```

Of course, for your game you need to replace the private attributes and method parameters so a board suitable for your game can be stored; for example, the parameter Move move can often be simplified and given as an integer number.

With this class Position, the first possibility of generating trial moves is to copy it and then perform a test move on that copied game position. This is done for all possible moves, and for each possible move, the position is evaluated. Note that with this procedure, you have to constantly copy the game board, which might result in performance problems and could therefore require optimization.

This trial move generation reads:

```
int maxValue = -LARGE_NUMBER;
Move bestMove;

// Loop all possible moves: We indicate this by
// a loop over 'all moves'. It depends on the actual game
// how a move is encoded and how all moves are looped, e.g.
// 'for (int i = 0; i < MOVES; i++)' or
// 'QListIterator<Move> it(moveList); while(it.hasNext()) ...'
for ('all moves' move)
{
```

```
// Copy the position: mPosition is the 'real' game
// position and includes the real game board as stored
// in your game class and on which the moves are performed
Position testPosition = mPosition.copy();

// Perform test move given as Move 'move'. Again
// depending on the game 'move' can be simply an
// integer number or two
testPosition.doMove(move)

// Evaluate test move
value = testPosition.evaluate();

// Update the best move
if (value > maxValue)
{
  bestMove = move;
  maxValue = value;
}
}// end loop
```

This is the easiest way to program the trial move generation and position evaluation.

The following alternative to copying the game position can be used when it is easy to do and undo the moves. The game position class has to be extended for this alternative so it can support such "undo" features. However, sometimes it can be more complicated to implement an "undo" than just copying the game board. Assuming that the Position class has an undoMove() method, we could replace the board evaluation inside the previous loop with:

```
...
// Perform test move
mPosition.doMove(move)

// Evaluate test move
value = mPosition.evaluate();

// Undo the test move
mPosition.undoMove(move)

// Update the best move
if (value > maxValue)
{
```

```
      bestMove = move;
      maxValue = value;
    }
    ...
```

Once all possible moves are tried, both the best move and the value of this move are known. The AI can then perform the real move `bestMove` on the real game board, which is included in `mPosition`.

```
// Perform the best move on the 'real' game board
mPosition.move(bestMove);
...
```

This concept of trial moves works surprisingly well for many simple games, especially if the position evaluation already respects some tactical considerations (e.g., "near wins"). However, all the long-term strategic decisions are neglected. In most games, such strategic planning is usually applied by human players. If the AI does not have this capacity, any simple trap the player creates will not be recognized, and unfortunately, the computer player usually wanders quite happily into situations that look good at first glance but aren't. This behavior can only be avoided by analyzing more than one trial move, that is, the consequences of a single move in the game ahead.

Cheating

Cheating is a very controversial topic for AI design. Should an AI engine have exactly the same information and resources that a human player has, or does the AI have access to additional information and resources?

An AI can often profit enormously if you provide it with information the player does not have. For example, instead of exploring an entire game map, the AI gets this information beforehand. This can also save computer performance, because often the AI does not need to perform unnecessary path searches or other calculations.

Another less drastic possibility to give an advantage to an AI that cannot compete with a human player is to simply equip the AI with more units or resources than the human player has. This is done in many computer games, and the players are used to the fact that a weak computer AI needs 10 times the resources the player does.

However, the question is, how does the player feel if he realizes the AI is cheating? Often, players find it very unfair if the AI does real cheating, such as checking cards in a card game that have not yet been uncovered. Generally more accepted is that the AI is equipped with more units or resources or has some beforehand map information. Because players are also annoyed by an AI that plays weakly, and if you could improve the AI by cheating, you perhaps should consider the possibility.

MIN-MAX GAME TREES

We will now continue and demonstrate a straightforward extension of the trial move concept that evaluates more than the outcome of one trial move by determining an entire sequence of moves. Ideally, these sequences should follow the entire course of the game. If the entire sequence of game play were known, the AI would win the game if the game could be won. However, since the amount of game positions grows exponentially with the amount of moves analyzed, it is usually only possible to determine the entire sequence for small games such as tic-tac-toe.

Performing searches to establish all possible moves is the main AI concept for traditional board-based games. It is called the *Min-Max game tree* method and can be applied to all games that have a deterministic movement sequence leading to clearly defined game states. Turn-based games that have a defined set of possible moves are typical examples and include games such as chess, tic-tac-toe, *Connect Four™*, or checkers.

The general idea behind this AI algorithm is to calculate all possible moves that can occur in the game to a certain time in the future, which is ideally the end of the game. The AI can then select a sequence of moves that will produce the best result. Again, the ultimate solution is a guaranteed win of the game regardless of the other player's moves. Figure 10.1 depicts a game tree for the Tic-Tac-Toe game.

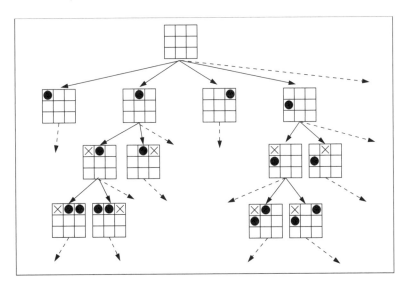

FIGURE 10.1   A game tree for the game tic-tac-toe is built. Two players place their pieces in turn on a game board. Note that for simplicity, not all possible moves are shown. Dashed lines indicate other possible game boards not shown here.

Note, however, that performing this form of game-tree move analysis, which covers many moves in the future, only makes sense when there are no random elements in the game (e.g., dice). For games that include chance factors, it is no longer possible to predict the correct move; you can only determine a move that has a fair probability of being successful. This can be achieved by assigning the probabilities for a certain event to each game tree node and then evaluating at each step in the Min-Max search the probability of the event together with the resulting board value. Nevertheless, if the randomness in the game is too strong, a tree search can often become useless.

In most game applications, a game tree search is limited by the amount of time and memory an AI algorithm can consume. The allotted time dictates the scope of the search and the number of positions that can be investigated. Consequently, it is impossible to obtain every possible sequence until the end of the game. Usually, in these cases, a search is performed up to a certain depth (a depth of 10 in a two-player game means that the first player makes five moves and the second player responds with five moves). The positions resulting from the move sequence up to this depth are then evaluated by the AI. This information is then used to choose the most favorable move.

The search depth can also be artificially limited to implement a weaker computer player. In this way, you can equip the AI calculation easily with levels: the AI on level one searches to depth one, on level two it searches to depth two, and so on.

In board games, it is also possible to use the AI algorithm to provide in-game hints to the human player. This is done by calculating a move with the AI for the human player but not performing it on the actual game; instead, it is shown as a hint. This is often seen in board games such as chess or checkers.

Building and Using a Game Tree

Having developed a method to evaluate a certain state or position in the game, it is then a straightforward task to apply this evaluation to the game positions that lay ahead; that is, those generated by all possible move sequences. Such a method is called building a game tree, and an example is shown in Figure 10.1.

In a turn-based game, each possible future situation can be determined from the current position by performing all possible moves to create all possible new positions. From each of these new positions, the next round of all possible moves is created, and so on. This process results in a tree-like structure, and each of the nodes on the tree contains one possible game position (see Figure 10.1). Obviously, this tree structure could be continued until the final set of moves at the end of the game. However, as this is an exponential growth, the amount of moves that can be calculated is quickly limited by memory and computing time. This growth will lead to such an enormous amount of positions that you can no longer calculate all of them. Nevertheless, for practical reasons it is also of interest to know how the possible positions grow in the first few turns, and this depends on the amount of possible moves per turn.

As an example, imagine three games in which you have 5, 10, or 100 possible moves each time for two players *A* and *B*. The amount of possible positions is then determined by the outcome of moving all pieces to every allowed location. In response to any move, the other player will do the same and move each of his pieces to every possible location. The numbers chosen for this example are realistic. For example, a game of chess has 20 possible moves in the opening move, and easily 100 possible moves during mid-game. A game of tic-tac-toe has 9, 8, 7, and so on moves, whereas a game of *Connect Four* always has seven possible moves until a column is completely filled, which will then reduce the amount of possible moves. The number of game positions created for such games having the possible moves (5, 10, 100) at each turn and for up to four moves in the future is listed in Table 10.1.

TABLE 10.1 Number of Game Board Positions Resulting from 5, 10, 100 Possible Moves Each Turn

	5 Possible Moves	10 Possible Moves	100 Possible Moves
move 1A	5	10	100
move 1B	25	100	10,000
move 2A	125	1,000	1,000,000
move 2B	625	10,000	100,000,000
move 3A	3,125	100,000	10,000,000,000
move 3B	15,625	1,000,000	1,000,000,000,000
move 4A	78,125	10,000,000	100,000,000,000,000
move 4B	390,625	100,000,000	10,000,000,000,000,000

Table 10.1 clearly shows that after only a few moves into the future, an enormous amount of positions is created. However, the amount of positions depends also on the possible moves each time. Its amount limits the search depth the AI can handle.

In a typical desktop game as discussed in this book and on a standard desktop computer, approximately 1 million positions per move can be calculated without optimizing the AI code very much. If you need to analyze more positions, optimizing the program code will become a major task of the AI programming.

However, regardless of how well the code is optimized, the huge amount of positions to evaluate will still prevent brute-force algorithms in complex games such as chess. In our example, not even four moves (each player moves twice) could be calculated. However, in simpler games, the calculation of four or five moves into the future is possible, and is often enough to play reasonably well.

Once the game tree, with all possible positions, is created, the resulting end positions are evaluated using the evaluation procedure described in the previous section. Each end position obtains a positive value for a good position for the player who made the current move, and a negative value for a bad position. This algorithm is shown in Figure 10.2.

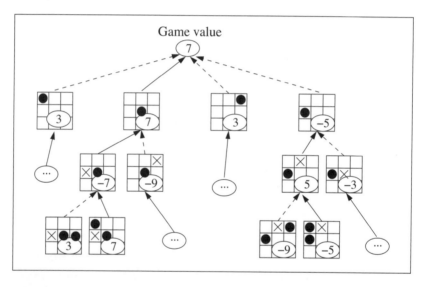

FIGURE 10.2 A game tree for the game tic-tac-toe is evaluated using the Min-Max algorithm. The numbers indicate the board values for the current player. For the end positions (bottom row), they are assigned by the board evaluation algorithm. These values are then back propagated by negating them each step following the Min-Max algorithm rules. Note that for simplicity, not all possible boards are shown, and arbitrary numbers are assumed for these incomplete branches. The solid arrows depict the resulting best movement sequence.

These values are then back propagated to the root of the tree using a *minimum-maximum* strategy. It is assumed that each player will make the best possible move. However, for the other player, this best possible move is of course a bad one. Therefore, on the next turn, the move is negated because the opponent will try to select the *worst* of the *best* possible moves of the other player, which is in turn his *best* move. This procedure is repeated until the results arrive back-propagated at the root of the game tree. The AI can then select the maximum of all possible moves, which will inevitably lead to a position having at least this game evaluation value. An even better value is reached when the opponent does not play his optimum move(s).

```
int gameTree(Position& position, int depth)
{
  int maxValue   = -LARGE_NUMBER;
  Move bestMove;

  // If the end of the recursion is reached or the game is
  // over then we really have to do some work by evaluating
  // the current position
  if (depth == 0 || position.isGameOver())
  {
    return position.evaluate();
  }

  // Loop all moves
  for ('all moves' move)
  {
    // Check whether the current move is possible. Only then do
    // we bother to create the test board and calculate the
    // value
    if (position.isValidMove(move))
    {
      Position testPosition = position.copy();

      // Make move on test board
      testPosition.doMove(move);

      // NEGATE value due to min-max algorithm
      value = - gameTree(testPosition, depth-1);

      // New max value found?
      if (value > maxValue)
      {
        bestMove  = move;
        maxValue = value;
      }
    } // end valid move
  } // end loop for all moves
  return maxValue;
}
```

This minimum-maximum strategy will provide the best possible moves a player can make and will result in the player winning the game if the board evaluation produces a value that accurately represents the game at the time of evaluation. However, this evaluation is crucial for the algorithm, but unfortunately, a good evaluation is often difficult to achieve.

Breadth-First versus Depth-First Search

There are two possibilities to build a game tree. The breadth-first strategy builds each level of the tree before the next one is started. For example, none of the second moves is performed until all the first moves are determined. This procedure then continues for all other levels.

The second strategy is the depth-first method. In this strategy, the first possible sequence is determined by moving from the start to the second, third, fourth move, and so on until the end of the search is reached, which is designated by a preset depth level or the end of the game. This position is then evaluated and back propagated. The algorithm then continues to evaluate the outcome of all other sequences. This type of behavior can be easily implemented by using a recursive algorithm.

Usually, a depth-first algorithm is more easily implemented and uses less memory than a breadth-first algorithm does. A breadth-first algorithm finds good solutions earlier in the move sequence. For more details on these search concepts, see the article [Beckert03].

Transposition Tables

In many board games, there is the possibility that a certain identical position can be reached in various ways. In a tree search, each of these possibilities will be represented as one branch of the tree, and consequently, the same calculations made for one branch are repeated for the other branch. Such a search will waste many computer resources, and the more possibilities exist to create the same situation, the more resources are wasted.

Transposition tables serve the purpose of storing all positions that have been already evaluated together with all data representing the search. This includes the position value and the best possible move that can be done in this position.

Usually, transposition tables are designed as hash tables, and each game position generates a hash key that serves as entry into this table. If the game tree algorithm generates a new move, the hash key of the resulting position can be calculated and a hash lookup in the transposition table will show whether this position is already available. If it exists, the search can take the stored values and return.

Alpha-Beta Pruning

The *alpha-beta pruning* concept is a method that allows you to reduce the time necessary to build a game tree by cutting off branches that do not contribute to the minimum-maximum search. If this pruning occurs early, many possible game moves are excluded from the evaluation and time is saved. In comparison to a standard game tree search (under optimal conditions; that is, with perfect move ordering), it is possible to double the search depth in the same amount of time using alpha-beta pruning.

When a game evaluation has found a better solution on a particular depth level than the currently analyzed one, the current sequence can be pruned from the tree since it no longer contributes to the evaluation. For example, in Figure 10.3 the leftmost branch guarantees a result of –7 for the opponent at node A. However, in the middle branch, node B will become at least –9 via the leaf B1. Therefore, the opponent will never play the middle branch B, and thus all further searches of this branch such as B2 or B3 can be omitted.

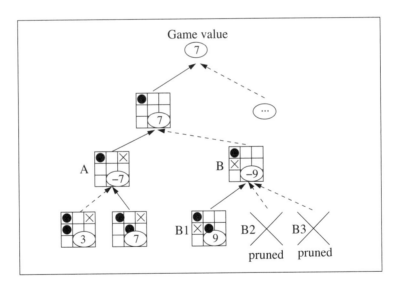

FIGURE 10.3 A game tree for the tic-tac-toe game employing alpha-beta pruning. Branch A is calculated first and yields a certain value (–7). If the search reaches leaf B1, it is already clear that the whole of branch B will result in a lower overall value (–9). Since the opponent will not allow this to happen, branches B2 and B3 do not need to be calculated. Note that you have to analyze at least B1 to get a board evaluation value for branch B.

To perform this pruning, it is necessary to store the best values both players can achieve during the search. Those values can then be compared to the current value on the current branch and the search can be either pruned or not pruned. These minimum and maximum values are called *alpha* for the best value player A can achieve, and *beta* for the best value the opposing player B can attain.

Obviously, alpha and beta have to be passed to the recursion since they are additional parameters. They will also be swapped and negated for each minimum-maximum step following the minimum-maximum algorithm rules.

```
int alpha_beta(Position& position,
               int alpha,
               int beta,
               int depth)
{
  if (depth == 0 || position.isGameOver())
  {
    return position.evaluate();
  }

  // Loop all moves
  for ('all moves' move)
  {
    // Check for valid moves
    if (position.isValidMove(move))
    {
      // Make the trial move
      Position testPosition = position.copy();
      testPosition.doMove(move);

      // Recurse tree, and SWAP alpha beta !
      value= -alpha_beta(testPosition, -beta, -alpha, depth-1);

      // prune tree?
      if (value >= beta)
      {
        return value;
      }

      // Update new best value
      if (value > alpha)
      {
        alpha = value;
      }
    }
  }
}
```

```
    return alpha;
}
```

In the alpha-beta algorithm, the search in one particular branch is aborted when the value of the current position exceeds the beta value. Obviously, it is preferable if this condition is reached as early as possible in the loop over all possible moves, because then fewer calculations need to be made. Consequently, it is beneficial if the possible moves are not tried in a random order, but sorted according to their position values. If the moves are perfectly ordered, alpha-beta can calculate twice as far ahead as the standard game tree search. However, in practice, the result will be somewhere between this optimum and the normal game-tree search.

Of course, when you do the game tree analyses you do not know the position values beforehand, because if you did you would not need to do the entire analysis. However, heuristic criteria can be applied to guess which move will be preferable to which other move. Sorting the moves according to such a heuristic criterion can speed up the alpha-beta pruning.

Applying alpha-beta pruning can reduce the search time. However, it is important to notice that it makes the tree search even more susceptible to faults in the evaluation algorithm than the normal tree search. It is therefore essential that the board evaluation return values that reflect the actual game situation.

Iterative Deepening

Often in a game tree search, it is unclear just how many positions have to be evaluated and how much time this will take. As seen in Table 10.1, the amount of positions can vary a great deal depending on the possible moves in each situation. Therefore, the amount of time needed for the search is difficult to judge, and by just defining a fixed search depth level, the search can take much longer than expected.

This problem can be solved by using the so-called *iterative deepening*, which searches a more shallow depth than the actual depth level suggests. After this briefer search is finished, the allotted time for the AI is checked, and if there is still some time remaining, the search is continued to a further level by either starting from the previous calculated end positions (if they are stored) or by recalculating the entire game tree. This is possible because a game tree search is exponential, and the move with the highest search depth will usually cost more time than all the other moves beforehand.

The iterative deepening can be even less costly when game positions evaluated earlier are stored in a transposition table. Then, the extended search can benefit from these stored positions and can continue searching from them. Therefore, only a small fraction of the search time is lost if the complete game tree is recalculated to the next depth level of the search! This procedure is iteratively repeated until the AI reaches the set amount of allocated time.

The Search Horizon

Obviously, the entire game tree minimum-maximum algorithm depends on the exact calculation of the values at the end positions in the tree (the search horizon). If they do not correctly represent the game, the AI will make moves toward a wrong goal and consequently lose the game.

However, there is a less obvious problem with this search algorithm: what will happen if a position on the end of the search tree looks promising, but just one or two moves later the game is lost or suddenly very disadvantageous because a deadly trap has evolved? Of course, the AI cannot see this and will happily play toward this position. This limited view of the AI is called its *search horizon*, and is depicted in Figure 10.4.

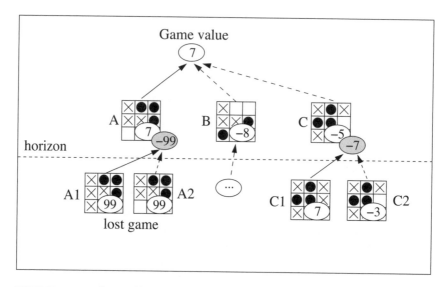

FIGURE 10.4 The problem of the game tree search reaching the search horizon for the tic-tac-toe game. The standard search before the horizon leads to position evaluation values depicted inside boards A, B, and C. Consequently, move A would be chosen. However, beyond the search horizon lurk the bad positions A1 and A2. Continuing the search until this level would lead to board evaluation values depicted inside the boards A1, A2, C1, and C2, and consequently would change the back propagation to the values depicted outside the boards. Now, move C becomes preferable.

In Figure 10.4, the standard search up to the horizon will lead to move A with the highest value (7). However, it is not noticeable for the AI that a very bad situation lurks just beyond the horizon. Searching beyond the horizon would change the board values to –99 for position A, resulting from both A1 and A2. If this information were known, move C (–7) would be chosen. Although move C also becomes worse than expected, resulting from C1, it is still not as bad as move A.

These types of problems can also develop when the arising bad situation can already be seen in some of the branches, but only become obvious in other positions after some intermediate moves. In these cases, the AI can perform delaying moves to avoid the bad situation in the game tree. Since these delaying moves shift the evaluation of the bad situation beyond the horizon of the search tree, the AI cannot see it and the evaluated positions still look reasonably good. Consequently, the AI will play toward them.

If such intermediate moves exist, the AI will actually perform all possible delaying moves to just shift the inevitable beyond its search horizon. However, such delaying moves can eventually result in an even worse situation than the one the AI was trying to avoid. These delaying moves often lead to multiple little mistakes and many little sacrifices. In the end, the original problem cannot be avoided and additionally the AI has made all the extra little mistakes, making for an awful result.

Historically, two ways of defeating the horizon effect have been tried: searching deeper, and improving the position evaluation: it always turned out that deeper searches were more successful. One way to allow for such extended searches (without analyzing too many more positions) is to not strictly limit the search in search depth. The AI analyzes the game for critical or changing situations, and only when these are detected are they then analyzed in greater depth to check their outcome. If this extended evaluation changes the game value drastically, it is obvious that a problem with the search horizon exists and the current branch has to be analyzed in more detail. Only if the situation is "quiet" is the search branch considered stable and can be used for evaluation (*quiescent search*). What game situations are critical depend on the actual game: for example, in a chess game, the capturing of a piece would be such a critical point.

SCRIPT-BASED AI

The script-based AI concept is very old in computer AI design, and originates from using a special script language that describes the behavior of the game units or characters. This script defines the entire behavior and actions of the AI characters. If scripts are flexible in design and enough situations are taken into account, scripted computer characters or game scenes can look very realistic, and can offer the player a very intense game play.

Script-based action can produce multiple effects; for example, the walking of a nonplayer character on the market place in a role-playing game; the patrolling of units in a maze-type game; the attack pattern of space ships in an arcade game; the reaction of an enemy battalion once a player enters its territory in a strategy game; or even entire cinematic sequences like the start of an invasion once the player enters the vicinity of the event.

In all cases, the general idea behind scripting is that a mini-language is developed and used that exactly describes the behavior of the game AI. The advantage of script languages are:

- The actual AI behavior is separated from the program code.
- The AI can be developed by nonprogrammers, who just have to learn a simpler script language.
- If the script language is interpreted and not compiled into the program, no recompilation is needed for changes to the AI.

Script languages can also be implemented in several ways. First, the script language can be interpreted at runtime. This requires a scripting engine that runs inside the main game program and interprets the script code. This can occur as interpreted script code or as precompiled byte-code. The former is easier to implement, while the latter is faster. This form of script engine is very flexible and allows you to have an AI that is independent of the program code. No recompilation is necessary if the AI is altered.

Second, the script language is actually not a script language but true C++ code. This can be done by auto-coding the resulting C++ code from a script, simply programming C++ code, or defining "script" preprocessor commands and using them inside the program. Although often the latter two are not considered proper AI scripting, for a small desktop game it might be a more feasible solution than invoking the full power of an AI scripting language. However, although very easy to implement, the disadvantages to this method include the strong dependency of code and AI scripts. Therefore, this type of script should only be used for small desktop games.

When applying a script language, the language has to be a balance between being specialized and flexible. Ideally, for your developed game you need a language that is small, specialized, and easy to parse and program. The extent of these criteria really depends on the type of game; for example, in role-playing games you might need spell-casting and speech dialogs that are unnecessary in strategy games that require more area and unit coordination commands. On the other hand, a script language also needs to be flexible and able to extend enough to allow a proper description and extension of the AI. To dismiss this aspect will result in much regret later when you plan extensions or new versions of your game.

To take these considerations into account, there are two possibilities for scripting languages: first, you can use existing scripting languages, in particular some that can be easily bound to a C++ program (e.g., Python). This has the advantage that you do not need to develop a new scripting language, but the disadvantage that these languages are sometimes nearly as complex as the C++ language, and therefore it may be hard to develop scripts for nonprogrammers. Second, you can develop your own scripting language that is tailored to your game and supports a small set of commands useful for your game. The advantage here is that the language is simple and usually easily understood by nonprogrammers. However, the main disadvantage is that developing script languages is very complicated. Like any other programming language, script languages also have to be scanned, parsed, and translated into the game program code, which can be a project on its own. Additionally, by being a new language, none of the possible script authors will be familiar with that language. Therefore, everyone has to learn this language from scratch, even though it may be rather easy to learn. The book [Rabin02] contains more detailed information on complex scripting languages.

Nevertheless, the idea of scripting is an easy and straightforward way to describe the behavior of game AI. It has therefore been used since the very beginning of computer games, and nowadays, all kinds of computer games employ scripting. Desktop games can especially benefit from scripting as a straightforward possibility to implement computer players.

With scripts, the behavior of the computer AI is modeled inside a predefined set of actions with a given set of conditions or events that will trigger these actions. No other behavior outside these predefined sets is possible.

Actions are the execution of some AI behavior or the change in state of game characters, units, or objects. Actions can be chosen from a pre-programmed set of possibilities that are defined for any particular unit or character. For example, a character can have the actions to *attack*, *withdraw*, *launch*, or *hide*. A typical example of a script commanding the current unit to attack an enemy would be:

```
Attack("Tank")
```

Actions can be *triggered* by certain changes in the environment. These changes are either notified by *events* or by actively querying (*polling*) the environment for certain conditions. These triggers describe the interaction of the game or player with the AI. An example of a trigger could be a character nearing an object, or the change in position of an object, the strength of an enemy, or the movement of that enemy into a certain area.

Note that it is generally better to opt for event-driven actions than to poll for conditions. In the case of events, anything happening is signaled by the creator of the event to the outside world. In the case of polling, each AI unit needs to query the state of all other items in the game world—most of them not offering anything of interest. Note that such event-driven AI programming can be further supported by adjusting the game world so it is "talkative"; that is, it broadcasts a lot of information to the AI units. This is often easier than making very intelligent AI units that have to figure out the state of the world. In the example of a strategy game, a trigger event could be the notification that a missile was launched, and an environmental check could be the distance to the next enemy units to see whether they are within firing range.

All triggers can be queried *conditional* using `if`, `then`, `else`, and `endif` statements. More flexible scripting language incorporates even more control structures such as loops, as you will know from real programming language.

```
if (trigger  == TRUE) then
  action()
endif
```

If and only if such a condition is TRUE will the corresponding `action()` be executed.

Actions or triggers can access information from the game engine or act on other objects of the game. This includes, for example, the ability to attack a certain unit: in the following example, `Tank47`

```
Attack("Tank47");
```

or the nearest enemy will be attacked, respectively.

```
Attack(NearestEnemy());
```

It is up to the designer of the scripting language which game objects are available and how they are accessed by the AI scripts.

Based on the pre-programmed conditions, all individual AI scripting statements are grouped into a script that creates the desired AI behavior. The following example describes an AI script in which an AI creature could have short- or long-range weapons, and depending on the distance to the enemy, a weapon is chosen. The script can either be activated in a polling loop or by an event. In both cases, the fact that an enemy is approaching will trigger it.

```
...
// If trigger 'distance' of object 'nearest enemy' is small
if (Distance(NearestEnemy()) < 10_meters)
  Wield("LaserSword")
  Attack(NearestEnemy())
// If trigger 'distance' of object 'nearest enemy' is large
elseif (Distance(NearestEnemy()) < 100_meters)
  Wield("PlasmaGun")
  Attack(NearestEnemy())
else
```

```
  // If trigger 'random' is small
  if (random() < 50)
    RunTowards(NearestEnemy())
  // If trigger 'random' is large
  else
    Hide(LocateCover())
  endif
endif
...
```

The next example shows an event-based AI script for a game in which the triggers are areas on the map that are entered by an enemy.

```
// An enemy group enters the area 'Homebase'
START_EVENT( EnemyEntersArea(Homebase) )
  Enemy = ...
  // Check the strength of the enemy
  if (AmountOfUnits(Enemy) > 10) then
    LaunchAirRaid(Enemy)
  else
    LaunchGroundAttack(Enemy)
  endif
END_EVENT
```

Early computer games were nearly 100-percent scripted. However, a purely scripted AI engine lacks flexibility, and the possibility to change its behavior and therefore actions will always be small or nonexistent. Actions that are not taken into account in the scripts will simply not happen, and conditions that are not foreseen by the programmers will have no effect. Especially when scripting actions are specifically designed for a particular game situation, the player has little choice but to follow this pre-designed track instead of being able to employ his own strategies. Modern games still rely heavily on scripted behavior, but nowadays, mix these types of script behavior with other AI strategies or even learning behavior and consequently create a more versatile game AI.

Although scripts might sound not very interesting, do not underestimate their significance to produce a good game AI. Having a large set of AI scripts with numerous triggers, effects, and actions for the game characters can create a very sophisticated behavior for the computer AI. Furthermore, in contrast to autonomous reacting AI, scripted AI can create a much denser atmosphere in the game.

If the scripting language is to be edited by a nonprogramming designer or even the user and players of the game, you need to have a scripting language that is very easy to understand, or design a tool or a graphical editor for the script rules.

FINITE STATE MACHINES

Finite state machines (FSMs) are another simple yet effective concept for AI engines. FSMs are often used in games in which the behavior of a unit or character can be characterized by a (small) set of possible internal states and the transitions between these states. An FSM describes a system consisting of a finite and discrete set of states of operation. At any one point, one of these states will be active. In addition to these states, a set of rules exists that defines when and how to leave the active state and which of the other states will then become active.

All the states in the system have the following (optional) properties:

- Upon entering a state, an *entry* action can be performed.
- Being in the active state, a *do* action is performed, which is the main action of the state. The *do* action continues until the state is left.
- When a state change occurs, an *exit* action can be performed.

Each state defines a set of transitions. These transitions determine which of the other states the state machine should switch into once the transition is executed. When a transition is executed the active state is left. This will happen if an external event has occurred which was associated with that transition. In addition, a transition is only allowed when a (guard) condition, also associated with the transition, is fulfilled. Figure 10.5 depicts a state machine with three different states that all contain the actions entry, do, and exit. The states are connected by transitions with their events and guards.

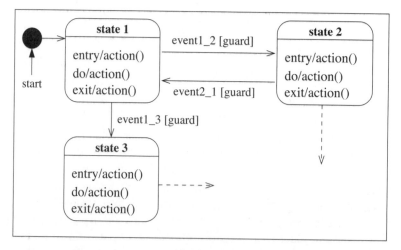

FIGURE 10.5 A finite state machine with three states containing their entry, do, and exit actions. Events will lead to a state change.

A finite state machine with many states can be used to represent any algorithm necessary for a computer AI. Normally, however, you should limit its complexity so that a typical AI unit or character has a set of a dozen states or so with only a few events and transitions associated to them.

The different states for a game character could include *idling, walking, running, exploring, attacking,* and *dodging.* A change from one of these states to another could be triggered by events such as "*the presence of an enemy*" (transition to *attacking*), "*the lack of an enemy for a certain amount of time*" (transition to *exploring*), "*the perception of an incoming object*" (transition to *dodging*), and so on. An example for a game AI state machine with the four possible states *hiding, idling, approaching,* and *attacking* is shown in Figure 10.6.

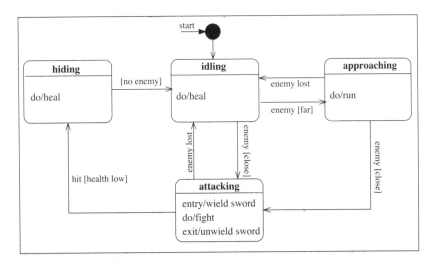

FIGURE 10.6   State transition chart for a computer character with four possible states (hiding, idling, approaching, attacking). The perception of an enemy or the internal health will trigger state transition events.

A state machine for a computer AI can be implemented in various ways. It is possible to directly implement it in C++ code, which is probably the most straightforward option. Alternatively, you could define preprocessor macros for states and state transitions, and with this choice the code becomes more readable [Rabin02]. There also exist tools [Uml05] that permit the design of state machines outside the actual program and allow you to include auto-coded program code into the actual program. Thus, you will retain a better overview of the situation and will not be lost in the details of the C++ program code.

The following code shows the main part of a state machine implemented by the first option; that is, directly into the program. This then implements a behavior that is similar, albeit more simplified, to the state machine shown in Figure 10.6.

```
// We assume all keywords to be defined beforehand, e.g.
// #define DISTANCE_FAR 10 or similar
...

// Retrieve any enemy in vicinity
enemy = enemyPresent();

switch(state)
{
  case 0:  // idle
    // Is there any enemy?
    if (enemy)
    {
      // Is the distance to the enemy close or far?
      if (distance(enemy) > DISTANCE_FAR) { state = 1; }
      else { state = 2; }
    }
    // No enemy?
    else { heal(); }
  break;

  case 1:  // approach
    // Did we lose the enemy?
    if (!enemy) { state = 0; }
    else
    {
      if (distance(enemy) < DISTANCE_FAR) { state = 2; }
      runTowards(enemy);
    }
  break;

  case 2:  // attack
    // Did we lose the enemy?
    if (!enemy) { state = 0; }
    else
    {
      // Hide if the health is low
      if (health < HEALTH_LOW) { state = 3; }
      else { attack(enemy); }
    }
  break;
```

```
  case 3:  // hide
    // If the enemy is gone go back to idle
    if (!enemy) { state = 0; }
    heal();
  break;
}
```

As mentioned previously, this type of state machine can also be implemented using preprocessor macros. You can define these macros to your liking and make the previous code easier to read. In the following example, we demonstrate the implementation of a state machine similar to the one depicted in Figure 10.6. However, this time we apply the state machine language proposed by Steve Rabin in [Rabin02].

```
// We assume all keywords to be defined beforehand, e.g.
// enum State {STATE_IDLE, STATE_APPROACH, ...};
// and #define DISTANCE_FAR 10 or similar
...

// Retrieve any enemy in vicinity
enemy = enemyPresent();

BeginStateMachine
  State(STATE_IDLE)
    OnDo
      // Is there any enemy?
      if (enemy)
      {
        // Is the distance to the enemy close or far?
        if (distance(enemy) > DISTANCE_FAR)
        {
          setState(STATE_APPROACH)
        }
        else
        {
          setState(STATE_ATTACK);
        }
      }
      // No enemy?
      else
      {
        heal();
      }
```

```
      State(STATE_APPROACH)
        ...


      State(STATE_ATTACK)
        OnEnter
          wieldSword();
        OnDo
          if (!enemy)
          {
            setState(STATE_IDLE);
          }
          else
          {
            if (health < HEALTH_LOW)
            {
              setState(STATE_HIDE);
            }
            else
            {
              attack(enemy);
            }
          }

        OnExit
          unwieldSword();

      State(STATE_HIDE)
        ...


    EndStateMachine
```

Without going into too much detail, there are also two principal extensions to a simple state machine. First, it is possible to have hierarchical or *nested* states in a state machine. In nested state machines, each state can contain its own finite state machine. However, any state change of the parent state will terminate any nested state as well. Second, a finite state machine can use *concurrent states*, which allow multiple state machines to be run simultaneously, and in doing so essentially behave as a single state machine. Both nested and concurrent state machines are depicted in Figure 10.7. Concurrent states are actually a useful extension since they can solve some of the problems that occur when the game states occur practically in parallel.

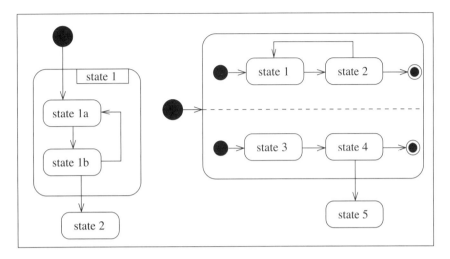

FIGURE 10.7 State transition chart for a nested (left) and a concurrent (right) state machine.

For a desktop game, these extra additions to the finite state machine are often not necessary. Furthermore, always keep in mind that your AI concept should be as simple as possible, since it is easy to lose track of what you are actually doing.

Finite state machines are one of the most-used design concepts in game AI. Consequently, you will find that nearly all state-of-the art computer games employ these state machines. They are easily implemented and a good way to create a simple, efficient AI model for a large variety of games. This also applies for small desktop games, and with these state machines, you will have an excellent way to implement your AI behavior.

BEHAVIORAL ARTIFICIAL INTELLIGENCE

In computer games, it is sometimes desirable to have computer characters that imitate a more human- or animal-like behavior. Characters that engage in social interaction will appear more realistic and believable to the human player if they follow the basic patterns of human behavior such as crying, arguing, or feeling tired. Examples of such games include the exceedingly popular Tamagotchis™, The Sims™, or Creatures™. Tamagotchis especially is an interesting application that can be developed in the scope of desktop games. The key to its success lies in the use of these behavioral systems. Furthermore, nonplayer characters in other games profit enormously from behavioral modeling.

In behavioral AI, the previously mentioned concept of a state machine is further extended so the state transitions are the result of fulfilled or unfulfilled needs of the individual [Doerner95]. Each individual is assigned a set of basic requirements or desires, which can include *hunger, thirst, fatigue, fear, attention, fun,* and so on. A certain behavior is triggered if a need crosses a given threshold level. Then, one or more corresponding actions are initiated and the computer AI will execute them in an attempt to reduce the need. Possible behaviors and their resulting actions could include the "*search for food*" and "*to eat*" if the individual is hungry, "*to sleep*" if it is tired, "*to talk*" if it needs attention, and so forth. Any action that is performed will have some effect on the individual and ideally reduce the imperative need. Such a need-driven system is depicted in Figure 10.8.

Note, however, that most of the resulting actions will not only feed back on the need that triggered them but also change others. For example, a successful search for food might result in less hunger, but simultaneously increase the tiredness of the character. These feedback models form a complicated control circuit. A problem that can arise with such complicated feedback systems is that they can start to oscillate between two (or more) behaviors, which results in a strange or monotonous behavior of the character. If these behavioral oscillations occur, they need to be dampened, and one way to reduce such unwanted behavior is to introduce a larger variety of possible actions for each need and give the individual the chance to fulfill the most urgent need and alternatively any need from a set of important ones.

In a computer program, these needs are modeled as internal counters. When the counters exceed a certain predefined threshold, they generate the necessary state transitions in the character, which results in the triggering of the corresponding action sequence (see Figure 10.8). These "need counters" can be connected to either internal or external stimuli, which can either raise or lower the corresponding desires. Internal stimuli are usually represented by either time-triggered effects or the interaction of various needs and actions with each other. For example, both fatigue or hunger build up with time, but being hungry can in turn reduce (or increase) fatigue. External stimuli are connected to the individual's perception of the environment, which includes the presence of other characters, the room it is in, items or just the general environment. For example, the presence of a friendly character can increase the fun value while a cold room or a rainy day can lower it.

The different behaviors that exist in AI-created characters can be generated by assigning weights to the internal or external stimuli. In addition, the trigger thresholds for the different needs can be set differently. Therefore, certain actions will affect the needs of one character but not those of another. This concept also reflects normal human behavior, since the desires of one person do not always mirror those of another; for example whereas one character might want more fun, another will strive for more food.

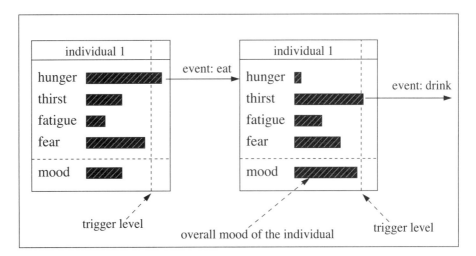

FIGURE 10.8 A behavior model for a computer individual. Certain needs (*hunger, thirst, fatigue, fear*) are modeled with their current values. The strongest need (*hunger*) will trigger a behavior event if it crosses a given threshold. The resulting action (*eat*) will change all the need levels and possibly initiate another need (*thirst*). Often, an overall mood or happiness value for the individual is also calculated and indicates how the overall needs of the individual are fulfilled.

In the end, this system of needs and desires builds a control circuit that creates a realistic behavior pattern. Although few typical desktop games require such a complicated control system, some desktop games have profited enormously from a detailed behavioral model (e.g., Tamagotchis). Note, however, that with these models it is very hard to plan or to foresee the reactions of the computer AI. The result might be an AI that resembles a nice, humanlike behavior, or it may just do strange things.

ADVANCED AI CONCEPTS

Nowadays, there is a tendency in computer games to use even more advanced AI concepts. Two key features of advanced AI concepts include learning and adapting to unknown situations, and both criteria allow the development of even more realistic computer AI. However, currently only a few computer games use these concepts. Many games simply do not require such advanced AI concepts, and if they do, often the game cannot spare the resources necessary to calculate them. Nevertheless, with the development of more powerful computers and games dependent on more realistic characters, the game world is beginning to focus on these advanced

AI technologies. Examples of games that use the advanced AI include Creatures™ and Black and White™.

The typical desktop games discussed in this book do not demand advanced AI concepts; therefore, we only provide a brief overview of some interesting AI alternatives so you can study them further if you so choose:

Computer *neural networks* **try to imitate the working of the human brain:** Neural networks are constructed from an interconnected set of primitive cells termed *neurons*, which receive input from other neurons to change their excitation level. When the excitation exceeds a certain threshold, the neuron is activated (it "fires"), and in turn starts to activate other neurons. A network of firing neurons creates a complex system, which can be trained in a learning process to perform a certain task. Since a network will not only recognize the exact input from the training but also similar input, it can be used to classify and recognize distinct patterns [Neural05a], [Neural05b], [Neural05c].

Fuzzy Logic **is an enhancement of the classical Boolean logic from only two Boolean elements (*true* and *false*) to a set of possibilities:** This originates from real life in which a clear true or false is often not sufficient because the truth is somewhere in the middle (*fuzzy*). For example, if we define a tall person as 6 feet in height, Boolean logic would state that someone 5 feet 11 inches is small, while we would probably still call him still "rather tall." Fuzzy logic allows such a description by allowing items to be partly members of a set (being 90% part of the "tall" set). Consequently, fuzzy logic also defines the typical logical operations such as negation, intersection, and union for these fuzzy sets [Fuzzy05].

Genetic algorithms **can be used for creating and training an AI or to implement intelligent behavior on a population or tribe level:** These algorithms try to imitate nature's way of inheriting information from one generation to the next using a set of genetic material (DNA). This DNA is comprised of a collection of genes, where each gene represents a certain trait or feature. Genes are inherited from the parent creatures, and genetic algorithms try to imitate this behavior by constructing genes in software. Forcing such genes under a selection process (only creatures that fulfill some environmental conditions will survive) will lead to an optimum adaptation to the environment, leading to the solving of the corresponding optimization problem [Rabin02], [Genetic05a], [Genetic05b].

SUMMARY

Games involving computer-based players require the design of a decent and robust AI engine, which is an essential addition to most computer games. Players will seldom choose to play a game if an AI is absent or if the AI is playing poorly. Exceptions are games that require just the human player, or multiplayer network games in which many human players play together. However, the choice of the AI algorithm largely depends on the needs of the particular game, and in this chapter, we presented some of the main approaches to game AI programming.

It is important to keep in mind that for the design of a game AI, the best system is often the simplest, not the most scientifically accurate. For example, if a simple script yields better results than a more accurate behavioral or neural network model, choose the script.

Additionally, the choice of the AI algorithms is frequently limited by the available computer resources, which is a principal problem on handheld computers. However, even on desktop computers, often much more performance is used for 3D world modeling than for AI. Sometimes, these restrictions can limit the design of your AI; thus, we recommend that you do not deprive your AI too much.

In the process of AI design, it is extremely important to keep the AI code as flexible as possible. The more modularly an AI is programmed, the more extensions are possible during the development and testing of the game. Often, you will notice that the design of a game AI is an iterative process where situations, conditions, and events have to be first tested and experienced before you can improve the AI built upon them. In the end, usually the testers of the game will provide critical feedback on how the AI behaves during game play.

The game tree algorithm is the standard method for board or similar games. Since most games cannot be analyzed up to the end, the game tree algorithms also involve a heuristic element, which is the actual evaluation of the game board. This evaluation algorithm will be the crucial difference between a good AI and a bad AI. The tree searches described in this chapter cannot be implemented when games include a random factor, such as dice games. However, depending on the amount of randomness, tree searches can be extended by a probability concept. Furthermore, in simple games, even a good game board evaluation algorithm can suffice and often works surprisingly well.

Although programmers sometimes think that scripted AI is not very advanced, or even a bit simple, script-based AI is actually a very powerful way to create sophisticated AI behavior in games. Scripted AI is usually easier to implement than a more complex AI model such as behavior AI and still produces a decent AI player. When combined with other AI concepts such as state machines, script-based AI is extremely useful for many computer games.

State machines are a fundamental part of game AI. They are robust and allow the easy implementation of numerous AI features. They also provide an excellent basis for many good AI algorithms. In fact, since general behavior dependencies are modeled by state machines, the game characters usually begin to act reasonably well. Nevertheless, do not expect wonders or a super-intelligent AI as soon as you program a state machine containing a few states.

Some modern computer games incorporate elements of behavior modeling, equipping characters with basic needs and desires so they appear more lifelike and interesting. This allows the character to pursue its own individual goals, which in turn makes the game appear more realistic.

In modern games there is a clear tendency to implement more realistic AI engines. Learning and adaptation, neural networks or fuzzy logic are concepts not yet used very often in game AI and even less in desktop games. However, it is likely that these concepts will be employed when the demand for more realistic AI is higher and more computer power is available for the AI algorithms.

Regardless of what AI algorithms you choose for your game, the goal of any game is still to create an AI that allows the player to play in a realistic game environment with or against a computer AI player that acts and reacts in a believable and intelligent manner.

REFERENCES

[Beckert03] Beckert, Bernhard, *Introduction to Artificial Intelligence, http://www. uni-koblenz.de/~beckert/Lehre/KI-fuer-IM/02Introduction.pdf*, 2003.

[Doerner95] *Dörner, D., and K. Hille, Artificial Souls: Motivated Emotional Robots,* IEEE Conference Proceedings, Vancouver, 1995.

[Fuzzy05] *Introduction to Fuzzy Logic, http://www.dementia.org/~julied/ logic/index.html*, 2005.

[Genetic05a] *Introduction to Genetic Algorithms, http://www.rennard.org/alife/ english/gavintrgb.html*, 2005.

[Genetic05b] *Genetic Algorithms, http://samizdat.mines.edu/ga_tutorial/ga_ tutorial.ps*, 2005.

[Neural05a] *An Introduction to Neural Networks, http://www.cs.stir.ac.uk/~lss/ NNIntro/InvSlides.html*, 2005.

[Neural05b] *Neural Networks, http://www.doc.ic.ac.uk/~nd/surprise_96/journal/ vol4/cs11/report.html*, 2005.

[Neural05c] *Artificial Neural Network Technology, http://www.dacs.dtic.mil/ techs/neural/neural_ToC.html*, 2005.

[Rabin02] Rabin, Steve, *AI Game Programming Wisdom*, ISBN: 1584500778; Charles River Media, 2002.

[Rabin03] Rabin, Steve, *AI Game Programming Wisdom 2*, ISBN: 1584502894; Charles River Media, 2003.

[Uml05] *UML Tools, http://www.jeckle.de/umltools.htm*, 2005.

11 Pathfinding

In This Chapter

■ The Game Map
■ The Terrain
■ Defining a Path
■ Pathfinding with a Gradient Approach
■ Pathfinding Using the A* Method
■ Moving Obstacles
■ General Performance Optimizations

Pathfinding in computer games is the task of defining a suitable trail between two locations on a map or in any other game area. In many games, the player commands the game unit or character to move from its current (start) location on the map, to one or more possible target locations. Often, the most direct passageway between these two locations is not accessible because obstacles may be blocking the way. Furthermore, the landscape on the map may also determine the ease with which a certain pathway can be traveled. Pathfinding basically reflects how a person travels in real life. For example, a journey from A to B in a car is relatively simple on a highway. However, the same distance on rough terrain such as through swamps or over hills would be more difficult and energy consuming, and crossing obstacles such as rivers would be impossible. Even if the highway were a detour around a swamp, which might be the direct passageway between points A and B, traveling on the highway would still be the "optimum" pathway. However, if the car had to be re-routed on a small street around a collapsed bridge on the highway, the path planner would choose this as a "good" alternative path. A typical map with landscape obstacles and two possible paths is shown in Figure 11.1.

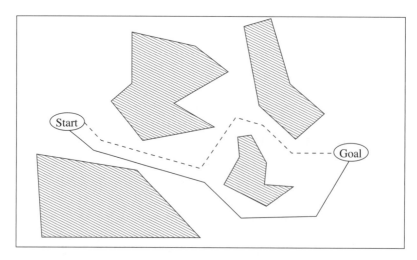

FIGURE 11.1 Two possible paths from the start location to the target location lead around impassable obstacles (shaded areas).

To create a path in computer games, the game engine has to find an optimal solution between the starting point and target location. Even when the map is extremely complicated or a path is not immediately obvious, the pathways still need to be located. Additionally, in computer games, both time and memory resources are particularly important factors, and therefore a path search must be completed even when there are limited resources. For a player to enjoy a game, the path search must succeed in fractions of a second instead of minutes or even hours.

Mathematically, such a path search is actually an optimization problem, and in principle, as soon as a path exists, the optimization problem is solvable and an optimum path can be found. The most straightforward method of locating the optimum path would be to analyze all possible routes and then choose the most appropriate one. Unfortunately, as the distance between the start and target points expands, the number of possible paths grows exponentially. Therefore, as the number of possible pathways increases, analyzing every route becomes impractical in terms of time and resource consumption. In computer games, a fast and efficient path-searching algorithm is required. Often, a fast algorithm that locates a good path is preferable to the perfect algorithm that finds the optimal path.

A typical application for pathfinding algorithms is in a strategy game in which units move around on a game map. In addition, board games (e.g., *Quintalign* or

Sokoban) in which pieces or characters can be moved around obstacles are examples of games that employ pathfinding algorithms. Furthermore, Non-Player-Characters (NPCs) in action or role-playing games are required to move from one location to the next, which is another application area for pathfinding algorithms. This brief list indicates that pathfinding occurs in many different game scenarios. Therefore, it is worthwhile to consider pathfinding algorithms for computer games you develop. Fortunately, the problem of pathfinding is a well-investigated topic, and good algorithms already exist.

In this chapter, we first discuss the general concepts of game maps, terrains, and paths. We then present two useful pathfinding algorithms [Astar04], [DeLoura00], [GameAi04] that can be easily implemented into desktop games. Both algorithms are implemented in the demonstration program `mypath` in the folder `examples/mypath` on the CD-ROM accompanying this book.

ON THE CD

THE GAME MAP

Before we can apply pathfinding algorithms to search for possible paths between two locations, it is necessary to represent or translate the game world or the game map into some internal computer representation. In this representation, the game world is partitioned; that is, split into discrete areas or cells. In essence, the computer then visualizes the map as a collection of cells; for example, a rectangular grid as depicted in Figure 11.2. Each of these cells corresponds to an area of the real game map and will be either marked "free" or "occupied" depending on the properties of the real game map. Additionally, all cells are interconnected so each cell has a clearly defined set of neighboring locations. However, the number of neighboring cells can be arbitrary and need not be the same for each cell. The task of the pathfinding algorithm is then reduced to planning a path from the start cell by moving through the defined consecutive neighborhoods until the target cell is reached.

This concept of discrete, interconnected cells on an abstract map is the most general model for all pathfinding algorithms. However, the exact type of partitioning of the game world depends on the actual game or type of game, and a clever setup of the game map can actually help and even speed up the pathfinding algorithm. Therefore, the partitioning has to naturally suit the game and game map. Most games divide the game world into a map of equally sized tiles that are square, rectangular, or hexagonal. This is very easy, as many games (strategy games or board games) are naturally based on a tile concept, and therefore the partitioning process is very natural. However, other methods of partitioning space divide the game world into very different entities (convex polygons or quad-trees), or use tiles of varying sizes. These ideas are rarely used for the type of desktop games we discuss in this book. Most games work efficiently with a regularly tiled world map.

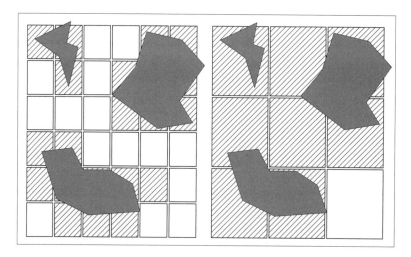

FIGURE 11.2 A map of a possible game world with free areas (white) and obstacles (dark) partitioned into cells. The cells are white for free cells and shaded for occupied cells, indicating how the computer will perceive the partitioned map. On the left, the chosen grid has small panels and allows a fair representation of the underlying map. However, on the right, the grid tiles are clearly too large, so the map representation is not as clear. For the sake of simplicity, the maps are constructed in such a way that cells partially covered by an obstacle are marked as occupied.

An important fact to consider when partitioning the game map into regular cells is the actual size of the cells. Cells that are too large will fail to represent the fine details on the map because there will be too many details spread over a single cell. However, very small cells will consume too much memory and result in paths with large numbers of steps, which will make the pathfinding process both time-retain and memory-consuming. Figure 11.2 shows two partitioning approaches for a game map. The tile layout shown on the left is clearly more suitable than that represented on the right, since the obstacle details on the game map are still clearly defined.

THE TERRAIN

Some simple games can suffice with a game world composed only of uniform free space and some impassable obstacles. Pathfinding in such a case has only to find a walkable path. However, the majority of games have a much more complex game world. In these game worlds, the landscape varies, and while some areas on the map will be easy to pass, others will be more difficult. The difficulty of crossing any particular area can even depend on the type of unit or character that has to move to the specified target location.

Pathfinding algorithms can take all types of terrain features into account, and can therefore plot a path that will minimize the route with respect to the arbitrary properties of each specific terrain. The level of difficulty that each terrain feature produces can be included in the pathfinding algorithms by assigning a certain *cost* to each location on the map—the higher the cost, the harder it will be to pass such a location. Impassable obstacles are then simply locations with infinite cost, as mountains would be for certain cars. In most cases, these pathfinding costs are directly related to movement costs or other movement properties of the units or characters that will use the path. Typical examples of such movement costs are the fuel consumption of a unit, the speed of a character, or the degree of danger in an area. Consequently, instead of just having a world map consisting of cells that are either occupied or free, we now have a world map in which all these movement costs are entered, which results in a *terrain* map. Figure 11.3 shows such a terrain map in which you can imagine the cell numbers to represent the heights of a topological map. Note, however, that often these terrains are not static and can even depend on a particular unit type.

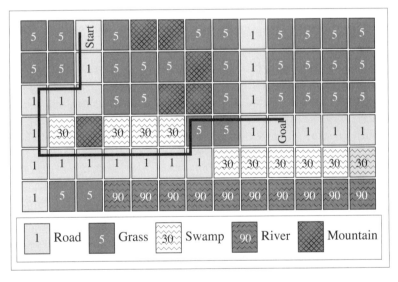

FIGURE 11.3   A game map showing the moving costs required for crossing different types of terrain (e.g., road: 1, grass: 5, swamp: 30, water: 90, mountains: impassable). A pathfinding algorithm will evaluate all "costs" and create a path that has a minimum overall cost as indicated by the line. In this example, this is achieved by avoiding the swampy areas and following the road.

A pathfinding algorithm will now not only count the geometrical distance between two locations along a free path but also calculate the movement costs of traveling over the different terrains. The total movement cost is the sum of all the individual terrain costs along the path. To a pathfinding algorithm, a path going over areas that are difficult to cross will appear longer. The pathfinding algorithm will automatically avoid these "bad" areas, since its principal function is to search for short paths.

In Figure 11.3, we show such a terrain map in detail. Using this strategy-game based map, we will assume that a unit has to travel from the start location ("Start") to the target location ("Goal"). From the plotted route, we can see that different areas have to be passed. For example, normal roads with a cost of 1 unit or grass areas (5 units) can be crossed with reasonable effort. Swamps, however, will cost 30 units, and rivers will cost 90 units, indicating that although these terrains are more complicated to cross, it is possible to do so. Nevertheless, we expect the pathfinding algorithm to avoid such expensive locations. Finally, there are also mountain areas that are impassable (infinite cost). The resulting path is marked as a line going from the start location to the target location. As expected, the path will avoid the river and swamps and stay on the roads and grass regions.

In this terrain example, to avoid crossing swamp fields (30 units), the pathfinding automatically plots a detour via roads and grass fields. Even if 5 grass fields or 29 road fields have to be crossed, the path will still have a smaller overall cost compared to wading through one swamp field. However, if a detour would be too long, the swamp route would be preferred, demonstrating that the pathfinding algorithm searches the most cost-effective route. You can try these different scenarios using the example program mypath on the companion CD-ROM. In this program, you can assign several obstacles to a game map and let a pathfinding algorithm find a way around them.

Within a complex or challenging game, the field costs can actually depend on the type of unit moving along the path. For example, if we consider that the unit moving along the path depicted in Figure 11.3 is a hovercraft unit, the swamp might be easily crossed, which would result in no movement penalties. However, a person without such a vehicle will have to either wade through the swamp at a high cost or follow the detour. Thus, the type of unit might incur varying penalties depending on its ability to handle swamps. These different movement costs will then lead to alternative paths, depending on the type of unit. Note that in some games, when a group of units has to stay together for protection reasons, some units might still have to follow a nonoptimal pathway, since this would be required by another unit of the group.

ON THE CD

DEFINING A PATH

In the previous section, we discussed how the shortest path on a game map is located. However, how do we actually describe such a path? We do so by defining a unique sequence of cells that contains all the necessary steps of the path. The first cell of the path sequence is the starting location on the game map. The following cells in the sequence are then consecutive steps of the path, and are the actual neighbors of each previous cell on the game map. The sequence of cells and therefore the path finally ends at the target location. Once the optimal path is chosen, each cell on the pathway through which the unit must travel is registered and linked to its neighboring cells.

In desktop games, such a sequence of cells can be conveniently stored in a linked list, or alternatively in an array. The elements of the list are then either pointers to the cells on the game map or indices or coordinates of the map cells. Both approaches are valid depending on how you store your original map. If the map is constructed of cells that contain multiple elements in a structure or class, it is more efficient to store them as pointers to these. Alternatively, when an array of primitive types is used to construct the game map, it is easier to just store the indices of the array elements or the coordinates of the map.

Using a tiled Cartesian x-y map as an example, it is possible to simply store the (x,y) coordinates of the cells as a linked list (e.g., of QPoints). In this example, a path on a 20×20 sized map can then be built as a list of (x,y) coordinates. If the example path then goes from position $(3,7)$ to $(7,9)$, the resulting path might look like

    (3,7), (4,7), (5,7), (6,7), (7,7), (7,8), (7,9)

Alternatively, the index numbers of the array elements can be stored. Assuming the index is $(x + 20 \times y)$, the same path sequence would yield

    143, 144, 145, 146, 147, 167, 187

PATHFINDING WITH A GRADIENT APPROACH

Once a game map is defined using interconnected cells, a pathfinding algorithm can be applied. In this section, we introduce the *gradient pathfinding* algorithm, which is a simple and easy-to-use pathfinding algorithm that works well on small maps or small, grid-based games. It is not as efficient as the A* algorithm, which we discuss in the next section, but serves as a good introduction to such algorithms since the mathematical application is easily understood. Furthermore, it can be easily implemented into a game program. The gradient pathfinding algorithm can be applied to games that contain only a few hundred grid cells such as puzzle board games, and its performance is more than sufficient in such cases.

The name *gradient pathfinding* stems from the type of search concept this algorithm uses. The search begins in a reverse manner at the target location and associates the actual distance or movement cost from this target location to each cell on the map. Depending on the terrain of each individual cell, this procedure builds up a new number-based (distance) map that is parallel to the real game map. In this new distance map, the target location is always the lowest number. Thus, if you consider these associated numbers heights, all the cells will become a hill or mountain area, and the target location is comparable to a valley; that is, the lowest point with a designated zero height. If you are on a hill or mountain, a valley can be reached fastest by following the path with the steepest descent; that is, the largest gradient. This is not always the wisest thing to do on a real mountain, but it is certainly the fastest. Such a gradient map is shown in Figure 11.4. The numbers indicate the actual distances from the target location, starting from zero. Impassable obstacles prevent a direct path in some areas. The path found by the algorithm is the steepest descent from the start location and is depicted by the bold line.

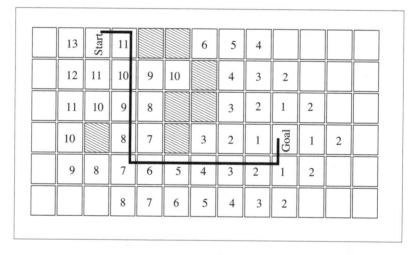

FIGURE 11.4 Gradient pathfinding principle. The algorithm creates a distance map that stores each cell's distance from the target. The depicted map only distinguishes between passable and impassable areas (shaded). The movement cost between two cells is therefore just the geometrical distance. The shortest path follows the steepest gradient from the start location ("Start") to the target location ("Goal") as shown by the line.

In the following sections, we describe the gradient pathfinding algorithm in more detail using an example program. The complete working example program can be found on the companion CD-ROM as part of the `mypath` program in the `examples/mypath` folder.

Creating a Distance Map

The key element for the gradient pathfinding algorithm is the creation of the distance map, which is a direct copy, in both shape and size, of the original grid of cells representing the world map. Typically, this distance map can be an array of the same size as the original game map. Each element on the distance map corresponds to its original on the real map at the same coordinates. All values in the distance map represent the actual distance of a cell on the map from the target location. Figure 11.4 shows a distance map using geometrical distances to the target. Instead of using the simple geometrical distance, it is possible to use general movement costs by considering the terrain of each cell.

At the beginning of the pathfinding search, the distance map has to be initialized. Each element should be marked "unused," so later it can be detected whether the element has already been processed. Since normal movement cost cannot be less than zero, such initialization can be done by filling the distance map with minus one (–1).

```
// Define the distance map: in this example the distance
// map is just a fixed size linear array of dimension
// WIDTH*HEIGHT. The (x,y) index into this map is simply
// x + WIDTH * y.
QMemArray<int> mDistanceMap;

// of this width and height
mDistanceMap.resize(WIDTH*HEIGHT);

// reset map
mDistanceMap.fill(-1);
```

Starting at the target location, the map is now constructed by assigning the movement cost for each cell to this target location. For the target location itself, this cost is obviously zero, because we are already at the target. The algorithm begins its calculation by making the target location the current working cell. For each current working cell (in the first step, the target cell), the cost to the target cell (for the target zero) is stored, and then all neighboring cells are processed in the same way by making them the current working cells in turn. This process is then repeated for the neighbors of the neighbors, and so on.

Once the movement cost or the distance from one cell to the target is known, it is easy to determine the cost from any neighboring cell to the target. This can be done without calculating the entire path; it simply has to add the current cost to the movement cost from the current cell to its neighbor. This is possible because the cost of the current cell already contains the running total of the path cost from there to the target location.

This algorithm has a recursive pattern, and a program can be implemented that automatically handles all the neighbors of every cell recursively (this recursion will search the map depth first). However, it is possible to search the map breadth first. In this case, a list of cells is maintained that contains all cells that have yet to be processed. This search list is filled by first storing the target location, then all its neighbors, then all of the neighbors of the neighbors, and so on. The algorithm then iterates the search list until it is empty, which means all possible grid cells have been processed.

In the example program, the cost association and the processing of the linked list is done by adding a path element at a given coordinate (*tx,ty*) of a rectangular map with the specified cost.

```
// Start search at the target cell (tx,ty) with zero cost
addPathElement(tx, ty, 0);
```

During the main pathfinding loop, the first item of the linked search list is retrieved, processed, and then deleted from the search list. When each new cell is processed, further items—that is, all neighbors of the current cell—are added to the search list for later processing. During the path search, it is possible that one of the adjacent cells of the current cell has already been processed. In the example, this would be noticed because the cell no longer contains the initial value of minus one (–1).

For such a cell, two possible scenarios exist. First, the cell can be safely ignored if it stores a distance value that is smaller than or equal to the current cost plus the cost of moving to that particular neighbor. In the scenario we created here, a new path to the same location would be longer, which we do not want. Second, if the cost of the neighboring cell can be reduced by this new path, the cost of this cell is updated with the newer, smaller value, and the cell is put back into the search list for further processing. This is necessary because all cells dependent on this cell will now have a shorter distance to the target and therefore need recalculation.

The following code snippet shows the details of the main loop for building the distance map. Here, the search list is looped until there are no more cells. Every cell can affect its neighboring cells; therefore, when each cell is calculated, all of its neighboring cells are added to the search algorithm. In addition, all the movement costs from these neighboring cells are updated with respect to the current cell's cost to the target location.

```
// Define the search list e.g. in the class header:
// our list stores (x,y) coordinates as QPoints
QValueList<QPoint> mSearchList;
...

// Loop the search list as long as there are items available
while(mSearchList.count()>0)
{
  QValueList<QPoint>::iterator it = mSearchList.begin();

  // Current (x,y) position on the map
  QPoint field = *it;

  // Remove the cell from the search list
  mSearchList.remove(it);


  // x and y coordinate of the current cell
  int x = field.x();
  int y = field.y();

  // Process the left cell: to keep the example simple we
  // ignore the border x=0!
  int cx = x-1;
  int cy = y;

  // Get current distance cost to the target
  int curCost = mDistanceMap[cx + WIDTH * cy];
  // Catch initial cell marker
  if (curCost < 0) curCost = 0;

  // Now the movement cost to the new cell and the current cost
  // are added
  int movementCost = board.at(cx + WIDTH * cy);
  int cost          = curCost + movementCost;

  // The cell is stored and added to the search list if the cost
  // can be reduced. This check is done by the addPathElement()
  // method.
  addPathElement(cx, cy, cost);

  // Repeat the cell processing for all other neighbors of the
  // current cell, that is right cell, top cell, bottom cell, ...
  ...
}
```

Finally, we show the method used to add a new cell to the search list. This method also checks whether such an addition is necessary; that is, whether the new costs are lower than the original cost. If they are not, the cell is not processed.

```
void addPathElement(int x, int y, int cost)
{
  // Check whether the cell was never processed (-1) or
  // whether the current addition can lower the cost to
  // this location
  if (mDistanceMap.at(x + WIDTH * y) < 0 ||
      mDistanceMap.at(x + WIDTH * y) > cost)
  {
    // Add the cell at position (x,y) to the search list
    mSearchList.append(QPoint(x, y));

    // Store the cost to the target in the distance map
    mDistanceMap.at(x + WIDTH * y) = cost;
  }
}
```

In gradient pathfinding, cells are typically re-processed if the direct path to the target is obstructed by terrain that contains a high movement cost such as a swamp. In the first processing round, a cell is added with the relevant high movement cost. A detour over the swamp via a bridge, for example, will reduce the overall cost of the pathway despite being longer in geometrical length. However, the new path is configured only when the search finds this bridge-containing cell; therefore, cells adjacent to the bridge also need re-processing.

Once the search list is empty, all possible path combinations are checked and the optimum path to the target is plotted. When the pathway is chosen, the distance map will also contain the overall movement cost from the start to the target. If no path exists between the two locations, the distance map will still have the "unused" value in the starting location's distance map cell. In our example, it would be minus one (−1); otherwise, an optimal path has been found.

Depth-First and Breadth-First Searches

Maps can be searched depth first or breadth first. A depth-first search typically results from a recursive implementation of a search algorithm. In a depth-first search, a single path is followed until it cannot be further extended or reaches the target location. If it did not reach the target location, it goes back one step and tries another direction. The search starts by generating very long paths. The ends of these long paths are then further probed until no more possibilities exist. However, during the search the paths are shortened by re-searching them.

A breadth-first search typically results from an iterative implementation of a search algorithm. In the breadth-first search, all possible paths are investigated in parallel by testing all first neighbors of the starting location, then probing all second neighbors of the starting location, and so on. In this algorithm, many short paths are created. For desktop games, when looking for an optimal path, both algorithms are more or less equivalent.

Creating the Path

Once the path distance map is built, the actual path can be created by simply following the steepest descent from the start location as shown in Figure 11.4. Thus, beginning at the start location, each neighboring cell is examined, and out of all of those cells, the neighbor with the lowest cost is selected for the next step. This process is repeated until the cost of the current step is zero, which indicates that the target location has been reached. All cells that are part of the pathway can be stored in a path list as described previously. The resulting pathway can then be used by units or characters in the game.

Optimization of the Gradient Path Search

Pathfinding can take a long time and can consume quite many computer resources. Therefore, it is essential to optimize the pathfinding algorithm. A very efficient way to do this is to stop the path search either when any path to the target location has been reached, or when the current path to the target cell is less than a specified length. The disadvantage to this premature end of the algorithm is that the algorithm will probably not find the shortest path. However, in many games, this is often unnecessary, and the resulting good pathway is more than adequate.

The next important criterion is to decide at what length the path is acceptable. By this, we mean in which cases the search can be aborted and in which cases the search has to be continued to find an even better path. A good indication for a suitable path length can be obtained by comparing the current cost (the current value of the start location cell in the distance map) with the cost for a direct straight-line path between the start and the target. This value is then multiplied by a specific user factor, which should represent the average movement cost for the typical terrain in the game. If the current path cost seems reasonable when compared to the straight-line value, the path search can be stopped prematurely. Note, however, that normally the algorithm will continue to reprocess the starting point values and thus lower the overall cost for the path from start to target, yielding better and better paths until the optimum path is found.

PATHFINDING USING THE A* METHOD

The A* (pronounced "A star") is the most commonly used pathfinding algorithm in computer games [Lester04]. It has been around for a long time (1968) and has proven very reliable and fast. As with other pathfinding algorithms, the A* algorithm uses the concept that each cell on a map is connected to its neighboring cells. Again, the distance between cells can be generalized to take into account the cost of moving from one particular cell to its neighboring cells. This is the movement cost for the cell, as depicted in Figure 11.3. In most computer games, such a map is typically based on a square, rectangular, or hexagonal grid. Figure 11.2 shows a typical game map on a rectangular grid.

In contrast to the gradient pathfinding algorithm, the A* algorithm begins from the start location and extends across the remainder of the map. It measures the distance it travels from the start location and additionally estimates the distance to the target location. This estimated distance value makes this process distinctly different from the gradient path search, because it takes both the start and the target into consideration. In particular, this additional information allows for a more directed search toward the target location; the search does not aimlessly wander around but is biased toward the target.

ON THE CD

In the following sections, we describe the A* pathfinding algorithm. The complete example program can be found on the companion CD-ROM as part of the `mypath` program in the `examples/mypath` folder.

Distance Measurement Functions

The A* algorithm measures the distance from the currently analyzed cell to both the start and target locations. The distance to the start location is precise because it is the sum of all cells analyzed during the process to reach the current cell. Additionally, the algorithm tries to estimate a distance or cost measurement to the target location. Both measurements together form the overall *cost function* of the A* algorithm. This overall movement cost, termed F, is always analyzed for the current cell and is determined by two functions, G and H. Function G measures the distance to the start location, and H measures the distance to the target location. The overall movement cost F is therefore F = G + H.

In detail, at any given cell under investigation, the algorithm calculates the movement cost G that would occur if the path were to extend from the start location to the current location. This cost G can be easily determined because the cost G to the previously analyzed cell is already known. To determine the new G value, the actual movement cost from the previous to the new location and the previous G value have to be added together, which yields the current overall cost G from the start location to the current cell. This process can be repeated for all the neighboring cells of the current cell, which leads to a recursive description. Such a search with the calculated path cost is depicted in Figure 11.5.

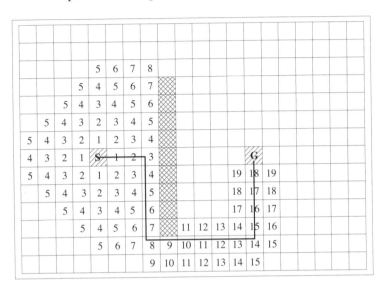

FIGURE 11.5 Pathfinding performed by the A* algorithm with an H function defined as the geometrical distance between two cells. The search begins at the start location and finds a path to the target location. The shaded cells in between these two are impassable obstacles that the algorithm must avoid. Cells that have been investigated by the path search have their movement cost entered. The shortest path found is drawn as a line connecting the start and target cells. Empty cells are those that have not been investigated by the algorithm. The capability of the A* algorithm to perform an effective and directed search can be seen by the high ratio of empty to investigated cells.

Alongside the movement cost function G, a second quantity is required. This function is called H and it is a heuristic cost function, because it *estimates* or *guesses* the cost from the analyzed cell to the target location. Contrary to the movement cost G, which is exactly known and is calculated on the part of the path already traveled, the heuristic cost to the target is not known because no part of that path has been explored. It is the task of the programmer to estimate this cost function. The performance and quality of the A* pathfinding depend on the choice and estimation of the H function.

You might argue that it sounds difficult or even impossible to estimate the cost H from any arbitrary location on the map to the target location before actually knowing the path. Remember, however, that only a guess or estimate is needed, and the cost value does not have to be precise. Once the A* algorithm has processed the map and the search reaches the target location, the overall cost will be determined only by G, and the estimate H is zero.

A good assumption for an estimation function H is to take a straight-line path from the current location to the target location and assume movement cost for normal terrain (e.g., cost = 1 unit). In this case, the cost H is directly related to the geometrical distance between the two locations. We discuss the effects of underestimating or overestimating the H function later in this chapter.

Shopping Lists

The A* algorithm describes a recursive search of the game map. However, here it is more efficient to change the recursion to an iteration and thus search the map breadth first. In the A* algorithm, this is done by introducing the so-called *shopping lists* that store the map locations that are still to be or already have been analyzed. Two lists of cell locations are maintained during the search: the *open* list and the *closed* list.

> **The open list**: The open list contains all cells that still need to be investigated during the path search. At the beginning of the search, the open list is initialized with only one item, the start location. During the search, all the neighboring cells of the cell currently being investigated are added to the open list so they can be processed in later steps.
>
> **The closed list**: The closed list stores all the cells that have already been examined during the path search. The closed list is initialized empty. Cells are moved from the open to the closed list once they have been processed by the algorithm.

During the pathfinding search, the algorithm examines one entry of the open list, determines the movement costs for this location, and then moves the item from the open list to the closed list. Throughout this procedure, new cells—that is, all the neighboring cells of the currently examined cell—are added to the open list. This will continue in the next step of the search loop and is repeated as long as there are still items in the open list. The search is completed when the list is empty.

Each entry or node in both lists should store at least the following items:

- The actual cost G for the current cell.
- The estimated cost H for the current cell.
- The location of the actual cell on the map (e.g., *x*-*y* coordinates, or a pointer to the map location).
- A link to the parent; that is, the previously visited node. This is used to trace the path once it is found. Following the links from one node to the next will produce the shortest path.

These noted items can be represented by the following general class definition for a list node:

```
class ANode
{
  public:
  ANode* parent;   // Parent cell
  int    costG;    // Cost from start location
  int    costH;    // Cost to target location
  <type> location; // Cell identifier, with <type> being
                    // e.g. integers or a pointer to a cell
};
```

For a rectangular grid, the location can be specified by the *x*-coordinate and *y*-coordinate. We can then define the ANode class as

```
class ANode
{
  public:
  ANode* parent;   // Parent cell
  int    costG;    // Cost from starting location
  int    costH;    // Cost to target location
  int    x;        // Cell identifier X
  int    y;        // Cell identifier Y
};
```

In the following examples, we use this ANode class as specialized for rectangular grids.

The A* Algorithm

We now describe the actual A* algorithm in more detail. First, we need a representation of the game world as a map of cells. For the following examples, we assume that this map is a rectangular grid of a fixed width (WIDTH) and height (HEIGHT). Additionally, we require the shopping lists, which can be any linked list type. Here we use a QPtrList that stores the previously defined ANode structures. Both the open and closed lists are initialized empty at the beginning of the algorithm. The start location is then added to the list with a movement cost G of zero.

In the following example, we pass the value of the current cell and its given movement cost to the addPathElement() method. This method will correctly handle the addition of nodes to the list and update the cost functions. Additionally, we provide the previous path node to the function so this information can be stored in the linked list node. Later, we will see that storing this information helps to retrieve the shortest path. Obviously, for the start location cell, the previous path element is not present; therefore, we just pass the argument NULL.

```
// Define lists of nodes
QPtrList<ANode> mOpenList;
QPtrList<ANode> mClosedList;

mOpenList.clear();    // Clear open list
mClosedList.clear();  // Clear closed list

...

// Start search at the starting location (sx,sy) with
// zero cost (0) and no parent (NULL)
addPathElement(sx, sy, 0, NULL);
```

The A* algorithm now has to process all cells on the map until a path is found. To do so, the algorithm has to loop through all entries in the open list until there are no more entries left. If the pathfinding loop ends in the latter way, no path could be found. Inside the pathfinding loop, the following commands have to be executed:

■ The item with the lowest overall cost F is extracted from the open list and made the current processed item. To avoid frequent searching of the entire list, the open list is sorted by the overall cost F. In this case, the first item of the list is also the item with the lowest overall cost F, and therefore you can just select the first item.

■ If the currently selected item happens to be the intended target location, the search is complete, a path has been found, and the search algorithm can be terminated.

■ Otherwise, all neighboring cells connected to the currently analyzed cell are considered for insertion into the open list. Each new insertion is placed in the list according to its total cost F parameter. Often, a cell that is about to be inserted is already present in the open or closed list. When this occurs, the cell has to be further analyzed to determine whether the current path will lower the movement cost G. If not, the cell is ignored; otherwise, the cell is removed from either list and re-added to the open list with the corrected cost. Although this procedure requires a search of both the open and closed lists, it allows a continuous reduction in the path length. When a new cell is stored in the open list, the current cell is stored as a parent to this newly added list item. Additionally, the costs G and H are updated for all newly added items. Impassable cells can be ignored at this stage.

■ The currently processed cell is now complete and can be moved from the open to the closed list.

The following code snippet shows this processing of the first list element. The element is taken from the open list, checked for being the target location, and if the target is not yet reached, all neighboring cells are added to the shopping list.

```
// Run the algorithm while there are still elements in the open
// list
while(!mOpenList.isEmpty())
{
  // Get first item from the list and make it the current item
  ANode* node = mOpenList.take();

  // Append the current item to the closed list. It does not
  // matter whether this happens here or at the end of this
  // method.
  mClosedList.append(node);

  // Check whether the target location is reached. We return
  // this location for information. Of course the check for the
  // target location is game dependent. Here, we just assume
  // (x,y) coordinates
  if (node->x == targetX  && node->y == targetY)
  {
    return node;
  }

  // Retrieve the board coordinates (x,y)
  int x = node->x;
  int y = node->y;

  // Add neighboring fields. We start with the field left of
  // the current cell. For the simplicity of the example we
  // ignore the border x=0.
  int cx = x - 1;
  int cy = y;

  // Add the cost of the current node plus the movement cost
  // from (x,y) to (cx,cy)
  int cost  = node->costG + costBetween(x, y, cx, cy);

  // Add neighbor to shopping list
  addPathElement(cx, cy, cost, node);
  ...

  // Repeat addition for all neighbors (right, top, bottom)
  ...
}
```

```
  // If no path was found we return NULL to the main program.
  return NULL;
```

The path element addition function now needs to add the path elements to the open list or update the lists if they fulfill the A* algorithm criteria; that is, they are not yet in the open or closed list, or alternatively they reduce the path cost.

```
void addPathElement(int x, int y, int cost, ANode* parent)
{
  ANode* cur  = NULL;
  ANode* node = NULL;

  // Check whether the node at (x,y) is in open or closed list
  // and the cost cannot be reduced. If so immediately return
  // to avoid double processing. If the cost can be reduced
  // the node is take away from the list and later on re-added
  // at the correct position in the open list.
  for (cur = mClosedList.first(); cur && !node;
       cur = mClosedList.next() )
  {
    if (x == cur->x && y == cur->y)
    {
      // Remove item from list if cost is reduced.
      if (cost < cur->costG) { node = mClosedList.take(); }
      // or return if no shorter path is found
      else { return; }
    }
  }

  // Do the same for the open list
  for (cur = mOpenList.first(); cur && ! node;
       cur = mOpenList.next() )
  {
    if (x == cur->x && y == cur->y)
    {
      // Remove item from list if cost is reduced.
      if (cost < cur->costG) { node = mOpenList.take(); }
      // or return if no shorter path is found
      else { return; }
    }
  }


  // Create new node or use the one found in the list
  if (!node) { node    = new ANode(); }
```

```
// Fill node with current data
node->parent   = parent;           // Parent node
node->x        = x;                // Store position x
node->y        = y;                // Store position y
node->costG    = cost;             // cost from start location
node->costH    = guessCost(x,y);   // Guessed cost to target

// Overall cost: This is used for the list insertion
int costF      = node->costG + node->costH;

// Find the position for insertion into the open list so
// that it stays sorted by overall cost F. Note, that we do
// this here with another loop over the open list which is
// not ideal for performance reasons but easier to
// understand for the example program. Optimize this for
// your game.
for (cur = mOpenList.first(); cur && node;
     cur = mOpenList.next() )
{
  // Overall cost of the current list element
  int curCostF = cur->costG + cur->costH;
  // Insert node if it is cheaper than the current list item
  if (costF <= curCostF)
  {
    int idx = mOpenList.at();
    mOpenList.insert(idx, node);
    node = NULL;
  }
}

// If node is still set it could not be inserted in the list
// and has to be appended at the end of the open list
if (node) { mOpenList.append(node); }
}
```

The A* algorithm can end in two ways. Either the loop over the open list ends, which means no path was found, or during the loop, the target location is reached. In the latter case, the loop can be terminated and the shortest path is available.

Creating the Shortest Path

When the target location is found by the A* algorithm, a suitable path is established and can be immediately used. Since all nodes in the closed list are linked to their corresponding parents—that is, the previous path element—the path is automatically produced in reverse order, from target to start. This reversed order also allows the start point to be recognized, as no further parent elements exist; hence, it is NULL. An example for a linked closed list is shown in Figure 11.6. The shortest path follows the depicted links between the cells, starting from the target and ending at the start location.

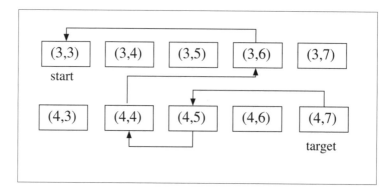

FIGURE 11.6 The closed list is depicted with the shortest path given by the linked cells from the target to the starting location.

Looping such a linked list inside the closed list allows you to easily retrieve the cell coordinates from the stored items. In our example, the (x,y) coordinates can be obtained directly from the (x,y) attributes of each ANode. In other applications, the location might also be a pointer to a map element. To create a path from start to target, these resulting locations have to be stored in reverse order, and then a game unit can move along them following the shortest path. The following example shows how a path can be retrieved in the correct order; that is, from start to target.

```
// The target location is returned as result of our A* search
ANode* target = findPathAStar(...);

// Retrieve the true cost of the path (if of interest)
int pathCost = target->costG;

// Define a path e.g. as list of QPoints
QValueList<QPoint> myPath;

// Walk the reversed path until no parent element, that is the
// starting location is found
while(target)
{
  // Get current location
  int x = target->x;
  int y = target->y;
```

```
    // Store location in your path list, e.g.
    myPath.prepend(QPoint(x, y));

    // Process next step
    target = target->parent;
}
```

The H Function: Under- and Overestimation of the H Function

The H function defines the heuristic cost from any location currently under investigation to the target location. The H function is a key feature of the A* algorithm because it allows an optimized, directed search toward the target. The original A* algorithm was designed so that the H function has to always *underestimate* the real cost to the target. This can be achieved by assuming the path is a straight line and has an ideal (minimum) movement cost per step (e.g., cost = 1 unit). In effect, no real paths can ever be shorter than such ideal paths unless there are jump gates or teleportation possibilities. In that case, such shortcuts have to be considered when calculating the heuristic function H.

If the H cost is underestimated, the A* algorithm guarantees that the optimum path to the target location will be found. Furthermore, it has been shown that the A* algorithm actually examines fewer map cells than any other algorithm using the same heuristic H function. However, examining fewer locations does not automatically mean that the resulting path search will be faster, but it is often a good indication.

The underestimated H function guarantees that the A* path search will find the shortest path, if it exists. As mentioned earlier, however, a good pathfinding solution is often more advantageous than an optimal one, since the latter usually requires extra calculations and further analysis of the map cells. Therefore, in computer games it can be very beneficial to drop the requirement of finding the shortest possible path. If so, it is not necessary to underestimate the H function anymore, and is actually possible to *overestimate* the heuristic cost H. The more the heuristic cost is increased, the fewer map cells are analyzed by the algorithm, and the faster the overall pathfinding becomes.

A method for overestimating the heuristic cost would be to replace the underestimated heuristic cost by another measurement. Normally, a straight line with an ideal cost (e.g., cost = 1 unit) between the start and target points is chosen as the underestimated heuristic measurement. This can be replaced by measuring a straight line in which every step is multiplied with a given factor, such as the average movement costs for a particular area (e.g., cost = 5 units).

In the example shown in Figure 11.5, the start and target locations are separated by 9 fields. Here, the underestimated heuristic cost will be a straight line crossing over 9 cells, and each cell has a designated cost of 1 unit; thus, the entire estimation has cost = 9 units. Using a more realistic approach that takes into account that the area is covered with grass, sand, or other terrain, we now have to multiply the original heuristic cost by the average movement cost. A mainly plain area, for example, could be assigned a cost of 3 units, which will yield an overestimated heuristic cost of H = 9 *3 = 27 units. Figures 11.7 and 11.8 depict the same path search as Figure 11.5, but with strongly underestimated cost in Figure 11.7 and overestimated cost in Figure 11.8. As you can see, the underestimated cost search investigates many more map locations than the overestimated cost does. The paths found in each example differ, but both are of minimum length. However, this is only by chance, and a more likely scenario is that the overestimated path search would return a longer path.

11	10	9	8	7	8	9	10	11	12	13	14	15	16	17	18	19		
10	9	8	7	6	7	8	9	10	11	12	13	14	15	16	17	18	19	
9	8	7	6	5	6	7	8	9	10	11	12	13	14	15	16	17	18	19
8	7	6	5	4	5	6	7		11	12	13	14	15	16	17	18	19	
7	6	5	4	3	4	5	6		12	13	14	15	16	17	18	19	
6	5	4	3	2	3	4	5		13	14	15	16	17	18	19		
5	4	3	2	1	2	3	4		14	15	16	17	18	19			
4	3	2	1	S	1	2	3		15	16	17	18	G	20			
5	4	3	2	1	2	3	4		14	15	16	17	18	19			
6	5	4	3	2	3	4	5		13	14	15	16	17	18	19		
7	6	5	4	3	4	5	6		12	13	14	15	16	17	18	19	
8	7	6	5	4	5	6	7		11	12	13	14	15	16	17	18	19
9	8	7	6	5	6	7	8	9	10	11	12	13	14	15	16	17	18	19
10	9	8	7	6	7	8	9	10	11	12	13	14	15	16	17	18	19	

FIGURE 11.7 In comparison to a moderately underestimated H function (Figure 11.5), a strongly underestimated H function will lead to the examination of more map locations. Compared to Figure 11.5, many more cells have been investigated (indicated by the movement costs inside investigated cells).

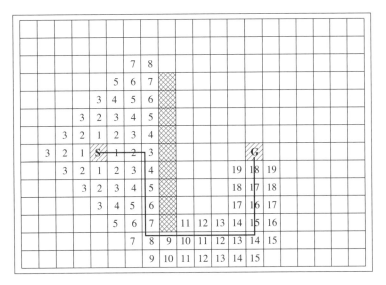

FIGURE 11.8 In comparison with the underestimated H function (Figures 11.5 and 11.7), overestimating the H function will lead to fewer examined locations (indicated by the movement cost inside investigated cells).

Optimization

If long paths on a huge map have to be evaluated, even the A* algorithm might consume too many computer resources, so it might be necessary to optimize the search algorithm. This can be easily achieved by two straightforward possibilities. First, one of the most time-consuming parts of the A* algorithm is the handling and sorting of the open list. When this task is more efficient, it can help reduce the search time. There already exist concepts for using binary heaps for such an open list, which will speed up the process.

The second possibility to enhance the algorithm is the modification of the heuristic function H. Although underestimation of the H function will always guarantee that the shortest path to the target is found, it may not be the quickest search because more map cells have to be investigated. This is in contrast to an overestimated H function. In fact, if a reasonable path will suffice, it can actually help to overestimate the heuristic cost H, since this will attract the search algorithm faster to the target. Unfortunately, this adaptation can produce higher path costs, and since the exact amount of overestimation can vary, it has to be experimentally found for each game. Nevertheless, overestimating the heuristic cost can be beneficial if you are able to limit the overestimation to a small amount. You can then achieve a fast path search resulting in fairly good paths.

MOVING OBSTACLES

Pathfinding algorithms generally work well in computer games. On a game map, the shortest path between any two locations can be easily found. However, a problem with pathfinding algorithms arises when the map contains moving obstacles that have to be avoided, such as strong enemy units traveling directly along your path. There are several ways to treat such moving obstacles. However, apart from blowing them all up, none is of general use, and you have to check which one can be used for your game.

One way to tackle moving obstacles is to include them as normal obstacles in the path search. How well this works depends on how fast the obstacles move compared to the unit you are intending to move on the path. If the obstacles are of similar speed or faster than your unit is, it is unlikely that the two units will arrive at the same location at the same time. The obstacles will no longer be at the position used for the pathfinding once your unit arrives there. In this case, it is better to ignore the obstacles altogether. However, whether you choose to include or ignore the obstacles, a worst-case scenario can happen: the moving obstacle moves in such a way that it blocks the unit moving on the calculated path. If both units follow pathfinding algorithms, it is even possible to create a deadlock situation, and then none of the units can move any more.

This problem can only be tackled by recalculating the path while the unit is moving on it. However, pathfinding requires a great deal of computer performance, and additional searches might not be desirable. An additional problem that can occur with moving obstacles on recalculated paths is that two units begin to move on oscillating paths. This oscillation can occur if one unit tries to evade the other unit, and vice versa, and can also develop into a deadlock.

A good solution for the treatment of moving obstacles is to first ignore them in the overall path search and only include them later in a local obstacle detection. When local obstacles are found on the path and in the vicinity of the moving unit, a local detour around them can be planned. This detour will lead back to the original path, once the obstacle is passed.

Yet another possibility to include moving obstacles in the path search is a movement prediction. If you know the movement of the obstacles on the map or can predict this movement, you know where the moving obstacles will be when the unit you are directing with the pathfinding reaches them. Therefore, pathfinding does not have to calculate its route according to the current location of the obstacles, but the actual location of obstacles when the path would meet them in the future. This method can work well but often requires knowledge that the game does not provide.

Overall, the handling of moving obstacles is difficult and should be avoided if possible. Fortunately, many desktop games do not require pathfinding with moving obstacles. The topics of path planning and moving obstacle avoidance are actually part of ongoing discussions in current research on cars, aircrafts, or moving robots.

GENERAL PERFORMANCE OPTIMIZATIONS

The gradient pathfinding algorithm and the A* pathfinding algorithm can be successfully applied to long paths on large maps. However, pathfinding on huge maps with many units can take up vast portions of the computer performance available for the game. Therefore, optimizations of path searches are always desirable. The time used for pathfinding depends on the number of map locations analyzed by the algorithm before the final path is found. Unfortunately, the number of locations grows very fast; that is, exponentially with the length of the path. It is therefore advisable to limit the number of map locations necessary for the path search.

There are several ways to reduce the number of cells, some of which depend on which algorithm is used. We have already seen in the description of the A* pathfinding algorithm that it analyzes fewer map locations than other algorithms do. It can be optimized further by adapting the heuristic distance function H. These two adaptations already increase the pathfinding performance.

Another important possibility to reduce the number of map locations investigated is to simply reduce their amount by defining larger grid cells on the map. A larger grid will drastically reduce the number of cells that are analyzed for the path search. However, cells cannot be made arbitrarily large, because the details of the map are then lost. A possible solution here is to introduce a super grid that combines a group of smaller grid cells into a bigger super cell. These super cells then have the averaged, minimum or maximum properties of the smaller cells and can serve to plan an initial coarse-grained path. When the entry and exit of each super cell is known, a finer local path can be planned inside each super cell. This procedure does work because of the exponential growth properties of the search. It is much faster to calculate several short paths than one longer one.

A similar approach to the super grid is the introduction of waypoints that define certain fixed intermediate locations on the path. As with super cells, these waypoints produce smaller paths that can be more easily calculated. Waypoints often occur naturally in a game; for example, cities or bridges that need to be passed.

If many units have to move on the same game map, it is usually possible to reuse parts of the path maps or planned paths. For example, the distance map can be used for more than one unit and reduce the calculations needed. Often, it is also possible to group units in a game as occurs naturally in many games, such as strategy games. It can then be possible to calculate the path only once for the group. However, keep in mind that different units might have different movement properties: you don't want a path planned to go through a swamp when some units can cross that swamp but one of the units cannot.

SUMMARY

Pathfinding is a very important part of many types of games, including strategy games, building games, action games, and some board games such as mazes and puzzles. Therefore, it is more than advantageous to have a good knowledge of pathfinding. However, many new game programmers are a bit frightened by the concept of pathfinding. At first, it seems that this is a quite complicated matter, but once the general principles are understood, it is not that difficult. In particular, gradient pathfinding allows an intuitively understood approach to the task of pathfinding. If you use the pathfinding example application `mypath` provided on the companion CD-ROM in the folder `examples/mypath`, the transfer to your game application should be relatively straightforward and easy to accomplish.

ON THE CD

In this chapter, we described two of the most important algorithms. The gradient pathfinding algorithm can be easily used in many desktop games that have small or medium-sized game maps; desktop board games are a good example. Furthermore, the gradient pathfinding algorithm can be easily understood, implemented, and tested, and because of its simplicity, it is a good practice algorithm for programmers new to pathfinding. The A* algorithm is widely used and has proved extremely efficient. One of this algorithm's main advantages is that no other pathfinding algorithm, using the same heuristic function H, can examine fewer map locations. In short, it is normally difficult to be faster than the A* algorithm.

The A* algorithm guarantees to find a path from the start location to the target location if one exists. Furthermore, A* will find the optimal path between these two locations if the heuristic distance function H underestimates the real cost between the current location and the target. However, underestimating the cost will result in better paths but will require longer search times. Therefore, it is often useful to overestimate H and go for a semi-optimal path that is longer but consumes fewer CPU resources.

REFERENCES

[AStar04] *A* Search Algorithm, http://en.wikipedia.org/wiki/A-star_search_ algorithm*, 2004.

[DeLoura00] DeLoura, Mark, *Game Programming Gems*, ISBN:1584500492; Charles River Media, 2000.

[GameAi04] *Pathfinding algorithms, http://www.gameai.com/pathfinding.html*, 2004.

[Lester04] Lester, Patrick, *A* Tutorial, http://www.policyalmanac.org/games/ aStarTutorial.htm*, 2004.

12 Particle Effects

You've probably seen special effects stemming from particle effects, but perhaps not realized how these effects are achieved. Particle effects can be observed in the form of smoke, explosions, water fountains, flames, snow, rain, and many other special effects. These effects are all based on the same principle; that is, they consist of many simple objects called *particles*, which together produce the desired effect. Each individual object is constructed from a simple graphic, often no more than a point, circle, or textured triangle. The movement of the particles usually follows a simple physical trajectory, and the appearance of the particles can change with time; for example, the particles can fade. Particles gain their power by appearing in huge quantities. Having just one particle is clearly not enough to achieve impressive graphical effects. However, displaying hundreds of particles on the screen in an orchestrated manner can create stunning effects.

Particles can also be used to depict other aspects of the game world. You might, for example, use them to display temporary information; in strategy games, you often see buildings that produce income every few seconds. They display this profit to the player through small text signs such as "$". Another task of particles could be the visualization of speech from characters; here, whenever a character says something, bubbles are displayed containing some symbols. These bubbles can be made from particles. In these cases, ready-made images are used as the particles.

In this chapter, we describe how particle effects are created, their implementation, and their relevance in desktop games. In the section "2D Particle Effects," we focus more closely on how effects can be implemented for the Qt canvas library. We then extend this model to cover 3D particle effects using OpenGL. Some of the more commonly required special effects, such as the generation of computer fire and explosions, are closely related to particle effects, and we conclude this chapter with these aspects.

CONCEPT AND ARCHITECTURE

In computer games, special effects such as snow, smoke, or explosions are produced by the animation of large amounts of simple objects. All of these objects are related to each other and follow the same or similar (physical) movement and animation rules. These special effects are called *particle effects*, and the simple individual objects involved are termed *particles*. All particles are collected in a *particle system*, which bundles and controls groups of particles with similar properties. Some examples of particle effects are shown in Figure 12.1.

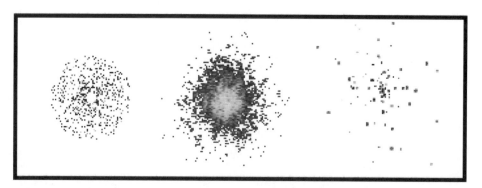

FIGURE 12.1 Examples of particle effects used in desktop computer games and described in this chapter.

A single particle is a very simple object that stores information about its state, including its position, movement, graphical, and animation properties. An individual particle is normally displayed using standard graphical elements such as colored dots, circles, lines, and textured triangles—even basic graphical shapes can be employed. Sometimes, however, particle effects can benefit from using more complicated graphical shapes or even frame animations. These ready-made particles create effects that require fewer particles and consequently save processing power.

The movement of particles contributing to a particular effect usually follows the same (physical) laws; the only difference between the individual particles is the setting of their initial properties. These distinct initial properties cause the particles to follow different trajectories and animations. Therefore, the desired effects arise from the actions of all these particles together. Another key feature of all particles is their life cycle. The life of the particle consists of its current *age* and its maximum age or *lifespan*. The current age counts the time the particle exists, which is correlated to its maximum lifespan. If this maximum lifespan is exceeded, a particle ceases to exist. When this happens, it is automatically removed from the display (sometimes, the life counter is also started at the maximum lifespan and counted down to zero). Often, other movement or animation properties, like the color of the particle, depend on the age of the particle; for example a particle can fade as it ages.

When programming particle effects, it is important that the individual particles be encapsulated in a way that the main program does not need to control them individually. When this has been achieved properly, the effect should operate alone.

The Particle Class

A particle is defined as a small object that contains all properties necessary for determining its lifespan, aging, display attributes, and most importantly, its trajectory. The following example defines some of the typical and essential attributes of a particle class. Depending on the actual application, you will need to modify or add attributes to this class.

```
class Particle
{
  public:
    // Properties
    ...
    unsigned int mLifeSpan;  // Life span
    unsigned int mAge;       // Time since creation

    QRgb mColor;             // Current color
    unsigned int mSize;      // Current size
```

```
    float mX;                    // Position
    float mY;                    // 2D: (x,y)
    float mZ;                    // 3D: (x,y,z)

    float mVx;                   // Velocity
    float mVy;                   // 2D: (vx,vy)
    float mVz;                   // 3D: (vx,vy,vz)
    ...

    // Methods
    void advance();              // 'Heartbeat' of the particle
    ...
};
```

The age (mAge) and lifespan (mLifeSpan) of a particle are used to determine when to remove a particle from the display and to calculate its age and age-dependent effects. The particles will be displayed until their age exceeds their lifespan. Both quantities are measured in either real time (seconds, milliseconds) or in game ticks, such as advance cycles of a canvas.

The color (mColor) and size (mSize) of a particle determine its appearance on the display. The color can be either QRgb or QColor, depending on how you want to specify the color components. When choosing QRgb, you can also set an alpha value (translucency) for the particles. An easy example for displaying a particle is to paint each particle as a filled circle with a given size using a particular color. It is also possible to paint a small graphical image instead of a geometrical form by storing a pointer to a graphical image or an OpenGL texture object ID number. Often, the color or size of the particle changes with age; for example, the particles fade out slowly.

The position (mX, mY, mZ) and the velocity (mVx, mVy, mVz) determine the location and trajectory of a particle, respectively. The position can be stored as absolute window coordinates or relative to a common origin (the particle system). The simplest case for particle movement is a linear movement with constant velocity. However, more complex physical trajectories can be implemented involving acceleration, gravity, and friction [Bourg01]. Therefore, with just a little effort, each particle can be constructed so it follows a realistic physical trajectory.

Usually, particles are simple objects that need fast access to their properties, and therefore the attributes are often kept public. Obviously, it is possible to make the attributes private, and define access sets and get methods for them all. For performance reasons, however, these methods should be made "inline." Finally, the advance() method serves as the heartbeat of the particle, and is called periodically to update, animate, and move the particle. The particle will also age each time advance() is called. Depending on the implementation of the particles, advance() can be either the advance() method of a QCanvasItem, which is then automatically called by the parent canvas, or a user-defined method that is called manually or by a periodic timer.

The Particle System Class

So far, the particle is just a simple object without any particular features or effects. However, the idea of particle effects is to use numerous particles at the same time—using even hundreds or thousands of particles for an effect is possible. Of course, trying to individually control all of these particles would be tedious, not to mention the amount of time required to allocate, initialize, and destroy them. Therefore, particles are grouped together in a container object, the *particle system*, which maintains a list of all the particles and keeps track of their status.

Concerning speed and memory allocation, it is particularly useful to not allocate and destroy particles whenever they should be inserted or removed from the game, but instead keep a pool of particles in memory even if they are unused. Whether a particle is used is distinguished by maintaining two administrative lists of particles; one list stores the currently active particles, and a second list holds the pool of unused particles. These lists are grouped in the ParticleSystem class.

```
class ParticleSystem
{
  public:
    // Construct the particle system
    ParticleSystem(unsigned int maxparticles = 0);

    // Destruct the particle system
    ~ParticleSystem();

    // Add particles to the system
    void addParticles(unsigned int amount)

    // Advance the system (heartbeat)
    void advance();

    // Activate one particle
    Particle* inject();

    // Inactivate a particle
    void remove(Particle* p);

    // Get all active particles
    QPtrList<Particle>* particleList();
```

```
    private:
     // The particle lists
     QPtrList<Particle> mActiveList;
     QPtrList<Particle> mPassiveList;
 };
```

Upon initialization, all particles are located in the passive list and only move to the active list when they should be displayed. The particles are then animated and follow their life cycle until the maximum age of the particle is exceeded. Then, they are hidden from the display and moved back to the passive list. This procedure avoids continuous allocating and deallocating of the particles. The particle lists are typically filled at program start, but if you run out of particles, the particle system can be also refilled during the program run.

```
// Create 'amount' of particles
void ParticleSystem::addParticles(unsigned int amount)
{
  for (unsigned int i = 0; i < amount; i++)
  {
    Particle* particle = new Particle();
    mPassiveList.append(particle);
  }
}
```

Particles are made active and a pointer to them is returned at the same time when using

```
Particle* ParticleSystem::inject()
{
  // Inject passive particle
  Particle* particle = mPassiveList.take();
  if (particle)
  {
    mActiveList.append(particle);
    article->mAge = 0;
  }
  return particle;
}
```

When a particle's lifespan is over, it signals the particle container to move it back to the passive list.

```
void ParticleSystem::remove(Particle* particle)
```

```
  {
    if (mActiveList.remove(particle))
    {
      mPassiveList.append(particle);
    }
  }
}
```

Unless the particles are implemented as QCanvasItems, where they will obtain their advance calls directly from the canvas, the particle system needs to move the particles. This is performed with the advance() method, which in turn invokes the particle's movement and animation method.

```
void ParticleSystem::advance()
{
  Particle* p;
  for (p = mActiveList.first(); p; p=mActiveList.next())
  {
    p->advance();
  }
}
```

Particle Effect Classes

Particles effects are created in two steps. First, a particle class needs to be defined that specifies the desired properties and behavior of the particles such as movement and color change (covered previously). For the second step, the particles have to be initialized with a certain set of parameters and then properly activated, which will bring the particles alive and display them on the screen. We can achieve this step with a simple, particle effect class. Note that in contrast to this particle effect class, neither the particle nor the particle system depends very much on the actual effect.

The particle effect inserts all particles necessary for the effect into the display with the appropriate set of initial parameters. Depending on whether you need one or more than one particle system for the desired effect, you can either subclass the particle effect from the particle system, or store a particle system as a private attribute in a new class ParticleEffect. In both cases, the effect class gains access to the particles via the particle system, and can activate and initialize them. Here, we will show the latter method because it is a bit more general and allows more than one particle system per effect. More than one particle system will be required in situations in which you have different particles or different particle behaviors combined into one effect (fire and smoke). If, however, you prefer to have fewer classes around, derive the effect class directly from the ParticleSystem.

Depending on the actual effect you want to model, all particles can be inserted either at once (like an explosion) or just a few periodically (sparkler effects, rain, snow). For an even more realistic effect, it is advisable to randomize the particle's initial parameter (direction, color, lifespan, amount) to a certain extent.

Examples of particle effect classes are snow, rain, explosions, smoke, or fireworks. Here, we show the class SnowEffect as a model for a 2D effect that creates snowflakes falling from the top of the screen. More specific examples can be found on the companion CD-ROM in the folder examples/myparticle.

```
class SnowEffect
{
  public:
    // Construct the particle effect
    SnowEffect()

    // The actual effect implementation
    void advanceEffect();

  private:
    // Either store one system
    ParticleSystem* mParticleSystem;

    // or alternatively store many systems
    QPtrList<ParticleSystem> mParticleSystems;
};
```

The advanceEffect() routine of the particle effect needs to be called only once to initiate the effect, or periodically when new particles need to be inserted into the system. Both of these requirements can be easily achieved by using a timer event (or the advance() method of a QCanvas canvas).

For the snow effect, we only need a simple particle class that is able to draw white and gray dots of varying sizes. The movement of the particles is basic; it should just follow a linear path with constant velocity. However, to create a more snow-like appearance, we'll make the particles jitter by using a random value to change the resulting x-position. We therefore re-implement the advance() method of the particle class as:

```
// Advance function of the particle of the previously
// described particle class. This advance() is called by
// the corresponding parent object periodically
void Particle::advance()
{
  // Change position and add a bit of randomness:
```

```
    // random(a,b) returns a random value between a and b
    // and RND_X is any number used for the wind
    x = x + vx + random(-RND_X, RND_X);
    y = y + vy;
  }
```

The effect function of the particle effect needs to be called periodically, and at every call inserts a few particles (in this example, three) at the top of the screen that have a slightly randomized direction, position, size, and color. Note that the maximum lifespan is calculated so the particles exactly cross the screen before vanishing.

```
void SnowEffect::advanceEffect()
{
  int cnt = 3;
  Particle* particle;
  while(cnt>0 && (particle = mParticleSystem->inject()))
  {
    // Select random angle and speed to set the velocity
    float angle = random(-0.05, 0.05) + 90.0/180.0*M_PI;
    float speed = random(0.6, 1.0);
    float vx    = cos(angle) * speed + 0.1; // add wind drift
    float vy    = sin(angle) * speed ;

    // Initially position the particle in a window of size
    // (width, height)
    float x0    = random(0, width);
    float y0    = 0;

    // Color the particle: We use white but randomly give a
    // gray shade
    float dark  = random(100.0, 115.0);
    QColor color = Qt::white;
    color       = color.dark(dark);

    // Size the particle: Random size
    float size  = random(1.0, 4.0);

    // Lifespan (in advance cycles): Adapted so that
    // the particle lives the whole time it moves
    // on the screen. ADVANCE_RATE is the amount of
    // screen advance cycles per second (e.g. 30)
    float life  = (height/vy)*ADVANCE_RATE;

    // Set particle parameters
```

```
        particle->mLifeSpan = life;
        particle->mSize     = size;
        particle->mColor     = color.rgb();
        particle->mX         = x0;
        particle->mY         = y0;
        particle->mVx        = vx;
        particle->mVy        = vy;

        // Decrease particle counter
        cnt--;
    }
}
```

2D PARTICLE EFFECTS

Many desktop games use a 2D canvas as the game view. Therefore, it is useful to learn how to implement particle effects for a Qt canvas. In this section, we demonstrate two different possibilities for this implementation. The first method is to integrate each particle as a sprite, which allows easy movement and animation of the particles as canvas items. However, using too many particles—that is, too many sprites—can lead to performance problems. The production indication of a factory in a strategy game or the speech indication of a character are possible applications for this type of particle effects. The second method is to manually draw the particles into an image and then display that image, which is more complicated to implement, but is faster. This method is useful for particle effects that use many small particles, such as fireworks or explosions.

Particles as Qt Sprites

To display a particle in a window display, it has to be drawn to the canvas and associated with the display view. The simplest way to do this in Qt is to model each particle as a sprite. Details on sprite implementation can be found in Chapter 6, "Canvas Games," and Figure 12.2 depicts the class dependencies for this case.

To create a particle sprite class, all QCanvasItem classes can serve as a base because only the most basic features of sprites are required. In this section and for the example program on the companion CD-ROM (in the folder examples/myparticle), we chose the QCanvasSprite as the basis for the particle sprite. The main methods necessary to display the particle are:

```
class ParticleSprite : public QCanvasSprite
{
  public:
```

```
// Construct the particle sprite
ParticleSprite();

// The bounding box
QRect boundingRect() const;

// The actual paint method
void draw(QPainter& p);

// Periodic advance
void advance(int phase);

// Collision detection
bool collidesWith(const QCanvasItem*) const
                    { return false; }
    ...
};
```

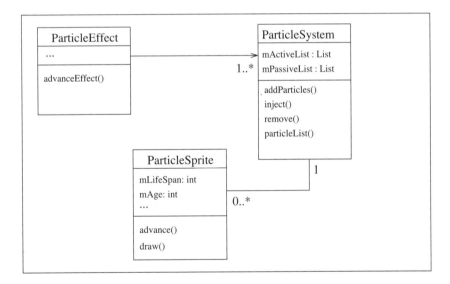

FIGURE 12.2 Class diagram for the particle effects using sprites as particles. Each particle is implemented as QCanvasSprite.

The draw() method is used to paint the sprite on the canvas using the QPainter object provided by Qt. With this system, everything can be achieved, from drawing a single pixel:

```
void ParticleSprite::draw(QPainter& p)
{
  // Prepare pen with the particle color
  QPen pen;
  pen.setColor(QColor(mColor));

  // Draw a point with this pen given a QPainter p
  p.setPen(pen);
  p.drawPoint(mX, mY);
```

to centering a line of length $(2 \times lx, 2 \times ly)$ around the particle:

```
  ...
  p.setPen(pen);
  p.drawLine(mX-lx, mY-ly, mX+lx, mY+ly);
```

or even painting a full QImage or QPixmap:

```
  ...
  p.drawImage(mX, mY, mImage);
}
```

When manually drawing a sprite, you need to let the canvas know how large your sprite is. To do so, the boundingRect() has to return the bounding box surrounding the particle. This rectangle has the size of the particle and is centered on the particle's position. For example, for a particle of a certain size (mSize) that is centered on the particle's position (mX, mY), it would be

```
QRect ParticleSprite::boundingRect() const
{
  // Increase size by +1 to avoid rounding errors for
  // odd numbers. If the box is too small Qt will cut
  // off the edges for the sprite.
  int rSize = (mSize+1)/2;
  QRect rect(mX-rSize, mY-rSize, mSize, mSize);
  return rect;
}
```

For the particle sprite, we ignore all collision detection; that is, when we implement the corresponding function we always return false, which signifies no collision. Checking for particle collisions is possible, but usually unnecessary, and costs a lot of processing time.

The main method for a sprite used in animation and movement is `advance()`. For the `QCanvasItem` classes, it is automatically and periodically called by the parent canvas, and thus sprites can use it to perform animation and movement. Our particle sprites do this, and count up their life counter. Once the counter exceeds the given maximum, the sprites are removed from the display.

First, the counter is checked.

```
void ParticleSprite::advance(int phase)
{
  ...

  // Increase age
  mAge++;

  // If the lifespan is exceeded, remove the particle
  if (mAge >= mLifeSpan)
  {
    hide();

    // Tell the particle container that the particle should
    // be removed. The system should be stored in the
    // particle upon creation.
    mSystem->remove(this);
  }
  ...
```

Then, the motion and color changes of the particle are performed.

```
  // advance() continued:
  ...
  else
  {
    // Change position
    newX = mX + mVx;
    newY = mY + mVy;
    move(newX, newY);

    // Change color (we for example remember the initial color
    // set upon creation in QColor mOriginalColor)
    int colorChange = 100.0 * (1.0 - ((float)mAge)/mLifeSpan);
    mColor = mOriginalColor.light(colorChange).rgb();
  }
}
```

Note that these types of linear movement would be performed automatically by Qt when setting a velocity to the sprite. In this example, we have calculated the position manually, since you will more than likely use a more complicated trajectory and then have to set the position manually. Also keep in mind that the QCanvasItem::advance() method has two phases (see Chapter 6), and movement is only done in phase one.

Besides the actual movement, there are other aspects to consider when changing the properties of the sprite; for example, its color. The canvas will not notice such changes in the sprite and consequently not update it in the next drawing cycle. To avoid this, the canvas has to be notified of a property change. There are two methods available, depending on whether an entire area of the canvas should be invalidated or just one pixel. For a single pixel, the canvas can be invalidated by

```
canvas()->setChangedChunkContaining(x(), y());
```

or for a larger sprite

```
canvas()->setChanged(boundingRect());
```

can be called to invalidate the part of the canvas in which the particle is positioned. Both will force a repaint of the appropriate canvas areas in the next update cycle.

Particles Inside Bitmap Images

As mentioned previously, a second way to use particle effects on canvases is to collect all the particles in one image and then draw this image as a single sprite on the canvas. This special sprite is then just a bitmap with a size that is determined by the maximum separation between the particles in their bounding box as depicted in Figure 12.3. The class hierarchy resulting from this particle concept is depicted in Figure 12.4. You can now observe that the actual sprite is used to store the particle system instead of the particle.

By displaying all particles in one image, we gain performance but have to move and draw the particles ourselves into the sprite image. Fortunately, this is not very difficult, since drawing the particles just requires you to loop the list of active particles and plot them on their current position in the corresponding sprite image. Furthermore, using one sprite for all particles allows you to apply additional effects to the particle sprites, such as blurring or smoothing necessary for fire and explosion effects.

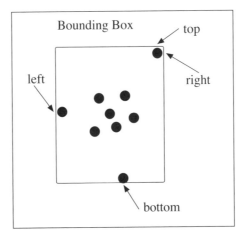

FIGURE 12.3 Bounding box or bounding rectangle of a set of particles (circles). The maximum separation of the particles determines the edges of the bounding box.

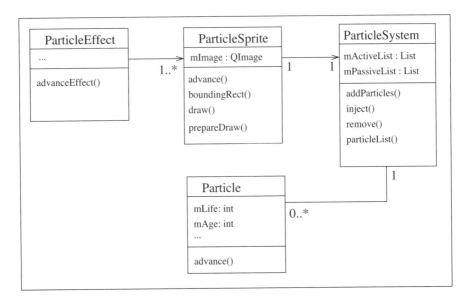

FIGURE 12.4 Class diagram for the particle effects using bitmap images. Here, a particle is just a simple container class, and the particle sprite contains all the particles collected in the container.

To obtain optimum display performance, the resulting sprite image should not be too large. Ideally, the optimum size would be that which is able to include all particles. However, since the particles can move, the size is generally not constant. To resolve this problem of constant size changing, there are two solutions. The first solution would be to choose a large enough sprite image so the maximum particle extension is covered, but only display the part of the image currently occupied by particles. The second possibility is to resize the image during the operation. This is costly, but is appropriate if the resizing does not occur at every update step and the size of the image will then be increased to cover additional update steps, such as making it 50% larger. The same logic obviously applies for making the resulting image smaller when the particles vanish from the canvas.

Using this particle effect implementation solves most performance problems. The only other problem you may experience is when the particles get very far apart, which results in the container sprites covering the entire canvas, which can cause QCanvas to hiccup a little. Nevertheless, the advantage of this concept is that there is basically no limit to the number of particles you can use.

The Implementation

The implementations of the particles and the particle system are straightforward and similar to the implementations previously described. However, on top of the particle system there has to be a real sprite that embeds the particle system (see Figure 12.4). Again, the sprite can be any QCanvasItem class—for example, the QCanvasSprite class—in which the draw() and boundingRect() methods are re-implemented.

```
class ParticleSprite : public QCanvasSprite
{
  public:
    // Construct the sprite
    ParticleSprite();

    // The bounding box
    QRect boundingRect() const;

    // The actual paint method
    void draw(QPainter& p);

    // Periodic advance
    void advance(int phase);

    // Collision detection
    bool collidesWith(const QCanvasItem*) const
                    { return false; }
```

```
  protected:
    // Prepare the internal image for drawing
    void prepareDraw();

  private:
    // The particle system
    ParticleSystem* mParticleSystem;
    // The internal display image
    QImage mImage;
};
```

The bounding rectangle now returns the size of the displayed part of the image that corresponds to the maximum extension of the particles (see Figure 12.3). Note that this distance is best updated on the fly; that is, when moving a particle inside the container. These values are then stored and returned by the bounding rectangle. For performance reasons, you should avoid looping all particles in the boundingRect() function.

For the display of the sprite, a QImage (we define it as QImage mImage) is associated with the sprite. This QImage has to be filled with the particles from the container during the advance() calls, and is the central feature for this type of particle effect.

First, we prepare the image in which to draw the particles.

```
void ParticleSprite::prepareDraw()
{
  // Reset the image to an empty transparent one
  // Note: A 'feature' of Qt3 does not allow to fill
  //       the alpha buffer unless it is switched off
  QRgb empty = qRgba(0, 0, 0, 0);
  mImage.setAlphaBuffer(false);
  mImage.fill(empty);
  mImage.setAlphaBuffer(true);
  ...
```

Unfortunately, when using a QImage, the graphics cannot be directly copied (*bitblt*) to the canvas, as a QPixmap would normally allow. Nevertheless, when compared to the faster QPixmap, a QImage allows easier pixel access.

Next, all active particles are looped and drawn into the QImage.

```
  // prepareDraw() continued:
  ...
  QPtrList<Particle>* list = mParticleSystem->particleList();
  Particle* p;
  for (p = list->first(); p; p = list->next())
  {
```

```
    // Ignore points which are not on the canvas:
    // offset is the origin of the container sprite
    if (!canvas->onCanvas(offset.x()+p->mX,
                                offset.y()+p->mY) )
    {
        continue;
    }

    // Offset
    int x  = -offset.x() + p->mx;
    int y  = -offset.y() + p->mY;
    // and color
    QRgb col = p->mColor;

    // Draw more pixels, circles, lines or images here if you
    // want different shapes. In this example we draw
    // particle just as a single pixel with a given color
    mImage.setPixel(x, y, col);
    }
}
```

Finally, the sprite's draw function has to paint the image, which now contains all the particles, to the screen.

```
void ParticleSprite::draw(QPainter& p)
{
  QRect rect = boundingRect();
  if (!rect.isNull())
  {
    // Draw full image
    p.drawImage(rect.left(), rect.top(), mImage);

    // Or alternatively draw only section specified by the
    // QRect clipping area. The clipping area corresponds
    // to the maximum particle extension and has to be
    // maintained by you.
    p.drawImage(rect.topLeft(), mImage, clippingArea);
  }
}
```

Since the particle objects are no longer part of the canvas, their advance method has to be called manually, which can be easily done via the particle sprite's advance() method.

```
void ParticleSprite::advance(int phase)
{
  ...
  // Tell the system to advance the particles
  mParticleSystem->advance();
}
```

All other attributes of the particles and the particle container are handled as shown previously.

3D PARTICLE EFFECTS

Particle effects can also be created very effectively when using OpenGL. The textures and hardware-accelerated rendering provided by OpenGL make it even easier to create realistic-looking particle effects. Furthermore, compared to canvas-based effects, OpenGL allows the processing of many more graphic objects and effects at the same time. Finally, with OpenGL, the entire system can be in 3D.

There are only a few differences between 2D and 3D particle systems. First, of course, there is a third coordinate. Second, when using OpenGL, the coordinates are not in the canvas space but in world space, which includes the *z*-coordinate. The last and main difference is that the particles usually have both color and texture associated with them. The color is used to tint the texture of the particle, which comes without any performance penalties on accelerated 3D hardware. This can be very useful, because instead of using numerous small, colored particles (which can be slow), or using a single big particle with a pre-rendered effect (which can look bad), you can apply multiple medium-sized particles that have both color and texture.

For the OpenGL effects used in desktop games, there are usually ten to a few hundred particles; the amount of particles depends on the type of effect you want to create. For example, smoke-type effects normally require more particles than explosions or (dust) cloud effects because they spread out more. Using a texture in a particle also allows the pre-rendering of certain parts of the effect, such as small smoke puffs. Having such pre-rendered textures reduces the amount of particles and thus requires less processing power. When using different colors to tint the particle's textures, you also obtain a color variety, which makes the effect look even better.

Implementation

Implementation of the OpenGL particle effects requires both a `Particle` and a `ParticleSystem` class. The `ParticleSystem` can be taken directly from the previous 2D examples. However, the `Particle` requires some minor modifications, including storing the color of the particle as an array of floats and adding a distance property to the particle. This is necessary to store the distance between the particle and the camera, which is then used for sorting the particles according to their depth. For the special meaning of "camera" in terms of OpenGL, see Chapter 7, "OpenGL."

```
class Particle
{
  public:
    // Properties
    ...
    unsigned int mLifeSpan;   // Life span
    unsigned int mAge;        // Time since creation

    float mColor[4];          // Current color
    float mSize;              // Current size

    float mX;                 // Position
    float mY;
    float mZ;

    float mVx;                // Velocity
    float mVy;
    float mVz;

    float mDistance;          // Distance from the camera
    ...

    // Methods
    void advance();           // 'Heartbeat'
    ...
};
```

The actual effect is organized by the ParticleEffect class, and to demonstrate how this is achieved we will now generate a smoke effect. Smoke effects come in many variations, and the effect created here represents a steady stream of smoke, like that emitted from a chimney. Another type of smoke would be a cloud of smoke or dust that you get from a collision. These effects are very similar to the explosion effects discussed later in this chapter; for now, we'll focus on how to implement a steady stream of smoke.

```
class SmokeEffect
{
  public:
    // Construct the particle effect
    SmokeEffect(GLuint texture);
```

```
  // The actual effect
  void advanceEffect();

  // Return OpenGL texture object id
  GLuint texture() const { return mTexture; }

private:
  // We need just one particle system
  ParticleSystem mParticleSystem;
  // OpenGL texture id
  GLuint mTexture;
};
```

Note that the constructor takes a texture argument. This is the OpenGL texture object ID that will be used to render the smoke particles. If you want to create a more complex effect, you could also pass an array of textures and switch between them during the particle's lifetime, which would result in animated puffs of smoke.

The advanceEffect() method can be used to create some new particles, and because we are not using any Qt canvas objects, we have to process the moving of the particles in accordance with their velocity. Similar to the 2D canvas effects, this method is called by a timer, which is synchronized with your screen updates (e.g., 30 times per second).

```
void SmokeEffect::advanceEffect()
{
  // Move all particles according to their movement rules
  mParticleSystem->advance();

  // Create new particles
  int cnt = 2;
  Particle* particle;
  while(cnt>0 && (particle = mParticleSystem->inject()))
  {
    // All the particles start at almost the same position
    particle->mX = random(-0.1, 0.1);
    particle->mY = random(-0.1, 0.1);
    particle->mZ = random(-0.1, 0.1);

    // The particle will not go straight up, but instead
    // will have a slight
    // angle, plus it's affected by wind
    particle->mVx = random(-0.2, 0.2) + 0.1;
    particle->mVz = random(-0.2, 0.2) - 0.05;
```

```
      // The particle will rise about 1 unit per second
      particle->mVy = random(0.8, 1.2);

      // We use gray color for the particles, but give them
      // slight variations in intensity of the color
      float intensity = random(0.3, 0.4);
      particle->mColor[0] = intensity;
      particle->mColor[1] = intensity;
      particle->mColor[2] = intensity;

      // Particle will be slightly translucent
      particle->mColor[3] = 0.7;

      // Size the particle using a random size
      particle->mSize = random(0.3, 0.5);

      // ADVANCE_RATE is the amount of screen advance cycles
      // per second (e.g. 30)
      particle->mLifeSpan = random(1.5, 4) * ADVANCE_RATE;

      // Decrease particle counter
      cnt--;
   }
}
```

Note that almost every property of each particle is randomized to a certain extent, which ensures that the effect looks more interesting.

Rendering

So far, we created the particles and the actual effect. We are now left with the main difference between 3D OpenGL and 2D canvas particle effects: the rendering of the particles. The actual rendering of the particles involved in the effect is performed by the renderParticles() method, which is called by the main rendering method, QGLWidget::paintGL(). All translucent objects in an OpenGL scene need to be sorted by their distances from the camera. When rendering two translucent polygons, the light in reality would pass through the farthest one first and then through the nearer one before reaching the camera. The blending in OpenGL does not function this way; therefore, to simulate this, we need to render those polygons in the order in which natural light would travel through them—that is, from farthest to nearest. This same process has to be performed for the translucent particles.

```
void renderParticles(ParticleSystem* system)
```

```
{
  // Calculate distance from camera for all active particles
  // and add them to a list: we subclass the QPtrList<int> in
  // our ParticlePtrList list to allow sorting
  ParticlePtrList distanceList;

  // Get access to the particles
  QPtrList<Particle>* list = system->particleList();
  Particle* p;
  // Loop through all particles
  for (p = list->first(); p; p = list->next())
  {
    // Calculate and store the (squared) distance
    p->mDistance = (cameraX - p->mX) * (cameraX - p->mX) +
                   (cameraY - p->mY) * (cameraY - p->mY) +
                   (cameraZ - p->mZ) * (cameraZ - p->mZ);
    distanceList.append(p);
  }

  // Sort the list: the farthest particle should now be the
  // first one in the particles list and the nearest particle
  // should be the last one in the list
  distanceList.sort();
  ...
}
```

When comparing the distances of the particles, it is sufficient to calculate and compare the squares of the distances. This procedure is much faster because it involves no square root calculations and still gives the same results from the comparison.

In Qt, a distance-based sorting of a QPtrList requires you to implement the compareItems() function of the QPtrList. If you did this in the class ParticlePtrList, the implementation of the distance-sorting algorithm would resemble:

```
int ParticlePtrList::compareItems(QPtrCollection::Item item1,
                                  QPtrCollection::Item item2)
{
  Particle* p1 = (Particle*)item1;
  Particle* p2 = (Particle*)item2;
  if (p1->mDistance < p2->mDistance) return  1;
  if (p1->mDistance > p2->mDistance) return -1;
  return 0;
}
```

Note that in Qt 4 when using a `QList<Particle*>`, the sorting is achieved by calling `qHeapSort()` on this list. However, this requires the particles to implement the < operator, which will then compare the distance of two particles.

Since a particle can be larger than just a single point, we usually render it as a quad. The problem here is that we need to supply coordinates of all four corners of the quad while only storing a single position for each particle. So, how do we get four coordinates out of one? The answer is a technique called *billboarding*, which will generate corner vertices so that the quad (billboard) will be aligned with the camera. To perform billboarding, we first need *up* and *right* vectors, which point upward and to the right in the viewport, respectively. We can obtain them from OpenGL's modelview matrix as shown in the following code snippet:

```
// renderParticles() continued:
...
// Calculate the right and up vectors from the modelview
// matrix
GLfloat modelview[16];
glGetFloatv(GL_MODELVIEW_MATRIX, modelview);
float right[3];
float up[3];
for (int i = 0; i < 3; i++)
{
  right[i] = modelview[i*4];
  up[i]    = modelview[i*4 + 1];
}
...
```

These vectors can then be scaled in accordance with the particle's size and added to the particle's center coordinate to obtain the coordinates of all quad corners.

Finally, we have to prepare OpenGL for drawing.

```
// renderParticles() continued:
...
// Save the OpenGL state
glPushAttrib(GL_COLOR_BUFFER_BIT | GL_DEPTH_BUFFER_BIT |
             GL_ENABLE_BIT | GL_TEXTURE_BIT);

// Enable the effect's texture
glEnable(GL_TEXTURE_2D);
glBindTexture(GL_TEXTURE_2D, effect->texture());
```

```
// Choose the blending function
glBlendFunc(GL_SRC_ALPHA, GL_ONE_MINUS_SRC_ALPHA);

// Disable writing to depth buffer
glDepthMask(GL_FALSE);

// Disable lighting
glDisable(GL_LIGHTING);
...
```

First, we save the current OpenGL state by `glPushAttrib()` and ORing the four different values relevant to us. We then enable the texturing and bind the OpenGL texture used in the effect. The next step, choosing the actual blending function, is very important, and here we use

```
glBlendFunc(GL_SRC_ALPHA, GL_ONE_MINUS_SRC_ALPHA);
```

to achieve a "natural" blending. This blending mode will interpolate between the source (currently rendered particle) and destination (already rendered part of your scene) values.

OpenGL provides many other blending functions, some of which are better than others in creating a particular effect. For example, if you want to generate an explosion or fire effect, it is better to use

```
glBlendFunc(GL_SRC_ALPHA, GL_ONE);
```

In this blending mode, OpenGL's color buffer is taken and incoming color values are added to it (additive blending), which is extremely effective for fire or explosion effects. In these effects, the colors of the particles add up, which results in brighter displays and even white areas when there are many particles together. This looks very realistic and similar to a real fire or explosion where the center of a flame is the hottest part and often looks white, while toward the edges of the flame, the temperature decreases and the colors become more yellow and red. Finally, we disable the writing to the depth buffer and lighting.

```
glDepthMask(GL_FALSE);
glDisable(GL_LIGHTING);
```

The writing to the depth buffer is disabled because in cases where there are many particles very close to each other, the depth buffer's precision is not good enough to distinguish between them. This results in ugly artifacts because some of the particles are partially hidden by others. The lighting is also disabled, since the particles are just flat quads facing the camera. When lighting is enabled, the brightness of the particles varies a great deal when rotating the camera, because the angle between a particle and the light changes.

Finally, we render all the particles one by one. For each particle, we first send its color to OpenGL, followed by the texture and position coordinates for every corner of the quad. Here, we also add the *right* and *up* vectors to the particle's position and therefore obtain all the coordinates of the quad.

```
// renderParticles() continued:
...
glBegin(GL_QUADS);

for (p = distanceList.first(); p; p = distanceList.next())
{
  // Set OpenGL's current color to the particle color
  glColor4fv(p->mColor);

  // Give the coordinates of the quad to opengl
  glTexCoord2f(0.0f, 1.0f);
  glVertex3f(p->mX + ((-right[0] + up[0]) * p->mSize,
             p->mY + ((-right[1] + up[1]) * p->mSize,
             p->mZ + ((-right[2] + up[2]) * p->mSize);

  glTexCoord2f(1.0f, 1.0f);
  glVertex3f(p->mX + (( right[0] + up[0]) * p->mSize,
             p->mY + (( right[1] + up[1]) * p->mSize,
             p->mZ + (( right[2] + up[2]) * p->mSize);

  glTexCoord2f(1.0f, 0.0f);
  glVertex3f(p->mX + (( right[0] - up[0]) * p->mSize,
             p->mY + (( right[1] - up[1]) * p->mSize,
             p->mZ + (( right[2] - up[2]) * p->mSize);

  glTexCoord2f(0.0f, 0.0f);
  glVertex3f(p->mX + ((-right[0] - up[0]) * p->mSize,
             p->mY + ((-right[1] - up[1]) * p->mSize,
             p->mZ + ((-right[2] - up[2]) * p->mSize);
}

glEnd();

glPopAttrib();
} // end renderParticles()
```

Note that the example `renderParticles()` function is meant to be used only when you have to render a single particle effect in your scene; however, most of the time this will not be the case. To render multiple effects, you should extend the example function so it incorporates a list of all effects as an argument. Then, all particles of all effects can be combined in one list, which is in turn sorted according to the distance of the particles to the camera. All particles are then rendered together in one go; if you render all the effects individually by calling the `renderParticles()` function for each effect, the blending will still not work correctly because particles from different effects might be in front of each other.

You will need to take extra care when your effects use different textures or blending functions. OpenGL does not allow you to change these parameters between a `glBegin()` and `glEnd()` pair. Therefore, you first need to call `glEnd()`, change the texture or blending mode, and then resume rendering by calling `glBegin()` again. Such rendering can be made easier if each particle stores a pointer to a texture and blending mode so the render function can then simply retrieve these values.

COMPUTER-GENERATED FIRE EFFECTS

There are different ways to create fire and explosion effects for computer games [Fire05] [Lode05]. Here, we present a very easy method to create quite realistic-looking fire effects for 2D canvas-based games. Later, we'll extend the idea behind these fire effects to explosion effects.

The principle of a fire is simple. Basically, a fire is fed from the embers at the bottom with heat, which rises to the top of the fire. During this process, the flames lose heat and appear darker. In a computer-generated fire, the heat is depicted by the color of the flames. A white to yellow glow at the bottom fades to darker red colors until it vanishes into the (black) background. This description already suggests a procedure on how to implement a computer-generated fire effect.

For fire-like effects, it is useful to employ a color palette that contains typical fire colors. Instead of using the RGB colors directly, a palette allows you to quickly address a color via the palette index. In addition, similar colors are easily retrieved because they have neighboring indices in the palette. Therefore, by increasing or decreasing the palette index, you will obtain a color that is a little brighter or darker. Consequently, palette handling is much faster and easier to program than direct handling of the RGB color values. For most fire effects, it is normally sufficient to choose a palette of about 200 colors. These typical color values can be stored in an array of the desired size.

```
QRgb mPalette[256];
```

Colors that are useful to create a fire begin with the dark colors such as black (0) and go via red to brighter colors such as yellow and white (255). An example of a palette is shown in Figure 12.5 and is provided as a color version

(12_5_palette_col.png) on the companion CD-ROM in the folder figures.

For storing the palette colors we use the class QRgb, which allows you to include alpha transparency. A color with a distinct red, green, blue, and alpha part can be constructed using

```
QRgb qRgba (int r, int g, int b, int a)
```

FIGURE 12.5   Example palette for use in fires and explosions.

The next step in creating the fire is the definition of a bitmap image on which the fire can be drawn. A QImage serves as the image storage.

```
QImage mImage;
```

This QImage can be embedded into any canvas sprite and drawn to the canvas as described previously for the particle sprites. Since the fire effect manages its own color palette, the effect algorithm cannot directly be applied to this RGB image. Consequently, the fire effect has to be processed in two steps: first, the algorithm is applied to a separate buffer where the index values are stored and manipulated. Second, once an animation cycle is complete, this extra buffer is copied to the actual image by looking up the RGB color values on the palette index and storing these values in the QImage. The intermediate buffer can be any data collection class, and for the example shown here, we chose a simple QMemArray storing integer numbers (the palette indices).

```
QMemArray<int> mFire;
```

However, a standard integer array int* or a Qt 4 QVector<int> will also suffice. For the sake of simplicity, the translation between the (x,y) coordinates of the image and the array index is performed manually as index = x + WIDTH * y.

Now it's time to actually draw and animate the fire. This is done in the animation method; for example, at each `advance()` call of the corresponding canvas sprite. The algorithm for the fire is now defined as follows: the fire is started at the bottom by supplying the embers with heat; this is achieved with our brightest colors (palette indices around 255). To have a good amount of randomness in the fire, the particles are randomly injected in the bottom line of the fire. Note that you can also inject the particles in another line besides the bottom row to produce more heat.

```
void FireSprite::prepareDraw()
{
  // Retrieve the image size
  QSize size = mImage.size();

  // Fill only the bottom row
  y = size.height()-1;
  for (x = 0; x < size.width(); x++)
  {
    // We do the manual (x,y) to index number
    // multiplication here
    int index = x + y * size.width();

    // Our random function returns a random value located
    // between the two arguments. Depending on this value
    // either a bright or a dark element is added. You can
    // of course also add in between elements. But these
    // two are enough to demonstrate the effect.
    int col;
    if (random(0.0, 1.0) < 0.4) { col = 0; }
    else { col = 255; }

    mFire.at(index) = col;
  }
  ...
```

The main trick of the fire algorithm is to propagate the heat upward to the top, while at the same time blurring or averaging the graphics around each processed pixel. This process will make the image look softer and more blended. In addition, the color of each pixel can be made darker; that is, shifted down in the palette index.

It is possible and actually recommended to randomly inject hot or cold sources (particles) into the flame. Alternatively, it is also possible to randomly weaken or strengthen the current particles' colors. Both of these tricks will produce a much more lively and realistic fire. This random process is left out in the example code snippet here so you can focus on the main algorithm. The source code `myparticle`

ON THE CD on the companion CD-ROM in the folder `examples/myparticle` includes these random effects, and Figure 12.6 shows some snapshots of different fire effects.

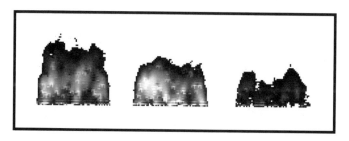

FIGURE 12.6 Example images of a computer-generated fire effect.

The main fire propagation looks like:

```
// prepareDraw() continued:
...
// Loop the whole image and propagate the fire
for (y = size.height() - 1; y > 0; y--)
{
  // Process row, except for left and rightmost pixel. This
  // is a bit cheated but simplifies the averaging
  // calculation.
  for (x = 1; x < size.width() - 1; x++)
  {
    // Shortcut for the index into the palette array
    int width   = size.width();
    int yOffset = y*width;
    int col;

    // Calculate average of surrounding pixels
    col = mFire[x-1 + yOffset] +
          mFire[x+1 + yOffset] +
          mFire[x-1 + yOffset-width] +
          mFire[x   + yOffset-width] +
          mFire[x+1 + yOffset-width] +
          mFire[x-1 + yOffset+width] +
          mFire[x   + yOffset+width] +
          mFire[x+1 + yOffset+width];
    col = col / 8;

    // Reduce color to make it go weaker
    col--;
```

```
        // Prevent palette from leaving the range 0..255
        if (col < 0) { col = 0; }

        // Propage particle one line upwards to raise the flame
        mFire[x + yOffset - width] = col;

        // Set pixel into image to painting it to the display
        mImage.setPixel(x, y, mPalette[col]);

      } // next column
    } // next row
  } // end prepareDraw()
```

Note that for the final step in the calculation loop, the actual color of the pixel is looked up in the palette and drawn into the real bitmap using:

```
        mImage.setPixel(x, y, mPalette[col]);
```

The resulting QImage can then be displayed on the canvas using the sprite's draw() method (see the implementation of the particle sprites earlier).

EXPLOSION EFFECTS

The combination of particle effects and computer-generated fires leads to the creation of computer-generated explosion effects. In principle, an explosion can be seen as a violent burst of fire stemming from a common center or core into which matter and gases have been ejected. The ejection can be either directed or undirected depending on the type of explosion.

Particle effects are ideally suited to model explosions. Essentially, the particles are ejected from the center of the explosion and their colors are selected from the fire palette (black, red, yellow) (see Figure 12.5). The overall particle sprite is then blended using the blending algorithm described in the previous section on fire effects. By applying this simple recipe, you will generate wonderful explosion effects. The actual details for the procedure of ejecting and moving the particles determine the exact shape of the explosion, and the overall effect will depend on the actual situation you simulate. For example, in space an equal ejection of particles to all angles will suffice, while on Earth, the explosion is influenced by gravity and friction. These effects have to be implemented in the trajectories of the individual particles. In addition to fire, real explosions are accompanied by smoke, which needs to be added to the computer explosion or the effect will be less realistic. The creation of smoke is performed in exactly the same manner as fire, but using a white, gray, and black palette.

In the following section, we show how to generate such explosions (see Figure 12.7) using a 2D canvas sprite that stores the particle system and the particles (see Figure 12.4). We propagate the particles depending on the actual explosion type; for example, space explosions. However, before actually drawing the particles to the image of the particle sprite, we apply the fire-blurring algorithm to create the explosion effect.

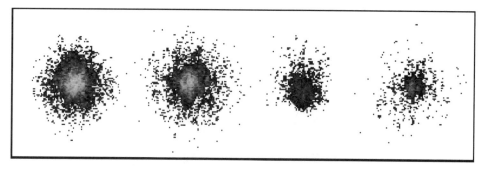

FIGURE 12.7 Snapshots of the animation of a computer-generated explosion using particle effects.

The particles will use a color from a fire palette (see Figure 12.5). This requires us to replace the color mColor attribute of the particle by an integer value, which then serves as an index to the palette.

```
class Particle
{
 ...
  int mPaletteIndex;   // Index color
};
```

Furthermore, because the particles are not directly drawn to the QImage anymore, they need to be propagated in an integer index buffer. This buffer mFire is an array of the same size as the QImage and contains integer values that correspond to the indices in the palette. The following example shows the prepareDraw() method of the particle sprite:

```
void ParticleSprite::prepareDraw()
{
  // Loop all particles
  QPtrList<Particle>* list = mParticleSystem->particleList();
```

```
Particle* p;
for (p = list.first(); p; p = list.next())
{
  // Fill the palette buffer with the particle index colors
  // 'width' is the width of the image
  x = p->mX;
  y = p->mY;
  mFire.at(x + y * width) = p->mPaletteIndex;
}
...
```

Immediately after setting, the buffer it is blurred, as described in the previous section on fire effects.

```
// prepareDraw() continued:
...
// Blur whole image analogous to the fire example
for (int y = size.height() - 1; y > 0; y--)
{
  for (int x = 1; x < size.width() - 1; x++)
  {
    // Shortcut for index into our palette array
    int width  = size.width();
    int yOffset = y*width;
    int col;

    // Calculate average of surrounding pixels
    col = mFire[x-1 + yOffset] +
          mFire[x+1 + yOffset] +
          mFire[x-1 + yOffset-width] +
          mFire[x   + yOffset-width] +
          mFire[x+1 + yOffset-width] +
          mFire[x-1 + yOffset+width] +
          mFire[x   + yOffset+width] +
          mFire[x+1 + yOffset+width];
    col = col / 8;

    mImage.setPixel(x, y, mPalette[col]);
  } // next x
} // next y
} // end prepareDraw()
```

To start an explosion, it is sufficient to just inject the particles into the sprite.

```
void ExplosionEffect::advanceEffect()
{
  // Move all particles according to their movement rules
  mParticleSystem->advance();

  // Do the remainder only for the initialization: we trace
  // this with a boolean flag mFirst
  if (!mFirst)
  {
    return;
  }
  mFirst = false;

  // Inject a lot of particles
  int cnt = 2000;
  Particle* p;
  while(cnt>0 && (p = mParticleSystem->inject()))
  {
    // Select random angle and speed to set (x,y) velocity
    float angle = random(0.0, 2 * M_PI);
    float speed = random(5.0, 300.0);
    float vx    = cos(angle) * speed;
    float vy    = sin(-angle) * speed;

    // Set lifespan
    float life  = random(60.0, 150.0);
    ...

    // Set the particle's properties , e.g. linear movement
    // originating from a common center
    p->mLife = life;
    p->mX     = 0.0;
    p->mY     = 0.0;
    p->mVx    = vx;
    p->mVy    = vy;
    ...

    // Decrease particle counter
    cnt--;
  }
}
```

Using linear movement with constant velocity for the individual particles, this example creates an explosion that could occur in space (Figure 12.7).

SUMMARY

Particle effects can be used in computer games to produce a variety of interesting effects, such as snow, rain, smoke, or explosions. An individual particle is a simple item that stores a small set of properties that allow it to fly on a physical trajectory and change its appearance (color, shape, size). However, the wonderful effects that can be achieved with these particles only become apparent when numerous particles (each with individual parameters) are used simultaneously. Another important application of particle effects is the use of ready-made images as particles. Here, you normally require fewer particles, but each particle consists of an already prepared image (such as a little "$" sign). These particle effects can then be used to illustrate the aforementioned raising of money from a building in a strategy game.

In this chapter, we demonstrated the relevance of 2D particle effects in creating basic effects for desktop games. To use such effects inside Qt, any sprite class can be used as a basis for the particle effect implementation. There are two ways to implement particles, the first of which is to model particles as individual sprites. This design works well for effects that require only a few particles. Alternatively, all particles are collected inside one sprite and are then manually drawn to an image that is displayed as the sprite. This procedure is applicable for effects requiring a large amount of particles.

Particle effects can also be generated using OpenGL, which is the most obvious choice when your game is already a 3D OpenGL game. When using OpenGL, it is much easier to create stunning particle effects, because you can apply hardware-accelerated textures and blending effects. The implementation of the 3D particles is very similar to that of 2D particle effects; you just have to additionally implement the OpenGL rendering code pertinent for the effect. The only tricky aspect to working with 3D OpenGL is that before rendering, you must ensure that all the particles are sorted according to their distance from the camera. When this is not the case, the translucent particles will not properly blend.

A topic related to particle effects is the creation of computer-generated fire. Here, a special particle propagation together with a blurring algorithm creates the typical appearance of fire. Applying particle effects and fire algorithms together also leads to realistic-looking explosion effects.

Often in computer games, it is easier to use preprocessed special effects and not create fire and explosions at runtime, and this is usually better for performance reasons. These effects can be created outside the program either by using a program [Blender05] that generates the desired effects and then stores them in bitmap image files, or by drawing such effects with a normal paint program (see Figure 12.8). Using a sequence of such images and playing it back will create a smooth animation. This also allows the display of special effects such as fire and explosions without using much processor time, because only the sprites' frames have to be displayed.

However, the disadvantage of this process is that you are limited to only a few different animation sequences, because each has to be stored and loaded from a file and therefore needs to be prepared beforehand.

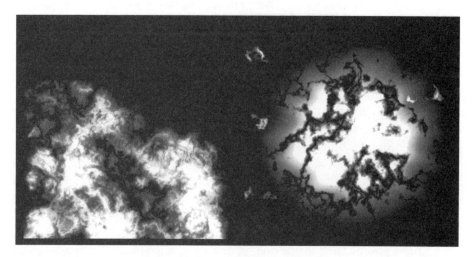

FIGURE 12.8 Ready-made flames and explosion drawn manually using a standard paint program.

REFERENCES

[Blender05] *Blender, http://www.blender.org*, 2005.

[Bourg01] Bourg, David M., *Physics for Game Developers*, ISBN: 0596000065; O'Reilly, 2001.

[Fire05] *Computer Fire, http://freespace.virgin.net/hugo.elias/models/m_fire.htm*, 2005.

[Lode05] *Computer Graphics Tutorial, http://www.student.kuleuven.ac.be/~m0216922/CG/fire.html*, 2005.

13 Math and Physics in Desktop Games

In This Chapter

- Coordinates
- Introduction to Scalars and Vectors
- Matrices
- Game Physics
- Random Numbers

Computer games that want to appear realistic to the player have to generate a game world that follows real physical principles. For example, if a player accelerates his vehicle, fires at an opponent, or throws an object, he expects these actions to occur as they do in the real world. If these actions behave very differently in the game, it may appear odd to the player (of course, some games might want to do this on purpose). Therefore, many games require a very detailed modeling of the real world's physical laws. In fact, many of today's games have already begun to incorporate increasingly realistic physical behavior in their game engines. Games such as action shooters, flight simulators, or car races try to excel by using very realistic physics engines.

Basic mathematical transformations are not only necessary for physical models but also appear in standard game applications. Rotations and translations can be applied to objects of the game world and to graphical images. These transformations even occur in simple desktop games. Nevertheless, the amount of math and physics necessary for a particular game clearly depends on the type of game. Some desktop games such as card games or word puzzles actually require only a little math and no physics. However, as soon as the game includes moving objects, such as the firing of bullets or missiles, you will find yourself applying the first physical principles. When you start to construct 3D games, additional and more complicated transformations such as 3D rotation will be necessary.

In this chapter, we remain within the scope of desktop games and present the concepts of coordinate systems, vectors, and matrices, and basic mathematical transformations such as rotations and translations by applying transformation matrices. Some of the most fundamental physical movement laws are important for the realistic behavior of an object or vehicles in a game. In the scope of this chapter, we concentrate on scenarios that are useful for desktop games.

Another necessary ingredient for many computer games is random numbers. Their use and implementation as a computer algorithm and the consequences arising from this implementation are also discussed here.

In the scope of this book, which focuses on desktop games, we can only give you a very first impression of the mathematical and physical laws useful for computer games. We selected some topics that occur in typical Qt or KDE desktop games and present them here. If you want to or need to dig deeper into this topic, we recommend the book [Bourg01].

COORDINATES

The most common way to determine the location of an object is to specify its Cartesian coordinates. These coordinates measure the distance from the coordinate system's origin to the object along each main axis. These axes are perpendicular to each other and are called the x-axis, the y-axis, and for 3D structures, there is an additional z-axis. An example of a 3D coordinate system is depicted in Figure 13.1. In a 3D environment, the coordinate measurement will contain three numbers, the (x,y,z) coordinates, whereas in a 2D environment, only two numbers, the (x,y) coordinates, are needed. Even if you are in a 3D environment, 2D behavior can be emulated by using a constant value as the z-coordinate, such as $z = 0$.

The coordinate origin is a special but arbitrary place in the coordinate system and can serve as a reference point for measuring the distances to the objects. For graphical or windowing applications the coordinate origin is usually defined by the graphics library. Qt canvas views locate the origin in the top-left corner while OpenGL places it in the lower-left corner. When you use coordinates outside of this graphic realm the origin can be placed anywhere, for example in the middle of a game map.

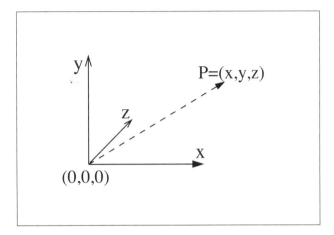

FIGURE 13.1 3D Cartesian coordinate system with the three
(x,y,z) axes and the coordinate system origin (0,0,0). The
position of any point P in this coordinate system is obtained
by specifying the measurements (x,y,z) along each of the
coordinate axes.

For desktop game applications, it is usually sufficient to use the typical screen
coordinates that are based on the Cartesian coordinate system. Note however, that
this is not the only possible coordinate system. Another important system would be
the radial coordinate system, in which the distance to the origin (radius) and an
angle is used to specify the location of a point in 2D space. Sometimes, these radial
coordinate systems can be useful for game objects that are based inherently on circular movements; for example, a spaceship in orbit around a planet or a rotating
turret. A combination of coordinate systems can be used in game applications,
since the coordinates of different systems can be converted to and from each other.

INTRODUCTION TO SCALARS AND VECTORS

Scalar numbers and vector quantities are used throughout mathematical and physical equations. As a short introduction to these topics, this section gives you a brief
overview on their definition.

Scalar Numbers

Scalar numbers is simply another term for the normal numbers we encounter in
daily life and computer programming. They can be described by a single number

(which is in contrast to vectors), and thus have no direction associated with them. An example of a scalar number would be the number "15," and an example of a physical scalar quantity would be the temperature. There is nothing special about scalars in terms of computer programming, but they are often referred to in combination with vector quantities, and it is important to distinguish between these two quantities.

Vector Quantities

A vector is a mathematical quantity that contains more information than a scalar number does. A vector defines both the direction and magnitude in one quantity: the vector. For instance, a vector quantity would be the velocity of an object such as an aircraft traveling 300 miles per hour in a northwest direction.

A vector is specified by two numbers in 2D and three numbers in 3D. Although it is possible to state the direction and magnitude of a vector, a vector is normally presented in terms of its components with respect to the coordinate system axes. In the aircraft example, this would be the velocity along the x-axis, the y-axis, and in 3D, the z-axis. A vector for the velocity (of the aircraft) can be written for 2D as column vector $\mathbf{v} = \begin{pmatrix} v_x \\ v_y \end{pmatrix}$, or alternatively as a row vector $\mathbf{v} = (v_x, v_y)$, and for 3D the column vector would resemble $\mathbf{v} = \begin{pmatrix} v_x \\ v_y \\ v_z \end{pmatrix}$, or as a row vector $\mathbf{v} = (v_x, v_y, v_z)$ (with v_x, v_y, and v_z being the velocities along the three coordinate system axes). Writing column vectors in the form of row vectors—that is, as $\mathbf{v} = (v_x, v_y, v_z)$—is called *transposing* the vectors. Here, we do not distinguish between these two formats.

Note that vectors are often denoted by a little arrow above their name so they can be readily distinguished from normal scalar numbers. Thus, you would write $\vec{v}$ instead of $\mathbf{v}$. Since within computer programming the denotation is not visible, this denotation is not performed within this chapter.

Vectors can be used for handling all quantities that have a direction and a magnitude. This is normally achieved with physical formulas, because many physical quantities such as forces, velocities, and accelerations are actually vector quantities. Vectors can be further used to specify the direction and length or the position of a point in a coordinate system. To do so, you first need to define where the vector should start; this could be at the coordinate system origin, for example. The end position of the vector is then the desired point in the coordinate system. Thus, we will also not distinguish between a vector $v = (x, y)$ and a point $P = (x, y)$.

Vectors can be used in mathematical and physical formulas, and allow addition, subtraction, and multiplication. Addition and subtraction work per element;

that is, for two 2D vectors $\mathbf{v}_1 = (v_{x1}, v_{y1})$ and $\mathbf{v}_2 = (v_{x2}, v_{y2})$, the addition becomes

$$\mathbf{v}_1 + \mathbf{v}_2 = \begin{pmatrix} v_{x1} + v_{x2} \\ v_{y1} + v_{y2} \end{pmatrix}.$$

An often-used vector operation is the dot product vector multiplication $\mathbf{v}_1 \cdot \mathbf{v}_2 = v_{x1} \cdot v_{x2} + v_{y1} \cdot v_{y2}$, which results in a scalar, not a vector, quantity. The magnitude $|\mathbf{v}|$ of a vector is its length and can be retrieved from the dot product of the vector with itself $|\mathbf{v}| = \sqrt{\mathbf{v} \cdot \mathbf{v}}$, which corresponds in 2D to $|\mathbf{v}| = \sqrt{v_x^2 + v_y^2}$. The angle φ between two vectors can also be calculated from dot product because multiplication of two vectors $\mathbf{v}_1$ and $\mathbf{v}_2$ yields $\mathbf{v}_1 \cdot \mathbf{v}_2 = |\mathbf{v}_1| \cdot |\mathbf{v}_2| \cdot \cos(\varphi)$, which when divided by the vector lengths results in the (cosine of the) angle between the two vectors. Often, the angle between arbitrary vectors is not of interest, but the angle toward one of the coordinate axes, preferably the x-axis, is. Calculating the dot products of a 2D vector $\mathbf{v} = (v_x, v_y)$ with the x-axis (1,0) and the y-axis (0,1) allows you to simplify the resulting equations so that, for example, the angle φ between the vector and the x-axis becomes $\varphi = \text{atan2}\,(v_x / v_y)$. Note, it is important to use the C-library `atan2` function instead of the `atan` function; otherwise, the quadrant (a 90-degree section of an arc) is not determined.

Sometimes, a quantity in the game is not known by its x- and y-coordinates, but instead by its magnitude and direction. Therefore, in the latter case, it is not the (v_x, v_y) values that are given, but the overall magnitude $|\mathbf{v}|$ and the angle φ between the vector and the x-axis. Such a description happens quite often for velocities. However, when moving the game objects to the desired target coordinates, it is normally necessary to know the x- and y-components to allow the settings of the screen coordinates. From the direction and magnitude information, these components can be calculated using again the dot product with the x-axis and y-axis as $\begin{pmatrix} v_x \\ v_y \end{pmatrix} = |\mathbf{v}| \cdot \begin{pmatrix} \cos(\varphi) \\ \sin(\varphi) \end{pmatrix}$. An example for such a situation could be a cannon turret that shoots bullets with a given speed (100 miles per hour) at a given angle (30 degrees).

In most programming libraries (standard C library), angles are given in radians 0...2π, not in degrees 0...360. However, some other libraries do use degrees (OpenGL), and you must be careful which units you use. If necessary, both values can be converted into each other: the radians values can be calculated from degrees by multiplying them by π/180 where π = 3.14159... as defined in math.h as M_PI. Degrees can be calculated from radians with the inverse formula; that is, multiplying by 180/π.

MATRICES

In a computer game, it is usually not sufficient to just define points or vectors; you also want to transform them. By *transforming*, we mean to change the position of a point in some way. This can be either the translation (movement) in any direction, the rotation around one of the axes, and so forth.

To simplify the handling of such transformations, the concept of *matrices* is introduced. Matrices allow the development of a compact formula that describes the transformation from one point P_0 to another P_1. Note, however, that using matrices is just an uncomplicated method for writing these transformations. These transformation equations can be directly applied equally well to the points you want to transform. Especially in 2D, this is often sufficient. However, in 3D, it is often more convenient to use matrices.

In the following, we present both possibilities so you can choose the one that suits you more. We use the original point $P_0 = (x_0, y_0)$ (2D) or $P_0 = (x_0, y_0, z_0)$ (3D), which will be transformed to the new point $P_1 = (x_1, y_1)$ (2D) or $P_1 = (x_1, y_1, z_1)$ (3D). We first discuss the basic transformations in 2D; the extension to 3D is trivial except for rotations that we discuss later.

Basics of 2D Matrices

In the 2D case, any point or vector has two coordinates (x,y). The original point P_0 can be transformed to any new point P_1 by the 2D matrix equations

$$x_1 = a \cdot x_0 + b \cdot y_0$$
$$y_1 = c \cdot x_0 + d \cdot y_0$$

These equations are the definition of the matrix $\mathbf{M}$

$$\mathbf{M} = \begin{pmatrix} a & b \\ c & d \end{pmatrix}$$

which is constructed by four (two by two) numbers and allows the transformation to be written in a compact format from the old point P_0 to the new point P_1, as $P_1 = \mathbf{M} \cdot P_0$.

It is possible to apply more than one transformation to a point by repeating this process. It is furthermore possible to construct more complex transformations by multiplying two transformations matrices together. If both $\mathbf{M}_1$ and $\mathbf{M}_2$ create transformations, then $\mathbf{M}_1 \cdot \mathbf{M}_2$ is the combined transformation of both. This is defined as matrixmultiplication.

$$\mathbf{M}_1 \cdot \mathbf{M}_2 = \begin{pmatrix} a_1 \cdot a_2 + b_1 \cdot c_2 & a_1 \cdot b_2 + b_1 \cdot d_2 \\ c_1 \cdot a_2 + d_1 \cdot c_2 & c_1 \cdot b_2 + d_1 \cdot d_2 \end{pmatrix}$$

Note that in matrix calculation, $\mathbf{M}_1 \cdot \mathbf{M}_2$ is usually *not* equal to $\mathbf{M}_2 \cdot \mathbf{M}_1$.

Such transformation matrices cover most transformations in 2D. However, one important case, the translation—that is, shifting a point in a certain direction—cannot be written using such a 2D matrix. There is one way to circumvent this problem and to introduce translations into matrix calculations, a concept frequently used in computer games and by Qt.

It is possible to introduce an artificial third coordinate into the 2D points, vectors, and matrices. This third coordinate (sometimes called the *w-coordinate*) allows the incorporation of a translation into the matrix, while maintaining all other normal matrix operations. The matrix multiplications will then include this translation in the original coordinates. It is important to note that this additional coordinate has no real meaning and must not be confused with the *z*-coordinate in 3D (although it looks exactly the same).

This type of matrix then contains nine (three by three) numbers, and the translation by (t_x, t_y) is listed as an extra column.

$$\mathbf{M} = \begin{pmatrix} a & b & t_x \\ c & d & t_y \\ 0 & 0 & 1 \end{pmatrix}$$

To apply such a matrix in the 2D case, all points have to be extended by an artificial third coordinate. Since this coordinate has no real meaning, it is always set to "1." Therefore, the point P_0 from the previous example is now defined as $P_0 = (x, y, 1)$.

Applying such a matrix to P_0 yields again $P_0 = \mathbf{M} \cdot P_0$, or in more detail:

$$x_1 = a \cdot x_0 + b \cdot y_0 + t_x$$
$$y_1 = c \cdot x_0 + d \cdot y_0 + t_y$$
$$1 = 1$$

These equations contain the translation (t_x, t_y) for the *x*- and *y*-coordinates.

Matrix multiplications using this extra translation column are particularly useful because Qt offers the class QWMatrix, which specifies exactly such matrix operations. In the following sections, the exact formulas for the most-used basic transformations are described in more detail. Note that in Qt, all of these transformations can be applied to individual points, objects, or even entire images.

QWMatrix Transformations

Qt offers the class QWMatrix to process the 2D matrix transformations of points or entire images. These Qt matrices are implemented as 2D matrices with an additional third coordinate for translations, as described in the previous section. QWMatrix provides methods to define the standard matrix operations such as translations, rotations, shearing, and scaling. Some of the most often-used transformations can be accessed directly by method calls to QWMatrix.

```
QWMatrix m;
m.translate(tx, ty);  // translate
m.rotate(phi);        // rotate (in degrees)
m.scale(sx, sy);      // scale
...
```

However, it is also possible to specify all matrix parameters yourself.

```
QWMatrix m;
// Specify the matrix coefficients
m.setMatrix(a, b, c, d, tx, ty);
```

The class QWMatrix also allows the combination of multiple transformations into a single matrix as described here:

```
QWMatrix m;            // default is the identity matrix
m.translate(10, -20); // first translate by (10,-20) pixel
m.rotate(25);         // then rotate 25 degrees
m.scale(0.5, 0.5);    // finally scale it to half size
```

and this combined matrix can then be applied to a distinct point by

```
// The coordinates can be integer or double values
m.map(x0, y0, &x1, &y1)
```

or, alternatively, the matrix transformation can also be applied to an entire pixmap using the xForm() method.

```
QPixmap pixmap;
pixmap.xForm(m);
```

Note that when rotating a pixmap, Qt will place the resulting image into a pixmap, which is the smallest image that contains all the transformed points of the original image. Consequently, the transformation can include unwanted translations that you have to correct by moving the images to a different position. Therefore, the outcome of an xForm() rotation might not always be what you expect.

2D Translations

Most movements in computer games are translations along one or more axes, depicted in the left-hand picture in Figure 13.2. The point P_0 is shifted by an amount t_x along the x-axis, by t_y along the y-axis, and results in the new position P_1 as

$$x_1 = x_0 + t_x$$
$$y_1 = y_0 + t_y.$$

This movement can also be achieved by the matrix multiplication using the translation matrix

$$\mathbf{M}_t = \begin{pmatrix} 1 & 0 & t_x \\ 0 & 1 & t_y \\ 0 & 0 & 1 \end{pmatrix}.$$

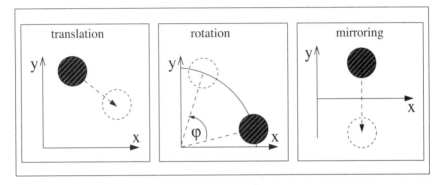

FIGURE 13.2 Three possible transformations on an object. The translation (left) moves an object to another location, the rotation (middle) rotates the object by a given angle φ around a center, and the mirroring (right) reflects the object in respect to an axis (here, the x-axis).

2D Rotations

When the movement of an object in a game is based on rotations, or an image should be rotated by a certain angle, you need to apply a rotation calculation. Such a transformation can rotate one point or all pixels of an image around a common center, which is usually the coordinate origin (in the case of an image, the image center). A typical rotation is depicted in the middle image in Figure 13.2.

Assuming that the center of the rotation is the coordinate origin (if this is not the case, the object has to be first translated toward it), the counter-clockwise rotation of the point P_0 by the angle φ results in the new point P_1.

$$x_1 = x_0 \cdot \cos(\varphi) - y_0 \cdot \sin(\varphi)$$
$$y_1 = x_0 \cdot \sin(\varphi) + y_0 \cdot \cos(\varphi)$$

Again, this can be achieved by the matrix multiplication using the rotation matrix

$$\mathbf{M}_r = \begin{pmatrix} \cos(\varphi) & -\sin(\varphi) & 0 \\ \sin(\varphi) & \cos(\varphi) & 0 \\ 0 & 0 & 1 \end{pmatrix}.$$

Note that clockwise rotation works by replacing φ with $-\varphi$.

2D Mirroring

Mirroring a point P_0 at the x-axis results in the reflected point P_1

$$x_1 = x_0$$
$$y_1 = -y_0,$$

which can also be achieved by matrix multiplication using the matrix

$$\mathbf{M}_m = \begin{pmatrix} 1 & 0 & 0 \\ 0 & -1 & 0 \\ 0 & 0 & 1 \end{pmatrix}.$$

An example of a mirror operation is shown on the right-hand side of Figure 13.2. Mirroring again is particularly useful when applied to images that are then flipped along one axis.

Mirroring around an arbitrary axis involves translating the axis to the origin, rotating the axis to the x-axis, and then applying the mirroring transformation. After the mirroring transformation, the rotation and translation have to be undone by rotating and translating in the opposite directions. Using matrix multiplication, these rotations and translations can be combined into one matrix, which is then applied to the point P_0 to achieve the mirroring. Ideally, this is performed at compilation, not at runtime.

2D Scaling

Scaling can enlarge or diminish both images and objects by a given scale factor. Again, this is particularly useful when applied to images. The scale factor can differ for the different coordinate axis and can thus distort the image.

Scaling by the factor s_x in the x-direction and by s_y in the y-direction will change the original point P_0 to

$$x_1 = s_x \cdot x_0$$
$$y_1 = s_y \cdot y_0,$$

which can also be written using the scaling matrix

$$\mathbf{M}_s = \begin{pmatrix} s_x & 0 & 0 \\ 0 & s_y & 0 \\ 0 & 0 & 1 \end{pmatrix}.$$

A scaling factor of one does not change the object. Scaling factors less than one make the object smaller, and factors larger than one enlarge it.

3D Transformations

From a mathematical point of view, the extension of transformations to 3D is easy. Most of the issues discussed for 2D also apply to 3D; in fact, we just replace the normal 2D coordinates (x,y) with the 3D (x,y,z) coordinates. The extension by the third coordinate for translations in 2D $(x,y,1)$ is also straightforward; we simply add a fourth coordinate $(x,y,z,1)$, and this last component only exists to support the translations. Accordingly, instead of using 3×3 matrices, we use 4×4 matrices.

For 3D applications, matrices are usually the primary form of transforming coordinates. One of the reasons for this is that 3D libraries such as OpenGL make extensive use of matrices, and it is convenient to use them in the actual game. Note, however, that using OpenGL calls to perform 3D matrix calculations in the game itself is not generally recommended, since it can hinder the overall performance. Yet another reason for using matrices instead of straightforward mathematical calculations is that fast code is much easier to write. Imagine the equations that would be necessary to apply multiple rotations on multiple points!

While most transformations explained for the 2D case can be easily adapted to the 3D case by just adding a third coordinate, rotations are a bit more difficult. In 2D, you always rotate around the "z-axis," but in 3D, you can freely rotate around an arbitrary axis. Therefore, two values are necessary to describe the rotation: the first value, the angle φ, is required to describe the amount of rotation, whereas the second value, a vector (x,y,z) of length one, describes the axis of the rotation. This axis is the line through the coordinate system origin and (x,y,z). A rotation is then performed by the following rotation matrix, in which we abbreviate $c = \cos(\varphi)$ and $s = \sin(\varphi)$:

$$\mathbf{M}_r = \begin{pmatrix} x^2 \cdot (1-c)+c & x \cdot y \cdot (1-c)-z \cdot s & x \cdot z \cdot (1-c)+y \cdot s & 0 \\ y \cdot x \cdot (1-c)+z \cdot s & y^2 \cdot (1-c)+c & y \cdot z \cdot (1-c)-x \cdot s & 0 \\ z \cdot x \cdot (1-c)-y \cdot s & z \cdot y \cdot (1-c)+x \cdot s & z^2 \cdot (1-c)+c & 0 \\ 0 & 0 & 0 & 1 \end{pmatrix}.$$

Note that by setting *x = 0, y = 0, z = 1*, the 3D matrix rotation is simplified to a rotation around the *z*-axis and equals the 2D rotations.

GAME PHYSICS

If a game is to have a realistic feel, the objects within the game, such as vehicles or characters, need to move in accordance with real physical laws—only then will the behavior of the objects appear "normal" to the user. This form of behavior in a game can be implemented by requiring that the game objects obey real physical equations. For desktop games, the main physical effects are forces and collisions on the objects' trajectories (their paths). The velocities and accelerations resulting from these interactions and the resulting changes to their paths need to be accurately described.

In essence, the more realistic a game should appear, the more physical equations need to be applied. Especially in 3D games or simulations, the correct physical description of the game will require the programmer to incorporate more complicated scenarios such as noncentral impacts, physically correct rotations, energy, and angular momentum conditions. Since most desktop games do not require such detailed descriptions, the following sections focus on simpler examples for physically correct movement as typically found in desktop games. In particular, we do not mention the effects of the spatial extension of an object on its movement. Advanced physics in computer games is further discussed in the books [Bourg01] and [Eberly03].

Desktop Game Scenarios

Vehicles in a game are usually powered by an engine or a rocket, and these engines generate an accelerating force on the vehicle. Unless you are in space, these forces are often compensated by friction. Together, both forces lead to constant velocity or accelerated movements.

When a vehicle or any other object enters a gravitational field—that is, on or near a planet—it will be under the influence of gravity, and this gravity will pull the object toward the ground. This gravitational pull then has effects on the movement of the objects; for example, bullets or missiles will follow parabolic trajectories, and objects in space will enter an orbit around the planet.

In games, objects often collide, and this can have two effects. With the first effect, you use the collision information as an indication that something has happened, such as the missile you fired made the spaceship explode. However, the precise treatment of an impact requires a physically correct description. Games in which such descriptions are necessary would be, for example, billiard games, since the exact resulting trajectories of two colliding balls are of utmost importance.

Usually, in desktop computer games you will change the position of an object in some kind of `advance()` method of the object. For canvas games, this is the `QCanvasItem advance()` method. Typically, using such `advance()` methods, the current position (x,y) of an object is updated with its current velocity (vx,vy), thus:

```
void advance(...)
{
  // For a Qt canvas item: oldX=x() and oldY=y()

  newX = oldX + vx * dt;
  newY = oldY + vy * dt;
  ...

  // For a Qt canvas item: setX(newX), setY(newY)
}
```

Often in computer games, velocities are just added to the current position as $x = x + vx$. Note, however, that a correct position update is actually achieved by first multiplying a velocity with a time step dt. Here, dt could represent the canvas advance time. Especially when you have synchonized advance steps and view updates in your game, we recommend doing this as well, because you become independent of the actual screen update time, and changes in the timing do not change the movement speed of your objects. Mathematically interested readers might be interested to note the following extra detail: the physically correct location x of an object with initial location x_0, initial velocity v_0, and constant acceleration a is retrieved by integrating the acceleration and the velocity over time. Both velocity and location become time dependent quantities.

$$v = v(t) = \int_0^t adt = a \cdot t + v_0$$

$$x = x(t) = \int_0^t v(t)dt = 0.5 \cdot a \cdot t^2 + v_0 \cdot t + x_0$$

However, our approach in this chapter sets velocity and position as

```
void advance(...)
{
  // Increase current velocity v by acceleration
  v = a * dt + v
```

```
// Increase current location x by current velocity
x = v * dt + x  // == (a * dt * dt + v * dt) + x
...
}
```

which is in fact only an approximation of the correct physical equation and is only applicable to small time steps. This procedure of adding up the changes in small time steps is called the *Euler* integration. When calculating the new positions within an `advance()` like method, this is usually a valid approximation because the advance steps *dt* are naturally very small.

Forces

Forces are the key elements that bring about change in the movement of an object. Actually, unless a force acts on an object, it will forever maintain its current movement state. This applies to an object that is at rest, or an object that is currently moving with a set velocity—the latter will continue to move with that same constant velocity. The object will never accelerate, decelerate, or make any bends or curves. This behavior is actually Newton's first law of motion.

If, however, a force acts on an object, the object is accelerated in the direction of the applied force. If the force is in the same direction as the movement, acceleration will occur. In contrast, if the force is in the opposite direction to the movement, a deceleration occurs. If the force is perpendicular to the direction of the movement, a curve is initiated. Note that a force of arbitrary direction can always be decomposed into a force that is in the direction parallel to the movement and into another component that is perpendicular to it. The acceleration a resulting from the force F is proportional to the applied force. The proportionality constant is the mass m of the object. Newton's second law of motion states $F = m \cdot a$.

In desktop computer games, there is usually a limited set of forces that can act on an object. These forces include:

The engine force: This force accelerates the vehicle and is normally constant $F = constant$. Typical examples are the engines of cars, planes, ships, or spacecraft.

The (dynamic) friction force: Friction decelerates a vehicle. Without an engine, friction will finally lead to a full stop of any vehicle. Friction forces are usually velocity dependent; that is, the faster a vehicle goes, the more friction it experiences. Often, friction can be assumed to be $F = u \cdot v^2$, with u describing the strength of the friction and v being the velocity of the vehicle. Note, however, that depending on the cause of the friction, you can get different force laws, but this is the most common form [Eberly03].

Gravity: The gravitational force pulls all objects toward the center of gravity. For vehicles close to the surface of a planet, the gravitational acceleration can be considered constant, pulling directly toward the ground. The gravitational force for an object of mass m is then $F = m \cdot g$, where g is the gravitational constant of the planet (on Earth, $g = 9.81 m/s^2$). However, for a spacecraft that is farther away from the gravitational source—the planet—the gravitational force yields $F = G \cdot m_1 \cdot m_2 / r^2$, where m_1 and m_2 are the masses of the spacecraft and the planet, respectively. r is the distance between them, and $G = 6.67 \cdot 10^{-11} m^3 kg^{-1} s^{-2}$ is the universal gravity constant acting as scaling factor.

Linear Movement with Constant Velocity

The most common and easiest movement of objects is a linear movement with constant velocity. In this form of movement, the objects follow a straight line and do not change their velocity during the movement.

Physically, this form of movement arises in two scenarios. The first is when there are no forces acting on an object; consequently, the object just keeps going with what initial velocity it has. This type of movement is not normally found on Earth, since forces such as friction constantly act on the objects. However, in space, a nonaccelerated spacecraft will fly with a constant velocity. In the second scenario, a constant velocity movement also occurs if forces act on an object, but all forces add up to a resulting force of zero. A typical example of this is a car or an aircraft. The engine yields a force in the direction of the movement, but the engine force is balanced by friction on the street and/or air resistance. When the forces are not balanced, there will be an accelerated movement; that is, the velocity of the object increases. However, friction forces depend on and increase with velocity. Therefore, at some point, the engine and the friction forces are equal, and the object will continue to drive with constant velocity.

Unless you are simulating such an exact acceleration, it is usually easier to ignore the initial acceleration in game scenarios and set the velocity to a constant. Both scenarios apply to many possible cases of movement in games, including vehicles, planes, ships, or spacecraft.

With each time step (e.g., each canvas advance step) of length dt, the object will change its position (x,y) to a new position, which depends on the velocity (vx,vy):

```
void advance(...)
{
  x = x + vx * dt;
  y = y + vy * dt;
}
```

Linear Movement with Constant Acceleration

Acceleration or deceleration occurs if the forces acting on an object do not balance. If the resulting force is in the direction of movement, acceleration occurs, and if it is opposite the direction of movement, deceleration is initiated.

A typical example for the use of accelerated movement is the movement of any object in a gravitational field where it will experience an acceleration toward the center of gravity; for example, on Earth, all objects are pulled toward the ground. Another example of accelerated movement is the start of a car or an aircraft. Here, the velocity is not yet constant, and the vehicle is accelerated until it reaches its cruise velocity. Using Newton's second law, the acceleration a on the object can be calculated from the force F, which acts on an object of mass m as $a = F / m$.

An acceleration (ax, ay) causes a constant change in the velocity (vx, vy) of an object, which in turn can be used to determine the position of the object.

```
void advance(...)
{
  vx = vx + ax * dt;
  vy = vy + ay * dt;

  x = x + vx * dt;
  y = y + vy * dt;
}
```

Orbits

If a force acts on an object perpendicular to its direction of movement, the direction of movement is changed. Should this force stem from a single center, like the gravitational force of a planet, the object will bend its path around the center of the force so the object is then in an orbit around the planet. Depending on the initial velocity of the object, different scenarios may occur. For example, if the object is very fast, it will not enter an orbit, but make a hyperbolic movement around the center of the force. In contrast, when the velocity is slower, the object will enter an elliptical orbit around the planet. A special form of elliptical orbit is the circular orbit. Here, the velocity in the direction of the movement is and stays constant, and the orbit is a circle around the center of the force. Figure 13.3 depicts the possible orbital movements, the positions, and the force involved.

The equations of motions for orbital movements are the same as the ones for accelerated movement in the previous section. However, the acceleration now depends on the position of the object. This is because the current force F will always be directed toward the location of the force center (cx, cy).

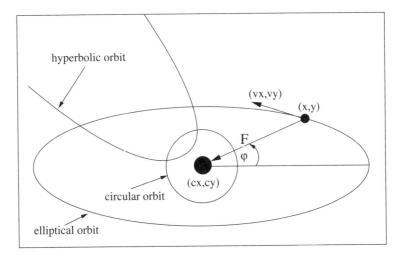

FIGURE 13.3   Possible orbits around a central force such as the gravit-ation of a planet: a circular, elliptical, and hyperbolic orbit are shown, together with the main parameters determining the orbits.

The acceleration (ax,ay) for our object at position (x,y) with mass m will be:

```
void advance(...)
{
  phi = atan2( (y-cy) / (x-cx) );

  ax = F/m * cos(phi);
  ay = F/m * sin(phi);

  // Continue with velocity and position as before
  ...
}
```

if phi is the angle between a parallel to the x-axis going through the force center and our object.

Parabolic Trajectories

Another useful example of accelerated movement is the trajectory of an unacceler-ated object in the gravitational field of the Earth. The object starts its movement with an initial velocity in any direction, and during flight is only affected by the Earth's gravity. Such movements result in parabolic trajectories, which are useful for computer games since they represent the firing of cannons, bullets, or dropping of cargo from a plane. Figure 13.4 depicts a typical parabolic trajectory.

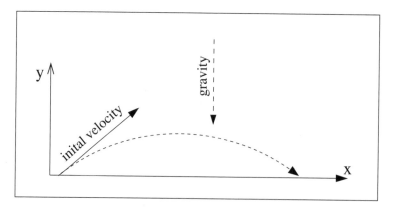

FIGURE 13.4   A parabolic trajectory for an object started with a constant initial velocity. During flight, only gravity acts on the object.

We apply the gravitational force into the negative y-direction (toward the ground) as $ay = -g = -9.81m/s^2$, to an object starting at (x,y) with the initial velocity (vx,vy). While there is no acceleration in the x-direction, the corresponding movement in the x-direction will continue with constant speed vx during the entire movement. The velocity in the y-direction is modified by the acceleration. Your movement code looks like

```
void advance(...)
{
  vy = vy - ay * dt;

  x  = x  + vx * dt;
  y  = y  + vy * dt;
  ...
```

At some point, the movement will hit the ground; thus, the movement code in the game has to check the y-position for valid values. If the ground is at $y = 0$, such a check would resemble

```
if (y <= 0.0)
{
  // stop movement
  ...
}
}
```

Impacts

Another very important topic in computer games is the physically correct treatment of collisions between two objects. The question here is, what actually happens when an impact between two objects occurs? Examples of such situations are two billiard balls hitting each other, or a bullet deflecting off a wall.

Unfortunately, a general and physically correct treatment of collisions is quite extensive. In the following section, we therefore analyze only the main impact scenarios that can be treated with reasonable effort in our games. In all of them, the colliding objects are considered *elastic* objects (billiard balls, rubber balls, steel balls). In this respect, the term *elastic* denotes that the objects are not deformed after the collision, and therefore no movement energy is absorbed by them. However, in principle, all formulas can be extended to the *inelastic* impact case as well [Bourg01]. Furthermore, only central impacts are discussed. By this, we mean that the objects are treated as if they would always hit right in their center, which is often a good approximation if the extensions of the objects are small compared to the movement area. If this is not assumed, the impact treatment gets much more complicated, and the objects change their speed and direction, and can also start rotating.

For an elastic impact, the key features are that the momentum and the energy of both objects are conserved before and after the impact. This condition allows you to derive their movement behavior.

Direct Central Impact

The direct central impact is the simplest case of a collision. Here, two objects move directly toward each other and have a frontal collision; that is, they hit each other along their line of movement as shown in Figure 13.5 (left). Imagine this scenario for the frontal collision of two objects A and B, which have the velocities *va* and *vb* along the lines of movement and the masses *ma* and *mb*. The velocities after the

collision are given as $va = \dfrac{(ma - mb) \cdot va + 2 \cdot mb \cdot vb}{ma + mb}$ and $vb = \dfrac{(mb - ma) \cdot vb + 2 \cdot ma \cdot va}{mb + ma}$.

These equations simplify a great deal when both objects have the same mass— *ma=mb*. Then, *va = vb* and *vb = va*. Now, the velocities of both objects are simply exchanged during the collision.

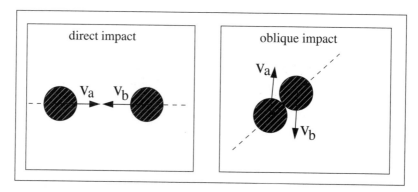

FIGURE 13.5   The left figure shows the direct central impact with velocities along the line of impact (dashed line). The right figure shows the oblique central impact where the velocities are not parallel to the line of impact.

Oblique Central Impact

Although the direct central impact is very easy to calculate, it is not the normal case in a game. It is far more likely that the two objects have different movement directions, but just happen to hit at some point in space. This behavior leads to the oblique central impact as depicted on the right in Figure 13.5.

Fortunately, the equations of the direct central impact can be directly transferred to the oblique central impact. This is performed by decomposing the movement of the objects into a movement that is parallel to the line of impact, and another that is perpendicular to the line of impact. This form of decomposition is depicted in Figure 13.6. Once this is achieved, the perpendicular velocities can be ignored because they are not changed during the impact. The impact only affects the velocities along the line of collision, and these follow exactly the same equations as described in the direct central impact. The only task remaining now is to split the velocities into the two components parallel and perpendicular to the line of impact.

Let us demonstrate this with an example: object A has the velocity $va=(1.0, 2.0)$, and object B has the velocity $vb=(-1.0,-3.0)$. For the sake of simplicity, both objects will have the same mass. The objects should be circles with diameter one, and the collision will occur on the x-axis, right at the coordinate system origin. The line of impact is then the x-axis, and thus the velocity components along the x-axis are the $vax = 1.0$ and $vbx = -1.0$. According to our previous equations, these components are exchanged while the perpendicular velocities stay constant, so the final velocities are $va=(-1.0, 2.0)$ and $vb=(1.0,-3.0)$.

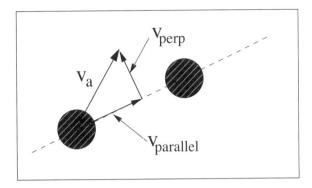

FIGURE 13.6 The velocity of the object A (v) is decomposed into one component parallel ($v_{parallel}$) to the line of impact, and one component perpendicular (v_{perp}) to the line of impact. The same decomposition is done with object B but is not depicted here.

Impact at a Wall

The collision of an object with a wall can be seen as a special case of an impact situation since one object, the wall, has an infinite mass and zero velocity. Using the impact equations, this situation results in a reversal of the velocity component perpendicular to the wall.

Using the same parameters as those in the previous example, object A with velocity $va=(1.0,2.0)$ hits a wall, which is along the y-axis. Afterward, the impact object A will have the velocity $va=(-1.0,2.0)$, and thus a reversed x-velocity.

RANDOM NUMBERS

Random numbers and their generation are an important task in computer games. Most games need a certain amount of randomness to generate an interesting game play. In games such as dice games or games in which you shuffle cards, the use of randomness is obvious. In other games, the behavior of the AI or the creation and appearance of opponents has a random component. Additionally, in many games, there are probability elements that directly relate to randomness; for example, a player has a 73% chance of hitting an opponent. This can be implemented by drawing a random number in the range [0...100] and checking whether it is above or below 73.

In most game programming, you will find a high demand for random numbers. However, strictly speaking, it is impossible to have true randomness for a computer program, which is an algorithm that runs in a fully determined way.

Using the same input, a program or algorithm will always create exactly the same output, which is no different for any algorithm creating random numbers. Therefore, computer-generated random numbers are never truly random, and so are termed *pseudo-random* numbers instead. Note that the only sources for true randomness are some physical processes in the realms of quantum mechanics, such as the decay of an atom or the noise generated in some electrical elements.

In most computer programs, including computer games, the generation of randomness is done in a different way. First, an algorithm is devised that generates a sequence of numbers. This sequence should be hard to predict, nonrepeatable during the runtime of the program, and the numbers should be distributed evenly on a given interval of numbers. If these conditions are fulfilled, the sequence of numbers will appear random to an observer. Nevertheless, these pseudo-random generators are still a mathematical algorithm, and will generate the same sequence of random numbers each time they are started. Whether this predictability is a problem or a feature depends on the actual application.

Usually, you will want to have different random numbers every time you begin a game, so the players do not always throw the same dice or draw the same cards when the program starts. This can be achieved by initializing the pseudo-random number algorithm with a quantity that differs every time the program is started. Often, the time or the process ID of the program is used for this purpose. On Linux, there is also a special device (`/dev/urandom`) that provides randomness to applications generated from "unpredictable" sources and events on the computer, such as keyboard input or external devices. All these inputs are random enough so that using them as a starting point for a pseudo-random algorithm will create unpredictable random numbers sufficient for the use in game programming.

However, there are two scenarios in which you actually want predictable random numbers; that is, the generated numbers appear random but always occur in the same sequence. Such predictable random numbers are useful when debugging a game because you can repeat the program behavior and possibly bugs, which is then much easier to analyze and correct. Furthermore, another interesting aspect is the possibility to generate actual game data by such predictable random numbers. Creating the same random sequence every time the program runs allows the generation of a game world that appears random, can be arbitrarily huge, and can still be recreated every time the program starts. Many years ago on computers with extremely limited memory, the *Elite*™ game used such an algorithm to create a basically endless universe. In that game, an arbitrary number of planets and star systems were generated and included traders and shops with a virtually endless amount of goods and prices.

Random Numbers in Qt and KDE

In C++ and Qt, random numbers can be obtained from the C Standard Library. To initialize the random sequence, a seed value can be set using

```
#include <stdlib.h>

// Choose any seed, here for example the value 10
unsigned int seed = 10;

// OR chose the seed from the current time
QTime t = QTime::currentTime();
unsigned int seed = t.second() +
                    60 * t.minute() +
                    3600 * t.hour();

// Use the seed as starting point for the random algorithm
srand(seed);
```

and random numbers can be obtained by the rand() function.

```
// Create a random number between 0..RAND_MAX
int rnd = rand();

// Create a random number between 0..200
int rnd = rand() % 200;

// Create a double random number between 0.0 .. 1.0
double rnd = (double)rand()/(double)RAND_MAX;
```

A fixed seed value will reproduce the sequence of random numbers. A varying random sequence is achieved by using the time or process ID or any other quantity varying when the program starts at the seed value.

KDE offers a random number system that is automatically initialized by system quantities such as the time, the process ID, or the random device /dev/urandom when available.

```
// "Truly random" random number
int rnd = KApplication::random();
```

A random number obtained with KApplication::random() is also a good source for a seed value for the class KRandomSequence (see Chapter 3, "Game Development Using KDE"). Using KRandomSequence instead of random() has two advantages. First, the class `KRandomSequence` offers a more convenient and faster method to access the random numbers.

```
KRandomSequence random;

// Get a integer random number between 0..max
int rnd = random.getLong(max);

// Get a double random number between 0.0 .. 1.0
double r2 = random.getDouble();
...
```

Second, it can be initialized with a seed value. Therefore, for game testing, this seed value can be set to a constant, and thus the same random sequence is reproduced for each game run. For the release version of the game, the seed is taken from `KApplication::random()` and a random game is generated.

Advanced Random Number Generators

In some special cases, you might want to program your own random number algorithm instead of using the system libraries of C or KDE. This might be the case if you construct your game data or game world from predictable random numbers. It is then possible that you do not want your game world to change if the implementation of the `rand()` function or the KDE library changes, and thus different random numbers are created. Note, however, that for desktop computer games, the reason for implementing your own algorithm is seldom the need for higher quality random numbers. This is only necessary if an application really requires a high degree of randomness such as cryptography.

There are several algorithms available for the generation of pseudo-random numbers. Linear congruential generators (LCG) are one of the most commonly used random generators. They generate a sequence of random numbers $r(n)$ as

```
r(n+1) = (a * r(n) + b) % m;
```

Although LCGs do not generate exceedingly high-quality random numbers, they are more than sufficient for most game applications. However, the quality of the random numbers depends on the choice of the parameters. The book *Numerical Recipes in C* [Press92] suggests the following parameters

```
a = 1664525;
b = 1013904223;
m = 2^32;
```

to create good random numbers. Note that with this choice of parameters and using 32-bit integer numbers, the modulo m can be omitted from the algorithm.

Another good alternative for a pseudo-random number algorithm is the Mersenne twister algorithm [Matsumoto98]. This is a fast algorithm that generates high-quality random numbers. The source code of the algorithm is available as open source at the Web site [Matsumoto05].

SUMMARY

Mathematical transformations are an important ingredient of games. Even if the game itself does not need many transformations, the game graphics usually will. In this chapter, we presented some basic mathematical concepts and the most useful transformations required to achieve good desktop games. These transformations can be applied to either a single game object or entire graphical images. Both types of transformations are inherently supported by the Qt library using the class QWMatrix, which defines 2D matrix operations.

Transformations in 3D are similar to the transformations in 2D except for 3D rotations. In 3D, a rotation can be around an arbitrary axis, resulting in a more complicated rotation matrix. Nevertheless, especially in OpenGL programming, 3D transformations are a key ingredient.

If the objects in a game are to move in a realistic fashion, they need to obey some basic physical formulas; if they do not, a movement on the screen will look unnatural or odd to a player. Nowadays, not only flight simulators rely on physically correct environment modeling. More and more modern computer games incorporate an increasingly realistic physical behavior into their game world, resulting in sophisticated physics engines.

Although desktop games usually do not require such elaborate physical treatment, even here some basic physical laws need to be followed. This particularly applies to the application of forces such as engine forces or friction, and collisions between objects. Both lead to a change in the movement trajectory of the game object, which needs to be accurately calculated. Pinball or billiard games are good examples of games in which real-world physics needs to be simulated, even in desktop games.

In addition to these aforementioned aspects, we provided an overview on some of the other useful movement concepts such as constant velocity or accelerated movements, and special movement cases such as orbits or parabolic trajectories.

REFERENCES

[Bourg01] Bourg, David M., *Physics for Game Developers*, ISBN: 0596000065; O'Reilly, 2001.

[Eberly03] Eberly, David H., *Game Physics*, ISBN: 1558607404; Morgan Kaufmann, 2003.

[Matsumoto98] Matsumoto, M., and T. Nishimura, *Mersenne twister: A 623-dimensionally equidistributed uniform pseudorandom number generator, ACM Trans. on Modeling and Computer Simulations*, 1998.

[Matsumoto05] *Mersenne Twister, http://www.math.sci.hiroshima-u.ac.jp/~m-mat/MT/emt.html*, 2005.

[Press92] Press, William H. et al., *Numerical Recipes in C: The Art of Scientific Computing*, ISBN: 0521431085; Cambridge University Press, 1992.

14 Qt Network Games

In This Chapter

- Internet Transport Protocols
- Networking with Qt
- Synchronization

Nowadays, multiplayer games are becoming increasingly popular [Topology05]. Many people like to play with and against other human players. These types of multiplayer features are best provided through networks; consequently, networking is now an important aspect of many games. The Internet has developed into the most important network, and therefore protocols used on the Internet such as TCP and UDP have become the primary options for game developers.

In this chapter, we present two different networking architectures: the client-server model and the peer-to-peer model. Both architectures can be implemented using the Qt and KDE network features. During the second part, there is a brief summary on the TCP and UDP protocols, accompanied by a practical presentation on how to implement a TCP network with Qt using the `QSocket`/`QServerSocket` pair.

Multiplayer games usually follow one of two main structures. The first and more commonly used configuration is the client-server architecture. Here, one program acts as the game server and handles the complete game flow and control. Players then connect to the game server using a game client, which may or may not be the same program.

The game server runs the actual main game program and sends out the game data to all game clients. A client that then receives the actual game situation from the server displays it to the local player on the computer screen. Apart from forwarding the input of the local player to the server, the client does not affect the game flow. A typical client-server network architecture is depicted in Figure 14.1.

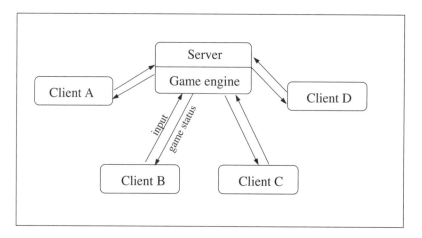

FIGURE 14.1   Network game: client-server architecture.

The advantages of this concept are a high amount of data integrity and security. All calculations are made by only one program, and except for network lags, very few synchronization problems are involved in the game. In principle, cheating by the players is also much harder since the server has control over the game. However, even with this scenario, it is not always possible for the game server to have full control over the game. Many of the popular games suffer from cheat programs, which either manipulate the client to reveal more information than the player should have, or employ programs that can produce a superior game input by automatically analyzing the current situation (e.g., automatically fire on approaching enemies).

A second approach for a network game architecture originates from cluster programming. With this structure, a program is split into many parts that are run on many different computers. All these parts have to communicate with each other. This architecture allows you to balance the calculation load equally on many computers. However, the disadvantage here, especially for games, is that the synchronization of the program race conditions is much harder to achieve (see the section "Synchronization"). This form of network architecture is called a peer-to-peer network and is depicted in Figure 14.2.

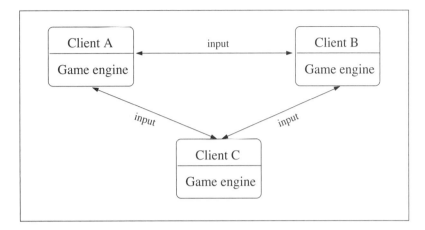

FIGURE 14.2   Network game: peer-to-peer architecture.

For network computer games, usually one computer acts as the coordinator or administrator and thus initiates and supervises the game. However, each of the participating peers can become the role of the coordinator, and this can even change at runtime.

The scenario that you choose depends mainly on your requirements. The client-server architecture is usually less convenient for the player, because in addition to running the client program, it is also required to start and host a server program. These criteria may make the game inconvenient for the player, especially when the game should also be played in single-player mode. However, client-server network games are more easily implemented and controlled, and provide better cheating prevention.

INTERNET TRANSPORT PROTOCOLS

Two main transport protocols can be used for Internet games. The first and most widely used protocol is the Transmission Control Protocol (TCP), and the other is the User Datagram Protocol (UDP). Generally, UDP is very unreliable, because in contrast to TCP, it does not guarantee the arrival of any sent data. Although you might consider UDP useless, it is still important in the field of multimedia or Internet games since it possesses much less latency than TCP does. However, for normal desktop games, TCP is usually the better choice.

TCP

TCP is the most important protocol used on the Internet. The TCP protocol provides several services that are important to network applications, including:

- A connection between two computers
- The transfer of data over the connection
- Dividing application data into packages on sending and reintegrating them on receiving
- Ensuring that all data packages arrive, and in the correct order

When employing TCP, the first step is to establish a connection with another computer to send data between them. The data sent is guaranteed to arrive correctly or not at all (lost connection). This is the reason why TCP is called a "reliable" transport protocol.

Even though the reliability of TCP is one of its most important features, it is simultaneously its greatest disadvantage. The requirement to ensure that all data is delivered and in the correct order without duplicates makes it necessary to add a certain latency to the transport protocol, which makes TCP unusable for applications that require low latency. Consequently, multimedia applications and some games still prefer UDP to TCP. However, for desktop games, the latency problem is not really an issue, and therefore TCP is clearly the better choice.

UDP

In contrast to TCP, UDP is a connectionless protocol. Data is "just sent" from one computer to another and one hopes that it arrives. As a result, it is an unreliable protocol, meaning that there is little or no effort to ensure that the sent data actually arrives. The protocol also does not inform you whether any data has arrived on the other side. It is even possible that data packages ("datagrams") arrive in the wrong order, and all these problems must be handled by the application. Reliability is not a crucial feature for some applications such as videoconferencing in which a few dropped frames do not alter its overall usefulness. The same principle applies to some games. For example, in a first-person shooter game, dropping a single move of a player may be an acceptable unreliability, as the game can recover from the drop using the information of one of the subsequent moves.

Since UDP does not provide any reliability, it does not require the overhead necessary for TCP. Concerning games, the most important result is that UDP has a very low latency. The latency originates only from the underlying network and not from the protocol. However, the price for this advantage is not having any reliability, which diminishes the application of the protocol for desktop games.

NETWORKING WITH QT

Qt provides several classes for networking. For TCP-based connections, QSocket and QServerSocket are available, where QSocket implements the actual TCP connections, and QServerSocket provides a TCP-based server. This server allows remote applications to connect to the server using a QSocket, for example. If you were to apply UDP, the QSocketDevice class must be used directly. Qt 4 provides true support for UDP in the class QUdpSocket.

For desktop games, TCP is usually the most appropriate choice, and we will therefore concentrate on building a network connection using TCP. Usually, when using the KGame framework (see Chapter 15, "The KGame Library"), you do not have to directly use either connection model, since this is done automatically. However, for a Qt-based game or a game that does not use the KGame framework, you will need to implement the network connection using the sockets yourself.

Listening to Connections

TCP is connection based; therefore, one computer must have some type of server running that is listening for new connections. This type of server is implemented using QServerSocket and is very easy to use; all you need to do is subclass QServerSocket and re-implement newConnection() so new incoming connections can be handled.

```
class MyServer : public QServerSocket
{
  Q_OBJECT

  public:
    MyServer(Q_UINT16 port, QObject* parent = 0)
          : QServerSocket(port, 1, parent)
    {
    }

    // Notifies that a new connection has arrived
    virtual void newConnection(int socket);

  signals:
    void clientConnected(QSocket*);
};
```

Now, re-implement the newConnection() method to create a QSocket for the new connection.

```
void MyServer::newConnection(int socket)
{
  QSocket* s = new QSocket();
  s->setSocket(socket);

  // Tell the outside world about this connection
  emit clientConnected(s);
}
```

This simple example implements a server that emits a signal whenever a new client connects. The QSocket object provided by the signal can be used to control the connection.

Such a server can be started easily in any program.

```
// The port that the server listens to:
// in this case just an arbitrary number > 1024
int port = 8459;
mMyServer = new MyServer(port);
if (!mMyServer->ok())
{
  // Error: could not listen on the specified port
  delete mMyServer;
  mMyServer = 0;
  return;
}

// Handle new connections
connect(mMyServer, SIGNAL(clientConnected(QSocket*)),
        this, SLOT(establishCommunication(QSocket*)));
```

The establishCommunication() slot used in the previous example should store the QSocket pointer somewhere in the program, so it is able to communicate with the other computer. In addition, you need to connect to the signals of this QSocket in the same way the client does.

Once the connection has been established, the two computers can communicate to each other in an analogous manner; that is, the server can talk to the client the same way the client talks to the server. Therefore, for the remainder of this chapter we will only discuss the side of the client, since the server works the same.

In Qt 4, the class QServerSocket has been replaced by QTcpServer. This class does not need to be subclassed anymore; instead, it emits the signal newConnection(), to which you can connect. There, a corresponding QTcpSocket object for the connection can be retrieved by calling QTcpServer::nextPendingConnection(); the server automatically handles the deletion of this object.

Connecting to a Server

Before a client can communicate to a server, it must first connect to the server. The most simplistic way is to create a new QSocket object and call connectToHost() on that object, which will then try to build the connection to the host. QSocket is non-blocking, which means all its methods return immediately without waiting for the initiated action to be completed. Therefore, when connectToHost() returns, the socket is not yet connected. Instead, QSocket emits several signals that indicate an action has been completed. The signal connected() signifies that the connection has been successfully established, whereas the signal error() indicates failure.

In the following example, the connection to another host is demonstrated. In addition to connected() and error(), we also connect the signals readyRead() and connectionClosed() to the QSocket. These signals are used once the connection has been established, and respectively control the reading from the socket and react to an ended connection.

```
mSocket = new QSocket(this);

// Signal indicating successful connection
connect(mSocket, SIGNAL(connected()),
        this, SLOT(connected()));

// Signal indicating a connection error:
// we treat it like a closed connection
connect(mSocket, SIGNAL(error(int)),
        this, SLOT(connectionClosed()));

// Signal indicating that the connection has been closed
connect(mSocket, SIGNAL(connectionClosed()),
        this, SLOT(connectionClosed()));

// Signal indicating that new data can be read from the socket
connect(mSocket, SIGNAL(readyRead()),
        this, SLOT(readDataFromSocket()));

// The host we connect to. In this case an IP address in a
// local network: internet names (like "www.kde.org" or
// "localhost") are also valid
QString host = "192.168.1.1";

// The port that we connect to: there must be a server
// listening on that port on the other computer
Q_UINT16 port = 8459;
```

```
// Actually connect to the host
mSocket->connectToHost(host, port);
```

As soon as the signal `connected()` has been emitted—that is, once the slot `connected()` has been called—the connection is up and ready for use.

In Qt 4, the `QSocket` class has been replaced by the `QTcpSocket` class. The example code remains working with that class, except for the signal `connectionClosed()`, which needs to be replaced by the signal `closed()`.

Exchanging Data

When a connection has been successfully established, the data can be easily sent through this connection using `QSocket::writeBlock()` (`QTcpSocket::write()` in Qt 4). Usually, this method is used in conjunction with either `QByteArray` or `QString` as argument. Both possibilities are shown in the following example:

```
QByteArray array;

// Write data into the empty QByteArray
QDataStream stream(data, IO_WriteOnly);
stream << QString("a string");

// Send the QByteArray
mSocket->writeBlock(array.data(), array.size());

// Send a QString
QString string = "another string";
mSocket->writeBlock(string.latin1(), string.length());
```

Receiving data, however, is not so easy. When data arrives and is read from the socket, the signal `readyRead()` is emitted. At this point, it is not guaranteed that all the data has been completely received; therefore, we need some way to find out when the data ends. A simple solution is to use line-based communication, which finishes every sending with an \n. When you have ensured this rule in your program, a `readDataFromSocket()` slot connected to the `readyRead()` signal of `QSocket` can be implemented like this:

```
void MyClient::readDataFromSocket()
{
  // Check whether a full line is available
  while (mSocket->canReadLine())
  {
    // Read the line
```

```
      QString line = mSocket->readLine();
      QString s = QString("line read: %1").arg(line);
      ...
   }
}
```

This algorithm will only read data when a complete line is received, and will continue reading data until no lines remain. The advantage of this algorithm is that it is very easy to understand and implement. However, it requires the program to ensure that every message is ended with a newline character, and when receiving the data, you need to read line by line. This can become inconvenient when working with binary data, for example.

To use arbitrary data, a more complicated algorithm is required, which requires the introduction of a header into our messages. Every message that is sent to the socket starts with a header containing

1. A magic cookie
2. The size of the data

The magic cookie is (for example) a single character, which is arbitrary but must be the same all over your program. The intention of this magic cookie is to reduce the likelihood that invalid data is read. The size of the data is simply the number of bytes of the following data (that is, without the header). The size is an unsigned integer and therefore 4 bytes, which makes the header 5 bytes. Note that this header is just one of many possibilities. The magic cookie, for example, is intended to find bugs in our network code, but it is not strictly necessary.

For reading both the data and the header, we need two new variables in the class.

```
bool mWaitForHeader;
Q_UINT32 mMessageSize;
```

The mWaitForHeader flag specifies whether the next data is supposed to be a header or the actual message. The mMessageSize variable contains the amount of data that is about to follow, and this is specified by the header. It is important that these variables be reset whenever the connection is lost or before a connection is made.

```
mWaitForHeader = true;
mMessageSize   = 0;
```

Using these variables, the readDataFromSocket() slot can be implemented.

```
// Size of the header.
// This is magic cookie (1 byte) + data length (4 byte)
#define SIZE_OF_HEADER 5

void MyClient::readDataFromSocket()
{
  // Stream the data from the socket
  // (instead of using QSocket::readBlock() manually)
  QDataStream stream(mSocket);
  if (mWaitForHeader)
  {
    Q_INT8 m;
    if (mSocket->bytesAvailable() < SIZE_OF_HEADER)
    {
      // Header incomplete. wait for more data.
      return;
    }

    // Read the cookie
    stream >> m;
    if (m != MAGIC_COOKIE)
    {
      qDebug("read error: Magic cookie mismatch");
      return;
    }
    // Read the size of the following message
    stream >> mMessageSize;
    mWaitForHeader = false;
  }
  ...
```

This half of the method only reads the header. If less than SIZE_OF_HEADER (5) bytes are available, not even the header of the message has arrived completely, so we cannot do anything except wait. Next, the magic cookie and the message size are read, and finally the mWaitForHeader flag is set to false. Once this point is reached, the actual data reading can begin.

```
// readDataFromSocket() continued:
...
if (mSocket->bytesAvailable() < mMessageSize)
{
  // Message still incomplete. wait for more data
  return;
}
```

```
    // Complete message available, now we can read it from
    // the stream
    stream >> ...;

    // The next message will again start with a header,
    // so reset the flag
    mWaitForHeader = true;
    mMessageSize   = 0;
}
```

When the complete message has arrived, it can be read from the socket. This can be done using the stream as suggested in the example, or alternatively by direct use of the `QSocket::readBlock()` method. Remember to reset the `mWaitForHeader` flag to `true`, and optionally reset the `mMessageSize` variable. Otherwise, the next message will be read as invalid.

Ending Connections

A connection can be easily closed by either side calling `QSocket::close()` or simply deleting the socket object, which in turn will notify the other side about the closed connection via the `connectionClosed()` signal. However, a connection may also be ended unintentionally through a broken network, for instance; in that case, the signal `QSocket::error()` is emitted.

As an aside, it is often beneficial to connect both signals to a `connectionClosed()` slot to tidy everything up. At the very least, you should delete the socket object on that computer.

SYNCHRONIZATION

When supporting network play, a game has to make sure the clients are always in sync. By this, we mean that at any moment, all the items relevant to the game are the same on all clients. Note, however, that "at any moment" refers to an abstract time in the game, such as game ticks (see Chapter 1, "Introduction to Desktop Gaming") and not necessarily real time.

This synchronization is usually easy to achieve with turn-based games. However, even then, it is necessary to ensure that if it's one player's turn, only that player can move. Otherwise, you can easily have the same problems as in non-turn-based games.

In non-turn-based games, it is of utmost importance to ensure that all messages are received by all clients in the correct order. As an example, imagine a game in which a game unit has 10 hit points (HP) and is destroyed if it reaches zero HP or less. The two players in the game try to do different things to the unit:

- Player A repairs this unit by giving it 10 HP.
- Player B attacks the unit subtracting 15 HP.

In this scenario, a race condition occurs because it depends on whose action is performed first:

Action of Player A first: The unit is first healed (10 + 10 = 20 HP) and then damaged (20 − 15 = 5 HP).

Action of Player B first: The unit is first damaged and destroyed (10 − 15 = −5 HP). The action of Player A cannot be performed any more.

This scenario is depicted in Figure 14.3. This condition is very natural in a non-turn-based game and can develop into a real problem if one scenario is performed on one client and the other scenario on the other client. In a network game, it is very likely that such situations occur, as the actions of the players must be sent over the network to each other. However, each player can instantaneously send a message to himself; that is, without a network.

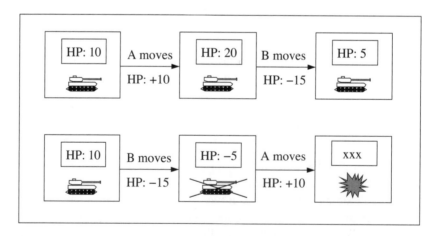

FIGURE 14.3   Race condition of a network game in which two players act on the same unit. Player A tries to repair the unit, and player B attacks it. Depending on which move is executed first, the result can be either a destroyed unit or a live one.

An obvious solution to this would be to make sure a client sending a message does not receive that message immediately, but in a strictly defined order instead.

For example, one client could be declared the "master" of the game, and all messages must be sent to it. This master then forwards all the messages to their final destination and automatically ensures that the messages are in the correct order.

When a pure client-server architecture is used, keeping the clients in sync is easier. This is because the server does the actual calculations alone and therefore cannot be out of sync since a client cannot get out of sync with itself. However, it still is possible that the network latency becomes so large that clients keep sending moves for a game situation that does not exist anymore, simply because they do not know that the situation has changed. Therefore, the server should be bulletproof concerning invalid moves.

In a peer-to-peer environment, keeping all the clients in sync can be very difficult, even if there is one master client that ensures the correct order of the messages. Since all clients do their own calculations of the game, it is necessary that at any time they do exactly the same calculations concerning game relevant calculations. If there is a small bug somewhere in the code, the clients can quickly become out of sync. This can even happen when using floating-point calculations on different processors [Dickinson01].

When two clients do become out of sync, they need to be either synchronized again or the game must be ended. A very easy implementation of synchronization would be to simply save the entire game to a stream on one client and then load that game on all other clients. An improvement to that solution would be to save and load only parts of the game, and ideally, those parts identified to be out of sync. These synchronization problems are difficult to handle and can be observed even in large commercial games. Occasionally, players end up playing different games without ever noticing, and a different player is then the winner on all clients.

SUMMARY

In this chapter, we described the two principal concepts used to implement network games. The client-server model has only one server computer that is responsible for all game calculations, but can have numerous clients that receive data. Alternatively, in the peer-to-peer concept, all clients do all the calculations themselves. Even though the client-server concept is more widely used, both models have advantages and disadvantages.

Problems particularly critical to desktop games include the fact that the client-server model requires a server to be started somewhere, either on one of the players' computers or a public host. In addition, this server needs to be known to other players. The peer-to-peer concept does not require such a server, but may prevent users who are behind a firewall from playing the game, since it usually requires that incoming connections be accepted.

Synchronization is harder to achieve in a peer-to-peer network than in a client-server network architecture. However, when a game is turn-based, synchronization is generally easier to achieve because there are natural synchronization steps at each move. Desktop games that are turn-based can therefore easily opt for both scenarios, while non turn-based games are more easily implemented with a client-server architecture.

Whichever concept is chosen, the game must use either TCP or UDP to support Internet gaming. UDP has advantages, especially concerning its extremely low latency. However, for desktop games, TCP is the preferred choice because it provides a reliable connection. Based on that choice, the `QSocket` and `QServerSocket` classes can be used to implement a nonblocking network game.

REFERENCES

[Dickinson01] Dickinson, Patrick, *Instant Replay: Building a Game Engine with Reproducible Behavior*, *http://www.gamasutra.com/features/20010713/dickinson_01.htm*, 2001.

[Topology05] *Network Topology, http://www.gamasutra.com/features/19970905/ng_01.htm*, 2005.

15

The KGame Library

The KGame library is an object-oriented gaming framework that is part of the KDE library libkdegames. It provides central, and often used, game functions in an object-oriented way, which makes it much easier to develop a desktop game because it allows you to concentrate on the actual game issues rather than the nitty-gritty details that arise during network programming.

KGame supports the writing of desktop games in various ways:

- It offers a neatly designed representation of a game, following the document-view-player-input model.
- It contains all support features necessary for networking, intended to be used primarily with the peer-to-peer concept.
- It provides support for computer players.
- It includes configuration, debug, and chat dialogs.
- It inherently enables an application to load and save games.

433

By using the KGame library, the programmer can concentrate on the actual game design instead of reinventing these standard game functions. The KGame library is added to your program by simply providing a -lkdegames to the linker.

ON THE CD In this chapter, we introduce the KGame library by first providing an overview of its architecture and then individually explaining the main classes necessary to set up a KGame-based desktop game. The program mykgame on the companion CD-ROM in the folder examples/mykgame implements an example game using the KGame framework.

THE ARCHITECTURE

The KGame library follows the document-view-player-input model as discussed in Chapter 1, "Introduction to Desktop Gaming," and depicted in Figure 15.1. By using the KGame architecture, a good design for most desktop network desktop games is automatically achieved. However, the KGame framework represents only the document-player-input side of this model, because a view is game dependent. As an example, in a canvas-based game, you may subclass KGame for your document and store the canvas in this object so the game flow can be controlled by the document class. However, the canvas view should be stored and managed by the main window of the application; that is, by the view.

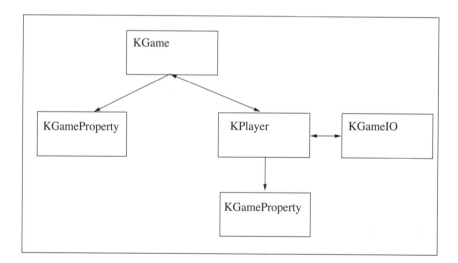

FIGURE 15.1   The KGame architecture.

The main classes of the KGame framework as depicted in Figure 15.1 are:

KGame: This class represents the game document. It manages the actual game and the players. Additionally, it provides support for networking and controls the game flow.

KPlayer: This player class stores the properties of a player. No input is performed by objects of this class; instead, this is managed by the IO classes. Properties of the player may include its name, score, health, and so forth.

KGameIO: This is the base class of all input classes. Every player can have input devices attached that determine how the player is controlled. For example, a human player can have a mouse and a keyboard input.

KGameProperty: The properties of a game should be implemented using this class. By using the KGameProperty objects instead of normal variables, the properties are automatically saved and loaded, so save game files and network games become easier.

THE GAME DOCUMENT

In the KGame framework, the game document class is represented by the KGame class. It contains all the relevant game data such as the game board or the maps. Furthermore, it handles the game, the move logic, and all the players. To implement the game document, the class KGame should be subclassed, and all relevant methods must be re-implemented.

```
class MyGame : public KGame
{
  Q_OBJECT

  public:
    // The GAME_COOKIE is a unique number identifying the game
    MyGame(QObject* parent)
      : KGame(GAME_COOKIE, parent)
    {
      ...
    }

    // Player handling
    virtual KPlayer* createPlayer(int rtti,
                                  int io,
                                  bool isVirtual);
```

```
    protected:
      // Player input
      virtual bool playerInput(QDataStream& msg,
                               KPlayer* player);
  };
```

Player Creation

Players are represented by the class KPlayer (see Figure 15.1) and are supposed to store all data relevant for a player. The player and thus the player data are associated to the game data via the KGame object. Due to the network features of KGame, the library must be able to automatically create new players when necessary, which should occur, for example, when a new client connects. The players from this new client are then automatically added to the current game, but are considered "virtual" players because they originate from the remote client and mirror its players.

Player creation is performed by calling the virtual method createPlayer(). This method needs to be implemented by your specific implementation to create an object of the correct player class. The player that needs to be created is identified by the rtti parameter. In the context of this book, we implement a single player class only, so using this parameter is not required even though the design of KGame allows you to implement more than one player class. The io parameter specifies which IO devices should be created for this player. If the player is a virtual player, it must not have any input devices because it will receive its input from the network; that is, from the input of the client from which this player originates.

A player creation is shown in the following code snippet:

```
KPlayer* MyGame::createPlayer(int, int io, bool isVirtual)
{
  // Create a player object: Use your own player class
  // instead of KPlayer if you subclass it
  KPlayer* player = new KPlayer();
  if (!isVirtual)
  {
    // Define something like this to add the IO modules
    createIO(player, (KGameIO::IOMode)io);
  }
  return player;
}
```

The KGame game class offers the possibility to add and remove players to the game, which is done, of course, in a network-transparent way. A player is added via

```
addPlayer(KPlayer* player);
```

and removed via

```
removePlayer(KPlayer* player);
```

Player Input

Handling input in a more generalized fashion is important for a game because it can receive input from a mouse, keyboard, joystick, computer players, or even a network connection. In essence, it makes the game more independent of the actual input scheme if all input is handled by one central input method. This input from a player is done with input device objects that in turn are connected to a player object (see Figure 15.1). A player can have an arbitrary number of these input devices.

This central treatment of all input is performed by the KGame method playerInput(). This method is called as soon as any input to the game is received. Its parameter is a data stream object that contains information about the move (the input) and the player object that created the input. The format of the data stream is up to the programmer and will be filled in the input device code, which is described later. Here, we assume that the data stream contains the x and y position of a move in an integer format.

```
bool playerInput (QDataStream& msg, KPlayer* player)
{
  // Platform independent integer variables
  Q_INT32 x,y;
  // Read the input into x and y
  msg >> x >> y;

  // Do something useful
  ...
}
```

Note that to be platform independent, it is recommended to use the Qt data types Q_INT32 (integer), Q_UINT32 (unsigned integer) instead of the normal C++ types.

This code is enough to read the player input that could arise from the network, the mouse, or a computer player. Of course, after receiving the information, you need to do something useful such as moving the player's vehicle to the specified coordinates.

Random Numbers

When using the peer-to-peer concept of equal clients instead of a server-client architecture (see Chapter 14, "Qt Network Games"), there is one important thing to notice about the use of random numbers: it has to be guaranteed that the random numbers are the same on all game clients. Only then can you rely on consistency in all clients. To support network consistent random numbers, the KGame class provides the method

```
KRandomSequence* random() const;
```

which returns a pointer to a KRandomSequence object. This random number generator is synchronized over the network and provides the same random number sequences to all clients.

Turn-Based Games

KGame provides special support for turn-based games, including the automatic selection of a new player after the current player has had its turn. By default, all players are called after one another and start again with the first player after the last player has moved. When a more complicated turn sequence is necessary, it can be implemented by overwriting the

```
// Last: The player who made the last turn
// Exclusive: Disable the input of all other players
KPlayer* nextPlayer(KPlayer* last, bool exclusive);
```

method. This method indicates which player has the next turn by returning the corresponding player object.

Important for a game is, of course, to detect whether the game is over and whether one of the players won the game. To do so, the KGame class offers the method

```
// Last: The player who made the last turn
int checkGameOver(KPlayer* last);
```

which returns a nonzero value if the game is over. If a game over is detected, the signal

```
void signalGameOver(int status, KPlayer* last, KGame* game)
```

is emitted. The first argument status is the returned value provided by the checkGameOver() method. Connecting to this signal allows all objects—for example, the main window—to react in an event-driven way to the end of the game. Moreover, the internal status of the game is automatically set to End so player input is no longer accepted.

Note that the methods `nextPlayer()` and `checkGameOver()` can be re-implemented in a `KGameSequence` object, which is then stored in the game object using `KGame::setGameSequence()`. By doing so, the implementation of the game class can be kept shorter and more readable.

THE PLAYER CLASS

A player object can be either an instance of the `KPlayer` class or a subclass of `KPlayer`. It is often useful to subclass the `KPlayer` class to store additional properties for the player. However, in contrast to the `KGame` class, this step is not essential.

Note that when adding properties to the player object, the `KGame` property system can be used. These properties are then automatically saved to and loaded from a save game file. In addition, they are automatically transmitted over the network to a connecting client.

A player in a game is represented by an object of a player class. Different *types* of players are represented by different player classes. Therefore, in most desktop games it is not required to implement different player classes. For example, in a chess game, you have two players, but only one type of player; therefore, one player class with two instances of this class is sufficient. However, the players are often distinguished by using different input devices (one player uses the mouse, and the other uses the keyboard).

`KPlayer` includes the methods `id()` and `userId()`, which must not be confused. The `id()` of a player is automatically set by the game object and is an internal administrative "name" of the player. In contrast, the `userId()` of the player can be used freely by the actual game application because it is not touched by the game library. The `userId()` should be used to identify the different instances of players in the same class. An example here could be a game of chess in which player *white* gets `userId` *1*, and player *black* gets `userId` *2*.

It is important for players to know when they are allowed to make input. In a turn-based game, only one player is allowed to make its input at any one time, whereas in non-turn-based games, all players can make an input continuously. The `KPlayer::setAsyncInput()` method is used to distinguish these two cases, and setting it to `true` allows asynchronous input; that is, input at any time.

INPUT DEVICES

An important feature of the `KGame` framework is the input devices of players. Any `KPlayer` object can store any number of `KGameIO` objects that are primarily responsible for the player input.

The IO devices are the connection of the player to the "outside world." They process the input from the corresponding real-world input devices—for example, the mouse or keyboard—and generate a valid move or input for the player to whom they belong. This move or input is then forwarded to the game object, which uses the `playerInput()` method to integrate the information into the game flow.

The IO device approach has two main advantages. First, the game is independent of the actual input. The game object just "sees" a move forwarded to it, and no distinction needs to be made from which source this move originates. Second, the possibility to have numerous IO devices per player and to exchange them at runtime is very beneficial.

Even computer AI players can be seen as abstract input devices. The reason behind this is that for a game, the input of a computer player is no different from the input from the mouse or the keyboard from a human player. In this respect, it is even possible to exchange a computer player with a human player, and vice versa.

An input device is added to a player using the `KPlayer::addGameIO()` method. Input for this player can then be made via the given device. More than one device can be added to a player, allowing, for example, parallel mouse and keyboard input. Note that only local players must have an IO input device. Network players are commanded via the network. Whether a player is a network player is determined by the *virtual* property of the player. An example from the input device creation might look like

```
if (!player->isVirtual())
{
  // This is a local player - add a IO device
  KGameMouseIO* io = new KGameMouseIO(gameView);
  player->addGameIO(io);
}
```

The preceding example uses the mouse as the input device. `KGame` provides several predefined input devices, and for noncomputer players it is usually sufficient to use these, as no subclassing is required. However, subclassing `KGameIO` to implement a new input device is also possible.

The following code example shows how to use an input device; in this case, a `KGameMouseIO`. We need to create and connect the device.

```
// Create the device
KGameMouseIO* mouse;
mouse = new KGameMouseIO(gameView);

// Connect the processing code to it
connect(input,
```

```
        SIGNAL(signalMouseEvent(KGameIO*,
                QDataStream&,
                QMouseEvent*,
                bool*)),
        gameView,
        SLOT(mouseInput(KGameIO*,
                        QDataStream&,
                        QMouseEvent*,
                        bool*))
    );

// Finally add it to a player
player->addGameIO(mouse);
```

Note that the library will destroy the IO device when the player is destroyed.

All game logic—how to react to mouse input to generate a valid input or move for the game—goes into the processing slot, which is connected to the signal. In this case, the name mouseInput() is chosen. An example for this slot might look like:

```
void MyView::mouseInput(KGameIO* input,
                        QDataStream& stream,
                        QMouseEvent* mouse,
                        bool* processInput)
{
  // Only react to key pressed not released
  if (mouse->type() != QEvent::MouseButtonPress )
  {
    return;
  }

  // Our player
  KPlayer* player = input->player();

  // Create a move
  Q_INT32 x,y;
  x = mouse->pos().x();
  y = mouse->pos().y();

  // And stream it
  // IMPORTANT: This format of the message is what you will
  // get back in the playerInput method of the game. It has
  // to be the same!
  stream << x << y;
```

```
    // Setting the processInput will stop Qt from processing
    // the event from here on additionally this causes KGame
    // to actually send the player input
    *processInput = true;
}
```

In this example, we were only concerned about the *mouse press* events; that is, we ignored other events such as *mouse move* events, which is the normal procedure for desktop games. After all checks are made, a move should be generated using the position of the mouse. Which data is actually put into the move output stream is up to the programmer; the library does not interpret this data, and it will be forwarded "as is" to the game object where it is received in the `playerInput()` method. Finally, the library is signaled that the input was processed by setting the Boolean pointer `*processInput` to `true`. This indicates that the input was handled by the user method. If the slot does not process the input, this return value is set to `false` (the default value).

Tracking is also possible for the mouse input device. When turned on, tracking will produce a continuous stream of input events with the mouse position in them. However, this should only be used when necessary because it produces a high event load.

Other input devices, such as the `KGameKeyIO` device, can be set up in an analogous way to the `KGameMouseIO` device.

COMPUTER PLAYERS

If a game can or should have more players than there are human players available, the computer usually takes over the role of the missing player. Implementing computer players is relatively easy, because the `KGameIO` design already abstracts the player input. Therefore, all we need to do is to use this `KGameIO` class, which is dedicated to computer player input.

There are two different approaches for the implementation of a computer player, and these result from the distinction between event-driven and observing (polling) computer players. In the first category, the computer player remains inactive until a special event happens, and then generates a reaction. For example, the event could be an enemy unit attacking, and the reaction could be to fire on it. The advantage here is that the computer player does not require unnecessary processing time. The disadvantage, however, is that initially a multitude of events needs to be specified and connected to the computer player. Second, there is the observing or polling computer player, which is periodically activated and checks the game to see whether any interaction is required. The main disadvantage here is that the computer player needs to check the entire game on every activation time.

For turn-based desktop games, the distinction between the two possibilities is not that large. The computer player is mainly called when the turn of the game changes. The computer player then calculates a move and is deactivated. This works very well for all types of games, such as card games, board games, and so forth.

Direct and Indirect Computer Players

In the KGame library, computer players are connected to the game via KGameIO objects, because the computer player also generates a form of input to the game. The game does not actually need to know where the input originates. This is particularly advantageous since it allows you to replace computer players with human players, even during runtime. For example, an actively playing human player who goes offline or leaves a game can be seamlessly replaced by a computer player.

The KGame library offers two types of computer players via two different KGameIO classes. The first is implemented in the class KGameComputerIO. This computer player reacts quickly to any query. No long calculations as can occur in a chess game should be done when this type of move is calculated, since the player is directly integrated into the main process of the game, and consequently, long calculations will block the main game and the GUI. The second computer player type, implemented by the class KGameProcessIO, is a player suitable for long calculations. This computer player runs in a separate process and does not block the main program or the GUI. However, this advantage has to be balanced against the additional overhead from the inter-process communication.

The Internal Computer Player

The class KGameComputerIO implements the direct or internal computer player (see Figure 15.2). Some of the basic methods necessary for a computer player are included in this class. However, for practical purposes you should probably overwrite these methods with your own, to implement a more specific computer player.

The KGameComputerIO class has some internal support for an observing computer player, and in comparison to a Qt canvas, an advance period can be set. The advance() method of the player is then periodically called to allow game interaction. After a given amount of advance() calls (the computer player's "reaction" time), the signal signalReaction() is emitted. Connecting to this signal allows a certain game action to be performed. An example would be

```
KGameComputerIO* computer = new KGameComputerIO();

// Call advance() every 50 ms
computer->setAdvancePeriod(50);
```

```
// Connect the reaction signal
connect(computer, SIGNAL(signalReaction()),
        this, SLOT(shoot()));
```

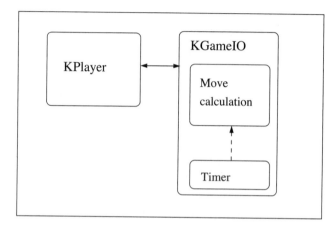

FIGURE 15.2   Direct computer player architecture.

Here, a computer player is created, and both its reaction and advance period are set. After each 50 ms, the slot shoot() is called, and at this point we are allowed to shoot at a target, for example. If the game is based on the Qt canvas class, the setAdvancePeriod() should not be used; instead, the KGameComputerIO::advance() method should be called using the QCanvas::advance() method. In addition, the re-action time of a computer player can be increased. For example, a hard computer player may shoot every 0.5 seconds, whereas an easy player would only shoot every 2 seconds. This can be implemented using the setReactionPeriod() method. The reaction period is given in advance calls so the player automatically adjusts itself to an increased game speed. The use of the reaction period is demonstrated in the following example:

```
KGameComputerIO* hard = new KGameComputerIO();
KGameComputerIO* easy = new KGameComputerIO();

// Call advance() every 50 ms
hard->setAdvancePeriod(50);
easy->setAdvancePeriod(50);

// The hard player emits signalReaction() every 0.5 seconds
// that is every 10 advance() calls
hard->setReactionPeriod(10);
```

```
// The hard player emits signalReaction() every 2 seconds
// that is every 40 advance() calls
easy->setReactionPeriod(40);

// Connect the reaction signal
connect(easy, SIGNAL(signalReaction()),
        this, SLOT(easyPlayerShoot()));
connect(hard, SIGNAL(signalReaction()),
        this, SLOT(hardPlayerShoot()));
```

For an event-driven computer player, the occurring events need to be dispatched to the computer player. For this, you need to subclass the class KGameComputerIO (or, alternatively, KGameIO directly) and connect these methods. The advance() and signalReaction() facilities are no longer needed.

The External Computer Player

The external computer player allows the addition of an external process as input to the game (see Figure 15.3). Long calculations, like those that arise from AI calculations, can now be performed there without blocking the main application. The advantage of using this input device instead of manually designing the process via KProcess is that it can be transparently plugged into the KGame framework.

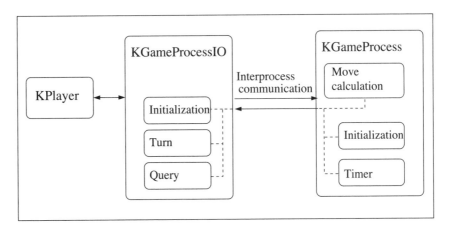

FIGURE 15.3 Indirect computer player architecture.

Since the external computer player is split into two processes, you also need to consider two classes. The IO side is conducted by the KGameProcessIO, and the KGameProcess is available for the external process. Usually, both classes can be employed without making any changes, and do need not be subclassed. When using these classes, the KDE library also takes care of all interprocess communication; therefore, you only need to implement the AI logic.

The `KGameProcessIO` Class

Objects of the `KGameProcessIO` class work like any other `KGameIO` device and are plugged into a `KPlayer`. Upon creation, it starts the external process and connects to it.

```
// Create the external computer player: provide the filename
// of the external process as argument
KGameProcessIO* computer = new KGameProcessIO(filename);
```

The main program can communicate with the external process in several ways. All of them are achieved by signals emitted by the `KGameProcessIO` device, to which you can react. These signals comprise:

`signalIOAdded()`: The input device was added to a player. This can be used to transmit the current game status or initial data to the external process.

`signalPrepareTurn()`: The external process is about to make a turn. This is used to prepare and start the actual calculation.

`signalProcessQuery()`: The external process actively queries the game for information.

All of these signals can be connected in the following manner:

```
connect(input, SIGNAL(signalPrepareTurn(QDataStream&,
                                         bool,
                                         KGameIO*,
                                         bool*)),
            this, SLOT(prepareTurn(QDataStream&,
                                    bool,
                                    KGameIO*,
                                    bool*)));
```

and in all cases, the called slot allows a message to be stored in a `QDataStream`, which is in turn sent to the external process. Furthermore, arbitrary messages can be sent to the external process using the method `sendMessage()`. The message format of all these methods and slots is game specific and thus user defined, and one example for such sending could resemble

```
// Create a QDataStream in a memory buffer: this is only
// necessary for the sendMessage() method, because the slots
```

```
// Already provide a stream as argument
QByteArray buffer;
QDataStream stream(buffer,IO_WriteOnly);

// Stream the actual (arbitrary) data
Q_INT32 number = 15;
stream << number;

// Send the message with an arbitrary ID (222):
// the last two arguments (sender, receiver) are of no
// importance for us
computer->sendMessage(stream, 222, 0, gameId());
```

The KGameProcess Class

The actual external process needs to use the KGameProcess class to establish communication. Usually, this can be done by creating a standard C++ main program, which creates an object of the class KGameProcess. This object then establishes the inter-process communication, and by connecting to the signals, it can react to the game messages. A simple possible main program could then look like

```
int main(int argc, char* argv[])
{
  // Note that all (debug) output must go to stderr
  // as stdout is used for the communication
  fprintf(stderr,"Computer player started\n");
  fflush(stderr);

  // Create the actual computer player which also
  // stores the KGameProcess and execute its event
  // loop
  Computer comp;
  return !comp.proc.exec(argc, argv);
}
```

Besides implementing the actual AI algorithm, the Computer class is a simple class that only needs to contain an object of the KGameProcess class and can then implement slots that are connected to all the signals provided by the KGameProcess. These signals are called in response to incoming messages from the main program, and comprise:

signalInit(): This signal is emitted when the process should be initialized. The data format is user defined.

signalTurn(): This signal is emitted when the computer player should generate a turn. Here, the AI calculation is started. Information sent back here goes directly to the `playerInput()` of the game and must follow the specified format.

signalCommand(): This signal is emitted when a generic message sent via the `sendMessage()` is received.

Note that the data format of all messages is defined solely by you. Consequently, you need to read the same types of data you sent out in the corresponding methods of `KGameProcessIO`.

Messages can be easily retrieved in all of these communication functions. An example of a command slot could look like

```
void Computer::command(int& msgid,
                       QDataStream& in,
                       QDataStream& out)
{
 // Check the message id for 222
 if (msgid == 222)
 {
   // Retrieve send number (15 in our example)
   Q_INT32 number;
   in >> number;
 }
}
```

Information, in particular the resulting moves, can be sent back to the game using `sendSystemMessage()`. In our computer player, the move generation, defined in the turn slot, could look like

```
void Computer::turn(QDataStream& in, bool turn)
{
  // Only react if a turn should be made
  if (!turn) { return; }

  // Prepare the output stream
  QByteArray buffer;
  QDataStream out(buffer, IO_WriteOnly);

  // Prepare an AI move to the field (5,7): note that
  // the format must exactly match your playerInput()
  // format
  Q_INT32 x = 5;
  Q_INT32 y = 7;
```

```
    out << x << y;

    // Send a player input command back to the game
    int id = KGameMessage::IdPlayerInput;
    proc.sendSystemMessage(out, id, 0);
}
```

Note that although the many options, signals, and messages might look frightening at first, this concept of an external computer player actually allows the easy creation of an AI player that resides in a separate process but still communicates via the signal-slot mechanism with the main program. All interprocess communication is automatically done by the library.

NETWORK GAMES

A network is an important ingredient in games these days, and KGame is designed to provide easy support for such networking. By using the KGame features, minimal effort is needed to provide network features to your game, and there are essentially three things necessary to this network support in a KGame-based game:

- Send all player input (all moves) using input devices as discussed in the section "Input Devices"
- Use the KGameProperty class for all game-flow-relevant data
- Connect to the network

Input devices are a central part of the KGame technology, and have already been discussed in this chapter. In this section, we discuss the two remaining items.

Network Properties

In network games, it is often necessary to ensure that some variables, such as the health of the players or the amount of money owned by a player, are exactly the same on all clients participating in the game; otherwise, the clients end up playing different games. The usual approach to this is to send out a network message containing the new value whenever a variable changes. The KGame library provides the template class KGameProperty to simplify this task. It is intended to be used for member variables of classes derived from KGame or KPlayer, as these are usually relevant to the game flow and therefore need to be the same on all clients (but it can also be used for other classes). A KGameProperty variable once initialized can be used like a normal variable, but when its value is changed, it automatically sends its value through the network to all clients. The same happens when a new client joins an already running game: all KGameProperty variables are sent to that client so it can take part in the game with little additional work by the programmer.

Furthermore, KGameProperty variables are saved automatically by KGame::save() and loaded by KGame::load(), so saving and loading games requires essentially no code other than using KGameProperty for all game flow relevant variables.

Every data type that can be streamed using QDataStream can also be used with KGameProperty; therefore, all basic data types such as int, double, and bool can be used directly, as well as Qt data types such as QString. A KGameProperty variable can be declared like any other normal variable.

```
KGameProperty<int> mHealth;
```

However, before use it must be registered to a so-called data handler in the constructor of the class.

```
mHealth.registerData(dataHandler()
                     KGamePropertyBase::PolicyDirty,
                     "health");
```

The dataHandler() method is provided by both KGame and KPlayer, and this is where the game properties are usually required. In other objects, you would need to create an instance of the data handler.

For the policy given as the second parameter, there are three values possible: PolicyDirty, PolicyLocal, and PolicyClean. This flag determines how the network update of a property is performed. A property having PolicyDirty automatically propagates its value to all other clients in the network once it has changed; thus, you do not have to worry about networking. A property with PolicyLocal, however, does not do any automatic networking and behaves like a normal variable. PolicyClean should generally not be used and is marked deprecated for KDE 4. If no policy is specified, PolicyLocal is used by default. Note that no matter which policy you use, a registered property is both saved and loaded by KGame::save() and KGame::load(), respectively. The third parameter to registerData() specifies a name of the property. This free string primarily serves debugging purposes.

As soon as the property has been registered to the handler, it can be used like normal variables.

```
mHealth = 100;
...

if (mHealth < 100)
{
  ...
}
```

Event-Driven Property Games

In addition to loading, saving, and transmitting over the network, properties are able to emit a signal when their values change. This allows the easy implementation of an event-driven game, by building all program events onto changes of the properties. For example, when the health of a player is increased, a widget that displays the health is not directly updated, but reacts instead on the signal that the property mHealth has changed. In this respect, it is also guaranteed that the widget is properly updated when a network change to the property or load game occurs.

For example, listening to a property change of a game object could be performed in the following manner:

```
connect(this, SIGNAL(signalPropertyChanged(KGamePropertyBase*,
                                            KGame*)),
        this, SLOT(propertyChanged(KGamePropertyBase*,
                                   KGame*)));
```

and the accompanying slot would read

```
void MyGame::propertyChanged(KGamePropertyBase* prop,
                             KGame*)
{
 // Find out which variable is changed by comparing ids
 if (prop->id() == mHealth.id())
 {
   // Do something like updating the health display
   ...
 }
}
```

Connecting to a Network

The use of the game properties makes any game using the KGame library automatically network aware. For connection to the network, the game object of the library builds on a network module that provides all functions necessary to connect to another game object via TCP/IP and hence the Internet.

In the KGame network design, there is only ever one client, the game master, to which all other clients connect. To play a network game, this client must offer socket connections on any port.

```
// Offer network connections to port 6783
bool mMyGame->offerConnections(6783);
if (!result)
{
```

```
    // error
    ...
}
```

The clients on the other side may want to connect to that master client once it begins to offer connections.

```
// Connect to a master on "localhost" on port 6783
connectToServer("localhost", 6783);
```

As soon as the client is connected, the signal `signalClientConnected()` is emitted to all clients (including the connecting client).

```
// Connect this slot to the signalClientConnected() signal
MyGame::clientConnected(Q_UINT32 clientId, KGame*)
{
  if (clientId == gameId())
  {
    // This client connected is the master
    ...
  }
  else
  {
    // A new client has entered the game
    ...
  }
}
```

Note that the task of actually initializing and synchronizing the network game is done by KGame. To achieve this, it adds the required KPlayer objects to the clients and transmits all properties to the new client. Once the network has been established, the property changes are automatically transmitted. You can also send customized messages using KGame::sendMessage(); however, if you use the property architecture, this is not usually required.

ADVANCED FEATURES

KGame is a large library that supports many aspects of game development, and provides features necessary to get started and continually aid the development of your game. Some of these more important advanced features are presented in this section.

Debug Facilities

A very important feature and a good way to debug a KGame-based game is the KGameDebugDialog. All that is required is the addition of a "Debug" entry to one menu, and a slot called by that item

```
void MyGame::debug()
{
  KGameDebugDialog* dialog =
                    new KGameDebugDialog(mGame, this);
  connect(dialog, SIGNAL(finished()),
          dialog, SLOT(slotDelayedDestruct()));
  dialog->show();
}
```

needs to be defined.

Invoking the slot from the corresponding menu will show a nonmodal dialog. This dialog consists of several pages (see Figure 15.4) that allow you to inspect all game properties and messages. More (user-defined) pages can be added by the method KDialogBase::addVBoxPage().

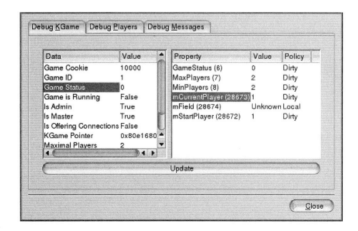

FIGURE 15.4 Game debug dialog.

If the game properties are of standard types (int, long, bool, etc.), their values will automatically be shown in the debug dialog. If they do not, it is possible to connect to the signal KGamePropertyHandler::signalRequestValue() and create a QString that shows the value of a user-defined type.

It is also possible to debug general game messages, since every message sent through the KGame object can be displayed. However, as every KGameProperty also sends messages, there will be many of them; fortunately, the debug dialog allows you to filter messages to limit the display to important messages.

Chat Facilities

A main feature of multiplayer game environments is the capability to chat between players, which allows them to speak about the game, its configuration, or just about anything. The KGame library does provide a chat widget that allows the sending and displaying of text messages between the different network clients. These types of widgets can be set up in the subsequent manner:

```
// The KGame object of your game
KGame* game = ...;

// The local player on this client
KPlayer* player = ...;

// A message ID that is not used for custom
// KGame::sendMessage() messages
int msgid = 10000;

// Create the chat widget
mChatWidget = new KGameChat(game, msgid, this);
mChatWidget->setFromPlayer(player);
```

The setFromPlayer() is required so the chat widget can identify the player who entered a message. This code is sufficient for full chat support.

Network and Game Setup Dialog

The configuration of the network and the game is provided by a standard dialog (see Figure 15.5), which provides a flexible way to set up all the relevant parameters of a game. Since not all games require such a high degree of configuration by the user, the various configuration possibilities of this dialog can be enabled and disabled. The configuration dialog also provides several general configuration pages, like those for the chat widget, the network, and the game configuration itself.

Upon creation of the dialog, it can be specified which of these options the game should allow you to configure via the dialog. Often, this will just be the network part. For example, a chess game cannot allow the number of players to be configured, since the minimum and maximum number of players is set by the program.

To provide a more flexible configuration but still use the standard dialogs, all dialogs can be extended with user-defined widgets. For instance, the network dialog often needs an option for the color a remote player should play. In a chess

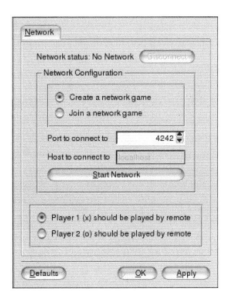

FIGURE 15.5   Game configuration dialog.

game, one could specify that the local player should play *white*, and the remote player should play *black*. To allow this transparently in the network configuration dialog, it is possible to add a user-defined widget to the dialog. Note that in a network game, only the *game admin* is able to change the game configuration; other clients can only view these parameters. An example for setting up such a user-defined dialog can be found in the program mykgame on the companion CD-ROM in the folder examples/mykgame.

ON THE CD

User-Defined Properties

For the majority of games, one of the predefined property types, such as KGame PropertyInt or KGamePropertyString, is usually sufficient. However, sometimes a custom data type is desired, and for this, the class KGameProperty is defined as a template class so any data type, including custom classes, can be used with it. This is extremely easy for all normal C++ types.

```
KGameProperty<float> mHealth;
```

This example provides an mHealth property that operates on the data type float. The property can then be used without additional work.

The only requirement for this property handling is that the << and >> operators are implemented for the user type, so the type can be saved to and loaded from a

QDataStream. The following code snippet demonstrates the construction of a custom class MyClass that stores one integer and one QString variable:

```
class MyClass
{
  public:
    QString mString;
    int mInt;
};

// declare the streaming operators
QDataStream& operator<<(QDataStream& s, const MyClass& m);
QDataStream& operator>>(QDataStream& s, MyClass& m);
```

and the corresponding implementation.

```
QDataStream& operator<<(QDataStream& stream, const MyClass& m)
{
  stream << m.mString;

  // We cast the int to Q_INT32 to be platform independent
  stream << (Q_INT32)m.mInt;

  return stream;
}
QDataStream& operator>>(QDataStream& stream, MyClass& m)
{
  QString string;
  Q_INT32 integer;

  // Read from the stream. Use the same order as
  // in operator<<()
  stream >> string;
  stream >> integer;

  m.mString = string;
  m.mInt = interger;

  return stream;
}
```

With these two implemented functions, a property using the class MyClass can now be declared and used just like any other property.

```
KGameProperty<MyClass> mMyProperty;
```

Loading and Saving

KGame provides support for saving and loading games to and from files. By calling KGame::save(fileName) and KGame::load(fileName), games can be saved and loaded without any additional work as long as all game information is stored in the property system of KGame.

Sometimes, however, it is desirable to save and load custom data or perform additional actions that cannot be covered by the game properties. In these cases, the methods savegame() and loadgame() can be re-implemented.

```
bool MyGame::savegame(QDataStream& stream,
                      bool network,
                      bool savePlayers)
{
  // Call the original implementation. Don't forget this,
  // otherwise the properties are not being saved
  bool ret = KGame::savegame(stream, network, savePlayers);
  if (!ret) { return false; }

  // Save custom data to the stream
  stream << ...;
  return true;
}

bool MyGame::loadgame(QDataStream& stream,
                      bool network,
                      bool reset)
{
  // Call the original implementation.
  bool ret = KGame::loadgame(stream, network, reset);
  if (!ret) { return false; }

  // Load custom data from the stream
  stream >> ...;
  return true;
}
```

The KPlayer class also provides save and load methods that can be re-implemented in the same manner. This allows custom data to be saved and loaded for the player as well. All these methods are called automatically by KGame.

SUMMARY

In this chapter, we presented the KDE-based gaming framework KGame, which supports game development and network game development in various ways. Its design is based on the document-view-player-input model, making it much easier to create a game that has a good design.

KGame provides the concept of player input classes through KGameIO. These classes are the actual interface to the real player, whereas the player class is merely a container of the player's data. Using this concept, there is little difference between a human player on a local computer, a network player, and a computer AI player, as they only differ by the way in which the input is transmitted to the game object.

KGame is particularly useful for turn-based games, which is the common game scenario for desktop games. However, even though KGame provides additional support for these kinds of games, it can be used for any other type of game as well. By using the game property system, games can be written to support network play with minimal additional effort. Furthermore, properties can emit signals whenever they change, so an event-driven game becomes possible. These properties are automatically saved and loaded, and therefore provide built-in support for save game files.

There are many advanced features provided by this library, and we mentioned the most important ones here. One of them is the debug dialog, which is very useful when developing a game or when searching for bugs. Another feature is the configuration dialog, which allows you to easily set up a network game. Both dialogs are often used in desktop games; thus, by using the classes provided by KGame, you do not have to invest a great deal of time developing them from scratch.

16 XML

The *eXtensible Markup Language* (XML) is a language widely used to describe data, especially when the data should be read, stored, or shared [Xml05]. For games, XML is extremely powerful when designing file formats. When used in conjunction with archive file formats such as *.tar (see KTar in Chapter 3, "Game Development using KDE"), sophisticated file formats often required for save game files can be easily developed. Other applications for XML include the design of protocols for inter-process communications or networking.

In contrast to binary formats, XML is presented in human-readable ASCII text and can therefore be easily modified and checked. For obvious reasons, this feature also simplifies the problem of debugging. Furthermore, it is very easy to convert an XML data file into a different format regardless of whether the new format is XML or non-XML. This is very important for file formats of old game data or save files that the player would like to remain relevant when using newer versions of a program.

This chapter serves as a step-by-step introduction to using XML with Qt. As an introduction, we briefly present the XML language and then show how to set up Qt for XML. Next, we show how to fill the Qt data structures with data and how to process this data. We emphasize its use within games and primarily focus on file formats, and therefore present reading and writing XML files. The example program `myxml` in the folder `examples/myxml` on the companion CD-ROM demonstrates this reading and writing of XML files.

ON THE CD

THE XML LANGUAGE

Before discussing how XML can be read or written using Qt, we first give a brief overview on the XML language [Harold04]. As mentioned earlier, XML is a language to describe data. It is not actually a file format because it does not give any semantics; that is, an interpretation to the data. Moreover, the same XML statement can have different meanings in different contexts. For example, in one program the XML line

```
<headline>GAME</headline>
```

could mean that `"GAME"` is the headline of something, which is usually the case. However, another program could interpret this same XML statement as something else; for example, `"GAME"` could also be a comment or a filename. Normally, however, to prevent confusion, a decent file format should use names that actually correspond to the content they describe, and the program should use these names accordingly.

NOTE

XML only defines the language of a file or the data format and does not specify the actual file format. This is in contrast to HTML, which appears similar to XML but specifies both the language and the file format.

The `<headline>` example already shows the main principle of XML, which is that all data must be located between so-called *tags*

```
<tagname> ... </tagname>
```

where `"tagname"` is an arbitrary name of your own choice. In XML, every tag `<tagname>` must have a corresponding closing tag `</tagname>`. However, if there is no content between these two expressions such as

```
<tagname></tagname>
```

this may be shortened to

```
<tagname />
```

The text between an opening and a closing tag is free plain text. Additionally, every tag may also have attributes associated with it and specify more details about that tag. Attribute names, just like tag names, can be chosen arbitrarily. In the example

```
<Level name="Level 1" />
```

a tag named `"Level"` has the attribute `"name"`, which has the value `"Level 1"`. Note that attribute values always need to be quoted in XML.

An important feature of XML is that the tags can be nested, such as

```
<Game>
  <Player name="John">
    <PowerUp name="Extra Speed" />
    <PowerUp name="More Health" />
  </Player>
  <Player name="Jack" />
  <SpecialItem>
    <PlayerWins />
  <SpecialItem />
</Game>
```

By *tag nesting*, the XML document builds a tree-like structure as depicted in Figure 16.1. Note, however, that the XML document can only have one root tag. In our example, this would be the `"Game"` tag.

XML files are plain text and therefore can be read with a simple text editor. However, sometimes this is not sufficient, since certain aspects of the file may need further explanation. These additional explanations can be included in the XML document using comments that are placed between <!-- and -->.

```
<Level>
  <!-- The next tag makes sure that the level can
       not be played in multiplayer games -->
  <SinglePlayer />
</Level>
```

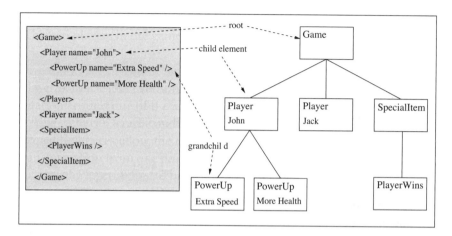

FIGURE 16.1 An XML file (left) is read into a QDom XML object (right), forming a tree-like structure.

Although plain text can be easily saved using XML, binary data can only be saved in an XML file with some additional effort. Therefore, it is usually more practical to separate the binary data into a separate file, instead of including it inside the XML file.

Combining both binary and text-based data with TAR archives creates powerful file formats for games (see the description of KTar in Chapter 3). To the user, the file seems like a single file, but the program is actually working with multiple files inside the archive. With this type of archive file, you can easily store binary files, like screenshots, next to XML files that contain the actual map or save game.

THE DOCUMENT

Qt provides two different ways to read XML files: a SAX2- and a DOM-based implementation. The SAX2 classes (QXml*) implement an XML parser, which reads an XML file and emits events when it locates tags within the file. Since SAX2 cannot write XML files, we will not present SAX2 any further; as for file formats in games (such as level or save game files), writing is usually required. However, it can sometimes (especially when developing the AI) be an interesting alternative if only file reading is required, because compared to DOM, parsing files is generally faster using SAX2.

QDom, the Qt implementation of DOM, first parses the whole XML data and then provides access to all its elements. It is not necessary to write any code for the actual parsing process since this is all performed by Qt. To use QDom, we first create an object of the class QDomDocument. The QDomDocument object represents the XML data in the memory.

```
QDomDocument doc;
```

As soon as a QDomDocument object is available, it must be filled with data. This can be done by loading existing XML data into the document, as described in the next section. Usually, loading data in this way is what you will do most often. Alternatively, if a new document is to be created, new elements can be added directly to the document (see the section "Modifying a Document").

LOADING DATA

To read from an existing XML file, the method QDomDocument::setContent() must be called.

```
QDomDocument doc;

// Load the document from a file
QFile file("file.xml");
if (!file.open(IO_ReadOnly))
{
  // Error
  ...
}
else
{
  bool success = doc.setContent(&file);
}
```

QDomDocument::setContent() is overloaded, and thus provides several possibilities to set the data. Two of these options, which are particularly interesting for game programming, would be to use QByteArray or QString as the data. By using one of these, a file can be loaded manually into the QByteArray or QString object first and then later copied into a QDomDocument. The QByteArray or QString object can be obtained from other means as well; for example, from a network stream or a KTar archive. Therefore, your program can exchange XML data without actually requiring any other disk file. Such an example can look like:

```
QDomDocument doc;
bool success;
```

```
// Obtain QByteArray from e.g. a KTar archive
QByteArray data = ...;
success = doc.setContent(data);
...


// Obtain QString from e.g. a network stream
QString string = ...;
success = doc.setContent(string);
...
```

It is important that the XML data conveyed to the QDomDocument does not contain any errors. If syntax errors are present, the QDomDocument is usually unable to load the data in the correct manner, and further processing is impossible. In this case, setContent() returns false and indicates an error has occurred. For debugging purposes, it is often necessary to find out which line in the XML data caused the error, which can be performed as:

```
QFile file("file.xml");
if (!file.open(IO_ReadOnly))
{
  return;
}

QString errorMessage;
int errorLine;
int errorColumn;
bool success = doc.setContent(&file,
                              &errorMessage,
                              &errorLine,
                              &errorColumn);
if (!success)
{
  QString s;
  s = QString("An error occurred while loading %1:"
              "%2 at line %3, column %4").
          arg(filename).
          arg(errorMessage).
          arg(errorLine).
          arg(errorColumn));
  qDebug(s);
  // stop further processing
  return;
}
...
```

As soon as the XML data has been loaded into the document, it can be processed as described in the following section.

PROCESSING DATA

Once the data has been loaded into the QDomDocument object, the application needs to do something with the data; that is, the data needs to be processed. In the most common case, the application will search for certain elements and read the assigned data, so it can use this data in some way. This is the case when the game uses XML for level or save game files, and then the assigned level or game data must be read from the file. However, even if the program needs to store additional data only, it still has to process the XML document to find the XML tags in which the data should be stored. Therefore, we present the task of processing data first, and extend this to storing data later.

Note that for many games, processing data may be totally sufficient already. For example, if the game uses XML for the level information, it may be sufficient to create the XML files using a normal text editor so the game needs to read the files only. However, using QDom, a level editor can get added later.

The DOM classes are organized in a hierarchical manner on a tree-like structure as depicted in Figure 16.1 with QDomDocument as the root. The QDomDocument contains the root element, which corresponds to the root tag on the XML structure (the XML file). This root element can be used to refer to all child elements that stem from the root element. This so-called document element can be retrieved using:

```
// Create a QDomDocument with data loaded from a file
QDomDocument doc;
QFile file("file.xml");
if (!file.open(IO_ReadOnly))
{
  return;
}
doc.setContent(&file);

// Retrieve the document root element
QDomElement root = doc.documentElement();
```

QDomElement objects are explicitly shared, which means that if you assign an object of this class to another object, both objects point to exactly the same XML element. Consequently, any modification to one element will simultaneously alter the other. This explicit sharing is demonstrated here:

```
// Create the first element
QDomElement element = ...;

// Assign the first element to the second
QDomElement element2 = element;

// Change the name of the second element
element2.setTagName("test");

// Both elements have the same name now
qDebug(element.tagName());       // "test"
qDebug(element2.tagName());      // "test"
```

The principle of explicit sharing applies to nearly all QDom classes because they are inherited from the QDomNode class. Therefore, creating QDom objects on the heap (that is, using new) is usually not required. Sometimes, however, performing this option can be beneficial; for example, if the QDomDocument is created on the heap, it can be kept in memory for the lifetime of the program.

An XML element always represents a start tag, everything inside this tag, and the corresponding closing tag. An object of the class QDomElement provides access to all of this data. The methods QDomElement::tagName() and QDomElement::attribute() can be used to access the tag name and the attributes.

Furthermore, the QDomElement can also have an arbitrary number of children, and depending on the XML data, these children can be other elements, text, or other data. In the remainder of this section, we discuss the processing of text and child elements. Other children, such as comments, are either not relevant when processing data or out of the scope of this book (e.g., CDATA sections).

Reading Text of Elements

Text children have a distinct method to access them: QDomElement::text() returns all the text inside an element, including all the text from possible child elements. In the example of a nested text tag

```
<description>
  You enter a <bold>secret</bold> level.
</description>
```

a call to QDomElement::text() on the element that is represented by the "description" tag would return the text "You enter a **secret** level."

Child Elements

For other elements, more direct control over their children is required. Therefore, Qt allows the iteration of the children within a QDomElement.

```
QDomElement e = ...;

QDomNode n;
for (n = e.firstChild(); !n.isNull(); n = n.nextSibling())
{
  // "cast" the node to an element
  QDomElement element = n.toElement();
  if (element.isNull())
  {
    continue;
  }
  // If the node is an element do something with it
  qDebug(e.tagName());
  ...
}
```

Note that a child of an element does not need to be another element; it can be a QDomText node, a QDomComment, or any other node. Therefore, checking whether the conversion call QDomNode::toElement() has been successful by employing the query QDomElement::isNull() is important.

Qt provides an easier system when trying to locate an element (or any child node) with a unique tag name. By using the method namedItem(), the iteration over all the children is unnecessary, since this method returns the first child node with the matching tag name. A returned child node can be different from an element node or may not exist at all. Therefore, it is advisable to check whether the requested element actually exists, which can be performed using QDomElement::isNull():

```
QDomElement e = element.namedItem("tagname").toElement();
if (e.isNull())
{
  // Error: There was no such child named "tagname"
  ...
}
```

With these two access constructs, complex file formats can be read easily. The following example resembles a simple XML save game file for a poker game:

```
<Game>
  <Player Money="100">
    <Name>John</Name>
    <Card Suite="Hearts" Value="7" />
    <Card Suite="Spades" Value="Ace" />
    <Card Suite="Diamonds" Value="10" />
    <Card Suite="Clubs" Value="King" />
    <Card Suite="Clubs" Value="Queen" />
  </Player>
  <Player Money="200">
    <Name>Bob</Name>
    <Card Suite="Spades" Value="10" />
    <Card Suite="Hearts" Value="Ace" />
    <Card Suite="Hearts" Value="Jack" />
    <Card Suite="Diamonds" Value="King" />
    <Card Suite="Spades" Value="10" />
  </Player>
  <Pile>
    <Card Suite="Spades" Value="2" />
    <Card Suite="Spades" Value="5" />
    <Card Suite="Hearts" Value="3" />
    ...
  </Pile>
</Game>
```

This file can be read with

```
void Game::loadFile(QDomDocument& doc)
{
  // Retrieve the element enclosed by <Game> and </Game>
  QDomElement root = doc.documentElement();

  // Loop all of its children
  QDomNode n;
  for (n = root.firstChild(); !n.isNull(); n = n.nextSibling())
  {
    QDomElement e = n.toElement();
    if (e.isNull())
    {
      continue;
    }

    // Query the tagnames
    if (e.tagName() == "Player")
```

```
      {
        loadPlayer(e);
      }
      else if (e.tagName() == "Pile")
      {
        loadPile(e);
      }
    }
  }
}
```

In this example, we forward the reading of the tags to two subroutines termed
loadPlayer() and loadPile(), which actually process their tags. The loadPlayer()
method could be written as:

```
Player* Game::loadPlayer(const QDomElement& element)
{
  Player* player = NULL;

  // Read the player's money
  int money = element.attribute("Money").toInt();

  // Read the player's name
  QString name;
  if (element.namedItem("Name").isElement())
  {
    name = element.namedItem("Name").toElement().text();
  }

  // Create a player object
  player = createPlayer(name, money);

  // Read the player's cards and add them to the player
  QDomNode n;
  for (n = root.firstChild(); !n.isNull(); n = n.nextSibling())
  {
    QDomElement e = n.toElement();
    if (!e.isNull() && e.tagName() == "Card")
    {
      addCard(player,
              e.attribute("Suite"), e.attribute("Value"));
    }
  }

  return player;
}
```

The `loadPile()` subroutine works in a similar manner to the `loadPlayer()` and consists of a simple loop calling `addCard()` for all child elements with the `tagName()` `"Card"`. Note that even if all the child elements of a particular element have the same tag name, it is still good working practice to check for the tag name. By performing this extra step, you can avoid errors if the file format changes.

Searching Elements

Sometimes, it is necessary to find all elements with a certain tag name, even if they are not the direct children of a particular parent element. For example, suppose you have an XML file such as

```
<Map>
  <House>
    <Room>
      <Enemy Name="hard enemy"/>
      <Enemy Name="easy enemy"/>
    </Room>
  </House>
  <Enemy Name="medium enemy"/>
  <House>
    <Room>
      <Enemy Name="hard enemy"/>
    </Room>
  </House>
</Map>
```

and want to retrieve the `Name` attributes of all `"Enemy"` tags. This could be achieved by first iterating all children in a tag and then recursively repeating this process. The result would be a list of all the `"Enemy"` elements in the file, and then the `"Name"` attribute of these elements can be retrieved. However, this process would require a lot of code.

An alternative is to use the `elementsByTagName()`, which does the aforementioned recursion and returns a list of all elements matching the given tag name.

```
QDomNodeList list = element.elementsByTagName("Enemy");
for (unsigned int i = 0; i < list.count(); i++)
{
  // We do not need to check if this is actually an element,
  // as elementsByTagName() returns elements only
  QDomElement e     = list.item(i).toElement();
  QString attribute = e.attribute("Name");
  ...
}
```

Always keep in mind that `elementsByTagName()` works recursively. Unfortunately, this can make the call to this method extremely slow as demonstrated in the following XML example file:

```
<Game>
  <Player Name="John" />
  <Player Name="Jack" />
  <Map>
    <Cell x="1" y="1" />
    <Cell x="1" y="2" />
    <Cell x="1" y="3" />
    <Cell x="1" y="4" />

    ...
  </Map>
</Game>
```

Imagine now that you store a map of 500×500 cells; therefore, 250,000 cell tags exist. If `elementsByTagName()` is used to retrieve all `Player` tags, Qt also needs to check all 250,000 cell tags—a very slow process. Consequently, using `elements ByTagName()` in this situation would be a mistake. To avoid it, you should manually iterate the children of the game tag. Now, only three tests for tag names are required to retrieve the players.

MODIFYING A DOCUMENT

As soon as the `QDomDocument` object has been created and optionally filled with existing data, every aspect of the document (including elements, attributes, and comments) can be read, modified, removed, appended, and saved at any time. This is the primary advantage of using `QDom` instead of the SAX2 `QXml` classes.

Creating and Modifying Data

The first thing to do when generating a new `QDomDocument` object, without any XML data, is to create the root element and append it to the document structure. Generally, when a new element is created, it is usually an orphan, meaning it has not yet been assigned to any parent. Unless it is added to a parent, it will not appear in the document structure. The root element of the document can be added by appending a newly created element to the document as shown in the following example. Note that there can be only one root element.

```
QDomDocument doc;

// Create a new element with tagname "Players" that belongs to
// doc. Note that it is NOT yet part of doc, it is not a child
// of it!
QDomElement root = doc.createElement("Players");

// Append it to the document that is make it the root element
doc.appendChild(root);
```

Other elements can be created in a similar manner, but instead of being appended to the document, they are added to another element (such as the root element). This latter element then becomes their parent. For example, to create the XML data structure

```
<Players>
  <Player Name="Jack" />
  <Player Name="John" />
</Players>
```

you can use

```
QDomDocument doc;

// Create the root element and append it
QDomElement root    = doc.createElement("Players");
doc.appendChild(root);

// Create the first player, set its name and append it
QDomElement player1 = doc.createElement("Player");
player1.setAttribute("Name", "Jack");
root.appendChild(player1);

// Do the same for the second player
QDomElement player2 = doc.createElement("Player");
player2.setAttribute("Name", "John");
root.appendChild(player2);
```

In addition, using the QDomNode::removeChild(), a previously appended child can be removed again.

In a similar way, text is also added to an element. The previous example could be modified so that the player's name is not an attribute, but a text element inside the Player tag. The XML structure would then resemble

```
<Players>
  <Player><Name>Jack</Name></Player>
  <Player><Name>John</Name></Player>
</Players>
```

and could be created by

```
// Create a document containing a "Players" root
QDomDocument doc;
QDomElement root     = doc.createElement("Players");
doc.appendChild(root);

// Create the first player
QDomElement player1 = doc.createElement("Player");
root.appendChild(player1);

// Create the name element
QDomElement name1 = doc.createElement("Name");
player1.appendChild(name1);

// Add text to the name element
QDomText text1 = doc.createTextNode("Jack");
name1.appendChild(text1);

// And the same for the second player
QDomElement player2 = doc.createElement("Player");
root.appendChild(player2);
QDomElement name2 = doc.createElement("Name");
player2.appendChild(name2);
QDomText text2 = doc.createTextNode("John");
name2.appendChild(text2);
```

Instead of creating all elements in one method, it is often more convenient to have a method that takes a QDomElement reference and then fills the element with data. However, for many tasks, such as creating new elements, these subroutines also require access to the QDomDocument. To avoid passing the QDomDocument reference to every subroutine, all nodes can return the document they belong to using owner Document(). The following example implements this:

```
void Game::save()
{
  // Create document and append root element
```

```
QDomDocument doc;
QDomElement root = doc.createElement("Game");
doc.appendChild(root);

// Create a player, save data to it and append it
// to the root element
QDomElement player = doc.createElement("Player");
if (savePlayer(player))
{
  root.appendChild(player);
}
}

bool Game::savePlayer(QDomElement& player)
{
  // Retrieve the document from the element
  QDomDocument doc = player.ownerDocument();

  // Append a new child element
  player.appendChild(doc.createElement("ChildElement"));
  return true;
}
```

This example also demonstrates that it can be useful to delay appendChild(). If the call to savePlayer() fails for any reason, the corresponding player element is never appended to a parent and will therefore be automatically destroyed as soon as the save() method is left. With this process, you can simply eliminate any elements that cannot be saved. Obviously, this should only be done for elements that are not critical to your data; for all other elements, an error should be generated.

Saving

When the XML document has been created, it should usually be saved to a file or sent over a network. To support such storage, the XML document can be converted into a string using QDomDocument::toString(), which can then be stored or sent over a network. The following example saves an XML document into a text file:

```
QDomDocument doc;
// Fill doc with content
...

QFile f("file.xml");
if (f.open(IO_WriteOnly)
{
```

```
    QTextStream stream(&f);
    stream << doc.toString();
    f.close();
}
...
```

SUMMARY

In this chapter, we presented a step-by-step introduction to XML using QDom. The most common approach starts by creating a QDomDocument, loads existing XML data into it, and then processes the data according to the file format. Additionally, QDom offers methods to modify its data, which allows you to implement save games or level editors for the game.

The processing of an XML document is the most important aspect presented in this chapter. An XML file can be represented by a tree structure to which QDom gives the developer access. The document element is the root of this tree, and all other elements can be accessed from there using the methods described in this chapter. Normally, this is done using namedItem() or by iterating over all children of an element. Additionally, a list of all children with a certain tag name, including all grandchildren, great-grandchildren and so forth, can be generated using elementsByTagName(). However, when large XML structures are involved, this convenient method can become extremely slow.

After the elements have been processed (that is, the desired elements have been found), or alternatively if a new document is created, data can be modified or added. This is usually done by either adding attributes to an element using set Attribute() or by adding new elements. Note that even the pure existence of an element can mean something to your program. The resulting document can be saved to a string, which can be used in various ways, including saving to a file or sending through a network.

XML can be useful to game programmers in many different ways, and is particularly practical for file formats and data storage. The tree-like construction of XML allows games to store and retrieve complex data structures, which is ideal for saving all types of files, especially save game files. For developers, there is the added benefit of being able to improve or modify the file format as the game evolves.

REFERENCES

[Harold04] Harold, Elliotte Rusty, and W. Scott Means, *XML in a Nutshell*, ISBN: 0596007647; O'Reilly, 2004.

[Xml05] *Extensible Markup Language, http://www.w3.org/XML*, 2005.

17 Open Source and Intellectual Property Rights

In This Chapter

- Intellectual Property
- Software Patents
- Open Source Licenses
- License Compatibility

Intellectual property rights such as copyright and software patents affect all software developers and, of course, game developers. You will be affected by these topics as soon as your work is supposed to be published or provided to anybody outside your own home. The effect of intellectual property rights on you and your games is twofold. First is the active side: by designing and developing a game, you create something new, and for this new creation, you will be given some legal rights. Second is the passive side: you will often use and incorporate other people's work into your game. When you use work completed by other people, you have to respect their active side and consequently the legal rights attached to them.

In this chapter, we present a basic introduction to the areas of intellectual property rights and focus on those aspects that are likely to affect Open Source desktop game programming. In particular, we discuss some typical Open Source license models and their implications for both the developer and user of game software.

Note, however, that this is an overview, not a legal handbook. If any of the discussed topics are of particular interest to you, follow the references provided in this chapter. These information sources will provide you with more in-depth knowledge into these legal matters.

INTELLECTUAL PROPERTY

The concept of physical property is very old. Items such as cars or houses are properties that usually belong to someone—their owner. The owner then has the right to decide what can and cannot be done with these items. In terms of a house, this includes the renting, selling, or even how the property is used; for example, as hotel or business. However, in the Middle Ages, it was recognized that intellectual items—that is, nonphysical things such as ideas, inventions, or designs—also had some value. For example, if someone has an idea on how to produce a new machine, this idea alone can be worth a great deal, because it allows the production of new items that nobody else can produce and the additional profit earned by selling them. Furthermore, a new invention or the creation of any work or artwork uses resources such as time, money, or energy. Without providing any form of protection to the original artist or inventor, someone else could just use or copy their ideas and work without the hassle or costs of the initial invention.

These issues led to the idea that a new invention and other intellectual creations should be protected by law, so nobody but the inventor could use them for a certain amount of time. This idea led to the definition and protection of intellectual property. The protection of intellectual property effectively grants a monopoly on that particular invention or creation. Someone else wanting to use it would have to bargain with the owner of the intellectual property, so that the owner would sell his or her rights. Otherwise, the use of the item by the interested party would be forbidden by law.

One of the first intellectual property protections was introduced by King Henry VI in England in 1449 when he granted a *patent* to a producer of stained glass, allowing him a 20-year monopoly on the production of that particular stained glass. Many more protections followed, first in England and later in continental Europe. Nowadays, the concept of intellectual property is firmly established in most countries and their laws.

There exist several different forms of intellectual property, the most common of which include:

Copyright: Protects the artistic works created by authors, artists, and composers; for example, writing, drawing, and music scores. Computer source code is also included here. Copyright protects a particular expression of such artistic work. A different work achieving the same or a similar result in a different way does not collide with the copyright of another person. Therefore, copyright protects mainly against copying.

Patents: Provide inventors with a monopoly right; that is, an exclusive use for their invention for a certain amount of time (usually 20 years). In contrast to copyright, a patent protects a specific idea and not the particular creative expression of the idea.

Trademarks: Protect the names, words, or phrases used to identify goods or services.

All of the preceding intellectual property rights provide some form of protection against the rights being used by others. Once the protection period has expired, the intellectual property will pass into the *public domain*; that is, the collection of all creative works (art, music, inventions, etc.) that are part of our human cultural heritage. Anything within this domain can be used without restrictions by anybody. An advantage of having a large amount of work available in the public domain is that it can serve as a foundation for new inventions and creations. For example, if you already know how to build a machine, you can design and build an even better machine.

From the preceding description of intellectual property, we can already see that there are two sides of the coin. An inventor will prefer his invention to be strictly protected so he can earn as much money as possible. If everyone could just copy an invention, the inventor would eventually realize that it is not worth his while to invent something new. On the other hand, having every invention strictly protected reduces the availability of items in the public domain; therefore, new inventions are harder to produce. In the long term, this also slows the overall invention process of humankind.

The problems of intellectual property described for the invention of a new machine also apply to the author of a computer program. Within this area, computer code, textual writing, graphics design, and music composing are all involved. The author of these items has to decide whether and in what way these items should be protected, or be available to others.

Software Copyright and Software Copyleft

Copyright protects a particular expression of creative work from being copied by others. This work can be text, graphics, music, or a software source code. If any work is copyright protected, you cannot use or copy this particular work without permission from the original author. Moreover, you cannot incorporate it or parts of it into your own work [Wikipedia05a]. However, many people believe that it is very handy to have a large amount of software available to incorporate into your own work, because this makes the development of new items much easier. Therefore, they tend not to protect their software and make it available to everybody for free. Other developers keep a tight protection on their software and guard it against any misuse.

Therefore, the application of intellectual property rights to software often splits software and software developers into different groups. For software, two main categories can already be distinguished. First, there is software that is generally free and available for others to use and incorporate into building new programs. This category comprises the *public domain* software, the *Open Source* software, and the *free* and *copylefted* software.

Second, there is *proprietary* software, which generally enforces strict restrictions to the user resulting in *closed source* code and *commercial* intent [Ravicher05], [Ifross05].

In the following section, we introduce the main categories for free and proprietary software.

The Public Domain

The public domain is the collection of all knowledge and creative work such as music, art, writing, and computer programs in which nobody has proprietary rights. Anybody can use and build upon work that is part of the public domain without any restrictions or fees. An item is usually entered into the public domain in two ways. First, items that have been under a copyright or patent protection lose this status after a certain amount of time. When these protections expire, the items automatically become part of the public domain and are freely available to everyone from that point on. Second, the author of a creative item can voluntarily transfer his item into the public domain, and in doing so, yield all of his rights to the item. Normally by law, the author of the work is automatically the copyright holder, and thus, before they can transfer their work into the public domain, they have to explicitly disclaim any proprietary interest in the work. For example, they must choose a license that will grant permission for actions usually forbidden by copyright laws (copying, modifications, redistribution, etc.). Note that the first way, copyright expiration, is very unusual for computer programs because of the very long time periods copyrights are owned. Usually, programs are no longer in use when such copyrights expire.

Open Source

Open Source software stems from the fact that the actual source code of the application is available to any user. However, the meaning of Open Source software goes beyond just showing the source code to the user. It also guarantees that the user of the software has certain rights when using or reusing the software. Perens

[Perens05] states that the Open Source definition can be seen as a "Bill of Rights" [Wikipedia05b] for the computer user. These rights given to the user allow the user to copy, distribute, or base his own work on the original software without any additional permission from the author of the software. This concept clearly differs from the traditional idea of intellectual property and copyright where only the author or producer of certain software has legal rights concerning the use or distribution of the software.

To make an Open Source-type program, the software has to be distributed under an Open Source license. These licenses allow the user to make copies of the program and distribute them. They give full access to the source code of the software and allow changes to the original software. The Open Source Initiative (OSI) [OSI05] has defined a set of rules that software must follow to be recognized as Open Source software. In the following summary, we list some of the key criteria required for true Open Source software:

Source code: The source code of the software must be available for free. Distribution of the software must be allowed in source and binary form.

Free redistribution: Open Source software must not require a royalty or fee for its use, distribution, or sales, even if it is used as a component of other software. Consequently, Open Source software can be used to build other applications.

Derived works: The software must allow modifications of the original work; that is, all derived work must be possible without limitations. Any work derived from the original has to be distributed with at least the same free terms as the original software.

Discrimination: The software must not discriminate against persons, groups, or any particular use or field of endeavor.

A detailed list of all requirements for Open Source software can be found at the Web site [OSSDefinition05].

Building software on Open Source software does not necessarily mean that the new and derived software has to be Open Source as well. There are Open Source licenses that both enforce or allow this aspect.

Nowadays, many large and successful software development projects are distributed as Open Source software. Linux, KDE, the Apache Web server, and the Mozilla Web suite are good examples of how Open Source programs can work.

Note that sometimes the term "Open Source" is misused by some people to describe their own form of distribution. Here, the source code is shown, but the original programmer still requires that you do not use, modify, or redistribute the software in any way. Such software does not match the definition of Open Source software.

Free Software

"Free software" is an ambiguous term because it can mean *free* as in *free beer*, or it can mean literally *free* as in *freedom*. With respect to software licensing, the second meaning was intended. Free software gives a certain freedom and rights to the user instead of the author. The Free Software Foundation [FSF05] pursues this approach for software licensing.

Copylefted Software

To emphasize the difference to copyrighted software where the author of the work holds all rights in the software and not the user, the term *copylefted* software was introduced, which means that the user obtains all rights over the software. Strictly speaking, copyleft has no legal meaning: to achieve such a legal meaning for copylefted software in practice, the software is first placed under normal copyright terms. The distribution aspects are then added, and these allow everyone the right to use, modify, or redistribute the software. However, these rights are only granted if they are not changed in any derived work.

Copylefted free software is very similar to Open Source software; however, the former goes beyond the Open Source definition. Whereas Open Source guarantees that the source code of the original software is publicly available and the rights to use and distribute the software are yielded to the user, copylefted software additionally requires that these rights of the original software be passed on to all derived works forever. This extra point implies that it is impossible to create a nonfree program that uses free software components.

Because derived work also has to be copylefted, such software licenses are sometimes referred to as "viral" licenses, meaning that once software is "infected" with such a license, it will spread to all derived work. Such behavior is intended by the creators of this type of license so a large pool of free software is produced and available for free to everyone. Note that the viral metaphor is somewhat exaggerated, but helps to distinguish between copylefted software and Open Source software that dose not necessarily enforce the licenses of the derived work.

For a typical example of how the Open Source and copylefted software licenses differ, you can compare the BSD license with the GPL license, both of which are discussed later in this chapter.

Software based on copylefted software must be redistributed as copylefted software. It is impossible to turn it back to nonfree or closed source software.

NOTE

Copyright and Proprietary Software

Contrary to copylefted software, copyrighted software means that the author of the work (software, writing, art, music, etc.) holds all rights over that particular piece of work. However, contrary to patents, a copyright does not protect an idea itself, but only the particular expression of the idea. This means that a similar but independently created work is possible without violating the copyright of other work. Therefore, although you are not allowed to copy parts of copyrighted software into your own program, you are allowed to reproduce the same functionality of the copyrighted software in an entirely new program. As an example, you are not allowed to redistribute your copy of Microsoft Word™ to a friend; however, you can redistribute a word processor you wrote that has the same functionality as Microsoft Word.

The exclusive rights of copyrighted software granted to the author of a work include the use, distribution, copying, and modification of it. Of these original rights, the author of the software can sell or lend some of the rights to the user of the software. The exact rights passed on depend entirely on the sales contract. Typically, this means no copying or redistribution, and no analyzing or modification of the original software code.

Software following this strict owner concept is called *proprietary* software. In this respect, the term *proprietary* stems from French-Latin meaning "privately owned and controlled" [Wikipedia05c]. To protect the ideas and the copyrighted software itself, commercial software is normally distributed without the source code and only in a binary form. Software available in this form of distribution is called proprietary *closed source* software.

Under the Berne Convention [Wikipedia05d] signed by most countries, anything written, including computer source code, will be automatically copyright protected, giving the author all distribution and usage rights. Note that normally no special process of registration is required to obtain the copyright (but certain steps are advisable to prove that the work was produced by the author at a set time). The exact rules depend on the country in which the software was developed and/or distributed.

However, having a copyright on some software or artistic work does not mean one cannot release it to the public domain. It is certainly possible to choose an appropriate license that basically yields all rights to the software, making it effectively part of the public domain.

Software Licensing and Distribution Models

We have seen that there are various ways to license software [FSFCategories05]. While the licensing of software is about rights, the distribution of software is more focused on money. Although often connected, these two issues are not necessarily linked.

Consequently, it is possible to distribute closed source copyrighted software for free, just as it possible to earn money by distributing Open Source software, although this is a little harder. However, this can indeed work for games or certain desktop programs. The Open Source license model requires that the source code be available for free. However, commercial distributors selling, for example, Linux distributions, earn their money with packaging, compiling, and additional services.

There are two main issues to consider when distributing your work. The first is whether to choose the Open Source/free software model or the closed source/proprietary software model. Second is deciding if the software should be distributed for free or sold commercially. These two issues have given rise to the following most used distribution models:

Public domain software: Non-copyrighted software that is also usually available for free. This software can be used for any purpose.

Open Source or free software: Licensed software, but with a license giving certain rights to the users, such as being able to use the source code for their own modifications. The source code of the software has to be available for free (except for a fee for providing the copy or the download). Compilation, packaging, or additional services can be charged.

Freeware: Typically closed source, proprietary software. The software cannot be modified or used as a basis for derived work, but can be used for free. Often, proprietary software is offered as freeware for private users, but sold as commercial software to companies. Although very similar in wording, freeware must not be confused with free software.

Shareware: Closed source software that is commercially sold and available for payment. However, the software can be tested before buying it. Often, a 30-day free trial period is provided so an individual can evaluate the program. After this, the program has to be bought.

Commercial software: Closed source, proprietary software that is only available for payment. This type of software does not normally give any rights to the customer besides being able to use the program. However, it is possible to get (or buy) additional rights if the author or distributor offers this option.

Figure 17.1 summarizes the various software-licensing models. Examples for games distribution following the Open Source idea can be found at the Web sites [Dmoz05], [KdeApps05], [Killefiz04], and [Osgaming05].

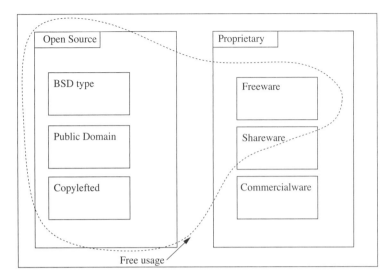

FIGURE 17.1 The Open Source licenses are depicted on the left. These licenses give source code and usage rights to the user of the software. On the right are the proprietary software models. Either type of model does not necessarily determine whether the software is free for use. The dashed line encircles the software that can be used for free.

SOFTWARE PATENTS

Patents, and therefore software patents, provide much stronger protection over a piece of work than general copyright laws do. Patents protect the invention; that is, the idea itself. With copyright protection, it would be possible to re-implement a software program so it has the same effect as the original program, as long as the source code is not directly copied. However, a patent also prevents any similar re-implementation and thus protects the actual idea.

To obtain a patent, a piece of software has to be novel and must also be inventive; that is, not identical to anything that already exists and not obvious. If a piece of *"prior art"* is found that destroys the novelty and/or inventiveness of the software, patent protection will not be available. However, the amount of inventiveness required is often arguable, because some trivial patents do exist. Additionally, many of the patents granted do not cover something that is a special idea; these broad patents are just worded cleverly and therefore granted. Furthermore, most patent laws require that the invention is capable of industrial application.

Note that software patents are possible in some countries, while other countries do not accept patents on software. You have to check whether your country issues software patents; for example, the United States issues software patents.

For Open Source developers, some problems arise from software patents. First, a patent also protects against independent reinvention of software. This means that if you create new software but are not aware that someone has already patented this idea, you will violate that patent anyway. Therefore, you can unknowingly violate a patent and may be sued. To avoid this, an extensive patent literature search should be conducted for any new creation. Second, broad patents may protect a general idea. Thus, someone having a broad patent on a crucial component can control the monopoly right in this area until the patent expires. Third, obtaining patents on your own is very difficult, expensive, and time consuming, often requiring patent attorneys and an even greater amount of money. This is normally not feasible for Open Source developers.

Concerning games, patents are usually only achieved in areas in which a large amount of money is involved, such as casino games, slot machines, and so on. You can see an example of such a game patent with US patent 6,612,927 at the US Patent and Trademark Office Web page [USPatents05]. However, general technologies or algorithms relevant for games are also sometimes protected. Compression algorithms are a good example for this category. Here, for example, the US patent 4,558,302 [USPatents05] for data compression algorithms (which ran out in 2003) had direct implications on several computer programs because it could be applied to encoding GIF images.

OPEN SOURCE LICENSES

To put a program under an Open Source license, there exist dozens of possibilities. Roughly, 50 to 60 licenses are recognized by the OSI [OSI05], [OsiApproved05] as true Open Source licenses. However, as a game author developing KDE or Qt games, you will fortunately encounter only a few of these licenses. In the following section, we briefly describe Open Source licenses used in the field of Qt or KDE programming.

The (Modified) BSD and MIT Licenses

The Berkeley Software Distribution (BSD) license originated at the University of California, Lawrence Berkeley Laboratory and is the foundation of the BSD Unix derivate. Almost identical to the BSD license is the Massachusetts Institute of Technology (MIT) license. Both licenses allow the customer, user, or programmer of the software to use the software in source or binary form free of charge. The original software can also be redistributed with or without modifications in accordance with nearly all conditions the user sets. This right includes the publishing or selling of the software, even as proprietary software.

The modified BSD license is especially used for free software publishing because it is one of the licenses that impose the least restrictions on the users of this software. Note, however, that older versions of the BSD license contain an "advertising" rule, which enforced that BSD software was mentioned as a component of the final product. Using this clause, authors who had initially used the BSD software would then often also want to appear as contributors to all other subsequent programs. Therefore, this paragraph was seen as an obnoxious part of the license and was finally removed in later versions.

The GNU General Public Licenses

General Public Licenses (GPLs) are issued by the Free Software Foundation and stress the free use of software [FSF05]. Remember that the term *free* refers to freedom, not price. The user of the software or the author of the derived work should have all rights to use, modify, or redistribute the software. This particularly includes free access to all source code of the application. To keep this freedom going, authors of derived works must pass the same rights to further users of their software. Compared to the BSD-type licenses, the GPL makes one fundamental difference to the user of the software. GPL licenses specify that anybody who has work derived from a GPL licensed product must place the newly derived work under a GPL license as well. This requirement enforces that any further published work based on GPL products is to be available as Open Source software forever. The Free Software Foundation does this intentionally to enforce the use of free software [FSF05]. In particular, the GPL license guarantees that the user or customer always receives free access to the source code, and can modify or redistribute it under the same GPL conditions.

However, the software can be sold under certain circumstances (additional services, executables, compilations, additional warranties), but the rights of the customer or user cannot be limited and access to source code of the program has to be always free. A typical example would be a Linux distribution like Suse Linux™. It is also possible to demand a small fee for providing a copy or download of the source code.

The widespread use of the GPL licenses, especially those for operating systems or general utility libraries, has made one problem with these licenses apparent. Strictly speaking, it is not possible to base commercial, closed source software on GPL libraries. Therefore, if a software system such as KDE were GPL, commercial software for KDE would not be possible. Therefore, a modified version of the GPL was released. This Lesser General Public License (LPGL), also formerly known as

Library General Public License, puts libraries and operating systems such as Linux under less-stringent conditions. Software development that changes the libraries themselves (work based on the library) needs to be placed under the same license conditions as well. Software that just uses or links with the libraries (work that uses the library) is free from any restrictions.

Typical examples for GPL/LPGL programs are the operating system Linux, and the desktop environments KDE and Gnome.

Apache Software Licenses

The Apache licenses are very similar to the BSD type licenses; they grant all rights to the software, the user, or to any derivative work. The licenses are available in version 1.1 and more recently in version 2.0. Both licenses grant any user a royalty-free right to use, reproduce, and derive one's own work from the software. All work derived from it can be distributed in source or binary form. To prevent unjustified promotion, written permission needs to be acquired before using the Apache organization for product promotion. Typical software products that use the Apache license are the Apache Web server, Perl, and the spam filter SpamAssassin.

Mozilla Public License

The Mozilla Public License (MPL) in version 1.1 can be seen as a compromise between the GPL and BSD licenses. It also enforces the free availability of the source code. However, it allows the author of derivative work to change the license type as long as the Open Source character is maintained.

Typical examples of the Mozilla source code include the Mozilla Web browser family.

The Q Public License

The Q Public License (QPL) is Trolltech's version of the GPL license and maintains many of the concepts in GPL licenses. The main differences are that changes made to the original software must be clearly marked and distinguished from the original code. The preferred form for such changes is a distribution of patches against the original program. Contrary to the GPL license, changes to the software do not need to be released under the QPL license. Any license can be used as long as free access to the source code is guaranteed, and the user has no restrictions in regard to the source code.

Contrary to the LPGL license, work that is only linked against QPL products needs to be available as Open Source software. Free access to the source code of the application also needs to be provided.

A typical example of the Q Public license is Trolltech's Qt library, which is available as a free version under the QPL or the GPL. (The Qt library is also available as a commercial version, and no license restrictions apply.)

This form of licensing issue of Qt is particularly interesting if you develop Qt-based software.

License Comparison

There exists a variety of Open Source licenses, and the type that will affect your program depends on two facts. If your work is based on a license like the GPL, you will generally have to remain with those forms of licenses. When no such initial restrictions apply, you have the choice of the license type under which your software can be distributed. BSD or MIT licenses are a good choice if you do not want to impose any restrictions on your software. Note, however, that other people can then modify and sell your products even as closed source. GPL or LGPL licenses are a good choice if you want to guarantee that your software and all products derived from it stay free and Open Source forever. Figure 17.2 depicts the different license types available and the level of protection or freedom your game application has with each.

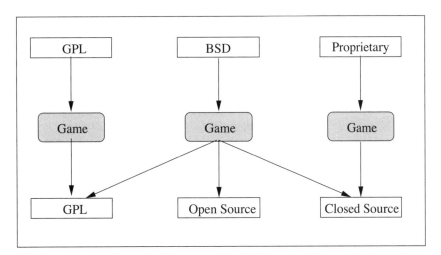

FIGURE 17.2   The choice of license type for a software will also determine the license for any future derived software. For example, if a game program builds on GPL software, it has to be published as GPL software (left). If it builds on BSD software, it can be published with any license the developer chooses (middle). If it builds on proprietary closed source software, it can generally not go back into the Open Source domain, because this would violate the rights of the original owner of the proprietary software (right).

A further source for possible licenses that also extend to artistic fields such as images, videos, text, and music is the Creative Commons Licenses [Commons05]. Here, a selection of licenses, ranging from very restrictive to quite open, are available, and together allow a various degree of rights sharing. Most of these licenses do not follow the Open Source policies.

All Open Source licenses try to ensure that the author of the software is not liable for any damage done by software; therefore, no warranty is given for using the software. Interestingly, the local law might not allow a complete exclusion of warranty. However, if the software is given away for free, warranty is normally very limited.

Using one of the already existing Open Source licenses for your product has the advantage that you do not have to be a lawyer or consult a lawyer to create a license that expresses your wishes and can withstand any legal arguing.

Finally, as long as you own the complete copyright of your program, you are free to change the type of license at any time. If you are not the sole copyright holder, you have to have the permission of all contributing authors before you can alter a license. However, once you have released a version of your software as Open Source, you cannot prevent it from being redistributed by other people. This is especially important when more updated versions of your software appear under other, stricter licenses.

LICENSE COMPATIBILITY

From the previous sections, you can conclude many things about license compatibility; that is, when you are allowed to include work of other people into your own work, and when you are forbidden. However, some typical misunderstandings can arise with software licenses.

The first misunderstanding that arises very often is about unlicensed work. Very often, you see some work (whether it be code, text, graphics, sound, or something else) somewhere (e.g., on a Web site) that you want to use in your project. Many people assume they are allowed to use this because "it was available on this Web site for free." This assumption is not true; to be allowed to use the work of someone else, you must have the permission of the copyright holder, typically the author. This can be either in the form of a license allowing the use or in an explicit permission. If you do not have such permission, you must not assume anything. All work is initially under normal copyright, and you have no right to distribute or use it under any conditions other than what the author intended. In the case of the Web site, you may watch the work on the Web site, but that is all. Concerning these copyright issues, it does not matter whether your project is Open Source/free software, commercial/proprietary software, or falls under any other category. You need the appropriate permission to use such work in your project.

Even if the work used is under an Open Source license (and your project uses an Open Source license), there is still no guarantee that you are allowed to use it. There is normally no problem if your project uses the same license as the original work. However, if you use a different license, the license of the original work needs to be compatible with yours. For example, if your project is under the GPL, you are allowed to include work into your application that is under the (modified) BSD license because it is compatible to the GPL (see Figure 17.2). However, if you use the (modified) BSD license in your project and the original work used GPL, you are not allowed to incorporate it, since the GPL is stricter than the BSD license. Concerning the GPL, you can find a list of compatible licenses at the Web site [FSF05].

If you want to use any work that is explicitly placed in the public domain, you are allowed to use this work, no matter which license (Open Source, proprietary, etc.) you use. Nevertheless, you must be careful that the work is actually public domain—do not confuse this with terms like "freeware," which means something very different.

In a proprietary project—that is, a project that uses a non-Open Source license—you are usually very limited about the work you are allowed to include into your project. A few Open Source licenses (such as the modified BSD license) grant you the right to include the work in your proprietary project. However, most licenses (such as all copyleft licenses) do not. In this case, you may choose to contact the author or copyright holder directly, for he may grant you a special right to use his work in your project. Regardless of the situation, you need to make sure that the one who grants you that right is actually the (only) author or copyright holder and is therefore allowed to grant you the right.

SUMMARY

When writing computer games, you must approach intellectual property rights from two directions. First, as an author, you will have copyright on all you create. Second, you will find yourself a user of intellectual property of others. This may be in the form of source code fragments, graphics, or even music. In computer game development, the main areas affected by intellectual property rights are the images and sprites, the source code, the music and sound effects, all text and writing, and some fonts, too.

Even though license issues are a difficult and complex topic, they are important for game development. In this chapter, we gave you a few guidelines on how to navigate the intellectual property world. However, we are not patent lawyers, so make sure you thoroughly understand the process.

There are two main license models available for software and software-related items. The Open Source or free software models propose that software should be available to everyone for free and as Open Source. This allows programmers to build new software on already existing software without additional costs or restrictions. Conversely, the closed source license models typically keep most or all rights with the author and are mainly used for commercial software. As an author, you must decide to which world you want to belong. Choosing an Open Source model allows you to obtain all the ingredients for your software as Open Source for free. The free sprites, free sound effects, and nifty game libraries help enormously to build a new game, since not everything needs to be reinvented.

However, you might want to earn a little money with your software. You want to sell your super cool new game; therefore, you might decide to sell it as proprietary closed source software so others cannot copy your work. If you choose such a proprietary model, you have to buy all additional parts of your game program from the commercial distributors—which can get quite expensive. If you prefer not to buy them, you will have to create all code, graphics, and sound effects from scratch. One compromise can be to sell your program using an Open Source license. However, you may find fewer customers, because anyone buying your game would also be allowed to distribute it, for free, to anyone else.

Buying is expensive, and recreating everything is time consuming. Both issues are often a major hindrance for new game developers. Therefore, basing your work on Open Source software can make development much easier. Especially if you are new to game development, you can profit enormously from Open Source software—obtaining free ingredients for your programs and learning from other people's experience and source code is an advantage not to be underestimated. However, if you use other people's free work, you either have to (GPL) or want to (BSD) publish your derived work as Open Source so other people can benefit from it and you give a little back to the software community.

Sometimes, it is possible to have a mixture of both models; the game software is published as Open Source software, but compilations or special distributions of the game are sold. Whichever model you choose is entirely up to you; the most important part is to have fun!

REFERENCES

[Commons05] *Creative Commons, http://creativecommons.org/licenses,* 2005.

[Dmoz05] *DMOZ—Open Directory Project, http://dmoz.org/Computers/ Open_ Source/Software/Games,* 2005.

[FSF05] *GNU Operating System—Free Software Foundation, http://www.gnu.org,* 2005.

[FSFCategories05] *Categories of Free and Non-Free Software, http://www.fsf.org/ philosophy/categories.html,* 2005.

[Ifross05] *Ifross, http://www.ifross.de,* 2005.

[KdeApps05] *Kde-Apps, http://www.kde-apps.org,* 2005.

[Killefiz04] *Zaurus Software Index, http://www.killefiz.de/zaurus/,* 2004.

[OSI05] *Open Source Initiative, http://www.opensource.org,* 2005.

[OsiApproved05] *Approved Licenses, http://www.opensource.org/licenses,* 2005.

[Osgaming05] *Open Source Gaming, http://osgaming.net,* 2005.

[OSSDefinition05] *The Open Source Definition, http://www.opensource.org/docs/ definition.php,* 2005.

[Perens05] Perens, Bruce, *The Open Source Definition, http://perens.com/ Articles/OSD.html,* 2005.

[Ravicher05] Ravicher, Dan, *Open Source Legal Issues, http://slashdot.org/ article.pl?sid=01/06/05/122240,* 2005.

[USPatents05] *United States Patents and Trademarks, http://www.uspto.gov,* 2005.

[Wikipedia05a] *Copyright, http://en.wikipedia.org/wiki/Copyright,* 2005.

[Wikipedia05b] *United States Bill of Rights, http://en.wikipedia.org/wiki/United_ States_Bill_of_Rights,* 2005.

[Wikipedia05c] *Proprietary, http://en.wikipedia.org/wiki/Proprietary,* 2005.

[Wikipedia05d] *Berne Convention for the Protection of Literary and Artistic Works, http://en.wikipedia.org/wiki/Berne_Convention_for_the_Protection_ of_Literary_and_Artistic_Works,* 2005.

18 A Practical Summary

In This Chapter

- The Game Design Document
- The Class Design
- The Implementation
- Artificial Intelligence
- Multimedia
- Building the Game
- The Result
- Game Enhancements

In the course of this book, we presented the necessary key ingredients to create a desktop game for Qt or KDE on various target platforms such as KDE/Linux, Microsoft Windows, and PDAs. Our goal was to show you that game development does not have to be difficult, and this is particularly true for small desktop games. We demonstrated that with limited effort and resources, you can produce an appealing game.

You will often notice that to get the games running, you frequently employ the same technologies. The first step is to set up a basic application, and we based this on Qt or KDE. Applying the document-view model on top of the basic application provides you with a good basis for the new game design. For the actual view—that is, the display of the game on the screen—you have several options. For instance, do you want a conventional widget-based view, a canvas that uses sprites, or 3D graphics that require OpenGL? Generally, multimedia effects such as music, sound effects, and graphics are of particular importance in games; games should play well, and look and sound good, too. As a game designer, you must become familiar with this idea and should not ignore multimedia aspects if you want to create a catchy game.

Some topics are special to games, and are not normally found in other desktop applications. They include pathfinding, the concept of artificial intelligence (AI), particle effects, or network games (with or without the KGame framework). In this book, we provided an introduction to these specialized topics so you can employ them in your own desktop games.

Furthermore, when developing games, you will encounter the topic of licenses and patents, and this is especially true for games developed using Open Source software. Questions that might arise here include, "What am I allowed to do, and what are the conditions of using this software?" Although this may seem like a boring topic, it is worthwhile to have a basic overview of the legal situation when programming with Open Source. In Chapter 17, "Open Source and Intellectual Property Rights," we provided a general idea about license issues and focus on those of particular concern for Open Source developers.

During this book, we demonstrated many features and technologies of game development. However, we did not put all the theoretical knowledge together and create a real game. Therefore, we conclude this book by combining all the key areas of developing a small desktop game. We begin by making a game design—that is, writing the game design document—which is then followed by some sketches of the actual class design. Finally, we present the implementation of the main classes used in our game, and focus on the code snippets relevant to the topics discussed in this book. Straightforward C++ implementations or obvious code parts are omitted in this chapter, but can be found on the companion CD-ROM. In fact, you can find the full source code of the working game in the folder `examples/consty`.

ON THE CD

THE GAME DESIGN DOCUMENT

It is always a good idea to start the design of a new game by writing down some of the main concepts first. A game design document is usually created for this purpose, and being the developers of this new game, we now proceed to formulate one. The key issues of game design and of the game design document are discussed in Chapter 1, "Introduction to Desktop Gaming." In short, however, it should contain all the information necessary to describe the game, including its idea and the key technologies used.

For small desktop games, these documents do not have to be overly extensive. Nevertheless, you will profit from collecting your ideas and presenting some of the first sketches of the game. An example of this type of sketch in shown in Figure 18.1. It is also much easier to attract other developers or artists to your project if you can show them a small description and some preliminary graphics of the game. Additionally, an initial concept can avoid many problems that often occur in real game development. Note, however, that even a good design document may need to be changed over time so it meets new requirements.

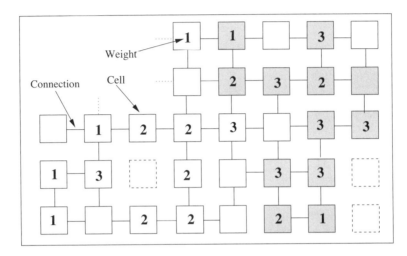

FIGURE 18.1 The game board, which is assembled from a rectangular array of cells that can be interconnected. Each cell can be either *not owned* (empty white cells) or *owned* by one of the two players (white or gray cells with numbers). Each owned cell can have a *weight* (number) associated with it. Player movement between cells is possible if they are connected. A cell without any connection can never be entered, and can therefore be omitted from the game board (dashed cells).

In the following, we present a game design document for our game. Note that we try to keep the specification in this chapter short because we want to demonstrate the idea, not every detail of the game. In your own game design document, you can be as detailed as you like.

Game Definition

Overview

- **Development name:** *Consty*
- **General description:** The game is a maze-type logic puzzle for two players (one human and one computer player). The aim of the first (human) player is to collect special items that are located around the game board, and after collecting

them, travel to the "goal" location. The second (computer) player has to prevent this by catching the first player. The game board is a "maze" constructed from a rectangular array of interconnected fields, where each field has a certain difficulty to be passed (called *weight*).

- **Genre:** Puzzle/maze type of game
- **Platform:** KDE

Rules and Game Flow

The following list describes the key game rules:

- The game board is an array of fields (cells). Each field can be connected to its neighbors to the left, right, top, or bottom (Figure 18.1). Moves are possible between neighboring fields having a connection.
- All fields can have an owner (one of the players) and a weight (one, two, or three). The weight of the field determines the amount of turns the opposing player must wait before he can own or cross that field. Thus, a higher weight makes it more difficult to pass the field for players who do not own it.
- Each player controls one or more units (depending on the level design). However, the first player usually has only one unit.
- All units start on defined locations (given by the level design).
- The players play in turns, and games always start with the first (human) player. A player commands all of his units in one turn.
- Possible moves for all units depend on whether the current field is owned by the current player, not owned, or owned by the opponent. If the current field has no owner or is owned by the current player, he can move to a directly connected neighboring field, increase the weight of the current field by one, or skip the move. If the current field belongs to the opponent, he can only decrease its weight by one. Only when the weight is reduced to zero does the opponent lose ownership of this field and other moves become possible.
- A field is owned as soon as its weight is increased to one.
- Weights can be changed by one each turn, up to a maximum (level-dependent) value (typically, three). Cells that have a weight serve by slowing down the opponent's moves because he cannot directly cross such cells, but instead must lower their weight to zero, which will delay his movement by the depicted number of weights.
- Each unit has a "life" counter, which is decreased by one every turn. If this counter reaches zero, the unit restarts from its start location.
- The start player has to "collect" a certain (level-dependent) number of special items by moving to the fields that contain them. Once all necessary special items are collected, the player has to reach the goal location to win the game.

- The second player has to catch the first player; that is, reach any field the first player is on to win the game.
- Figure 18.2 illustrates these rules by displaying the game board with interconnected cells, start location, goal location, and special items.

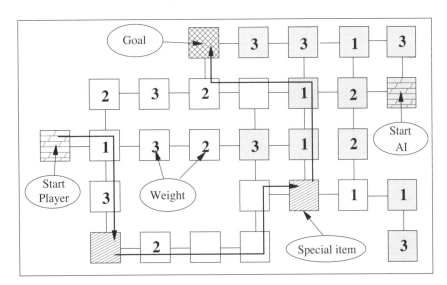

FIGURE 18.2 Each player has a starting location on the game board. Player one has to move over the special item cells to the goal, while player two has to try to catch player one. Movement is only possible between connected cells. A possible path for player one is shown as the arrowed line connecting start and goal. White cells belong to player one, and gray cells to player two. Empty cells have no owner. Moving over an opponent's cell will slow the movement depending on the cell's weight.

Scoring

A score is given for collecting special items from the game board (50 points) and for reaching the goal. The faster the goal is reached, the more points are awarded. The exact number depends on the design level.

Architecture

The game employs the KDE KGame framework (see Chapter 15, "The KGame Library"). This framework provides a basic game design, allows easy loading and saving, and permits network games.

The input of the player and of the AI player is done using the KGame IO modules. More details on the KGame game architecture are discussed in the section, "The Class Design."

User Interface

Introduction

The introduction screen shows a welcome message to the player and will disappear once the game is started the first time.

Game Screen

The main game screen will serve as input for the moves of the player and displays the current game situation. The screen depicts a maze built from a rectangular array of interconnected cells. All cells can have different weights and owners, and some of the cells have a special meaning, marked as special items, and start and goal locations. Figure 18.2 shows a sketch of the game screen, including these special cells.

Interface Specification

The game is mouse controlled. Moves are performed by clicking on the target field. Special moves like skipping a turn or changing a weight are invoked by pushbuttons (*Change Weights*, *Skip*). Starting a new game, loading or saving a game, and exiting the program are done using the *Game* menu.

Multimedia

The game will incorporate graphics and background music; for more information on these aspects of game programming, see Chapter 9, "Sound and Graphics." The details for *consty* comprise the following.

Graphics Type

The graphics are based on a 2D Qt canvas view in which the game elements can be drawn using sprites (see Chapter 6, "Canvas Games").

Graphics

The two players are distinguished by the colors red and blue. All cells owned by one of the players, their weights, and the player's units are drawn in these colors or shades of these colors. The following graphic elements are needed:

- The player and opponent sprites as colored circles.
- The special items (little diamonds).
- The starting and goal locations (a flag and a door).

- Cells with connection lines to their neighbors.
- Weight indications, which are filled circles (1–3) in the colors of the players and are located inside the cells.

All sprites contain several images (frames) that consist of the various states of the items. For example, the cell sprite contains all 16 different connection possibilities to its neighbors, and the weight sprites are constructed from several frames, where each frame displays a different amount of colored circles. Figure 18.3 depicts some frames of the weight and cell connection sprites. Depending on the game situation, one of these frames is shown for each sprite.

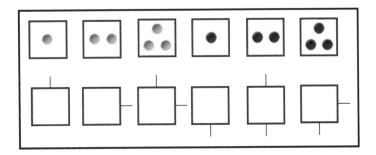

FIGURE 18.3   Two frame sequences, with the first depicting the cell weights that are represented by filled circles of two different colors. The second shows the cell connections, drawn by lines connecting to other cells.

Sound

A repeating background tune accompanies the game. The tune should be unobtrusive so the player is not disturbed. It should also be able to be switched off. Actions of the player such as moving and the end of the game are accompanied by short sound effects.

Artificial Intelligence

The second player will be controlled by an AI computer player. The AI will be script based and implement some basic rules on how to catch the first player. A main element of the AI player will be a pathfinding algorithm that can calculate the distances to various locations on the game board by respecting the weights of the fields. In this version of the game, the AI should not change the weights of cells unless it needs to reduce the weight of a cell so it can continue to move.

Level Design

The levels are "mazes" of interconnected cells. The connections between the cells and the initial weights of the cells are determined by the level designer. Some cells are given a special meaning; these are the start and goal location(s). Both can be placed arbitrarily on the game board. Furthermore, it is possible to optionally place special items on the game board. If they are present, a certain number of them need to be picked up by the first player before he can run for the goal. This amount is also specified by the level designer.

The human and the AI player have an arbitrary amount of units that will start from the given start locations. These starting places are also determined by the level design. Each of the units has an individual "life" counter, and if it reaches zero, the unit has to restart from the starting location. This counter is also part of the level design because it can influence the game strategy.

The level design should generally allow more than one route to win the game. The levels are stored in KDE resource files (ASCII), and one possible level is depicted in Figure 18.2.

THE CLASS DESIGN

The *consty* game should follow the usual design concept of a desktop game and consequently employ the extended document-view model; that is, the document-view plus the player and input classes, discussed in Chapter 1. This type of design is also used by the KDE KGame library, and thus we have chosen to base the *consty* game on KGame. However, if you want to develop the game for Qt or Qtopia, you can easily drop the KGame dependency.

To implement the extended document-view model, we need an *application* object, a *main window*, a *game document*, a *view*, and *players* together with their *input* devices. Additionally, we require a *sound server* to play the background music and the sound effects. An overview of these classes and their relationships is depicted in Figure 18.4.

The application (KApplication) is used to communicate with KDE, and the main window (MainWindow) represents the application, its frame, menus, and status bar to the user. This basic application configuration is discussed in detail for KDE, pure Qt, and Qtopia in Chapters 3–5.

The document class GameDoc (derived from the KGame class itself) represents the game data (by storing the actual game board Board) and the game flow logic (via methods like nextPlayer() and gameOver()). Since the game should be able to be stopped at any time and, when desired, continued later, the game document needs to be able to load and save itself. This save game handling is inherited from KGame by using loadgame() and savegame(). Furthermore, the GameDoc class should handle the input of all players to the game (using `playerInput()`). Most of these key methods are already defined by `KGame` and only need to be overwritten for our specific extensions. Figure 18.5 shows the class design of the game document and how it incorporates the actual game board and interacts with the players.

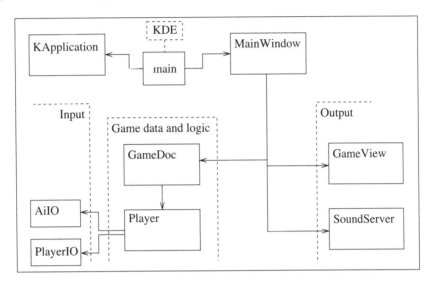

FIGURE 18.4 The game design overview showing the application, the main window, the document, the player and IO objects, the view, and the sound server.

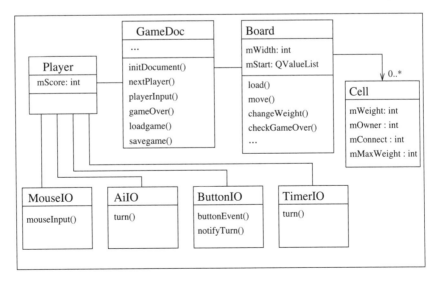

FIGURE 18.5 Class diagram of the game document and its dependencies. For all classes, the key attributes and methods are depicted.

Attached to the GameDoc is the player class Player. It is derived from the corresponding KPlayer class and its purpose is to store all player-related data and handle the player input devices. Fortunately, KPlayer already handles most of the game flow and input issues of a player, and thus our derived class Player needs to do little more than store the score or the points of the player (mScore).

Each player can be controlled by an arbitrary amount of input devices. The human player can use the mouse, a pushbutton, or an automatic timed input, which for convenience reasons will perform an automatic weight change move if the player has no choices left; that is, if his unit is on a field owned by the second player. This is so the player is not bored from having to constantly click the *Change Weight* button. The computer player is controlled by the AI engine, which invokes the AI script from another input device. All input classes are derived from the KGameIO modules, but react on different events to create the game inputs. For example, the MouseIO representing the mouse input will be invoked on mouse clicks, while the AiIO is automatically started as soon as it becomes the computer player's turn. However, both will send the same type of input to the game and thus create valid moves.

Also attached to the document is the actual game board, termed Board, which contains information such as its size, the player's start locations, the goal, and the locations of the special items. The board is made from a rectangular array of interconnected cells (see Figures 18.1 and 18.2). These cells are stored inside the board as an array of Cell objects. Each cell is a simple object and contains the basic attributes necessary to describe a game board location, such as its owner, its weights, and the connection to neighboring cells.

The board and the cells contain methods that allow you to query the state of the board or the cell (e.g., the cell owner, the weight, or the possible connections to other cells). Most of these methods are trivial and are omitted in Figure 18.5 for space reasons.

Since the game document allows both the loading and saving of a game, the board and the cell also need to support the loading and saving of their state. With this concept, for example, the loading of a game basically just invokes the loading of the board, which in turn invokes the loading of the cells.

The view and display part of the game is collected in the GameView class, the purpose of which is to manage the display and window drawings. Since we combine a canvas and traditional Qt widgets, such as pushbuttons, we organize all view elements in a master view, the GameView. This view internally manages the buttons (QPushButton) and the canvas view (CanvasView). The class design of this view concept is shown in Figure 18.6, and its layout in Figure 18.7.

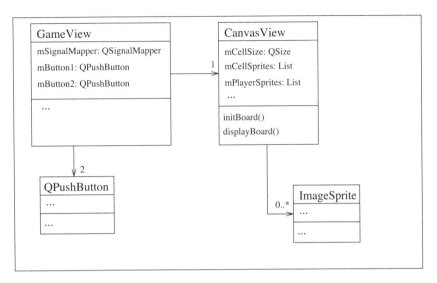

FIGURE 18.6 Class diagram of the game view and its dependencies. In the classes, only key attributes and methods are depicted.

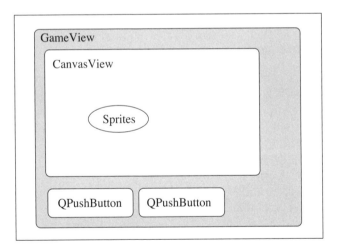

FIGURE 18.7 The game view: a canvas view and two push-buttons are combined in the master game view.

The main graphical display is handled by the CanvasView class. For the display of the game board, the items and players image sprites of the class ImageSprite are used. These sprites are based on a QCanvasSprite (see Chapter 6) and support multiple frames that can be loaded from files. Even if a sprite does not do much more than what the base class QCanvasSprite offers, it is usually a good idea to subclass the original sprite classes, because you are then more flexible if you decide to implement additional features later. In our game and for convenience, all sprites are loaded at the beginning of a level and stored in lists inside the view during runtime.

Finally, we require a sound server, which must be able to play back looped background music and individual sound effects. The sound server will be based on aRts and thus allow immediate implementation of these features. However, we wrap all calls to aRts in the class SoundServer so we can maintain independence from the actual sound library. For example, we could then easily replace aRts by QSound or Sound when moving to a different platform (see Chapter 9).

THE IMPLEMENTATION

ON THE CD

After describing and designing the game, we can now continue to actually implement the necessary classes. The complete game and all classes are included on the CD-ROM accompanying this book in the folder examples/consty. You can use this source code to look up details and to extend the game. In addition, the full API documentation generated with doxygen can be found in the apidoc directory on the CD-ROM. We will therefore not show the full source code in this chapter, but instead concentrate on some of the key parts important for a desktop game.

Setting up the KDE Application

Developing a standard KDE application requires you to follow a typical setup sequence (see Chapter 3, "Game Development using KDE"). The program starts with the C++ main() function in the main.cpp program. Here, the application is instantiated, the application data is set, the main window is created, and the event loop is run.

```
int main(int argc, char* argv[])
{
  // Create the application data, the exact parameters
  // are listed in Chapter 3
  KAboutData* aboutData = new KAboutData(...);
  ...

  // Create new application object
  KApplication app;

  // Enable the locale for libkdegames
  KGlobal::locale()->insertCatalogue("libkdegames");

  // Check whether the application is restored
  if (app.isRestored())
  {
```

```
    RESTORE(MainWindow);
  }
  // or whether we create it new
  else
  {
    MainWindow* mainwindow = new MainWindow();
    mainwindow->show();
  }

  // Run the application's event loop
  return app.exec();
}
```

KDE applications require a main window that needs to create the GUI and provide slots to handle menu calls (actions). Our game will have some menu items such as *New Game* or *Load Game*. Additionally, the game document and view need to be instantiated. This is done in the file `mainwindow.cpp`.

```
MainWindow::MainWindow()
        : KMainWindow(0)
{
  ...

  // Add the source directory to KDE search path, to allow
  // running of the application in the development directory
  KGlobal::dirs()->addResourceDir("data", SRCDIR +
                            QString::fromLatin1("/.."));

  // Create a document and a view and initialize them
  mDoc   = new GameDoc(this);
  mView  = new GameView(mDoc, this);
  setCentralWidget(mView);
  ...

  // Set up the menus etc
  initGUI();
  createGUI(QString::null);
  ...
}
```

The `initGUI()` call is actually used to define the actions, menus, and menu items. This is comparable to the one shown in the setup in Chapter 3, and therefore you can refer to that chapter if you require further details or explanations.

The KGame framework (see Chapter 15) allows you to start a new game easily by just changing the status of the game document object. The implementation of the menu slot that corresponds to the *New Game* menu could look like

```
void MainWindow::fileNew()
{
  // End anything still running
  mDoc->setGameStatus(KGame::End);
  // Init the board and clear the old game out
  mDoc->setGameStatus(KGame::Init);
  // Run it
  mDoc->setGameStatus(KGame::Run);
}
```

In this slot, any ongoing old game is ended, the game board is initialized, and a new game is started. All calls to setGameStatus() are processed in the GameDoc object, where the appropriate actions are executed. In the case of the KGame framework, this is done by the internal KGame properties. When not using KGame, you would implement the setGameStatus() method independently in the game document.

The game also should support loading and saving. As an example, we show the file open dialog routine invoked from the *Open Game* menu. It uses the KDE file open dialog to retrieve the filename and then in turn tells the game to load this file.

```
void MainWindow::fileLoad()
{
  // Store the application dialog settings.
  QString dir = QString(":<consty>");
  // Filter directory for "*.dat" files
  QString filter = QString("*.dat");
  // Show the file dialog
  QString file;
  file = KFileDialog::getOpenFileName(dir, filter, this);

  // Load the game
  if (!file.isEmpty()) { mDoc->load(file,true); }
}
```

ON THE CD The program source code on the companion CD-ROM also contains some extra methods that are invoked when the game status changes. These alterations, such as switching the player or a game over, are displayed to the user in the main window as status bar text or in a message box.

The Game Document

The game document object of the class `GameDoc` is derived from the `KGame` class. This class provides the game-over logic, serves as a container for the game data (the game board), and describes which player has the next turn. The class definition in the file `gamedoc.h` reads:

```
class GameDoc : public KGame
{
  Q_OBJECT

  public:
    GameDoc(QWidget* parent);
    // Game logic: next player
    KPlayer* nextPlayer(KPlayer* last,bool exclusive);
    ...

  protected:
    // Game move input
    bool playerInput(QDataStream& msg,KPlayer* player);
    // Start up: create a new player
    KPlayer* createPlayer(int rtti, int io, bool isvirtual);
    // Start up: create a new input device
    void createIO(KPlayer* player, KGameIO::IOMode io);
    // Game logic: check for game over
    int checkGameOver(KPlayer* player);
    // Load and save games
    bool loadgame(QDataStream& stream,
                  bool network,
                  bool reset);
    bool savegame(QDataStream& stream,
                  bool network,
                  bool saveplayers);
    ...

  public slots:
    // KGame notification
    void propertyChanged(KGamePropertyBase* prop,
                         KGame* game);
    ...

  private:
    Board* mBoard;
};
```

In the file `gamedoc.cpp`, we implement the actual game logic and game flow methods. The constructor is used to initialize the KGame object properly, which mainly requires the initialization of the property handling (for further details, see Chapter 15). Obviously, this part can be omitted when not using the KGame library.

The players are now initialized and added to the game. This is performed directly after the game document construction is complete, and we specifically show this step because it demonstrates how players can be easily added to a KGame game.

```
Player* player = (Player*)createPlayer(1, PLAYER_IO, false);
player->setUserId(1);
player->setName(i18n("Player %1").arg(1+i));
addPlayer(player);

// And the same for the second player
...
```

The `createPlayer()` method, called by this initialization, stems from KGame and needs to be overwritten. Note that when using the KGame library, this is the only place a player can be created. If you do not use the KGame framework, you have a bit more freedom when creating the players.

```
KPlayer* GameDoc::createPlayer(int rtti, int io, bool isNet)
{
  KPlayer* player = (KPlayer*)new Player();

  // If not virtual (network) insert an IO device
  if (!isNet) { createIO(player,(KGameIO::IOMode)io); }

  return player;
}
```

In the next step, the input devices for the players are created. Depending on whether the player is a human player or an AI player (distinguished by the IOMode variable), the corresponding classes are instantiated and plugged into the players. In accordance with the actual input task, some additional parameters are passed to the input devices. For example, for the human player, this is the view to access the mouse, and for the button, we need access to the button signals, which are provided by a QSignalMapper object.

```
void GameDoc::createIO(KPlayer* player, KGameIO::IOMode io)
{
  // Create the human interface
  if (io & PLAYER_IO)
```

```
  {
    new MouseIO(this, mView->canvasView(), player);
    new ButtonIO(this, mView->signalMapper(), player);
    new TimerIO(this, player);

    ...
  }
  else if (io & AI_IO)
  {
    new AiIO(this, player);
  }
}
```

Note that the constructors of the IO devices couple them automatically with the player objects. The player objects also perform the destruction of the input devices.

Loading and saving a game is done by the corresponding loadgame() and savegame() methods. Here we need to manually stream the game board to or from a save file, and this is easy with the KGame framework since the file data stream is already provided. If you do not use KGame, you would work in a similar way but would have to manually open the file and stream.

```
bool GameDoc::loadgame(QDataStream& stream,
                       bool network,
                       bool reset)
{
  // Load the game board
  mBoard->loadgame(stream);

  // load the new game (KGame only)
  bool res = KGame::loadgame(stream, network ,reset);

  // If so we need to redraw the sprites
  mView->canvasView()->displayBoard(mBoard);

  ...
}
```

Saving is completely analogous to loading and therefore not demonstrated here.

The key method for processing the game input is the playerInput() method, which is called by the KGame framework if any move input by any IO has occurred. When not using the framework, you can manually call playerInput() from your input devices.

```
bool GameDoc::playerInput(QDataStream& msg, KPlayer* player)
{
  ...
  // Read the move from the stream. The format is defined
  // entirely by our IO classes
  msg >> pl >> moveType >> moveX >> moveY >> unit;

  // Several move types are supported in our game (defined
  // in global.h)
  if (moveType == MOVE)
  {
    // Perform the move (sprite and logic)
    mBoard->move(pl, unit, moveX, moveY);
    mBoard->reduceLife(pl, unit);
  }
  else if (moveType == SKIP)
  ...
  else if (moveType == CHANGE_WEIGHT)
  ...

  // Tell the view to redraw the sprites
  mView->canvasView()->displayBoard(mBoard);

  // Delayed continuation of the move sequence
  QTimer::singleShot(300, this, SLOT(moveFinished()));
  ...
  return false;
}
```

Note that in the KGame framework we can return false from the playerInput() method and thus prevent the library from automatically continuing with the next turn. We can then invoke the next turn manually by calling a single-shot timer at the end of playerInput(), which will continue the game after it runs out. This trick can be used to create a small delay in the movement sequence, but is also an ideal place to start a sprite movement animation.

The purpose of the nextPlayer() method is to determine which player and which unit can make the next move. In our game, this is not so straightforward, because each player can have more than one unit, and all units are moved in turn before the players are switched. This rule has to be respected in the nextPlayer() method. Again, when using the KGame framework, the nextPlayer() method is already provided by the library, but we will overwrite it and implement our unit-based turn concept (within the KGame framework, you could also create a KGameSequence object and plug it into the game instead of directly overwriting this method).

```
KPlayer* GameDoc::nextPlayer(KPlayer* last, bool)
{
  // How many moving units are left
  int moveUnits = ((Player*)last)->moves();
  // Switch player if no move units are left
  if (moveUnits <= 0)
  {
    if (last->userId() == 1 )
    {
      mCurrentPlayer = 2;
    }
    else
    {
      mCurrentPlayer = 1;
    }
    moveUnits =
       mBoard->moveUnits(mCurrentPlayer.value());
  }

  // Find the player object belonging to that player
  Player* next = getPlayer(mCurrentPlayer);
  // and allow it to make the next turn
  next->setTurn(true, true);
  ...

  return (KPlayer*)next;
}
```

A specialty of the KGame framework is that it notifies us as soon as any KGame property has been changed (again see Chapter 15 for details). Here, we are interested in a game status change such as the game being started or stopped. We react to this accordingly in a slot.

```
void GameDoc::propertyChanged(KGamePropertyBase* prop,
                              KGame*)
{
  // Find out which variable is changed by comparing id's
  // Game Status changed (Run, Init, End,...)
  if (prop->id() == KGamePropertyBase::IdGameStatus)
  {
    // If the game status is changed to 'run':
    if (gameStatus() == Run)
    {
```

```
        // Set the start player
        nextPlayer(0, true);
    }
    // If the status is changed to 'initialization':
    else if (gameStatus() == Init)
    {
        // Initialize the game
        initGame();
    }
  }
}
```

Any other property could be queried in the same way. If you develop outside the KGame framework, you will not have this property method and probably react to emitted Qt events in a similar manner.

Finally, the check for *game over* is forwarded from the document to the actual board, because here all the cells and positions are stored and a check for *game over* is easier.

```
int GameDoc::checkGameOver(KPlayer*)
{
    // If the game is not over, return 0
    return mBoard->checkGameOver();
}
```

The Board

The main part of the game data is the actual game board, which stores the fields as an array of cells (see Figure 18.2). Board and cells are mainly standard C++ container classes storing the data together with some convenience access methods. The key properties of the game Board defined in the board.h file are the size of the game board and the array of cells.

```
Class Board
{
  public:
    Board(int width, int height);
    ...

    // Read the level definition from file
    void importLevel(QString filename, int level);
```

```
            // Load and save the current game board
            void loadgame(QDataStream& stream);
            void savegame(QDataStream& stream);
            ...

        private:
            // Game board size
            int mWidth;
            int mHeight;
            // Amount of specials to remove
            int mSpecial;
            // Array of cells
            QPtrVector<Cell> mCells;
            ...
    };
```

The Cell class defined in cell.h describes a single cell on the game board, mainly with its weight, owner, and connections.

```
    Class Cell
    {
      public:
        Cell();
        ...

        // Load and save the current cell
        void loadgame(QDataStream& stream);
        void savegame(QDataStream& stream);
        ...

      private:
        // Cell properties
        int mWeight;
        PlayerType mOwner;
        Sides mConnections;
        ...
    };
```

ON THE CD
We only comment on two interesting board methods that relate to Qt and KDE game development, and refer to the documented files on the companion CD-ROM for more details. First, the board is able to import a game level from disk. The level is stored in an ASCII file formatted as a KDE resource file.

```
[Board]
width=10
height=6
specials=2

[Player]
life1=99
...
```

These files can be read very easily using the KSimpleConfig class, which loads exactly this type of KDE resource file (see Chapter 3).

```cpp
void Board::importLevel(QString filename, int level)
{
    // Open a config file for reading: the level number
    // is inserted into the filename as "board%1.rc"
    KSimpleConfig config(filename.arg(level), true);
    config.setGroup("Board");
    // The board size
    mWidth          = config.readNumEntry("width");
    mHeight         = config.readNumEntry("height");
    ...

    config.setGroup("Player");
    mMaxLife1       = config.readIntListEntry("life1");
    ...

    // Read cell weights: here, the key depends on the actual
    // board row to read
    QString key = "..."; // e.g. "row5"
    config.setGroup("CellCount");
    QValueList<int> blockList = config.readIntListEntry(key);
    ...
}
```

By using KSimpleConfig, we can load various types of data, including integer numbers, strings, and lists. A non-KDE alternative to KSimpleConfig would be QSettings.

In the second method, a game is loaded and saved using data streams. Consequently, the game board also needs to load and save its data to and from the stream. In the KGame framework, there is already a QDataStream available, which we can use for this purpose. Outside this framework, any other IO streams will function identically, and instead of using binary data, it is then possible to store the game data as XML (see Chapter 16, "XML").

The board (and the cells) performs this storage handling, which is now listed for the case of loading.

```
void Board::loadgame(QDataStream& stream)
{
  // Load board properties
  stream >> mWidth >> mHeight >> mSpecial;
  ...

  // Load all cells
  mCells.resize(mWidth*mHeight);
  for (int i=0; i<mWidth*mHeight; i++)
  {
    Cell* c = new Cell();
    c->loadgame(stream);
    mCells.insert(i, c);
  }
}
```

Obviously, saving works analogously.

```
void Board::savegame(QDataStream& stream)
{
  stream << mWidth << mHeight << mSpecial;
  ...

  // Save all cells
  for (int i=0; i<mWidth*mHeight; i++)
  {
    mCells[i]->savegame(stream);
  }
}
```

The Player

The player objects store all the information that is both relevant and individual to a player. In our game, there is not much player information. Consequently, the player class is very simple and only a little bit different from the base class `KPlayer`. We specify it in the `player.h` file as

```
class Player : public KPlayer
{
  Q_OBJECT
```

```
public:
  Player();

  ...

private:
  KGameProperty<int> mMoves;
  KGameProperty<int> mScore;

  ...
};
```

We mainly use this class to define some additional properties that hold the player's score and the number of moves a player has left.

The implementation in the file `player.cpp` is straightforward. In the `KGame` framework, you need to register the properties with the `KPlayer` property handler (see Chapter 15). For non-`KGame`-related games, this process of registration is obviously unnecessary.

The Input Devices

Our game supports several different input possibilities. Two main input categories are the human player and the AI computer player. However, the human player has several ways to make his input, and we could either combine these various inputs into one large input class or implement small input classes that are then specialized to handle a particular input type. Here, we choose the latter system.

The human player now has three different inputs, whereas the AI consists of only one input class (see also Figure 18.6). This leads to the following four types of input:

- Mouse button input arising from clicking on the game board.
- Pushing a pushbutton.
- For convenience, a timer is also used as input, which automatically creates a move for the player if there is no choice left.
- The AI algorithm input.

We focus here on the aspect of the mouse input for the human player. This class `MouseIO` subclasses the `KGameMouseIO` and must perform two principal tasks. First, in the constructor, the mouse event signal is connected to a local slot, which is called as soon as a mouse event occurs.

```
MouseIO::MouseIO(GameDoc* doc,
                 CanvasView* view,
                 KPlayer* player)
```

```
            : KGameMouseIO(view)
{
  connect(this, SIGNAL(signalMouseEvent(KGameIO*,
                                        QDataStream&,
                                        QMouseEvent*,
                                        bool*)),
            this, SLOT(mouseInput(KGameIO*,
                                  QDataStream&,
                                  QMouseEvent*,
                                  bool*)));

  player->addGameIO(this);
}
```

Second, the mouse event slot has to process the mouse input, which involves checking for the correct button, the current location on the game board, and whether the move is legal. If everything is all right, we can create a move input into the game.

```
void MouseIO::mouseInput(KGameIO* input,
                         QDataStream& stream,
                         QMouseEvent* mouse,
                         bool* inputProcessed)
{
  // First perform checks whether the game is running, it's the
  // player's turn, the left mouse button is pressed, ...:
  // we omit these checks here
  ...

  // The player
  Player* player = (Player*)input->player();

  // Obtain the actual game board point from the mouse
  // coordinates
  QPoint point = mView->translateMouseCoord(mouse->pos());

  // Create a move
  Q_INT32 moveType, moveX, moveY, pl, unit;
  moveType = MOVE;
  moveX    = point.x();
  moveY    = point.y();
  unit     = player->moves();
  pl       = player->userId();
```

```
    // Check whether this is a legal move
    if (!board->legalMove(pl, unit, point.x(), point.y()))
    {
      return;
    }

    // Now stream the move: The stream format is defined here
    // and needs to be read from the stream in exactly this form
    // in the GameDoc
    stream << pl << moveType << moveX << moveY << unit;

    // Indicate that the processing was successful
    *inputProcessed = true;
}
```

The View

The view of the game is split into several subwidgets that are managed by a grid lay-out manager (Chapter 2, "Qt Primer"). One of the layout cells contains the actual canvas view, while the others hold the pushbuttons. This layout situation is depicted in Figure 18.7. More widgets can be easily added to the layout and used in a game extension to display the status or information about moves, scores, and high scores.

The Game View

The file gameview.h is very simple and defines the game view.

```
class GameView : public QWidget
{
  Q_OBJECT

  public:
    GameView(GameDoc* doc, QWidget* parent = 0);
  ...

  private:
    CanvasView* mCanvasView;
    QPushButton* mButton1;
  ...
};
```

To allow easier communication of the control buttons with the actual game input logic, we do not directly connect the buttons to the input devices, but instead map them using a QSignalMapper (see Chapter 2). This signal mapper sends a signal with a user-defined parameter (here, the parameter corresponds to the move type) to the input device.

The file gameview.cpp contains the implementation of the game view. In brief, a Qt grid layout is constructed and the resulting canvas view will span a full row. The buttons are then arranged in individual cells below the canvas.

```
GameView::GameView(GameDoc* doc, QWidget* parent)
        : QWidget(parent)
{
  // Create a new signal mapper for the ButtonIO communication
  mSignalMapper = new QSignalMapper(this);

  // Make a grid layout
  QGridLayout* grid = new QGridLayout(this, 3, 3 );
  mCanvasView = new CanvasView(doc, this);

  mButton1 = new QPushButton("Skip move", this);
  connect(mButton1, SIGNAL(clicked()),
          mSignalMapper, SLOT(map()));
  mSignalMapper->setMapping(mButton1, SKIP);

  mButton2 = new QPushButton("Change weight", this);
  connect(mButton2, SIGNAL(clicked()),
          mSignalMapper, SLOT(map()));
  mSignalMapper->setMapping(mButton2, CHANGE_WEIGHT);

  grid->addMultiCellWidget(mCanvasView, 0, 0, 0, 3,
                           Qt::AlignLeft|Qt::AlignTop);

  // Add the first four widgets with (row, column)
  grid->addWidget(mButton1, 1, 0 );
  grid->addWidget(mButton2, 1, 1 );
  grid->setColStretch(3, 10);
}
```

The clicked() signal of the buttons is connected to the signal mapper so later we can connect to this signal mapper instead of the buttons.

The Canvas View

The most important part of the view is the actual canvas view, the specific details of which are described in Chapter 6. Here, we only briefly recap some if its key features.

In our game, the canvas view is defined in the file canvasview.h.

```
class CanvasView : public QCanvasView
{
  Q_OBJECT

  public:
    CanvasView(GameDoc* doc, QWidget* parent = 0);


  ...
};
```

The implementation is done in the file canvasview.cpp. In this example, the view is set up and a standard canvas with its properties is initialized.

```
CanvasView::CanvasView(GameDoc* doc, QWidget* parent)
            : QCanvasView(parent)
{
  // Scroll mode
  setVScrollBarMode(AlwaysOff);
  setHScrollBarMode(AlwaysOff);

  // Initialize canvas
  QCanvas* canvas = new QCanvas(parent);
  canvas->setDoubleBuffering(true);
  canvas->setBackgroundColor(QColor(0, 0, 128));
  canvas->setAdvancePeriod(15);
  setCanvas(canvas);

  // Set (fixed) size and position
  move(0, 0);
  setFixedSize(QSize(400, 300));
  canvas->resize(width(), height());
  ...
}
```

The main task of the view is to load the sprites from file and display them on the screen according to the status of the game board. The loading is performed using a QCanvasPixmapArray, which loads a sequence of files (which have to follow a certain naming convention) from the given data directory and allows you to store this sequence as individual frames in a sprite.

```
// Find the image directory
QString dir = kapp->dirs()->findResourceDir("data",
            "pic/player0000.png") + QString("pic/");
```

```
// Load images (player0000.png, player0001.png, ...)
QCanvasPixmapArray* pics;
pics = new QCanvasPixmapArray(dir+QString("player%1.png"),4);
...


// Set up sprite with a z-coordinate, the image array and the
// canvas
ImageSprite* sprite = new ImageSprite(100, pics, canvas());
sprite->move(..., ...);
sprite->show();
...
```

In our game, both the loading and the display of the sprites are split into two methods so the sprites are loaded on initialization of a new level and then stored in class attributes (QPtrVector, QPtrList). When displaying the sprites, they are re-trieved from these collections. For the sake of simplicity, the handling of these lists is omitted here, but can be found in the source code on the companion CD-ROM.

ON THE CD

The weight and cell connection sprites are positioned on the game board so that each sprite corresponds to one cell. Depending on the content of each cell (owner, weight, connections), the actual symbol (frame number) of the corre-sponding sprites is chosen. For this to function, the sprites store all possible images, and an example displaying these frames is shown in Figure 18.3. This procedure al-lows you to retain all sprites during the game even if the contents of the cell change.

```
// Display the start frame for start cells (the frame
// keywords CELLFRAME_START, ... are defined which
// correspond to the actual frame images loaded)
if (cell->isStart())
{
  cellSprite->setFrame(CELLFRAME_START);
}
...
// Display the weight in the color of player 1
else if (cell->owner() == PLAYER_1)
{
  cellSprite->setFrame(cell->weight());
}
...
```

The Sprites

The sprites displayed in the canvas view are basically QCanvasSprite items. How-ever, we subclass the QCanvasSprite class to give us more flexibility.

```
class ImageSprite : public QCanvasSprite
{
  public:
    ImageSprite(int z, QCanvasPixmapArray* a, QCanvas* c);
};
```

We use the constructor to specify the *z*-coordinate of the sprites, which allows us to display the player sprites on top of the weight sprites, which are on top of the background cells. All other methods are taken directly from the base class QCanvasSprite, but compared to directly taking the base class QCanvasSprite, the use of our sprite class ImageSprite allows for easier game extensions.

Each sprite stores a sequence of frames, which are used to show all the different function possibilities, such as the various weights or the different connections of the cells. Figure 18.3 depicts several different sprite frames.

The Sound Manager

As described in Chapter 9, aRts has some drawbacks for sound effects in games that relate in part to the latency time of aRts. However, for a small KDE game, it is still the best option available because you do not have to incorporate additional sound libraries into your game.

Our game has simple background music and only a few sound effects. Both are manageable with aRts, and the availability and ease of use compared to other sound libraries makes it a good choice. When you want to transfer this game to Qt or Qtopia, you can easily replace the aRts play() calls by those from QSound or Sound. Their behavior is very similar and equally unproblematic.

The sound of the game is managed by a sound manager. This object can load and play music or sound effects using aRts (or QSound). Having a sound manager makes the game more independent from the actual applied sound library. Our sound manager is uncomplicated and allows only the playback of sound files. The playback can be either performed once or repeatedly continued. The sound manager is defined as the class Sound in the file sound.h.

```
#include <arts/kartsserver.h>
#include <arts/kartsdispatcher.h>
#include <arts/kplayobject.h>

class Sound : public QObject
{
  Q_OBJECT

  public:
    // Construct the server and specify the sound
```

```
    // directory location
    Sound(QString dir);
    // Start play back of a sound
    void play(QString file, bool loop = false);

  protected slots:
    void timeout();

  ...

  private:
    // Initialize the aRts communication
    KArtsDispatcher mDispatcher;
    // The aRts sound server
    KArtsServer mSoundServer;
    ...
};
```

Here, it is of particular importance to create an object of the type KArts
Dispatcher. Although we do not directly use this object, it maintains the internal
connection to aRts.

The initialization of aRts and the playback of sound and music are done following the guidelines described in Chapter 9. In the file sound.cpp, we implement
the sound management and here, the main method is play(), which can play back
any sound format supported by aRts.

```
// The play object factory
KPlayObjectFactory factory(mSoundServer.server());

// Create a play object. The filename to the sound is
// stored in 'url'.
KPlayObject* playObject = factory.createPlayObject(url, true);

// Play the play object if it got created
if(playObject && !playObject->isNull())
{
  playObject->play();
  ...
}
```

To clean up the play objects when they are no longer needed and to support
playback looping, we use a QTimer (see Chapter 2). This timer periodically checks
the status of all ongoing sound effects, and if they have finished, it either repeats or

removes them. Note that QSound and Sound already provide sound looping, and thus the timer method is no longer required. However, for our aRts implementation we use the timeout() slot called by a timer and perform these checks. The details of this cleanup and looping can be found in the corresponding file sound.cpp on the companion CD-ROM.

ARTIFICIAL INTELLIGENCE

Artificial intelligence applicable for the board games discussed in this chapter can be implemented in various ways (see Chapter 10, "Artificial Intelligence"). Scripted AIs usually create a good computer player in simple board games. An alternative is Min-Max game trees, which use a board evaluation.

Our game could be analyzed by a Min-Max tree search, but we do not use this implementation technique for the following two reasons. First, the game requires quite a deep movement analysis, and therefore numerous positions need to be calculated to obtain a strategic valuable move. With limited computer resources, this is only possible after optimizing the tree search so that many unfavorable moves are not evaluated. This is quite a complicated task and one we feel is not justified for this game. Second, in Chapter 10, we already presented an example game using a Min-Max tree search: therefore, we decided here to demonstrate how an AI script approach can create the computer player.

Scripted AI

We first define a very basic set of scripting commands for the AI engine. Using these commands, we can then construct a basic strategy that the computer player can follow. For the sake of simplicity, we implement the scripting code directly in C++ using the C/C++ preprocessor.

In the script, we defined the following types of script commands:

Movement commands such as DO_CHANGE_WEIGHT, DO_MOVE, DO_SKIP: These commands will execute one of the possible actions of the computer player.

Property queries such as CANNOT_MOVE, SPECIALS_AVAILABLE, TARGET_IS_BLOCKED: These statements query some of the properties or states of the game.

Distance function queries such as DISTANCE(): The distance between two locations on the game board is a key element of our game, and the AI strategy clearly depends on its accuracy. Note that a distance on the map has to reflect the weights of the cells, because following a path needs more turns if it crosses cells with high weights owned by the opposing player.

Locations such as `MY_LOCATION, GOAL_LOCATION, PLAYER_1, INTERSECT()`: These properties represent locations or player positions on the board. They can be used as parameters for the query functions.

Our script in the file `ai.script` reads:

```
// Check whether a valid move is possible.
// If not change weight of the cell
if (CANNOT_MOVE)
{
  DO_CHANGE_WEIGHT
}
else
{
  // Differ the strategy when special items are available
  if (SPECIALS_AVAILABLE)
  {
    DO_MOVE(PLAYER_LOCATION)
  }

  // Make some checks on the distance between the AI and
  // the goal, the player and the goal and the AI and the
  // player. Depending on this move either toward the
  // player, the goal or intersect the player's path to the
  // goal
  else if (DISTANCE(MY_LOCATION, GOAL_LOCATION) <
          DISTANCE(PLAYER_1, GOAL_LOCATION) &&
          DISTANCE(MY_LOCATION, GOAL_LOCATION) >3)
  {
    DO_MOVE(GOAL_LOCATION)
  }
  else if (DISTANCE(MY_LOCATION, GOAL_LOCATION) >=
          DISTANCE(PLAYER_1, GOAL_LOCATION))
  {
    DO_MOVE(INTERSECT(PLAYER_1, GOAL_LOCATION, 50))
  }
  // As default follow the player
  else
  {
    DO_MOVE(PLAYER_LOCATION)
  }

  // Make sure the selected path is free
  if (TARGET_IS_BLOCKED)
  {
```

```
        DO_SKIP
    }
}
```

In this script, we first test whether the computer player can move. No move is possible if it lands on a cell that is currently owned by the human player. The only option left for the AI is to change the weight of the cell until the cell is no longer owned by the human player. If this restriction does not apply, the AI checks some game scenarios. First, if the human player still needs to pick up special items from the game board, the computer tries to follow him. In this case, the human player cannot yet win the game by entering the goal. However, if there are no special items left, the computer player will move either toward the human player or toward the goal to block his path. Finally, it is possible that the computer player cannot move because it is enclosed by other AI units. In this case, the path is blocked and the AI simply waits a turn. Note that this can create a deadlock situation and can only be avoided by cooperative AIs, which requires an algorithm that respects all computer units.

The strategy implemented in this small script is not a particular clever strategy; nevertheless, the AI plays fairly well. We tried to keep the strategy simple so the script does not become unnecessarily complicated; improvements on this implementation in the AI strategy are now up to you. Two extensions are already obvious. First, you will notice that our AI strategy does not plan cooperative moves of the AI units; they all move independently. Thus, a better strategy could be devised if the movements were coordinated. Second, the computer player does not analyze the board for strategic valuable positions; it basically just follows the player.

Pathfinding

One key ingredient for the AI strategy is to know the shortest path and the length of that path between two arbitrary locations on the game board. Without this knowledge, it is impossible to know how to reach a selected location in the fastest possible manner, and for the AI to decide where to move. When calculating such a path, the different weights and the owners of the board cells have to be respected, because cells that are owned by the opposing player will delay a move until the weights are completely removed; therefore, these paths are effectively much longer.

This type of situation is ideal for the application of the A* pathfinding algorithm described in Chapter 11, "Pathfinding." It will find the shortest path between two locations and calculate the actual movement costs with respect to the weights of the cells. Therefore, it will automatically prefer a geometrically longer path with lower weights to a geometrically shorter path with higher weights.

For the implementation of A*, we use the algorithm from Chapter 11. The algorithm presented there is generic and requires only two alterations for our purposes here. In the first, we pass our game board to the algorithm so it can find the connections between the cells and the corresponding weights. In addition, when adding new cells to the open or closed list, we query our game board as to whether connections to the neighbors actually exist. When new locations are added, this is determined by movement costs, which are derived from the weight and the owner of the board cells.

All other ingredients of the A* algorithm such as the open and closed lists stay unchanged, and therefore we do not repeat their source code here. Details can be found in the files `astarpath.h` and `astarpath.cpp` on the companion CD-ROM. Instead, we now show how to calculate and retrieve a path in the AI calculation. The path between the two locations `QPoint current` and `QPoint target` is calculated as

```
AStarPath* astar = new AStarPath();

// Calculate the path for our game board and a given player
astar->calculatePath(mBoard, mPlayer,
                  current.x(), current.y(),
                  target.x(),  target.y());

// List of cells along the shortest path
QValueList<QPoint> list = astar->getPath();

// Cost of the path, that is length and weights
int cost = astar->pathCost();

// A typical movement would go to the first entry of the path
QPoint go = list[1];
```

On small maps, like the one in our game, A* is fast. Consequently, it is not necessary to store the retrieved paths, nor is it a problem to calculate many paths during each AI turn.

MULTIMEDIA

After implementing all source code classes, we are now ready to create and integrate the music, sound, and graphics elements. This is pure artistic work that you can do with your favorite paint and music programs, or assign to an available artist. Figure 18.8 shows some of the resulting artistic items created for the game.

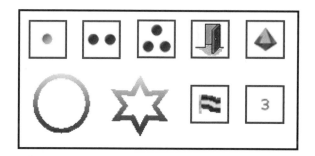

FIGURE 18.8 Screenshot of some sprites created for our game.

BUILDING THE GAME

The game is created using the standard KDE build and Makefiles as presented in Chapter 3. These include:

ON THE CD

- The automake Makefile.am for the main and source directories
- The KDE build files from the admin directory (included on the companion CD-ROM)
- Program icons
- The GUI resource file constyui.rc for menu definitions
- A desktop file that specifies the KDE properties of the game

Figure 18.9 shows a screenshot of the resulting directory structure. The build process can be started as usual using:

```
make -f Makefile.cvs
./configure
make
make install
```

In the subdirectory consty, you can also generate the API documentation with make apidox, which will then be stored as HTML files with an index document doc/html/index.html.

admin	4,0 KB	Folder
consty	4,0 KB	Folder
data	4,0 KB	Folder
board1.rc	1,4 KB	Plain Text Document
pic	4,0 KB	Folder
cell0000.png	206 B	PNG Image
<more>	0 B	Empty Document
sound	4,0 KB	Folder
gameover.wav	382,5 KB	WAV Audio
<more>	0 B	Empty Document
src	4,0 KB	Folder
board.h	4,2 KB	C Header File
Makefile.am	750 B	Makefile
<more>	0 B	Empty Document
consty.desktop	205 B	Desktop Config File
constyui.rc	387 B	Plain Text Document
cr16-app-consty.png	363 B	PNG Image
cr32-app-consty.png	963 B	PNG Image
cr48-app-consty.png	1,2 KB	PNG Image
Makefile.am	278 B	Makefile
configure.in.in	418 B	Plain Text Document
Makefile.am.in	1,3 KB	Makefile
Makefile.cvs	458 B	Makefile

FIGURE 18.9 Screenshot of the file explorer showing all files necessary for the build process. Multiple similar files are left out and replaced by <more>.

THE RESULT

Finally, after implementing all source files, creating the sound and graphics, and managing the KDE build process, we now have a finished game that can be started and played. Figure 18.10 shows a screenshot of the resulting game.

ON THE CD

The full source code, the sound, and graphics are included on the companion CD-ROM in the folder `examples/consty`.

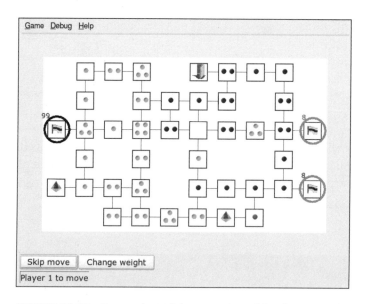

FIGURE 18.10 Screenshot of the game board for the example program. A color version (`18_10_consty_col.png`) can be found on the companion CD-ROM in the folder `figures`.

GAME ENHANCEMENTS

The game we presented in this chapter is a working desktop game. However, for the sake of simplicity, we did not implement some enhancements that would make this game more interesting for a real player. We leave this aspect as a practice task for you. You can use the game as a foundation and try to implement some new features.

A few possible features are listed in the following inventory, and we indicate the level of difficulty to implement that enhancement:

- Implement more levels and allow the user to choose one (easy).
- Instead of allowing the user to choose a level freely, store the levels the user managed to solve. Once a level is solved, the user automatically goes to the next level. In addition, the user can always select any level he has already played (easy).
- Count the score for the player as described in the game design document and display it on the screen. In addition, allow the player to enter his score in a high-score table (easy).
- Allow the player to switch the sound effects on and off (easy).
- When closing the application and restarting it, you can reload the game parameters from the KDE configuration files (e.g., go to the last played level) (easy).
- Add advanced graphics (explosions, etc.) and sound effects (medium).

- Introduce an animated introduction graphic instead of the simple welcome text (medium).
- Introduce an animated movement when the player moves, wins, or loses (medium).
- Implement an animated game-over sequence; for example a firework (see Chapter 12, "Particle Effects") (medium).
- Enhance the computer AI player by implementing a more sophisticated script, including more possibilities such as cooperative AI units (hard).
- Allow the computer player to be replaced by a network player so two players can play the game together (see Chapter 14, "Qt Network Games," and Chapter 15) (hard).
- Write a level editor that allows you to write and edit level files with a GUI (hard).

SUMMARY

Game development is easier than you might believe. In addition, it is a rewarding and enjoyable pastime because you do an imaginative task and create something unique and cool. Game development can be a great deal of fun when you begin to design and develop your own games and notice that players enjoy them, or when helping to contribute to other Open Source games. This is particularly true when you develop with a good and friendly team of developers such as the people in the KDE community.

Many technologies presented in this book such as pathfinding or artificial intelligence Min-Max tree searches can be easily applied to other games. You can take the models and classes described in the corresponding chapters and adapt them for your own use and games, or follow the references provided for a more extensive study of these topics. With this basis, we hope that you will quickly obtain a pathfinding search or AI that you can implement in your own games.

In this chapter, we combined most of the topics discussed in the scope of this book and used them to develop a small desktop game. By following the outline of this chapter and referring to the accompanying chapters to enhance your knowledge of the different specialty points, you can quickly program the basic elements of a small game. You can then continue with this example program or branch out with your own developmental ideas—so, let's get going.

Appendix

A About the CD-ROM

The companion CD-ROM contains the source code and documentation for all the example programs used to demonstrate the techniques described in this book. In detail, it contains:

■ The example programs (`examples` folder)
■ The API documentation for the example programs (`apidoc` folder)
■ Free tools and games (`tools` folder)
■ The figures in the book (`figures` folder)

You can access most documents from the index page (`index.html`) in the root directory of the CD-ROM. Please read that file first.

To access the source code or the programs, copy the CD-ROM to your hard drive and then open the corresponding directories (don't forget to change the directories to read/write mode if you want to compile the programs).

Code Examples

The example section contains the demonstration programs for the features, algorithms, or program examples discussed in the book. The example programs are divided into different categories for Qt 3, Qt 4, KDE, PDAs, and Microsoft Windows and are in the folder `examples`. Note: to compile the example programs from one of these categories, the corresponding development packages need to be installed on your system.

API Documentation

The API documentation section contains the complete API documentation for the example programs. The API documentation is generated using Doxygen and is in the folder `apidoc`.

Tools

The CD-ROM also contains some free development tools and Qt/KDE games. These programs are all Open Source or freeware and developed by third-party developers. We provide them "as is" and without any guarantee that they can be installed and work on your computer. The exact requirements, the compiling, installation, license details, and authorship details can be found inside the corresponding packages. These programs and tools are in the `tools` folder as compressed packages.

Figures

The CD-ROM also contains all the figures shown in the book (as color versions where appropriate) in the folder `figures`. An overview is provided by the file `images.html` in the same folder.

Copyright and Licenses

Unless otherwise noted in a program or in the folder where a program resides (for example by a file called LICENSE or COPYING) all files on the CD are covered by the copyright as stated in the README file.

The tools and examples in the folder tools are third party applications under an Open Source license (for example the GPL license) allowing free redistribution. However, for the exact license requirements refer to the license files accompanying these applications.

System Requirements

The is no special requirement for the computer, graphics card or processor. A slower system will just run the examples slower whilst a faster system will run them faster. However, the examples for the various operating systems require certain **development** libraries to be installed. In detail:

- ∑KDE examples: KDE 3.x on Linux
- ∑Qt 3 examples: Qt 3.x on either Linux or Microsoft Windows
- ∑Qt 4 examples: Qt 4.x on either Linux or Microsoft Windows
- ∑Qtopia examples: Qtopia 1.7.x or greater with the Qtopia emulator on Linux

Additionally, the OpenGL and OpenAL examples require the development libraries of OpenGL and OpenAL respecively.

Appendix

B

Software License

GNU GENERAL PUBLIC LICENSE

GNU General Public License
Version 2, June 1991
Copyright (C) 1989, 1991 Free Software Foundation, Inc.
675 Mass Ave, Cambridge, MA 02139, USA

Everyone is permitted to copy and distribute verbatim copies of this license document, but changing it is not allowed.

Preamble

The licenses for most software are designed to take away your freedom to share and change it. By contrast, the GNU General Public License is intended to guarantee your freedom to share and change free software—to make sure the software is free for all its users. This General Public License applies to most of the Free Software Foundation's software and to any other program whose authors commit to using it. (Some other Free Software Foundation software is covered by the GNU Library General Public License instead.) You can apply it to your programs, too.

When we speak of free software, we are referring to freedom, not price. Our General Public Licenses are designed to make sure that you have the freedom to distribute copies of free software (and charge for this service if you wish), that you receive source code or can get it if you want it, that you can change the software or use pieces of it in new free programs; and that you know you can do these things.

To protect your rights, we need to make restrictions that forbid anyone to deny you these rights or to ask you to surrender the rights. These restrictions translate to certain responsibilities for you if you distribute copies of the software, or if you modify it.

For example, if you distribute copies of such a program, whether gratis or for a fee, you must give the recipients all the rights that you have. You must make sure that they, too, receive or can get the source code. And you must show them these terms so they know their rights.

We protect your rights with two steps: (1) copyright the software, and (2) offer you this license which gives you legal permission to copy, distribute and/or modify the software.

Also, for each author's protection and ours, we want to make certain that everyone understands that there is no warranty for this free software. If the software is modified by someone else and passed on, we want its recipients to know that what they have is not the original, so that any problems introduced by others will not reflect on the original authors' reputations.

Finally, any free program is threatened constantly by software patents. We wish to avoid the danger that redistributors of a free program will individually obtain patent licenses, in effect making the program proprietary. To prevent this, we have made it clear that any patent must be licensed for everyone's free use or not licensed at all.

The precise terms and conditions for copying, distribution and modification follow.

GNU GENERAL PUBLIC LICENSE

TERMS AND CONDITIONS FOR COPYING, DISTRIBUTION AND MODIFICATION

0. This License applies to any program or other work which contains a notice placed by the copyright holder saying it may be distributed under the terms of this General Public License. The "Program," below, refers to any such program or work, and a "work based on the Program" means either the Program or any derivative work under copyright law: that is to say, a work containing the Program or a portion of it, either verbatim or with modifications and/or translated into another language. (Hereinafter, translation is included without limitation in the term "modification.") Each licensee is addressed as "you."

Activities other than copying, distribution and modification are not covered by this License; they are outside its scope. The act of running the Program is not restricted, and the output from the Program is covered only if its contents constitute a work based on the Program (independent of having been made by running the Program). Whether that is true depends on what the Program does.

1. You may copy and distribute verbatim copies of the Program source code as you receive it, in any medium, provided that you conspicuously and appropriately publish on each copy an appropriate copyright notice and disclaimer of warranty; keep intact all the notices that refer to this License and to the absence of any warranty; and give any other recipients of the Program a copy of this License along with the Program.

You may charge a fee for the physical act of transferring a copy, and you may at your option offer warranty protection in exchange for a fee.

2. You may modify your copy or copies of the Program or any portion of it, thus forming a work based on the Program, and copy and distribute such modifications or work under the terms of Section 1 above, provided that you also meet all of these conditions:

a) You must cause the modified files to carry prominent notices stating that you changed the files and the date of any change.

b) You must cause any work that you distribute or publish, that in whole or in part contains or is derived from the Program or any part thereof, to be licensed as a whole at no charge to all third parties under the terms of this License.

c) If the modified program normally reads commands interactively when run, you must cause it, when started running for such interactive use in the most ordinary way, to print or display an

announcement including an appropriate copyright notice and a notice that there is no warranty (or else, saying that you provide a warranty) and that users may redistribute the program under these conditions, and telling the user how to view a copy of this License. (Exception: if the Program itself is interactive but does not normally print such an announcement, your work based on the Program is not required to print an announcement.)

These requirements apply to the modified work as a whole. If identifiable sections of that work are not derived from the Program, and can be reasonably considered independent and separate works in themselves, then this License, and its terms, do not apply to those sections when you distribute them as separate works. But when you distribute the same sections as part of a whole which is a work based on the Program, the distribution of the whole must be on the terms of this License, whose permissions for other licensees extend to the entire whole, and thus to each and every part regardless of who wrote it.

Thus, it is not the intent of this section to claim rights or contest your rights to work written entirely by you; rather, the intent is to exercise the right to control the distribution of derivative or collective works based on the Program.

In addition, mere aggregation of another work not based on the Program with the Program (or with a work based on the Program) on a volume of a storage or distribution medium does not bring the other work under the scope of this License.

3. You may copy and distribute the Program (or a work based on it, under Section 2) in object code or executable form under the terms of Sections 1 and 2 above provided that you also do one of the following:

a) Accompany it with the complete corresponding machine-readable source code, which must be distributed under the terms of Sections 1 and 2 above on a medium customarily used for software interchange; or,

b) Accompany it with a written offer, valid for at least three years, to give any third party, for a charge no more than your cost of physically performing source distribution, a complete machine-readable copy of the corresponding source code, to be distributed under the terms of Sections 1 and 2 above on a medium customarily used for software interchange; or,

c) Accompany it with the information you received as to the offer to distribute corresponding source code. (This alternative is allowed only for noncommercial distribution and only if you received the program in object code or executable form with such an offer, in accord with Subsection b above.)

The source code for a work means the preferred form of the work for making modifications to it. For an executable work, complete source code means all the source code for all modules it contains, plus any associated interface definition files, plus the scripts used to control compilation and installation of the executable. However, as a special exception, the source code distributed need not include anything that is normally distributed (in either source or binary form) with the major components (compiler, kernel, and so on) of the operating system on which the executable runs, unless that component itself accompanies the executable.

If distribution of executable or object code is made by offering access to copy from a designated place, then offering equivalent access to copy the source code from the same place counts as distribution of the source code, even though third parties are not compelled to copy the source along with the object code.

4. You may not copy, modify, sublicense, or distribute the Program except as expressly provided under this License. Any attempt otherwise to copy, modify, sublicense or distribute the Program is void, and will automatically terminate your rights under this License. However, parties who have received copies, or rights, from you under this License will not have their licenses terminated so long as such parties remain in full compliance.

5. You are not required to accept this License, since you have not signed it. However, nothing else grants you permission to modify or distribute the Program or its derivative works. These actions are prohibited by law if you do not accept this License. Therefore, by modifying or distributing the Program (or any work based on the Program), you indicate your acceptance of this License to do so, and all its terms and conditions for copying, distributing or modifying the Program or works based on it.

6. Each time you redistribute the Program (or any work based on the Program), the recipient automatically receives a license from the original licensor to copy, distribute or modify the Program subject to these terms and conditions. You may not impose any further restrictions on the recipients' exercise of the rights granted herein. You are not responsible for enforcing compliance by third parties to this License.

7. If, as a consequence of a court judgment or allegation of patent infringement or for any other reason (not limited to patent issues), conditions are imposed on you (whether by court order, agreement or otherwise) that contradict the conditions of this License, they do not excuse you from the conditions of this License. If you cannot distribute so as to satisfy simultaneously your obligations under this License and any other pertinent obligations, then, as a consequence, you may not distribute the Program at all. For example, if a patent license would not permit royalty-free redistribution of the Program by all those who receive copies directly or indirectly through you, then the only way you could satisfy both it and this License would be to refrain entirely from distribution of the Program.

If any portion of this section is held invalid or unenforceable under any particular circumstance, the balance of the section is intended to apply and the section as a whole is intended to apply in other circumstances.

It is not the purpose of this section to induce you to infringe any patents or other property right claims or to contest validity of any such claims; this section has the sole purpose of protecting the integrity of the free software distribution system, which is implemented by public license practices. Many people have made generous contributions to the wide range of software distributed through that system in reliance on consistent application of that system; it is up to the author/donor to decide if he or she is willing to distribute software through any other system and a licensee cannot impose that choice.

This section is intended to make thoroughly clear what is believed to be a consequence of the rest of this License.

8. If the distribution and/or use of the Program is restricted in certain countries either by patents or by copyrighted interfaces, the original copyright holder who places the Program under this License may add an explicit geographical distribution limitation excluding those countries, so that distribution is permitted only in or among countries not thus excluded. In such case, this License incorporates the limitation as if written in the body of this License.

9. The Free Software Foundation may publish revised and/or new versions of the General Public License from time to time. Such new versions will be similar in spirit to the present version, but may differ in detail to address new problems or concerns.

Each version is given a distinguishing version number. If the Program specifies a version number of this License which applies to it and "any later version," you have the option of following the terms and conditions either of that version or of any later version published by the Free Software Foundation. If the Program does not specify a version number of this License, you may choose any version ever published by the Free Software Foundation.

10. If you wish to incorporate parts of the Program into other free programs whose distribution conditions are different, write to the author to ask for permission. For software which is copyrighted by the Free Software Foundation, write to the Free Software Foundation; we sometimes make exceptions for this. Our decision will be guided by the two goals of preserving the free status of all derivatives of our free software and of promoting the sharing and reuse of software generally.

NO WARRANTY

11. BECAUSE THE PROGRAM IS LICENSED FREE OF CHARGE, THERE IS NO WARRANTY FOR THE PROGRAM, TO THE EXTENT PERMITTED BY APPLICABLE LAW. EXCEPT WHEN OTHERWISE STATED IN WRITING THE COPYRIGHT HOLDERS AND/OR OTHER PARTIES PROVIDE THE PROGRAM "AS IS" WITHOUT WARRANTY OF ANY KIND, EITHER EXPRESSED OR IMPLIED, INCLUDING, BUT NOT LIMITED TO, THE IMPLIED WARRANTIES OF MERCHANTABILITY AND FITNESS FOR A PARTICULAR PURPOSE. THE ENTIRE RISK AS TO THE QUALITY AND PERFORMANCE OF THE PROGRAM IS WITH YOU. SHOULD THE PROGRAM PROVE DEFECTIVE, YOU ASSUME THE COST OF ALL NECESSARY SERVICING, REPAIR OR CORRECTION.

12. IN NO EVENT UNLESS REQUIRED BY APPLICABLE LAW OR AGREED TO IN WRITING WILL ANY COPYRIGHT HOLDER, OR ANY OTHER PARTY WHO MAY MODIFY AND/OR REDISTRIBUTE THE PROGRAM AS PERMITTED ABOVE, BE LIABLE TO YOU FOR DAMAGES, INCLUDING ANY GENERAL, SPECIAL, INCIDENTAL OR CONSEQUENTIAL DAMAGES ARISING OUT OF THE USE OR INABILITY TO USE THE PROGRAM (INCLUDING BUT NOT LIMITED TO LOSS OF DATA OR DATA BEING RENDERED INACCURATE OR LOSSES SUSTAINED BY YOU OR THIRD PARTIES OR A FAILURE OF THE PROGRAM TO OPERATE WITH ANY OTHER PROGRAMS), EVEN IF SUCH HOLDER OR OTHER PARTY HAS BEEN ADVISED OF THE POSSIBILITY OF SUCH DAMAGES.

END OF TERMS AND CONDITIONS

Appendix: How to Apply These Terms to Your New Programs

If you develop a new program, and you want it to be of the greatest possible use to the public, the best way to achieve this is to make it free software which everyone can redistribute and change under these terms.

To do so, attach the following notices to the program. It is safest to attach them to the start of each source file to most effectively convey the exclusion of warranty; and each file should have at least the "copyright" line and a pointer to where the full notice is found.

> one line to give the program's name and a brief idea of what it does.
> Copyright © 19yy name of author

This program is free software; you can redistribute it and/or modify it under the terms of the GNU General Public License as published by the Free Software Foundation; either version 2 of the License, or (at your option) any later version.

This program is distributed in the hope that it will be useful, but WITHOUT ANY WARRANTY; without even the implied warranty of MERCHANTABILITY or FITNESS FOR A PARTICULAR PURPOSE. See the GNU General Public License for more details.

You should have received a copy of the GNU General Public License along with this program; if not, write to the Free Software Foundation, Inc., 675 Mass Ave, Cambridge, MA 02139, USA.

Also add information on how to contact you by electronic and paper mail.

If the program is interactive, make it output a short notice like this when it starts in an interactive mode:

Gnomovision version 69, Copyright © 19yy name of author
Gnomovision comes with ABSOLUTELY NO WARRANTY; for details type 'show w'.

This is free software, and you are welcome to redistribute it under certain conditions; type 'show c' for details.

The hypothetical commands 'show w' and 'show c' should show the appropriate parts of the General Public License. Of course, the commands you use may be called something other than 'show w' and 'show c'; they could even be mouse-clicks or menu items—whatever suits your program.

You should also get your employer (if you work as a programmer) or your school, if any, to sign a "copyright disclaimer" for the program, if necessary. Here is a sample; alter the names:

Yoyodyne, Inc., hereby disclaims all copyright interest in the program 'Gnomovision' (which makes passes at compilers) written by James Hacker.

signature of Ty Coon, 1 April 1989
Ty Coon, President of Vice

This General Public License does not permit incorporating your program into proprietary programs. If your program is a subroutine library, you may consider it more useful to permit linking proprietary applications with the library. If this is what you want to do, use the GNU Library General Public License instead of this License.

Index